D1552565

Murder in Marrakesh

Murder in Marrakesh

Émile Mauchamp and the French Colonial Adventure

Jonathan G. Katz

INDIANA UNIVERSITY PRESS
BLOOMINGTON AND INDIANAPOLIS

This book is a publication of

Indiana University Press
601 North Morton Street
Bloomington, IN 47404-3797 USA

http://iupress.indiana.edu

Telephone orders   800-842-6796
Fax orders   812-855-7931
Orders by e-mail   iuporder@indiana.edu

The paper used in this publication meets the
minimum requirements of American National
Standard for Information Sciences—Permanence
of Paper for Printed Library Materials,
ANSI Z39.48-1984.

Manufactured in the United States of America

Library of Congress Cataloging-in-Publication Data

Katz, Jonathan Glustrom.
    Murder in Marrakesh : Emile Mauchamp and the French
colonial adventure / Jonathan G. Katz.
      p. cm.
    Includes bibliographical references and index.
    ISBN-13: 978-0-253-34815-9 (cloth : alk. paper)
    ISBN-10: 0-253-34815-3 (cloth : alk. paper)
    1. Mauchamp, Emile, 1870–1907—Death and burial.
2. Physicians—France. 3. French—Morocco.   I. Title.
    DT324.92.M385K37 2006
    964'.04092—dc22
    [B]   2006015062

1 2 3 4 5 12 11 10 09 08 07 06

For Tanya and my children
Madeleine, Suzanne, Julian, and Sophie

We can study files for decades, but every so often we are tempted to throw up our hands and declare that history is merely another literary genre: the past is autobiographical fiction pretending to be a parliamentary report.

Julian Barnes, *Flaubert's Parrot*

Contents

Acknowledgments

In a casual conversation, Susan Gilson Miller once remarked to me that "in Morocco, no one dies without a reason." Her offhand observation became the title of chapter 7, but it could well be the subtitle of this book. At the outset of my research, I never thought that the reason—or reasons—I uncovered for Émile Mauchamp's death would be at once so complex and so banal. Yet as I discovered, the very banality of the Mauchamp affair, like its complexity, makes it no less an accurate reflection of the colonial experience.

This book had a long gestation, and support came from many sources and in many forms. Grants from the Fulbright Commission and the American Institute for Maghrib Studies afforded me the opportunity to do archival research in Morocco over an extended period of time. The National Endowment of the Humanities provided me with the opportunity to do archival research in France. Travel grants from the Valley Library at Oregon State University similarly allowed me to make trips to Paris and Princeton. At the very outset, the Center for the Humanities at Oregon State University generously awarded me a term of residency where, unencumbered by teaching, I could get my bearings on what was then a new topic.

In Morocco, the efforts of Saadia Maski and Daoud Casewit of the Moroccan–American Commission for Educational and Cultural Exchange made my stay particularly pleasant and productive. My colleagues at Université Mohammed V were unstinting with their time and encouragement. I particularly want to thank Mohamed Aafif, Abd al-Ahad al-Sabti, Abd al-Majid al-Qadduri, Abdurrahmane El Moudden, and Khaled Ben Shrir. Hamid Moumou, the extraordinarily energetic librarian at the Bibliothèque Royale in Rabat, deserves special mention for opening many doors that might otherwise have been closed. Elie Goldschmidt, Stacy Holden, Hanna Muaz, and David Zaffran were likewise of great help to me in Morocco as well as great friends.

Over the course of the years many libraries and archives made their resources available to me. I particularly want to thank the archivists of the Archives du Ministère des Affaires Étrangères in Nantes, the Alliance Israélite Universelle in Paris, the Public Records

Office in Kew, and the Direction des Archives Royales in Rabat. In my work I also made extensive use of collections at the Bibliothèque Nationale de France, the Institut du Monde Arabe in Paris, the British Library, the Library of Congress, the Firestone Library at Princeton, and the library of the Tangier American Legation Museum. In Rabat the staffs of the Bibliothèque Générale, the Bibliothèque Royale, and the Bibliothèque de la Source were especially helpful. Members of the Société d'Histoire et d'Archéologie de Chalon-sur-Saône received me warmly when I arrived unannounced at their offices, and they graciously permitted me to reproduce photographs that appeared in their *Mémoires*. The librarians at the Bibliothèque Muncipale in Chalon were similarly helpful in providing me with materials. The Interlibrary Loan office at my home institution of Oregon State University did a superb job locating hard to find materials and bringing them to Corvallis.

Many people read part or all of an earlier draft of this book and provided me with valuable comments. I remain grateful for their insights and expertise even when I did not always share their interpretations. They include Terry Burke, Julia Clancy-Smith, Moshe Gershovich, Emily Gottreich, Susan Gilson Miller, Michael Osborne, Mary Jo and Bob Nye, Larry Rosen, and Daniel Schroeter. Others aided me through their response to presentations I made at conferences and at the University of Michigan and UC Santa Barbara. My colleagues in the Department of History at Oregon State University were especially helpful in their critique of early chapters of the book. I also wish to thank C. R. Pennell for providing the illustration of Mauchamp's murder that was in his personal collection.

Lastly, I want to thank my wife, Tanya, and my children for enduring with good spirits the periods of separation that *Murder in Marrakesh* sometimes required of me. Researching a book like this has many pleasures, but it can cause some minor hardship as well. I leave it to the reader to decide whether it was worth the effort.

Note on Transliteration and Names

For Arabic words, I have employed a simplified system of transliteration based on the one found in Hans Wehr's *A Dictionary of Modern Written Arabic*. In a few instances I have used a spelling that approximates common pronunciation, for example, *mellah* instead of *mallah* or *millah* to describe the Jewish quarter. I have deliberately left out diacritical marks that distinguish between various Arabic consonants. Anyone who knows Arabic will know where the dots and the long-vowel signs should go. General readers will not be perturbed by their absence. With two exceptions (the word *ʿar* and the name Ibn Yaʿish) I have similarly left off the apostrophe and inverted apostrophe that commonly stand in for the *hamza* and the letter *ayn*.

Rendering Moroccan personal and place names into English is particularly vexing, and no solution is entirely satisfactory. A Moroccan name in either Arabic or Berber, its French version, and its English variant are often widely divergent. In most instances I have transliterated Moroccan names according to how they would appear in written Arabic. In personal names that have a patronymic, I give preference to *bin* or *Ibn* ("son of") instead of the French *ben* or *Ben*. I have also done this in the case of Berber names that use *ould* or *wold* to mean "son of." Hence, I refer to Driss bin Minu instead of Driss ould Mennou, as he typically appears in French sources.

There are exceptions. I refer to the government official Ibn al-Ghazi as Bel Ghazi, a name by which he was universally known at the time and which is the spelling preferred by his descendants today. The Algerian-born translator Si Kaddour ben Ghabrit, who later had significant career in France, is best known by the French version of his name. Presenting his name any other way then did not make much sense.

The same logic applies to two other significant figures. In English transliteration, the names of the two sultans who reigned on the eve of the French protectorate are Abd al-Aziz and Abd al-Hafid. In deference to common usage at the time, I refer to them as Abdelaziz and Moulay Hafid. Similarly, I render the name of the governor of Marrakesh as Abdeslam al-Warzazi rather than Abd al-Islam.

Occasionally, Moroccan proper names are preceded by Si, Hajj, or Moulay. Si is an abbreviation of Sidi, "my lord," and a title of respect. Hajj is bestowed on someone who has made the pilgrimage to Mecca. Moulay, roughly the equivalent of "prince," designates a member of the sultan's family.

For place names, I use English spellings when applicable, hence Marrakesh instead of Marrakech. Readers should be aware that the cities of Essaouira and El-Jadida were universally known to Europeans a century ago as Mogador and Mazagan.

Lastly, for simplicity's sake, I give the titles of French books in English. Their actual titles may be found in the notes and the bibliography.

Principal Characters

Abdelaziz	sultan
Abdi, Aissa bin Umar al-	*qaid* of the Abda
Abdi, Allal	Algerian-born French chancellor in Essaouira
Abu Himara	"the Rogui," a pretender to the throne
Anflus	*qaid* of the Haha
Bel Ghazi, Kaddour	Moroccan official sent to replace al-Warzazi
Ben Ghabrit, Kaddour	Algerian-born French interpreter
Berrino	Italian businessman, friend of Mauchamp
Bin Karrum al-Jaburi, Ahmad	Moroccan governor of Oujda
Bin Majjad, Umar	French consular agent in Marrakesh
Bin Sulayman, Abd al-Karim	Moroccan foreign minister
Bouvier, Paul	French businessman in Marrakesh
Charbonnier	Frenchman attacked in Tangier
Corcos, Yashu'a	Jewish banker in Marrakesh
Cunningham Grahame, R. B.	British critic of French policy
Delcassé, Théophile	French foreign minister
Dubief, Ferdinand	French politician, Mauchamp champion
Falcon, Nissim	headmaster of school in Marrakesh
Gaillard, Henri	French consul in Fez
Gentil, Louis	geologist and eyewitness to events in Marrakesh
Gironcourt	Frenchman attacked in Fez
Glawi, Al-Madani al-	"Grand Lord" of the south, backer of Moulay Hafid
Glawi, Thami al-	Al-Madani's younger brother, pasha of Marrakesh
Guillemin, Henri	Mauchamp's biographer
Hafid, Moulay [Abdel]	viceroy in Marrakesh, later sultan
Holzmann, Judah	German doctor in Marrakesh
Houel, Christian	French journalist
Jaurès, Jean	French socialist leader

Jeannier	French vice-consul in Mazagan
Jonnart, Charles	governor-general of Algeria
Kattani, Muhammad al-	religious leader in Fez
Kouri, Nooman	French consul in Essaouira
Lassallas, Jean Denaut	Compagnie Marocaine agent in Marrakesh
Lennox, Alan	British vice-consul in Marrakesh
Linarès, Fernand	formerly Moulay Hassan's physician
Lowther, Gerard	British minister to Morocco
Lyautey, Louis-Hubert	French general and first resident general
Maclean, Sir Harry	British military adviser to sultan
MacLeod, James	British consul in Fez
Madden, Archibald	British vice-consul in Essaouira and Casablanca
Mauchamp, Émile	humanitarian doctor
Muhammad Sghir	Hajj Abdeslam al-Warzazi's business agent
Muqri, Muhammad al-	Moroccan official in Tangier
Nairn, Cuthbert	British missionary in Marrakesh
Niehr, Emile	German consul in Marrakesh
Ollivier	captain of the *Galilée*
Peffau-Garavini	friend of Mauchamp
Pichon, Stephen	French foreign minister
Raisuli, Ahmad al-	kidnapper and resistance leader
Regnault, Eugène	French minister to Morocco
René-Leclerc, Charles	French journalist, Mauchamp friend
Saint-Aulaire, Comte de	French chargé d'affaires in Tangier
Saint-René Taillandier, Georges	French minister to Morocco
Sarrien	French politician, Mauchamp champion
Terrier, Auguste	pro-colonial leader of Comité du Maroc
Turris, Muhammad al-	Abd al-Aziz's representative in Tangier
Vaffier-Pollet, Ernest	French supporter of Moulay Hafid
Warzazi, Abd al-Majid al-	son of Marrakesh governor
Warzazi, Hajj Abdeslam al-	governor of Marrakesh
Warzazi, Muhammd al-	son of Marrakesh governor
White, Herbert	British minister to Morocco

Murder in Marrakesh

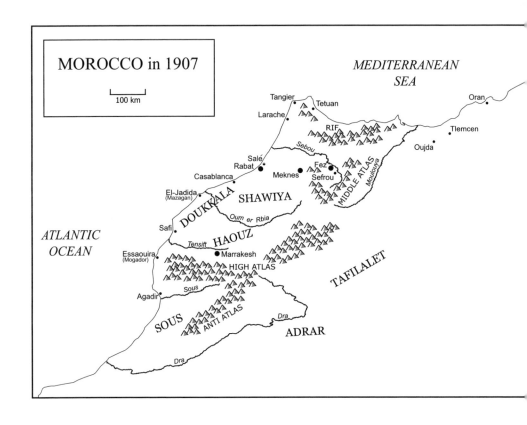

MOROCCO in 1907

100 km

MEDITERRANEAN
SEA

ATLANTIC
OCEAN

Tangier
Tetuan
Larache
RIF
Oran
Tlemcen
Oujda
Salé
Rabat
Casablanca
Meknes
Fez
Sefrou
El-Jadida
(Mazagan)
DOUKKALA
SHAWIYA
MIDDLE ATLAS
Moulouya
Safi
Oum er Rbia
Tensift
HAOUZ
Essaouira
(Mogador)
Marrakesh
HIGH ATLAS
TAFILALET
Agadir
Sous
SOUS
ANTI ATLAS
Dra
ADRAR
Dra

Introduction

People are not, generally speaking, conscious hypocrites.

Henri Brunschwig,
French Colonialism, 1871–1914: Myths and Realities

This book is about a murder and its consequences. It seemed like a senseless murder at the time when it took place in Marrakesh on March 19, 1907. It is thus a book about yesterday's news, now long beyond the reach of living memory. Some of the most important details are obscure. They were obscure even when they were first recounted. Today, the Mauchamp affair remains the kind of forgotten historical event often relegated to footnotes. It is, however, an event worthy of our renewed consideration, for Émile Mauchamp's life and death is a story about good and bad intentions and the inability of differing peoples to accept one another for what they are. A century after the fact—especially now, at a time when relations between Muslims and non-Muslims are still plagued by mistrust—the story retains its significance. In its broadest outline, it is the story of a Western power ostensibly justifying the occupation of a Muslim country in the name of a lofty, universal ideal. The analogy to events of our own day scarcely needs comment.

The outward facts of the case were fairly simple, if tinged with tragicomic irony. Émile Mauchamp was a physician sent by the French government to open a public clinic in Marrakesh. Arguably, medical clinics like the one operated by Mauchamp were desperately needed in Morocco. Mauchamp often saw upward of a hundred patients a day. But—as with much foreign aid in our own time—ulterior motives accompanied France's humanitarian gesture. In addition to being a doctor, Mauchamp was a fervent French patriot and, it emerges, an inveterate political intriguer. In Marrakesh, he worked tirelessly to further the colonial interests of France. And so, when rumors about him were spread through the markets of

Marrakesh in the middle of March 1907, they were quickly believed. It was said that Mauchamp had brought wireless telegraph equipment with him on his return from a vacation in Europe. It was said that the pole on the roof of his home in the midst of the "native" quarter was an antenna. It was said that Mauchamp was a spy who sent messages back to his superiors in Casablanca and Tangier.

Called from his clinic into the narrow street outside his house, Mauchamp argued with the crowd that the pole was nothing. His protestations did not cool tempers. Knives were drawn. The first blows fell upon Mauchamp as he was pressed against a door. Finally, as his lifeless body was stripped and dragged to a vacant lot, looters plundered his house. Other Europeans in Marrakesh first learned of the murder later that day when a Moroccan offered to them for sale a tennis racquet that they recognized as belonging to Mauchamp.

News of the murder reached Paris, where outraged deputies, crying for justice, demanded satisfaction from the Moroccan government. Elevated to a point of national honor, the incident became a major diplomatic affair. French troops stationed in neighboring French-held Algeria and led by General Lyautey moved across the border to occupy the Moroccan city of Oujda. In theory, they were to leave when the Moroccan government met a long list of demands set forth by the French. But as chance would have it, Mauchamp's death was followed in succeeding months by other horrendous attacks on Europeans in Morocco. France retaliated with an escalating series of military campaigns that would cost Moroccan lives by the thousands. In 1912, France finally succeeded in establishing a protectorate over Morocco and installed Lyautey as its first resident general. Although France never officially annexed the country, it deposed sultans at will and governed Morocco much like a colony until 1956, when Morocco gained independence. In brief, the French troops that entered Oujda in reprisal for Mauchamp's death would not leave Morocco for another fifty years.

The complex narrative of Mauchamp's murder, a cause célèbre at the time, and the subsequent French occupation have been distilled over the past century by historians to a single sentence: "After the murder of a French medical missionary at Marrakesh in March 1907, Prime Minister Georges Clemenceau ordered the occupation of Oujda, the most important Moroccan city in the east and just kilometers from the Algerian border."[1] So much for the barest outline of the story as it appears in a recent account of Franco-Moroccan relations. But of course there is more to tell.

I came across Mauchamp by accident in a computer search on North African magic. Magic and occult practices interested me to the extent that they intersected with dreams and Sufism, the subject of an earlier book I was writing.[2] In this context Mauchamp's name popped up on the screen as the author of *Sorcery in Morocco*.[3] The obscure volume was hard to obtain, even though Nina Epton, author of a curious little book called *Saints and Sorcerers, A Moroccan Journey*, writes that "students of the secret arts will recognize [Mauchamp's] name at once."[4] When it finally arrived, the yellowed tome bore the gloomy words "posthumous work" on its title page. A heartrending letter—written by Mauchamp's father and addressed to one Jules Bois, who edited the work and penned its introduction—served as the book's preface. "After the crime in Marrakesh," Pierre Mauchamp's letter to Bois begins,

> I received from the French legation a packet of papers, gathered through the efforts of some friends of my unfortunate son from his pillaged house. Not without dolorous emotion did I open the packet which contained a quantity of writings and some photographs, all in shreds and horribly soiled with blood and mud. I later learned that the murderous plunderers had killed each other as they fought to divide the booty.[5]

Pierre Mauchamp goes on to say that he found among these bloody papers of his "martyred" son the manuscript of a study on Moroccan magic. This work, the product of the younger Mauchamp's rare leisure moments, would serve as his final testament, bearing witness to "his French heart, [and] his ardent love of truth, science and humanity." The author could put only the first, introductory chapter in final literary form before he died; the remainder of the published text consisted of notes. They were, according to the father, "the complete and particularly exact translation of revelations cleverly extricated not without effort or without danger from the *talib*s, the Moroccan sorcerers." The book was, he wrote, a testament to his son's "physician spirit of observation" and a reflection of long years lived among Muslims.

Mauchamp's portrait of the Moroccans (and, by dint of reflection, his portrait of himself) is not pretty. His hubristic claim to understand Arab and Berber behavior and his malevolent critique of Moroccan customs and folklore are in fact the best (or worst) examples of the scholarship pejoratively labeled "Orientalism."[6] But even if Mauchamp's racist views are not entirely unexpected, they are at the very least disappointing. One would hope that his "French heart" and his "ardent love of truth, science and humanity" would allow him to rise above the prejudices and misconceptions of his times. But Mauchamp could not escape being a product of an era in which the ardent love of science and an abstract conception of humanity were fully compatible with racism. While Mauchamp's scholarly efforts served to reinforce preconceived notions of Arab and Berber irrationality and inferiority, his death confirmed the stereotypical view of North Africans as a violent people.

Mauchamp's posthumous study was not the only literary product to emerge as a consequence of his murder. Barely a year after his death, a full-length biography of Mauchamp appeared in serial form in the regional scientific publication of Saône-et-Loire, the department where Mauchamp's father had been a mayor of Chalon-sur-Saône.[7] This adulatory account of Mauchamp's life and especially his death, touchingly assembled by Henri Guillemin, a former teacher of Émile's from the local lycée, is replete with testimonials to the late doctor's character and scientific achievements.

With their parallel if antithetical representations of their respective protagonists, these two texts—Mauchamp's work on Moroccan magic and his biography by Guillemin—offer us a fortuitous juxtaposition. Nameless Moroccans are gripped in the vise of superstition; Mauchamp, the European exponent of hygiene, is portrayed as the exemplar of reason, a young and heroic embodiment of *la mission civilisatrice*, France's historic and self-proclaimed mission to bring "civilization" to the rest of the world. In compiling his tribute to Chalon's native son, Monsieur Guillemin managed to compose a full-fledged hagiography. Moroccans have a name for this genre: *manaqib*, "a book of virtues." The impulse to memorialize is universal. Only the names have been changed.

Doesn't the young Doctor Mauchamp deserve our sympathy? His medical work in Morocco and prior to that in Palestine, where he served for five years, was heroic—or, at the very least, not overtly exploitative. Without too much difficulty one can trace a line from Mauchamp to Bernard Kouchner and Médecins sans frontière (Doctors without Borders). French medical ethics—what the French call its *déontologie*—have always been informed by a sense of selfless devotion to higher aims. And yet, as one reads the introductory chapter of his *Sorcery in Morocco* (words that are indisputably Mauchamp's own, according to his father) one cannot avoid a sneaking suspicion, first ventured by historians sympathetic to Morocco's struggle for in-

Figure 1. Portrait of Émile Mauchamp. Reproduction courtesy of *La Société d'histoire et d'archéologie de Chalon-sur-Saône.*

dependence, that maybe Mauchamp got what he deserved. Reading *Sorcery in Morocco,* it is impossible to overlook Mauchamp's shocking and virulent racism. Of course, historical truth is altered by one's perspective. Our twenty-first-century point of view was certainly not held by his French contemporaries. They preferred to represent the doctor as a poster child for the French civilizing mission.

We can determine with relative ease what Mauchamp thought of the Moroccans and what his French compatriots thought of Mauchamp. The texts are only all too explicit. But French sources obviously tell only half the story. What did Moroccans think of Mauchamp and his compatriots? What was the Moroccan response to the French "civilizing" mission? And finally, if we are to have perfect symmetry (for shouldn't we demand that the rules of "otherness" apply both ways?) what representations of themselves did the Moroccans produce when they chose to size up the Europeans?

These specific questions are difficult to answer. Although Moroccan archives contain various documents in Arabic that deal with the affair, the official correspondence of the Makhzan—as the Moroccan government was known—is typically perfunctory. The disparity between the prolix European consular correspondence and the tightly folded scraps of paper that passed between Marrakesh, Fez, and Tangier—usually conveyed by couriers on foot—is striking. Today economists talk about an "asymmetry of information" that puts developing nations at a disadvantage in emerging globalized markets.[8] A century ago this asymmetry of information was already a factor in the French takeover of Morocco. Nevertheless, the disparity was not simply the result of Europeans commanding the varied technologies of fact production and accumulation. Rather, if knowledge is power, as is commonly asserted, I suspect that tight-lipped Moroccan officials had their own reasons for not wanting to expend too much of their symbolic capital. As a consequence, one labors in vain to uncover a full, representative *Moroccan* account of the Mauchamp affair. As a researcher, I can only state the obvious, that a mob in Marrakesh definitively expressed its views when it killed Mauchamp.

Some of Mauchamp's French eulogizers liked to imagine that a rejection of European science, medicine, and technology was the root cause of the doctor's murder. In this assessment, they were mistaken. If nothing else, the assault on Mauchamp reflected a *political* response on the part of Moroccans in Marrakesh. Intuitively they understood that the activities of Europeans such as Mauchamp irrevocably undermined their country's independence and sovereignty. For all the asymmetry of information it was the Europeans, and especially would-be civilizers such as Mauchamp, who failed to comprehend the true implications of the colonial encounter.[9]

"The Protectorate, a political parenthesis and an accident of History" reads the awkward headline in the Moroccan French-language daily *Le Matin*.[10] In a special twenty-four-page supplement, the paper commemorated the eighty-eighth anniversary of the signing of the Treaty of Fez, which codified France's domination of Morocco, on

March 30, 1912. "The shortest colonial occupation in history," proclaimed another headline in the same issue.

One could quibble with the slightly exaggerated boast. Libya, wrested by Italy from the Ottoman Turks in 1911 and given its independence in 1951, edges out Morocco for the honor of being "the shortest colonial occupation." But on the whole, the claim is true. Libya, after all, was an Ottoman province, not a sovereign country, when Italy seized it. This is an important distinction.

With a history of independence going back over a millennium, Morocco had been ruled since the middle of the sixteenth century by descendants of the Prophet Muhammad, the so-called *shurafa*. The first of the Sharifian sultans were drawn from the Saadi clan. Later they were displaced by the Alawis, whose descendant Mohammed VI occupies the throne today. What the headlines of the Moroccan *Le Matin* mean to suggest is that the French occupation was an aberration or a brief intermezzo, and that following the departure of the French—and with the monarchy again firmly in control—things returned to their normal order.

Whatever historic inaccuracies there may be in this account, the newspaper's intent is clear. Moroccan nationalist sentiment requires minimizing the effects of the French Protectorate. What the newspaper glosses over is the extent to which the ruling family depended on the French to remain in power. Without the French, would there be a Moroccan monarchy today? The question is not an accusation, but merely an acknowledgement that the French remained in power throughout the Protectorate through a kind of symbiosis with the royal family. Similarly, without condoning the French takeover of Morocco (the balance sheet of French accomplishments in the country remains murky and open to dispute), it is nonetheless undeniable that Morocco was irrevocably changed by its colonial experience. Indeed, one can scarcely imagine what Morocco would be like today had it not been for the intrusion of the French.[11]

France's legacy of North African conquest began with the seizure of Algiers in 1830. With the collapse of the local Turkish ruler's authority in western Algeria (and hoping to forestall the arrival of the infidel French), the citizens of the western city of Tlemcen appealed to the Moroccan sultan Abd al-Rahman for support. Justifiably reluctant to become embroiled in a conflict with a European power, the sultan nevertheless felt compelled as a Muslim leader to send troops into Algeria. The army was soon withdrawn when a menacing French warship appeared in the Tangier harbor. However, Morocco's continued support for the leader of the Algerian resistance, Abd al-Qadir, had disastrous consequences. As tensions mounted over the next decade, war between Morocco and France briefly flared in August 1844. While French ships bombarded the ports of Tangier and Essaouira (referred to by Europeans as Mogador), a French force of eleven thousand men routed a Moroccan army nearly three times its size at the Battle of Isly near the Moroccan border town of Oujda.[12]

The French victory over Morocco, however, did not give France a predominant role in the affairs of the Sharifian empire. Throughout the remainder of the nineteenth century England rather than France benefited most from a close relationship with the Makhzan. This relationship derived to a large degree from the extraordinary personal influence of John Drummond Hay. The British diplomat, who first visited in Morocco at the age of fifteen and learned Arabic fluently, succeeded his father in the role of consul general after the latter's death in 1844. Over the next forty years he would be the single most important European in Morocco. Preaching a gospel of free trade that appealed to Morocco's merchants but ultimately undermined the sultan's authority, he negotiated a treaty in 1856 that opened Morocco's doors to foreigners. Morocco offered the world grain, hides, and other agricultural products while providing a market for European manufactured goods and—in response to Morocco's newfound taste for sweetened mint tea—sugar.[13] Offering his services as mediator between Morocco and France, Drummond Hay used his influence to curb France's aggressive tendencies. The British diplomat's motivation was hardly altruistic, and on occasion Drummond Hay encouraged Morocco's leaders to make damaging economic and political concessions to the European powers. In many ways England's policy toward Morocco mirrored its approach to the Ottoman empire that was similarly languishing in the East. Looking across from Gibraltar, England preferred to see a weak but independent Morocco occupying the southern shore of the Mediterranean rather than a European rival such as France. The same logic later applied in the case of an expansionist Spain, which defeated Morocco in the Tetuan War that took place in 1859–1860.

As in the case of other Middle Eastern and North African countries, Morocco responded to European aggression by attempting to reform its military along European lines.[14] These efforts, which began soon after the defeat at Isly, continued in fits and starts over the remainder of the century but failed to achieve the desired results. Rather than keep Europeans out, the sultan's recourse to European instructors and the importation of modern European weapons only further increased Moroccan dependency on foreigners. Moreover, finding themselves unable to finance a large, standing professional army that was needed to ensure domestic stability as well as protect Morocco's borders, the country's sultans in the second half of the nineteenth century increasingly resorted to the *mahalla*. This institution consisted of a large, free-floating army of loyal tribal forces and camp followers, led by the monarch or other royal princes. The sheer size of the *mahalla* was intended to intimidate recalcitrant tribes into submission and aid in the collection of rural taxes. The sultan Moulay Hassan, in particular, spent much of his reign (1873–1894) either on campaign or traveling between his capital cities of Marrakesh, Fez, Rabat, and Meknes. European observers frequently commented on Morocco's traditional division of territories into tax-paying lands under the sultan's direct control (*bilad al-makhzan*) and those tribes—and occasional cities—that inclined toward rebellion (*bilad al-siba*). The dichotomy reinforced for European observers the overwhelming impression of disorder and anarchy and led them to underestimate the true nature of Morocco's nationalist feeling.[15] At the start of the twentieth century, many Moroccans, in both the cities and the countryside, were disaffected toward their government, but their hostility toward the Makhzan and its policies did not in any way incline them to favor European intervention.

Compounding Morocco's political difficulties, the country entered the global commercial network of the nineteenth century with an economy in shambles. In addition to frequent, devastating droughts and epidemics, Morocco suffered from an ongoing monetary crisis that more than once sent the value of Morocco's currency plummeting. The opening of trade to European merchants and the elimination of commercial monopolies formerly held by the sultan further adversely affected state revenues. Morocco became a powerful magnet for European speculators of all nationalities. Meanwhile, the extension of commercial privileges to indigenous Moroccans, the so-called protection system, further undercut the sultan's authority. Both Jews and Muslims (and on occasion even prominent officials of the Makhzan itself) worked on behalf of European missions and businesses and became protégés of the foreign missions. This status gave them immunity from taxes, military service, and criminal prosecution while providing an additional pretext for European intervention in Morocco's affairs. Apart from eroding Moroccan sovereignty over its citizens, the protection system allowed European businesses to operate in the interior. Despite the Conference of Madrid convened by Britain in 1880 to curb the abuses of the protection system, the practice of granting protection and, in many instances, naturalizing Moroccans as foreign citizens only increased throughout the next three decades.[16]

As was the case in other North African and Middle Eastern states, the ever growing indebtedness to European bankers ensured European domination over Morocco's economy. Loans were initially contracted in 1860 as a result of the disastrous war with Spain. Among the conditions for its withdrawal from conquered territory (it held onto the enclaves of Melilla and Ceuta as it continues to do today), Madrid imposed an indemnity of 100 million Spanish pesetas on the already bankrupt Makhzan, a figure roughly equivalent to $485 million in today's dollars.[17]

In 1894, Moulay Hassan died while leading a *mahalla* on campaign in the southern region of Tafilalt. His favorite son, Abdelaziz, then only thirteen years old, assumed the throne thanks to the efforts of the royal chamberlain Si Ahmad bin Musa. Ba Ahmad, as the chamberlain was known, managed to keep the sultan's death a secret until the corpse was safely back in friendly territory. He then used the occasion of Abdelaziz's accession to destroy his own political rivals and replace them with members of his own family. Until his death in 1900, Ba Ahmad ruled unchallenged as vizier and regent. Continuing to lean heavily on Britain for diplomatic support, he attempted to uphold Moulay Hassan's policies, but domestically the regime's legitimacy was undermined. By increasing his own personal power, Ba Ahmad had forever disrupted the delicate balance of forces on which Morocco's monarchy depended. In 1896, Ba Ahmad brutally suppressed a rebellion in the region of Marrakesh by the Rahamna tribe made on behalf of a rival claimant to the throne, Abdelaziz's brother Moulay Muhammad.[18]

In 1899, after suppressing another tribal revolt, this time by the Misfiwa, the vizier decorated the walls of Fez with the heads of fifty rebels. A revolt in the Rif mountains to the north was put down with equal ferocity. "The theatrical violence was, as always, designed to show that the Makhzan was still powerful."[19] But this was an illusion. The treasury was depleted, and under Ba Ahmad the economic situation worsened. Efforts to issue a new silver coinage failed to forestall the collapse of the local currency. Harvests continued to be poor, while for most of the last decade of the nineteenth century imports exceeded exports. Fueled by Makhzan expenditures and indemnities owed to Spain and the other powers, the foreign debt soared.

Following Ba Ahmad's death, the sultan Abdelaziz determined to take control of Morocco's affairs. At the time the sultan was still in his teens and faced a daunting task. During his reign, whole sections of the country would pass out of Abdelaziz's control into the hands of assorted rebels, pretenders to the throne, and brigands. Of a curious and open-minded temperament, the young monarch unfortunately manifested his interest in things European by filling his palaces with foreign gadgets and novelties and staging extravagant fireworks displays. "Here, everything has been completely turned upside down," a European visitor to his court wrote. "The sultan amuses himself with bike riding, automobile driving, and photography. Every evening there are fireworks or some less innocent games."[20] Abdelaziz would eventually be deposed in 1908 at the hands of his half-brother Moulay Hafid, an event set in motion by Mauchamp's murder.

Abdelaziz's contemporaries tended to label the young sultan as incompetent. Moroccans criticized his abandonment of tradition. Europeans were prone to see him as superficial and malleable. These assessments were certainly unkind, for the challenges Abdelaziz faced were virtually insurmountable. Although committed to military, political, and fiscal reform and determined to build Morocco's infrastructure, Abdelaziz could pursue this agenda only at the expense of contracting ever larger loans. And with the loans and contracts there arrived more and more Europeans. No longer confined to the diplomatic missions in Tangier or the palace in Marrakesh or Fez, their presence in Morocco's towns and countryside only further alienated ordinary Moroccans. As one historian aptly labeled it, the country entered the "the age of the traveling salesmen."

For decades, what had prevented one European nation or another from taking over the Moroccan kingdom outright was not the strength of Morocco's army or the ferocity of its tribes—although as both France and Spain would soon discover, the expense and difficulty of conquering Morocco was high. Rather, Morocco had remained a sovereign nation largely at the indulgence of the European powers, who, in their competition to acquire territory in Africa, were unwilling to see one country press its advantage over another. During the second half of Abdelaziz's reign, that longstanding point of view abruptly changed. With the forging of the diplomatic agreement known as the Entente Cordiale in 1904, France conceded England's control of Egypt in exchange for a free rein in Morocco. Meanwhile, Spain struck a deal with France, making sure that in the event of Morocco being divided, it too would receive its fair portion of the country. After all, Spain had an interest in Morocco that extended back for centuries.

Within France itself, a new attitude toward Moroccan affairs had also begun to emerge at the start of the new century. Representing an assortment of business, military, and Algerian settler interests, the so-called *parti colonial,* or colonial bloc, within the French legislature began to call for a more aggressive stance toward the acquisition of Morocco. The Comité du Maroc, the Morocco Committee, was formed, dedicated to promoting before the French public the idea of a takeover of Morocco. These efforts quickly paid off. Most French leaders disagreed only as to *how* France should acquire control of Morocco, not whether it should. Even the socialist leader Jean Jaurès, the most vocal critic of a French military venture in Morocco, spoke ardently of upholding "civilization's duty."

Initially, following the lead of Théophile Delcassé, the minister of foreign affairs, French diplomats opted for a gradual approach of peaceful penetration that called for extending French economic and cultural influence. Sending doctors such as Mauchamp to open clinics in Morocco's cities was a notable example. On the other hand, weaning the sultan and his court away from their longstanding reliance on British advisers and inaugurating a reform program of French inspiration was another key aim. The latter policy, known as the "Makhzan policy," rested on the premise that only by a strengthening of the sultan's rule could a more coherent, centralized Moroccan state—one conducive to French domination—ultimately emerge.[21]

Other advocates of a French takeover, especially members of the army and French colonists in the Oran region of Algeria adjacent to Morocco, favored a radically different approach. Eyeing the disorder of the frontier, where the sultan's authority was weak, this "forward" wing of the colonial lobby advocated a so-called tribal policy. This policy advocated gaining control of Morocco by overcoming tribal resistance and acquiring territory either by outright conquest or by bribing the tribes into submission. The policy had already been tentatively tested. Seeking to extend the Trans-Sahara railroad further south, French troops seized the oasis of Tuat, at least nominally a Moroccan possession, in 1900.[22] The seizure elicited no response from London. Meanwhile, the Makhzan, in no position to challenge France, meekly consented the following year to conduct negotiations with the French designed to restore security to the Algerian border. Nevertheless, when France presented a comprehensive reform program to the sultan in Fez in 1904, the program met with stiff resistance and was rejected by a special council of notables convened by the sultan. Seeking to counter the increasingly insistent French designs over Moroccan territory, the Makhzan responded much as it traditionally did in terms of its own domestic politics—that is, it sought to reach a stasis by balancing one opposing force against another.

Over the preceding decade, led by the Mannesmann Brothers mining interests, Germany had begun to play an increasingly important commercial role in the south of Morocco.[23] Especially after Kaiser Wilhelm's surprise visit in March 1905 to Tangier, it seemed that Germany would assume the role of Morocco's protector. At the Conference of Algeciras, held in Spain the following year and attended by representatives of the major European powers and the United States, Moroccan negotiators hoped to constrain French ambitions by internationalizing reform efforts.[24] But Germany quickly disappointed Morocco. On the contrary, despite some gestures in the direction of internationalizing reform efforts, the Act of Algeciras signed at the conference in reality gave France a free hand to pursue its own interests.

These developments did not go unnoticed by ordinary Moroccans. Algeciras confirmed for many Moroccans a growing conviction that the Makhzan served French interests. In separate incidents throughout the country Europeans, and especially Frenchmen, came under physical assault. Mauchamp's death provided the catalyst for changes that would irrevocably seal Morocco's fate. The retaliatory occupation of Oujda and, a few months later, the French naval bombardment of Casablanca abruptly put an end to the gradualist approach. The military had trumped the diplomats. In place of peaceful penetration, France would opt for a program of military conquest, euphemistically called "pacification."

As for Moroccans, various segments of society, chief among them the tribes of the Haouz region of Marrakesh and the Shawiya region adjacent to Casablanca, no longer viewed the sultan Abdelaziz as the country's legitimate ruler. Searching for an alternative, one who would lead them in a jihad against France, they eventually settled on Moulay Hafid. The concept of jihad, with its connotations of struggle and sacrifice, lay at the heart of the Alawi dynasty ever since its founding in the seventeenth century.[25] But in the eyes of many, Abdelaziz had failed in his responsibilities. He no longer fought corruption within the society, nor could he maintain the state against the incursions of the infidels.

Thus, against the backdrop of Mauchamp's death in Marrakesh, Moulay Hafid, the sultan's half-brother and viceroy in the south, launched his bid to become sultan. Under the circumstances, deposing his brother was not difficult, but even Moulay Hafid could not resist the enticements of the French. Like his predecessor, he found himself compelled to turn to the French intruders for aid in ruling his unruly country. The new sultan was caught in an impossible position. To the Europeans, he had to present himself as a leader seeking peace; to his Moroccan subjects, the leader of a holy war against the French. With the signing of the Protectorate agreement in March 1912 and his abdication a few months later, a reluctant Moulay Hafid formally consigned his country to its fate.

Rooted in a political and moral economy of its own, the conventional algebra of power sees the illegitimate application of imperialist force as being met with legitimate indigenous resistance. A half century after Mauchamp's death, the Moroccans regained their independence and sent the French packing. Mauchamp was forgotten. In Rabat, the capital city so nicely laid out by Lyautey, and elsewhere, Moroccans renamed the streets after their own heroes.

In its briefest telling, modern Moroccan history is a story of loss and recovery (and, for the French colonists, loss again). The difficulty in piecing together this story comes from the fact that it is never quite clear what is lost and what is recovered. Physical territory? National sovereignty? Cultural identity? In this vein the Mauchamp episode played a significant role as a symbolic marker. Mauchamp's murder underscores the fact that a violent death engenders not only rituals of mourning but also rituals of vengeance. It serves us well to remember that what is today an arid footnote at one time stirred great passions.

Accounts contemporaneous with Mauchamp's death uniformly extolled Mauchamp as the martyr of the French civilizing mission and as an exemplar of European science. The good doctor was interested only in saving lives. In this colonialist narrative the Moroccans who attacked Mauchamp could only be savages. The narrative's appeal is obvious. At its root is the dismal irony of a young humanitarian doctor torn to shreds by the very people he intended to aid. In some sense, it was a variation of an old theme and a recurrent fear—Captain Cook meeting his death at the hands of the Sandwich Islanders, explorers in Africa falling victim to cannibals.[26]

Curiously, the broad outline of Mauchamp's life and death was already familiar to French readers long before it ever appeared on the front pages of the Parisian press. In 1896 H. G. Wells offered the public a brilliant fable of colonialism bearing the title *The Island of Doctor Moreau*. By the time of Mauchamp's death, the popular novel had already gone through five editions in France. In the book Wells tells of an eccentric biologist living in virtual isolation on a tropical island. Science and modern medicine provide him with the means of turning beasts into humans. In his laboratory—the so-called "House of Pain"—the objects of this experiment are subjected to a harsh discipline. But if they survive, the doctor provides them with a final gift, a code of behavior, "the law." The erstwhile beasts can now declare themselves men, but the experiment ends in dismal failure. How could it have ended otherwise? The transformed animals revert to their true nature and in a bout of savage frenzy slay their maker.

Of course, there are places where the analogy to Mauchamp breaks down. Moroccans are not and never were beasts. But then neither was Mauchamp the mad doctor of science fiction. As our story will confirm, the experience of Émile Mauchamp was, if anything, only all too normal.

Writing his memoirs in the wake of World War II, the elderly French diplomat Saint-Aulaire recalled the feverish days of the Franco-German rivalry that provide the backdrop to the events described in this book. His words still resonate today.

> One hesitates to recall those events, dramatic in themselves, but which, if they are not entirely forgotten today, seem insignificant in scale to more recent events or those in which the nightmare weighs upon the future and replaces our ancient dreams of perpetual peace. . . . The events of 1905–06 merit the attention of whoever takes an interest in the chain of cause and effect. They are the prologue of a gigantic drama of which we still do not know the outcome.[27]

Murder in Marrakesh is divided into two parts. The first half deals with Mauchamp's life. The second outlines the events that followed in the wake of his death. In the course of telling of Mauchamp's story, I touch on several themes: medicine, colonialism, violence, vengeance, mourning, and memory. In this fashion I hope to shed light on what the colonial adventure meant to its participants and the effect it had on the lives of all those who came under its thrall.

Part 1. Life

1

Civilization's Martyr

Funeral in Chalon-sur-Saône

The spring of 1907 was an especially dolorous time for France. On March 12 an accidental explosion of munitions blew up the 12,000-ton warship *Iéna* in the port of Toulon. One hundred eighteen men died.[1] The following week, in an episode of obvious sentimental appeal, the famous chemist Marcellin Berthelot and his wife died within hours of one another. News of Mauchamp's death reached Paris just as Berthelot and his wife's coffins were being installed in the Panthéon amid enormous pomp and ceremony.

While the *Iéna* and the Berthelots may have squeezed Mauchamp's death out of the headlines for a day or two, Mauchamp's murder and Lyautey's incursion into Morocco soon took their rightful places on the front pages of the Parisian dailies. On March 30, a picture of Mauchamp on horseback occupied the cover of the weekly newsmagazine *L'Illustration*. By the time his corpse arrived on French soil, Mauchamp was already a household name in France. In his native town of Chalon-sur-Saône, elaborate preparations for his funeral were already in place. Some twenty thousand to thirty thousand people, among them important national dignitaries, would turn out for the event.

Mauchamp's coffin arrived in his hometown from Marseilles by train on the morning of April 10. Accompanying the corpse was Mauchamp's friend from Marrakesh, the geologist and explorer Louis Gentil. A Chalonnais commercial photographer named Barthelmy documented the scene at the station and the funeral the following day in a series of postcard shots taken almost on an hourly basis. The first photo shows Mauchamp's coffin being unloaded from

Figure 2. Mauchamp's coffin on view at the Chalon city hall, April 10, 1907. Reproduction courtesy of *La Société d'histoire et d'archéologie de Chalon-sur-Saône*.

the train's baggage car.[2] The French tricolor flag and many of the floral wreaths from Tangier, including one made entirely of daisies supposedly given by the Moroccan sultan, accompanied the corpse on the journey.

The next shot, taken a half hour later, shows a small crowd assembled at the gate of the railway station. At the fore stood Mauchamp's father Pierre, attended by Mauchamp's two brothers-in-law and surrounded by local dignitaries. The cortège then somberly walked to the square of the Hôtel de Ville, the city hall, where the body was to rest in state until its burial the following day. An honor guard of local firemen accompanied the hearse.[3]

The ground floor of the city hall was draped in black. The coffin, decorously surrounded by enormous wreaths, rested on a black stage erected under the peristyle of the city hall and protected under a black awning. The decorations, later praised by the local paper, *Le Courrier*, were the work of local architects and decorators. "In the middle of the central entrance, the drapes opened to show the high catafalque upon which rested the body. From all other sides hung hangings, among which the lamps, lit and cloaked in mourning, gave off a sad and yellow glow which one sees in mortuary chambers."

Before this dais, a small crowd of men, women, and children assembled. A photograph shows some leaning on bicycles; one ornately dressed woman leads a dog. Eventually, an estimated fifteen thousand people passed before the coffin, covered by the French tricolor, to pay their respects. Inside, in the city hall vestibule, the mayor of Chalon offered the condolences of the municipal council to Mauchamp's father and assured the grieving man that the entire nation and "*la patrie* [the homeland] that was Chalon" shared in his grief. The elder Mauchamp replied that while the sympathetic remarks were intended to assuage his grief, he remained at the moment inconsolable, knowing that his son, who had died for the glory of the nation, had been horribly mutilated by his assassins.

What the newspaper account did not say was that for Mauchamp's parents this was the second unspeakable tragedy within a year. Mauchamp's younger sister Alice, married to a civil engineer in Montpellier and the mother of two, had died of typhoid barely eight months earlier in July. In a moment of bitterness and disillusionment, Mauchamp himself had written from Marrakesh, "And to think during this time I was struggling here against an epidemic of typhus . . . spending my time saving a bunch of these savages while the leading professors of the faculty at Montpellier couldn't wrench from death my poor little sister, so sweet, so good, so young."[4]

Louis Gentil, Mauchamp's friend from Marrakesh, took the occasion to speak of the events that he himself had witnessed. Without hesitation, he claimed that Mauchamp had been killed on the formal order of the Moroccan government. "The truth," *Le Courrier* quoted Gentil as saying, "was that Mauchamp was drawn without defense into an ambush by some people who pushed him into the street."

The reception scene was repeated at the train station the following day. Only this time, instead of a coffin being unloaded, a carload of dignitaries disembarked. Barthelmy's photograph, taken precisely at 1:18 PM on April 11, shows a line of men in top hats and waistcoats exiting the imposing doors of the Chalon station and mounting one of three horse-drawn carriages assembled there. The so-called ministerial train, arriving from Lons-de-Saunier, held Stephen Pichon, the minister for foreign affairs, and a host of dignitaries. Together with the press, they filled thirteen carriages. Driving along Chalon's main thoroughfare, they stopped to pay their respects at the home of Mauchamp's parents, an apartment in the place de Beaune, today located over Chalon's Café Neptune. Finding the Mauchamp family not at home, the visiting officials then made their way to the place de l'Hôtel-de-Ville.

On a gray, rainy afternoon, with shops and offices closed and the entire town draped in black, an estimated twenty thousand Chalonnais assembled in the square before the city hall and filled the adjacent side streets. Others looked on from the windows of the surrounding buildings. The crowd included members of some ninety-five local societies, each with a banner, grouped in compact bands in a semicircle facing the city hall. Behind them, a battalion of the 56th stood in two rows, with bayonets in their rifles, ready to march. The town band played a funeral march composed especially for the occasion by its director.

At 1:50 PM the foreign minister and his entourage arrived. Mounting the stand, Pichon took his place to the left of the coffin. The accompanying senators ranged themselves around the minister.

Some two weeks earlier, on April 2, a dockside ceremony had taken place in Tangier as Mauchamp's coffin was being loaded on a ship for the voyage home. There Eugène Regnault, the French minister to Morocco, said that in attacking Mauchamp, the mob sought to destroy civilization itself, "of which he was in their eyes a living symbol."

"We know, Messieurs," he went on to explain, "that the evolution of peoples cannot be accomplished without setbacks nor without victims." Instead of pursuing a tranquil life at home, Mauchamp preferred the dangers of life abroad, "dominated by a noble ambition to serve his country in serving humanity."[5]

Now in Chalon, the eulogies resumed in a similar vein. The crowd stirred as Pichon pinned the cross of the Legion of Honor on a pillow set at the head of the coffin. Before his death legislators from Saône-et-Loire had lobbied unsuccessfully on Mauchamp's behalf for the decoration; the irony of the posthumous award as a chevalier or knight was not lost on anyone.

The band played a funereal tune. And then, with head uncovered and text in hand, the foreign minister, speaking in a clear, strong voice, began the first of the eight tributes to be delivered that day.

Pichon lauded Mauchamp as an "apostle" who gave himself entirely to his country and humanity, who, despite his short career, "fell bravely in full youth on the field of honor." Having undertaken only the most difficult challenges and rendered the most useful ser-

Figure 3. Mauchamp's funeral in Chalon, April 11, 1907. Reproduction
courtesy of *La Société d'histoire et d'archéologie de Chalon-sur-Saône.*

vices, Mauchamp met his end as the victim of a "sudden and monstrous explosion of Muslim fanaticism." Mauchamp's "inspiration,
always the same, was to add materially and morally to France and,
by this, to serve brotherhood."

> Doing good, caring for the unfortunate, healing the sick, popular-
> izing science, substituting it for the trial-and-error that is the law of
> ignorant races, and spreading by solidarity the benefits of civiliza-
> tion, that was the form which Dr. Mauchamp gave his patriotism.
> He found in the daily practice of these principles, the clear and firm
> notion of which he owed to the French Revolution, the most rational
> and sure means to express his love for his country.

Pichon himself had served as a diplomat in China and until the
preceding year had been France's resident general in Tunisia. He
described Morocco as a natural field for "the generous ardor of
[Mauchamp's] proselytism." There one found a population waiting
to be attached to France for instruction and to grasp the benefits of

European progress. Pichon also romanticized—in a way that Mauchamp himself almost never did—the charms of the East.

> He found there as well, without doubt, the seduction that the sweetness and poetry of the Orient exerts upon souls. . . . In Marrakesh, under the golden light of a limpid sky, not far from the snowy peaks of the Atlas, at the foot of minarets and mosques, amid the dangers that surrounded him, alas, in this inhospitable city, there mingled with the rigorous accomplishment of his humanitarian duties a part of the dream that seizes us in the lands of Islam, when we have felt the mystery of their impenetrable charm.

Pichon assured his listeners that the parliament and the government had acted with rare unanimity in demanding the punishment of those responsible for Mauchamp's death. The occupation of Oujda would continue until French demands for satisfaction had been met.[6] Pichon's remarks were followed by those of the mayor, two deputies, and a senator. Other eulogizers included a doctor who, on behalf of the local medical corps, recounted Mauchamp's career, and Guillemin, his former high school teacher and future biographer. These speakers, too, like Pichon, struck "big" civilizational themes, relating Mauchamp's pursuit of science and humanitarianism to the discharge of his patriotic duty as a Frenchman. Owing to the time constraints imposed by the foreign minister's schedule, two additional speakers—Jacques Bigart, a representative of the Alliance Israélite Universelle, the Jewish organization that maintained a school in Marrakesh, and Dr. Marius Baudrand, a personal friend from Paris—did not get an opportunity to speak, although their texts were later published.[7]

Louis Gentil, the geologist who had traveled with Mauchamp on his recent return to Marrakesh and who was one of the last people to see him alive, spoke last. He stressed the nature of Mauchamp's medical work and the personal loss felt by the small French community of Marrakesh for the young doctor in whose home they had gathered in the evenings for tennis and amiable conversation. Grandiosely, Gentil concluded his remarks by calling on the ordinary Frenchman to consider the famed Kutubiyya minaret of Marrakesh. "This giant minaret, built to the glory of an ancient civilization, now stands as a new marker of French civilization, because it shelters, o my dear friend, the altar where you were consumed for science and humanity."[8]

Toward 3:15, with the speeches concluded, the long funeral cor-

tège formed. Behind the mounted gendarmerie and at the head of
the many civic delegations, each with its flag or banner, marched or-
phaned children from the Hospice Saint-Louis. Two coaches loaded
with flowers preceded the hearse bearing Mauchamp's coffin. Acting as pallbearers were Guillemin, Mauchamp's old teacher, two of
his former medical colleagues, and three old childhood friends. The
entire cortège stretched 1,500 meters as it wended its way through
the streets of Chalon to the town's Eastern Cemetery. Among the
mourners were a surprising number of Mauchamp's acquaintances
from Morocco. These included the merchants Bouvier, Boule, and
the Amieux brothers as well as Vaffier-Pollet, the representative of
the Comité du Maroc, the Paris-based organization that promoted
French business and political involvement in Morocco. Also in attendance was Gabriel Veyre, author of a recently published and widely
celebrated account detailing his experiences as sultan Abdelaziz's
photography instructor.

At the cemetery, where the gates were initially shut to all but
family and officials, Mauchamp was buried in a civil ceremony. This
gesture reflected the young doctor's personal view that religious
belief was antithetical to the pursuit of science; this view was representative of the widespread anticlericalism in French republican
circles at the time.

The foreign minister and the other officials extended their condolences one last time before catching the 4:28 train back to Paris.
With their departure the crowd was now admitted into the cemetery. The mourners passed silently and somberly before the family
and the grave.

By 5:30 the "impressive and unforgettable ceremony" was complete. It was, in the hyperbolic words of Guillemin, "a veritable
triumph in death."

> The mourning for Mauchamp far exceeded the limits of his small
> hometown [*sa petite patrie*] and even those of France. It extended
> beyond the borders to the entire world of civilization, and there is
> no one in the bright universe who could remain indifferent. If the
> death of a soldier killed in battle merits glory, what strong and lofty
> admiration ought to be given to a man like Mauchamp, a benefi-
> cent apostle of peace, stoned by the very ones whom he came to
> enlighten, console and heal?[9]

L'Express de Lyon concluded its account of the funeral more mat-
ter-of-factly: "There was neither any accident nor incident."

Over the coming months and years the memorialization of Mauchamp in Chalon-sur-Saône continued. Not long after Mauchamp's death, Henri Guillemin composed a biography of his most famous student. Appearing initially in seven installments from 1907 to 1909 in *Le Bulletin de la Société des Sciences Naturelles de Saône-et-Loire*, the department's scholarly journal, Guillemin's admiring work stresses Mauchamp's devotion to science and reason, his selfless humanitarianism, and his dutiful patriotism.

Mauchamp, we are told, displayed the characteristic indifference to danger that marked a man of honor. He faced the challenge of each new epidemic like a brave soldier going into battle.[10] Beyond that, Mauchamp was cultivated, with an interest in art as well as science, and was a *causeur étincelant*, a captivating speaker. Most importantly, Mauchamp had not forgotten his roots. Guillemin depicts him as ever loyal to the city where his father, a career civil servant and long-time member of the city council, had served as mayor from 1899–1904. Throughout his Oriental adventures, Mauchamp himself remained an occasional contributor to the very same *Bulletin*.

At Mauchamp's funeral Lucien Guillemaut, the senator from Saône-et-Loire, also acknowledged the civic role played by Mauchamp's father. Guillemaut drew for his listeners the lesson that humanitarianism begins at home. "It is under the paternal aegis, by the examples permanently found in the family, that the young Mauchamp early on felt develop within himself feelings of human solidarity." The senator ended on an inspiring note, calling Chalon and the adjacent plain of la Bresse, the place of origin of Mauchamp's father, "this little homeland alongside the great French homeland." Chalon and the nation would piously keep alive Mauchamp's memory as a model of goodness, of the greatness of the fatherland, and of devotion to humanity.[11]

Speeches such as those delivered at Mauchamp's funeral and the small-town pride that suffuses Guillemin's biography demonstrate the sense of "connectedness" that French men and women in the provinces felt to the larger affairs of state. As historians of the period have often noted, the early Third Republic allowed the participation of the "middle middle class," the *bonne bourgeoisie*, in national politics in ways that had been restricted earlier in the century.[12]

According to Chalon's mayor, Mauchamp was motivated equally by a love of France and a love of humanity. "The second sentiment was born naturally of the first, because Dr. Mauchamp held that France ought to spread out in the world and extend its peaceful influence in disseminating generously on those who are still deprived the benefits of civilization." The mayor paid homage to Mauchamp's father as well, telling his listeners that "we can admire [the son's] tranquil courage, without being surprised by it, because we know in which school our compatriot had been reared."[13]

In short, the civilizing mission began at home.

La mission civilisatrice

To its proponents and practitioners, the idea that France had some special mission to bring civilization to the *indigènes,* or natives, was a self-evident proposition. Indeed, *la mission civilisatrice,* the civilizing mission, was such a commonplace phrase at the time that it required and received little comment. Despite the idea's ubiquity, it has received surprisingly little attention from scholars. Indeed, the typical response toward the French civilizing mission and its British equivalent, "the white man's burden," has been a cynical dismissal.[14]

Tempting as it may be to label Mauchamp a self-righteous hypocrite—or for that matter, following Marxist critics, to condemn the entire notion of a civilizing mission as either a pious fraud or a post facto rationalization—the evidence suggests otherwise. Men such as Mauchamp were sincere in their convictions regarding the inherent superiority of French cultural norms. Indeed, Mauchamp would have been the first to agree with sentiments later expressed by the socialist politician Léon Blum:

> We acknowledge the right and even the duty of superior races to attract those who have not arrived at the same degree of culture and to call them to the progress realized thanks to the efforts of science and industry. . . . We have too much love for our country to disavow the expansion of its thought, [and] of the French civilization.[15]

To many in France, the conviction that their particular version of post-Enlightenment, bourgeois, republican, scientific culture was in fact the universal civilization to which the entire world aspired was incontrovertible. Furthermore, France had a special obligation to extend the benefits of this civilization beyond its own borders. Indeed, the most striking aspect of the narrative of Mauchamp's life and death is the ethnocentrism—one can go so far as to say, narcissism—of the accompanying French discourse concerning France's civilizing mission.

Viewed in this light, the charge made by many that Mauchamp was sent to Marrakesh in October 1905 primarily as a spy both simplifies and exaggerates the political nature of his mission.[16] In fact, before his martyrdom and apotheosis, Mauchamp's incessant letter writing to Tangier marked him as a nuisance to his superiors in the foreign ministry. Reductionist explanations fail to answer the question of why politically motivated humanitarianism should take a particular form, in this case, that of a medical mission.

The genesis of the French civilizing mission can be found in the seventeenth-century encounter between the early French settlers and the native peoples of North America. On the ground, church and colonial officials pursued a twin policy of converting and "Frenchifying" the Indians. It was left to the intellectuals back home to ponder the nature of cultural diversity.[17] For French moralists, in viewing other peoples at a distance, the quandary hinged on how to reconcile the relationship between the universal and the particular. Their predilection for reason and order naturally led the French *philosophes* of the Enlightenment to uncover general principles. At least theoretically these should be applicable to all of humankind. But it comes as no surprise that the universal truths they espoused just happened to be the very customs and beliefs to which they themselves as Frenchmen—and the self-proclaimed proponents of human progress—subscribed.

Even in this earliest stage, the idea of a French civilizing mission was often confused and contradictory. As they swept across Europe, the armies of the Republic and later those of Napoleon were simultaneously represented as liberators and as conquerors. To be conquered by France—at least according to the French—*really* meant to be liberated from the reactionary constraints of the *ancien régime,* as the feudal social order of prerevolutionary Europe was known.

Not surprisingly, the notion that civilization could be both universal and simultaneously French did not fly everywhere. This was especially true in Germany, where thinkers in the early decades of the nineteenth century chafed under Napoleon's rule. In place of civilization German intellectuals offered a parallel explanation of human society that emphasized the concept of *kultur,* or culture. The French idea of "civilization" stressed the purported similarities that united peoples. In contrast, the German concept of "culture" recognized inherent differences in the identities of individual ethnic groups and nations. The concept of culture therefore was an implicit critique of the homogenizing nature of civilization.[18]

And yet for all the potential for territorial expansion latent in the idea of the civilizing mission, one finds its first true application not overseas but closer to home in Europe. There, beginning in the mid-nineteenth century, the European middle and upper classes sought to impose their values on the lower levels of their own national societies. The civilizing mission was carried to the slums and backward rural corners of Europe just as much as it was to North Africa or Indochina.

Likewise, the lines between colony and *métropole* or between colonizer and colonized were not tightly drawn. Colonial policies were very often extensions of metropolitan concerns confronting the mother country.[19] For example, Mauchamp's specialist training in infant hygiene—a concern that continued to absorb him in both Jerusalem and Marrakesh—clearly reflects France's homegrown metropolitan preoccupation with a declining birth rate and high infant mortality. Middle-class civilizers such as Mauchamp naturally extended their fields of operation overseas when the opportunity presented itself. By the same token, it comes as no surprise that Mauchamp should inveigh with equal ardor against the superstitions of the Bretons (who after all were ostensibly French) and the customs of Morocco's Arabs and Jews.

At the outset, concepts of political and moral reform underlay the idea of a civilizing mission. To these there soon adhered the notion of scientific accomplishment as the key determinant of civilization. Some historians have argued that, beginning in the eighteenth century, the ever-growing discrepancy in technological and material culture between Europe and the rest of the world was the overriding factor in the West's global domination. Racial arguments of European superiority were thus a later accretion in the process.

In the French case, beginning in the early 1800s, the idea of technological progress as the key to civilization was especially prominent among the followers of Saint Simon, many of whom—graduates of the École Polytechnique, the preeminent scientific institution of its day—filled the ranks of the military. These officers gravitated to Algeria. If society in Europe was to be recast along rational lines, even more urgent was the need for social reconstruction in North Africa. There they found alleged vestiges of feudalism—identified in the French mind with Arab tribalism and often contrasted with the supposed democratic values of the sedentary, village-dwelling, monogamist Kabyle Berbers. The strong French anticlerical tradition also played its part in the desire to remake North Africa and North Africans. Islam as a religion (not unlike the Catholic Church) was seen as obscurantist and as a hindrance to social progress.[20]

In short, while economics and politics may have provided the most closely argued theoretical justifications for imperialism, the loudest, most persistent, and ultimately most successful appeals were those made to French patriotism and humanitarianism. "The task of penetration and civilization in Morocco," wrote Jules Bois in his introduction to Mauchamp's posthumous book on witchcraft, "ought henceforth no longer to be the work of one party but that of every Frenchman who thinks of his country and the services which it continues to render on behalf of humanity."[21]

During the late nineteenth century French colonial policy in North Africa and elsewhere fluctuated between two theoretical poles, known respectively as *assimilation* and *association*. In its coarsest outline, assimilation maintained that the *indigènes*—that is, Arabs and Berbers—could rise to the level of European civilization under proper tutelage. In effect, natives could become Frenchmen. This goal was of course utopian, paternalistic, and condescending, but it was not—and here one needs to emphasize the point—necessarily disingenuous or mean-spirited.[22] Rather it was offered in the same generous and self-referential universalizing spirit that had long characterized French attitudes toward France's civilizing mission on the whole. As one French theorist wrote, "Thus we are often naïve enough to believe that that which makes us happy will make everyone happy, that all of humanity must think and feel as France does."[23]

Apart from the many practical difficulties in implementing a policy of assimilation, the chief obstacle of course was that the "natives" did not want to be assimilated. In particular, the policy ran up against the shoals of the Islamic religion, regarding which the French by and large had little understanding and less tolerance. Whereas in Algeria Jews could become naturalized French citizens as a result of the Crémieux law of 1870, subsequent laws extending citizenship to Muslim Berbers and Arabs contained an unacceptable "catch." Acceptance of French legal authority implied a renunciation of Islamic law and, by extension, Islam. Only a few thousand Muslim Algerians ever became French citizens.[24] What ultimately remained of the concept of assimilation was a misappropriated and watered-down notion that Algeria's half million European settlers (rather than its native inhabitants) be granted representation in the French chamber of deputies and senate. Simultaneously functioning as a colony of settlement for Europeans and a colony of economic exploitation,

Algeria remained a kind of hybrid experiment, a "mixed polity" in the language of that day.[25]

By the end of the nineteenth century additional factors emerged to weaken the previously unassailable conviction that native peoples could and should be assimilated into French society. First, so-called scientific attitudes regarding race and racial difference led to the construction of strict racial hierarchies. These categories, which placed Europeans at the summit of human evolution, served to undermine cherished French sentiments regarding brotherhood and equality. Secondly, colonial theorists in France began to examine the administrative practices of the rival colonial powers, Britain and Holland. There they found much to admire in the decentralized organization and utilitarian attitudes that characterized these regimes. The motive for colonial possessions, according to this line of thought, was profit, first and foremost. "The Englishman hasn't the false pretension to be loved," Jules Bois wrote regarding the British in India. "He wishes to be comfortable and to 'make money.' His goal has been attained."[26]

A third and final factor that led French colonial theorists to abandon the idea of assimilation was the emergence of colonial sociology. This new discipline, which celebrated its first international congress in conjunction with the Paris International Exposition of 1900, rejected the idea that cultural differences could be mitigated. These later theorists instead called upon colonial administrations to respect native institutions and customs as far as possible. In the name of science, "colonial practice was to be based on empirical evidence. Observation, investigation, analysis became the key words used."[27]

Thus spent, the doctrine of assimilation was replaced in the minds of colonial theorists by the new policy of association. In principle, association presumed the close cooperation between the French and the native populations, "each doing what best suited its abilities and stage of development."[28] As the technologically more advanced party, France would henceforth be a tutor to its colonial subjects. As might have been expected, the transition from assimilation to association was to a large extent one of name only. But whereas assimilation was paternalistic, association was proprietorial. While it obviously required that a few natives be educated to make the process of colonial rule easier, it made no demand that the mass of Arabs and Berbers be turned into Frenchmen and Frenchwomen. The policy of association, which provided for indirect rule rather than outright appropriation, would be most famously applied in Morocco. There the Protectorate agreement of 1912 left the monarchy intact. Unlike Algeria, Morocco was never formally declared a French possession.[29]

Among its proponents, association was most closely identified with the Protectorate's first resident general, Louis-Hubert-Gonzalve Lyautey (1912–1925). In his own words, the Protectorate was

> not the domination of a vanquished people by a conqueror, but a free association of two nations; one of them is ours, which provides you with a superior administration, the resources of the most advanced civilization, and the material means to draw on the better part of the resources of this beautiful empire, our force guaranteeing moreover against foreign intervention and anarchy; the other country, yours, still with its integrity under the shelter of this tutelary protection, guarding its laws, its institutions, its free exercise of its religion, developing in peace and in order its riches and prosperity.[30]

One of the most celebrated figures in French colonial history, General (later Marshal) Lyautey stood out among his contemporaries. In an age of republicanism, he remained a monarchist. And although he was an intellectual with refined, aristocratic tastes, his reverence for tradition did not prevent him from becoming an imaginative social innovator. His sympathetic and somewhat romantic attitude toward native peoples was formed by his military experience as a young officer in Algeria. In his later service in Indochina and Madagascar he carefully absorbed the lessons in colonial administration formulated by his commanding officer, General Joseph Gallieni. Combining military force and political persuasion, the latter's colonial policy depended on winning the confidence of the local inhabitants.

Lyautey would later carefully emulate Gallieni's approach in the pacification of Morocco. Known as *la tache d'huile*, or oil stain, it was a "go slow" strategy of military conquest.

> Immediately after the pacification of some territory, permanent posts, political centers and means of communication were to be established. Then the advance would continue slowly; the region would be cleared of the enemy with the help of the local inhabitants now won over to the French cause and duly armed for their new task. Provisional posts would be established in the newly acquired regions, and the process would thus continue until the whole region had been conquered and pacified.[31]

Under Lyautey, political "native affairs" officers were attached to military posts for the twin purposes of surveillance and negotiation with local leaders. Moreover, the posts, in that they provided local markets, also served as economic centers. And finally, in an effort to integrate social services and pursue a "hearts and minds" strategy, Lyautey authorized the creation of mobile medical units to tour the surrounding countryside. Just as medicine stood at the core of Théophile Delcassé's diplomatic policy of peaceful penetration, so too medicine was seen as central to the policy of military pacification that followed. As Lyautey himself famously quipped, "A doctor is worth a battalion."

The Formation of a Civilizer

The second of four children, Émile Mauchamp was born in Chalon-sur-Saône on March 3, 1870. His father Pierre, originally from Sens, one of the smaller towns of the surrounding plain of la Bresse, had moved to Chalon as a young man in 1855. There he held a variety of positions in the local administration, culminating in a term as the city's mayor. Mauchamp's biographer Guillemin makes much of the weekly visits to the local prison undertaken by the elder Mauchamp and the efforts he undertook to rehabilitate convicts. Such paternal devotion to the ideals of social justice, Guillemin insists, inspired Mauchamp to pursue medicine as a career.[32]

The young Émile's childhood was not without blemish, however. Despite his record as an outstanding student at the local *collège*, or middle school, his biographer writes that Émile was "unjustly reprimanded" for an unidentified prank committed by one of his classmates. Whatever the circumstances, the episode had significant consequences for the young Émile: His parents sent him away to attend the lycée in Lons-le-Saunier, a city even smaller than Chalon, some forty miles away. After three years he returned to his hometown where he completed his secondary education before heading off to Paris to study medicine.

In Paris Mauchamp already exhibited many of the same qualities that he would later demonstrate overseas in Jerusalem and Marrakesh, namely, a combination of heroic selflessness and driving personal ambition. After completing his initial studies and an internship in surgery, Mauchamp in 1896 came to the attention of Gaston Variot. As Variot would write in an obituary for Mauchamp in the journal *La Clinique infantile* (The Children's Clinic), the two men shared a common regional tie in addition to a mutual interest in pediatric medicine. Under Variot's direction Mauchamp worked—"without any worry as to danger or infection"—in the diphtheria service of the Trousseau children's hospital. Moreover, over the next two years Mauchamp would often join Variot on his weekly Friday rounds at the children's clinic in Belleville, then a working-class suburb of Paris.[33]

Mauchamp could not have chosen a better mentor. In fin-de-siècle France, Gaston Variot was a well-known name, a leader in the campaign for better healthcare for mothers and newborns and one of the founders, along with the physician-activist Pierre Budin and the politician Paul Strauss, of the League against Infant Mortality.[34] In 1889, on his return from a study tour of pediatric hospitals in London and Edinburgh, Variot spearheaded efforts to restructure the delivery of public healthcare in Paris. By 1901 three separate smaller hospitals, each designed to counteract the spread of contagious disease, replaced the old Trousseau hospital. Moreover, again following the English model, Variot established outpatient clinics, among them Belleville, where nursing mothers could be educated about infant hygiene. He also established *gouttes de lait*, literally, "drops of milk," clinics where mothers could receive sterilized milk for their infants.

Becoming an ardent disciple of Variot and his methods, Mauchamp undertook to write a thesis (as French medical students were then required to do) entitled *L'Allaitement artificiel des nourissons par le lait sterilisé* (The Artificial Feeding of Nursing Infants by Sterilized Milk).[35] Totaling 661 pages, Mauchamp's exhaustive study far exceeded the normal medical thesis in length. Despite the reservations of one examiner, who found the study filled with excessive (but perhaps not uncharacteristic) moralizing, Mauchamp received his doctorate in medicine in 1898 with highest marks. Variot himself was unstinting in his praise: "There cannot be a more important work in France than *L'Allaitement*."[36]

Mauchamp's moralizing is evident on the very first pages of his work. He notes that it might appear ironic that the author of a book entitled "Artificial Feeding" should in fact, be in perfect agreement with Dr. Adolphe Pinard, at the time France's leading advocate of breastfeeding.[37] Despite the detailed case Mauchamp makes for sterilized cow's milk as a substitute for breast milk, he makes it clear that a healthy mother's breast is by far the preferable means of feeding an infant. What Mauchamp objected to then was not breastfeeding per se but the use of wet nurses, particularly paid wet nurses. These he described in no uncertain terms as "prostitutes of a particular kind," women who, for money, neglected the care of their own children. His language is unambiguous: "We wish to show that the wet nurse is a very abnormal and immoral product of civilization and we wish to possess the power to hurl upon this institution the most complete discredit."[38]

Calling them pitiless "monsters," Mauchamp also had choice words for those modern women who preferred to send their children to wet nurses rather than take responsibility for nursing their infants themselves. Worse yet were those women—"unfeeling, egotistical beings"—for whom motherhood was odious and who failed to perform their maternal function.[39]

While the Roussel law of 1874 ostensibly regulated the use of wet nurses in a quest to reduce infant mortality, some two decades later the situation still remained dire. The quality of wet nurses was inconsistent, and mothers often employed three to four different women in the course of a year. The figures mustered by Mauchamp in support of his cause are indeed depressing. More than five thousand wet nurses serviced Paris annually, he says, but of those who left their own infants in the countryside, their children suffered a premature mortality rate of 77 percent. Meanwhile, Pinard, the mother's milk advocate, asserted that there was not a wet nurse in Paris whose own child had reached six months of age.[40]

Legay, another authority quoted by Mauchamp, even made recourse to Darwinian arguments in decrying this situation: "It is profoundly immoral to let one part of the population sacrifice itself for another, all the more so since the best of the mothers employed as wet nurses comprise the production of healthy infants whose disappearance is a sensible loss for the race and the greatest breach of the law of natural selection."[41]

Legay's citation of Darwin is notable; even in 1899, French scholars were still reticent in citing, let alone accepting, his views. Meanwhile, other studies cited by Mauchamp claimed that between one-fourth and one-third of the twenty thousand Parisian infants sent each year to the countryside to nurse soon died.[42]

With this broadside, the twenty-eight-year-old Mauchamp sought to make his mark on French public health policy. In this regard it should be noted that physicians like his mentor Variot enjoyed inordinate prestige in the national life of France of this period. Indeed, in total numbers doctors were second only to jurists in the legislature of the early Third Republic.[43] Even the prime minister himself, Clemenceau, had studied medicine before embarking on a political career.

Choice of a medical career meant more than mere social advancement. It also implied a commitment to a certain set of progressive and scientific values. Few doctors who obtained their degrees in Paris "could escape the ideological trappings of medical instruction in the capital."[44] These trappings included philosophical materialism and positivism and, by extension, anticlericalism and petit-bourgeois radicalism, all attitudes that shaped the Third Republic's approach to questions of public hygiene and other social issues. Mauchamp's choice of pediatrics for his specialty and his subsequent research on infant formula are especially significant; they reflect a high-minded seriousness in attempting to solve what was perceived at the time as France's number-one social problem, a demographic crisis manifested in a declining birthrate and high infant mortality.[45] Thus Mauchamp's devotion to science and his patriotism went hand in hand. In the aftermath of defeat in the 1870 Franco-Prussian war and in the tense atmosphere preceding World War I, questions of natality and puericulture—as efforts to improve infant care were called—were political as much as social or medical concerns. In simplest terms, Germany's population was growing, and France's was not.

France was not alone in its preoccupation. Early in the twentieth-century Belgium and England also took turns wringing their hands over depopulation and infant mortality.[46] On the one hand, the demands of maintaining an empire required ever more able-bodied men and women to serve in the colonies. On the other, European colonial doctors and administrators such as Mauchamp could not refrain from imposing on their subject populations overseas the attitudes toward birth and childrearing that they formed in the *métropole*.

Like many ambitious French students of the time, Mauchamp had, during the course of his medical studies, undertaken a stay in Austria and Germany. Upon receipt of his degree, smitten by the travel bug, he took a position with the interior ministry as a *médecin sanitaire maritime,* a naval medical officer. The position carried him to ports through much of southern Europe and South America, and Mauchamp's résumé for this period reads like a chronicle of infectious disease: the plague in Portugal, yellow fever in Brazil, typhus in Salonica and Smyrna.[47] All these experiences stood as good preparation for his appointment by the foreign ministry in June 1900 as a government doctor at the French Hôpital Saint-Louis in Jerusalem.

A Doctor in Jerusalem

Mauchamp took the Palestine assignment not without some anxiety. At the end of February 1900, he pondered whether to accept the position, and during a stop in Constantinople, he wrote directly to the French consul in Jerusalem to whom he posed a series of questions:

> Chiefly, I should like to know how many doctors there are appointed by the government to the French hospital and how many French doctors there are in the city? How many foreign and native doctors? What would the situation be like for a French doctor to establish himself there now? Could one find there sufficient, paying clientele either among the locals or the tourists? Is there in Jerusalem a *society* [underlined in original] which one could frequent and make some agreeable contacts? Is the city generally well-off and are the French doctors there viewed favorably? Finally, will housing and the cost of living be expensive, and would they not serve to eat up completely a modest wage?[48]

The consul offered a disquieting reply two weeks later. Regarding "society," the doctor would find none, only the members of the consular corps and a small number of foreign merchants. The city's inhabitants were poor; there was certainly not enough of a paying clientele for a doctor to make a real living. The consul further cautioned Mauchamp: It would be difficult to find a decent house for less than eight hundred to one thousand francs, and the quality of the local cooks was decidedly inferior.[49]

As discouraging as this news might have been, Mauchamp remained undeterred. He accepted the offer but wrote again to the consul in July, this time from Chalon-sur-Saône, asking permission to delay his departure till early September. He had just returned from the Black Sea and wanted to spend time with his family and visit the International Exposition, then in full swing in Paris. Apologetically, Mauchamp again demanded information about housing—whether he could find a furnished place in Jerusalem and what he should bring with him from France. The consul's reply this time was terse. Mauchamp's predecessor had simply lived in a hotel.[50] Mauchamp continued to postpone his departure, finally arriving in Jerusalem in November. Apart from a few months of leave, Mauchamp would spend the next four and a half years in Palestine.

Despite the impression the consul's correspondence might have given, Jerusalem at the turn of the century was hardly a dreary or moribund place. Driven by Jewish immigration, its population over the previous two decades had doubled. According to one reliable estimate, in 1900 there were thirty-five thousand Jews living in Jerusalem, with the city's remaining twenty thousand inhabitants divided equally between Christians and Muslims.[51] A "new" Jerusalem had emerged alongside the old city. Occupying an area twice as big as the "old" Jerusalem bounded by the city walls, it was where nearly half of this swelling Jewish population lived. In addition, a vast floating population of tourists and Christian pilgrims also crowded old Jerusalem's narrow streets. The largest group of pilgrims, some ten thousand of them in 1904, were Russian Christians.[52] A narrow-gauge, single-track train laboriously carried visitors and immigrants from the coast to the holy city.

Like the rest of Palestine and Syria, Jerusalem was subject to Turkish authority. Nonetheless, the city had become the object of a lively rivalry among the European nations. Midway through the nineteenth century and in the wake of the Crimean War, France and Russia in particular clashed over who should be the custodians of the holy sites. As the self-avowed protector of all Christians living within the Ottoman empire, the Russian tsar supported the claims of the Greek Orthodox Church. France, backing the Franciscans in their capacity as the Custodians of the Holy Land, represented Latin claims. In the absence of a satisfactory solution, a status quo emerged, with control of various sites—and even rooms within sites—being carefully divided among religious sects. Even when France took an anticlerical direction at the turn of the century, it continued to present itself as the champion of the Catholics in the Middle East and engaged in a heated diplomatic rivalry with Italy. Britain and Germany, meanwhile, competed over who would represent Protestant interests in the city. Engaging in what one historian has called "spiritual imperialism," each European nation supported philanthropy of all kinds, becoming the patron of hospitals, orphanages, schools, churches, and other charities.[53]

In particular, Kaiser Wilhelm II's 1898 visit to the city served as the occasion for a kind of urban renewal.[54] Two years after the event, a British observer noted that

> the visit of the German Emperor is still marked with a white stone in the history of Jerusalem. Roads were made, gates were opened,

the town was even cleaned in his honor, and he showed his warm appreciation of the welcome, general, and well deserved, by the truly cosmopolitan and Catholic spirit in which he presented to his subjects, in the Holy City, two sites, one for the erection of a Lutheran, the other of a Latin Church.[55]

European rivalries also manifested themselves in more mundane matters. In 1900 German and French authorities each opened special post offices in Jerusalem. Russia, Italy, and Austria all followed suit. Meanwhile, the Turkish government, sensing competition, opened additional branches in the new Jewish quarters.[56]

Resident Arabs were naturally disquieted by these changes. Meanwhile, the Jewish population continued to grow, especially after the creation of political Zionism and the resulting second wave of Jewish migration, from 1905 to 1914, known as the Second Aliyah.[57] "Nowhere was the fear of eventual Jewish statehood felt more strongly than among the Arabs of Jerusalem. When, at the end of 1900, the Ottoman authorities promulgated regulations making Jewish entry to Palestine, and also Jewish land purchase, easier, a number of Jerusalem Arabs holding positions in the local government collected signatures to protest to Constantinople."[58]

Jerusalem would be Mauchamp's proving ground for Marrakesh in more ways than one. In addition to thriving professionally as a doctor, he amply displayed his physical hardiness in a series of desert explorations. Moreover, in Jerusalem he developed a taste for politics. If the emerging conflict between Jews and Arabs seemed to have escaped his attention, he nonetheless quickly understood the nature of the European rivalry for influence in the Middle East. Mauchamp's experience in Jerusalem would not go unnoticed when the French foreign minister Théophile Delcassé, crafting his policy of "peaceful penetration," looked for a candidate to post to Marrakesh.

Although staffed by doctors on the government payroll, including those like Mauchamp who were staunchly anticlerical, the Hôpital Saint-Louis in Jerusalem was a religious institution founded by the Franciscans in the 1880s and, to judge from Mauchamp's account of it, a somewhat rundown place. Eager to emulate Variot's Belleville model, he established weekly consultations for nursing mothers. Reporting on his activities on behalf of puericulture in *La Clinique infantile*, he praised the nuns attached to the hospital and nursery. "Alongside the propaganda designed to save souls," he wrote, "there is a proselytism which saves the body and which gives immediate and palpable results." Moreover, the work of infant care added to France's prestige. "There is no more certain claim to the gratitude of the natives nor a better means of attracting them than preventing their children from dying."[59]

Later, when Mauchamp was living in Marrakesh, he received a packet with more than fifteen letters from friends and former colleagues in Jerusalem. Among them were long and affectionate letters from four nuns with whom he had worked and one from a priest who wrote, "I swear that I would prefer a skeptic and an out-and-out unbeliever like you if he possessed at least everything that you have deprived us of by leaving." Even before Mauchamp met his premature death, his framed photograph hung on the wall in the hospital waiting room in Jerusalem.[60]

To further the gospel of puericulture and to advertise his regular consultation hours for nursing mothers, Mauchamp wrote and distributed a dozen-page booklet in both Arabic and French versions, offering guidance on the feeding and care of infants.[61]

Beyond his activities as a pediatrician, Mauchamp also won recognition during his service in Jerusalem for his work related to various epidemics. In 1901 he dealt with an outbreak of smallpox. Next, in the fall of 1902, the consular corps in Jerusalem put Mauchamp in charge of efforts to protect the city from a cholera epidemic that was then raging in Palestine. Mauchamp won an Ottoman decoration for his successful efforts, and, according to a report submitted by Auguste Boppe, the French consul general in Jerusalem, he earned for the Hôpital Saint-Louis a "first place" among hospitals in the city. With its reputation established even among the Bedouins of the desert, the consul enthusiastically wrote, it was to the French hospital that Jews, Christians, and Muslims alike turned with confidence.

At medical meetings held by the local authorities in Jerusalem, Boppe wrote, "our compatriot did not cease to contribute his unwavering sang-froid, his perfect understanding of questions of hygiene, [and] the certainty of his judgment and knowledge. . . . We saw his counsel prevail and his opinions predominate in the decisions taken. It is hardly excessive to affirm that, owing especially to his initiatives, his energy and his tenacity that the city of Jerusalem was spared the scourge."[62] Shortly following Mauchamp's death, Boppe's report was reprinted in *Le Courrier,* one of the two local dailies in Chalon-sur-Saône, where, with predictable hyperbole, it was observed that

Mauchamp by his deeds served not only the Ottoman sultan and his subjects but the cause of France and all humanity.[63]

Mauchamp's letters home show him enthusiastic about his work in Jerusalem.[64] In June 1902 he wrote that he remained in perfect health despite his work among the sick and that he hurried about "at a speed that I must have gotten from papa, and which is becoming legendary here where they are used to conducting themselves *à l'orientale*." In an official record dating from the period, Mauchamp's superiors gave him high grades: "Good conduct, correct bearing, well-regarded," and then added somewhat comically, as if to explain the above remarks, "No relations with active Army officers" and "Doesn't know how to ride a horse."[65]

During Mauchamp's mission to Gaza, however, his letters home took on a more somber tone. At six each morning, with the aid of Ottoman troops, he began house-to-house searches for the dead and sick in the peasant villages. "We did this every day, eating at impossible hours, scarcely sleeping, because it has to be settled very quickly."

> Despite [the opinion of] four of my five of my colleagues who absolutely thought they saw cholera everywhere, I affirmed that it was it was matter of typhus, from pernicious attacks, arising among populations stretched by the harsh summer, misery, congestion, dirty drinking water, rotten fruit, overripe melons, etc.; these are the things that dispose them to contract illnesses which would not kill resistant organs but which strike them down in a matter of hours.

Having made preparations against the further outbreak of cholera, Mauchamp requested a six-day rest period for the overworked soldiers. Writing to his parents, he contrasted his humanity with that of the brutal Ottoman gendarmerie captain. Moreover, his quick expedition to Gaza restored calm. "I acquired here an authority such that the counsels I give are immediately executed."[66]

In another letter, dated November 3, 1902, he extolled the virtues of his European sensibility in Jerusalem. "Happily, there's a bit of European energy to shatter the torpor, prevent exactions, denounce speculations, and undertake useful work. It only costs a bit of effort and fatigue. But the result is the salvation of many unfortunates."[67]

Three weeks later, in a letter dated November 20, Mauchamp offered his assessment of the epidemic's prospects in Jerusalem. To allay the fears of his parents, he used humor to disparage the local risks of the disease.

> The Holy City is always sheltered from every contagion; it's only natural that the Holy Sepulcher, the Mosque of Omar and the Temple of Solomon be respected. Besides, winter has just come to us prematurely, which is excellent here from the point of view of the epidemic; however, very disagreeable cold rains: how I miss our good sun! The south of Palestine, Gaza, etc., is improving and the scourge is extinguishing itself. In contrast, Jaffa has been ravaged for ten days, and the panic there is considerable, the cases there being violent. . . . My poor Bedouins of Arabia are being decimated in their tribes, and today the border towns are infected.[68]

Finally, the doctor relayed to his parents an account of a pernicious rumor that circulated in Jerusalem. Later, in letters home from Marrakesh, he would similarly inveigh against a German-trained rival named Holzmann for also spreading rumors that he was plying his patients with a slow-working poison.[69]

> Here they accuse doctors of the worst misdeeds. A bizarre phenomenon, I alone have escaped the mistrust, and Muslims, Greeks, Latins only want to come to my hospital since I'm the only one—according to them—who doesn't poison suspected patients. I just snatched from the police two or three poor devils, found sick in the street, whom they wanted to take to a house outside the city without any care. I forced them to my hospital; they are completely healed; besides, they didn't have cholera!

Mauchamp emerges from his letters as a man proud of his accomplishments and therefore all the more zealous in claiming what was his due. As the cholera epidemic abated in December of 1902, Mauchamp found time to deal with an irksome Italian colleague, a doctor Savignoni who had put up posters in Hebrew stating his affiliation with the French hospital. While this was "good advertising" for the French hospital, as he wrote to the consul Boppe, it was simply not true that Savignoni was on his staff.[70]

To his mother back in Chalon, he wrote on January 14, 1903, that his career in Palestine had gotten off to a better start "than I dared to hope, and if I've had to expend some effort, I've been well compensated for it." Finding challenge in his medical work, Mauchamp wrote that there is "nothing astonishing" in his staying longer in Palestine than he had originally expected.[71]

Midway through his Palestine stay, Mauchamp took a three-month leave and at his own expense joined a French scientific mission to the Sinai, the Red Sea, and the Jordanian desert.[72] The party, thirteen in all, set off on February 11, 1902, from Port Tewfik at the Suez Canal. Their immediate destination was the monastery of Saint Catherine in the Sinai Desert, but the expedition got off to an incongruous start when, just a few hours after mounting their camels, they ran into a group of more than four hundred Russian marines coming back from an outing in the desert. A month later, following assorted and sometimes difficult negotiations with the Bedouins for safe passage, the French explorers arrived at Petra, the real object of their long desert ramble. Although the explorer Burckhardt had first visited the Nabataean ruins in 1812, nearly a century later it was still no mean achievement for Mauchamp and his companions to reach the ancient site. Petra captured Mauchamp's imagination, and he waxed romantic in his descriptions of the picturesque ruins at sunset.

Mauchamp's few months in the desert also allowed him to form a favorable impression of the Bedouins. According to his biographer Guillemin, Mauchamp had a special affinity for the desert Arabs. "By his tact, the goodness of his heart and his disinterested devotion, he knew to earn the confidence and unalterable friendship of these defiant and wild people." Enthusiastically, Guillemin writes of a shaykh named Abu Ghush: "For this powerful tribal chief to love Émile, wasn't this to love France a bit?"[73]

The Bedouins' alleged enthusiasm for Mauchamp was reciprocated. Mauchamp, who never stinted in his criticism of retrograde Morocco, "did not know how to contain his almost lyric appreciation for the Bedouins of great Arabia," wrote Jules Bois in his introduction to Mauchamp's posthumous book.[74]

Living in their uncomplicated, rude barbarity, the "real" Bedouins, according to Mauchamp, enjoyed a healthy primitivism. "Even if they are miserable and often have to replace costly tobacco in their *chibouk* with dried up camel dung, they are the masters of their destiny, and having no obligations toward anyone, can play out the fantasy of their beautiful freedom."[75] In Mauchamp's eyes the Bedouins were also veritable republicans. "A tribe of great Bedouins offers a very simplified but exactly realized image of the perfect Republic where the three superb words [*Liberté, Egalité, Fraternité*] which symbolize the ideal in ours, correspond among them to certain realities."[76]

The alleged superiority of the Bedouins to other Arabs was a common belief among European travelers and writers on the Middle East. Whereas Mauchamp was wont to see republicans, his British contemporary Wilfrid Blunt praised the Bedouins of the Najd region of Arabia for their aristocratic virtues.[77] Significantly, Mauchamp's positive image of Bedouins as "pure" Arabs would contribute to his later impressions of the racial and moral degeneracy of the supposed "mixed"-blooded Moroccans.

The following year, in May of 1903, Mauchamp was granted another official leave. It is not clear what he did during these four months, but before his departure, he managed to submit a fifty-seven-page handwritten report.[78] This document not only summarizes the details of his own service from November 15, 1900, to January 1, 1903, but ambitiously documents the state of healthcare in Jerusalem. As he earlier demonstrated in his lengthy dissertation on the benefits of sterilized milk, Mauchamp had a talent for assembling and reporting data. In this case, he provided details regarding every hospital and clinic in Jerusalem. Undoubtedly his motives were patriotic; the success of the Hôpital Saint-Louis could be measured only in comparison to the efforts of hospitals sponsored by other nations. The growth of the Hôpital Saint-Louis under Mauchamp's direction was indeed impressive. He had doubled the personnel and tripled the number of beds. The daily average number of hospitalized patients had grown from eight to ten to between thirty and forty. Outpatient consultations had grown to between two hundred and three hundred persons in place of twenty-five to fifty.

In January 1905 Mauchamp was granted a third leave. This time, setting out in February 1905, Mauchamp toured Syria and Egypt. In Aleppo he was the guest of the local governor, and in Damascus he enjoyed the hospitality of Saleh, the son of Abd al-Qadir, the famous Algerian patriot-in-exile. In Palestine and Syria Mauchamp had grown accustomed to receiving a warm reception from local notables. While on leave, Mauchamp unsuccessfully sought a post in Egypt, and it may be that he learned of the prospect of an opening in Morocco at this time.

Mauchamp finally returned to Europe in June 1905, where, in addition to visiting his family, he made a tour of Belgium and Holland. Something of an aesthete as well as a man of science, Mauchamp filled his letters home to his father with descriptions of paintings, sculpture, and cathedrals. With his friend, the painter

Louis Cambier, Mauchamp visited the atelier of Constantin Meunier, a Belgian sculptor who had just died that year. The family was still in mourning, and the sculptor's daughter played for the visitors the funeral march from Wagner's *Siegfried*. "I've rarely had impressions more strong, more great, more beautiful," Mauchamp wrote of the moving scene, "and this will be one of my most pure reminders of this voyage where I have only seen beautiful things, and how many!"[79]

From Amsterdam Mauchamp again wrote his father, this time gushing effusively as he recalled all the paintings by Rubens, Van Dyck, Memling, Rembrandt, and Hals that he had seen in recent weeks. "With that I'll furnish my memory and ruminate on beautiful art in hours of solitude during my stay in Morocco. Through reminiscence, the Flemish chiaroscuro will refresh me, when I find myself in the shade in the lands of the Maghreb!"[80]

Only one episode in Guillemin's account of Mauchamp's stay in Palestine gives a presentiment of the difficulties he would later face in Morocco. From Guillemin we learn that Mauchamp was an avid photographer.[81] One day, Mauchamp attempted surreptitiously to take photographs of the holy mosque in Hebron. After narrowly eluding the guards, he then courted the risk, according to Guillemin, of being stoned by fanatical Muslims. In Hebron, nothing happened. In Marrakesh, Mauchamp would not be so lucky.

2

The Road to Marrakesh

Medical Diplomacy

Beginning in 1904, Théophile Delcassé, the French foreign minister, threw his avid support behind the idea of sending French doctors to Morocco and created a Moroccan Medical Aid Service.[1] While entirely consistent with the official policy that France should extend its influence in Morocco through means of "peaceful penetration" rather than outright military action, Delcassé's decision also reflects the success of other medical missions—such as the Hôpital Saint-Louis in Jerusalem—in countries other than Morocco. <u>Medicine made for good public relations</u>. By 1905, some twenty French doctors, most sent by the state and a few with private practices, were active in Morocco. Almost all were stationed exclusively in the cities along the coast, where they competed against some thirty other English, Spanish, and German doctors.[2]

The use of doctors and medicine for political ends was not of course new. As early as 1845, Henri Salvandy, a French minister of education, addressed a medical conference at which he spoke of the "seduction" of "medical diplomacy."[3] In the case of Morocco at the turn of the century, the Quai d'Orsay—as the foreign ministry was known—regretted that there was no longer any Frenchman to take the place of Fernand Linarès. The famed Doctor Linarès lived in Morocco from 1877 to 1902, and in his capacity as court physician to the sultan Moulay Hassan was an important liaison between the French and the Makhzan.[4] In frequent communication with the French legation in Tangier, he promoted French interests at the expense of Germany and Britain, and when fighting broke out

Still does

between Spain and Morocco over Melilla in 1893, Linarès helped negotiate a settlement.[5]

The Spanish and the British, inspired Dr. Linarès's success, sought to introduce their own medical diplomats. The Spanish doctor Joaquin Cortès arrived in Fez in 1891 as part of a Spanish military mission; after being called as a doctor on various occasions in the palace, he was accredited as an official Spanish diplomatic representative in 1894. He remained in Morocco for another ten years.[6] The British, for their part, pinned their hopes on Dr. Egbert Verdon. His favor in the court dated to 1898, when he was called in to heal the ministers of war and finance. Verdon's brother Navil was a military instructor under Sir Harry Maclean, the sultan's British-born chief military advisor.[7] After Linarès retired, Verdon effectively became the sultan's physician, but the French would not let this claim go unchallenged. In 1904 a lively rivalry emerged between Verdon and Dr. Jaffary, a physician from Marseilles employed by the French mission in Fez. Jaffary achieved his first success when he delivered a baby for one of the sultan's wives. He would later announce another triumph over the English doctor Verdon with a message delivered by carrier pigeon to the French legation in Tangier: "I was called yesterday to place suppositories in two of his Majesty's negresses. We can do no better than that at peaceful penetration."

In his memoirs the former French chargé d'affaires Saint-Aulaire dryly commented that "this was revenge for Waterloo, or at least Fashoda."[8] As the veteran diplomat himself observed, international competition in Morocco took forms unknown to the chancelleries of Europe. Unlike the humorless Mauchamp, Jaffary in Fez seems to have fully appreciated the irony of his service in the sultan's harem as an instrument of peaceful penetration. "In Morocco, the new order is to deliver infants only by means of forceps."[9]

Toward 1885 various Presbyterian missionary societies also introduced doctors to Morocco. These operated mostly in urban areas. In many instances patients would be obliged to endure readings of the gospel before receiving medical treatment. Apart from attracting potential converts, offering treatment had another advantage. "It served as a lure to financial supporters in the metropole, who preferred medical humanitarianism to religious proselytizing."[10]

In addition to governmental and religiously sponsored missionaries, European medicine was also represented in Morocco by private physicians who had come to make their fortunes among the European settler communities of the coast. One student of the professional classes in Morocco has characterized these doctors as settler-adventurers. "Committed advocates of colonial takeover, who frequently sought to supplement their incomes by extramedical activities, these doctors were swiftly drawn into politics, from yellow journalism to espionage."[11]

The most famous of these settler-adventurers was Felix Weisgerber, a ship's doctor who established a practice in Casablanca in 1896. According to his memoirs, he was one of only three doctors practicing in Casablanca at the time; the others included a Spanish doctor subsidized by his government and a missionary sent from London. Nevertheless, despite the lack of competition, Weisgerber found it hard to support himself. The European clientele was small, while the Moroccan Jews, Weisgerber complained, tended to pay for their families' medical care in advance at a low yearly rate, thus assuring for themselves "the most for their money." "As for the Muslims, they were still little accustomed to using the European *toubib* [physician] and still less to paying for it."[12] For this reason, Weisgerber seized the invitation a year after his arrival to accompany the vizier Ba Ahmad and his *mahalla* on campaign. The trip provided Weisgerber with an opportunity to indulge in his hobby of geography, making maps that would later prove useful to the French forces in their invasion of the Shawiya. Barely ten years later, Weisgerber was already an "old hand" in Morocco and an active champion of French interests there.

Most of the doctors attracted to Morocco in this period were from petit bourgeois families who lacked social connections and financial support and thus found it difficult to establish practices in European cities. Colonial practice escaped the invidious social distinctions of the metropolitan cities and could be set up from scratch, not purchased at a high price as was usually the case at home.[13] The colonies also provided the opportunity to participate in the European civilizing mission, the adventure of colonial pioneering, and, not least, the rumored ease with which sizable fortunes could be rapidly accumulated. Morocco was one of the last colonial areas opened to European penetration, but it was close to Europe and temperate in climate.

Five years before Mauchamp ever set foot in Morocco, the sultan Abdelaziz voiced suspicions about the activities of European doctors in his realm. In a letter to a subordinate, the young sultan wrote that it had come to his knowledge that among the Christians who had established medical practices in the coastal towns there were some who routinely took measurements of young Moroccan men. In addition, the doctors hired the youths to sew cotton cloth. Although the reference to measuring the youths suggests that the doctors were collecting anthropometric data—a favorite kind of nineteenth-century anthropological investigation—what was really going on and how widespread these alleged activities were is impossible to discern from Abdelaziz's account. It may well be that that the doctors were simply using young Moroccans to prepare bandages and that the hiring of the youths was in fact an isolated incident. In any event, the sultan instructed the official to talk to the young men's fathers and to threaten them with punishment. If the youths were townsfolk and they still persisted in their contact with the doctors, they were to be summarily drafted into the "Felicitous Army," as the sultan's forces were styled. On the other hand, if the youths had come to town from the tribes, the *qaid,* or tribal governor, was to give the sultan the names of the appropriate officials, and he would transmit his orders directly.[14]

When the manuscript of this edict was donated to the archives in Rabat, it received the Moroccan government's Hassan II Prize for the Best Manuscript or Archival Document, and one Moroccan historian has subsequently referred to the incident outlined in the letter as a "doctors' plot."[15] But the reality is more complicated. The sultan's real concern seems not to have been the practice of European medicine per se but the fact that Muslim youths might be contaminated by frequent and recurring contact with Europeans. As the letter itself says, these youths lacked the ability to know "what is beneficial and what is harmful."

A different set of rules of course applied to the sultan. Widely criticized during his reign for being too familiar with Europeans, Abdelaziz—like his father before him—routinely consulted European physicians. Moreover, there is no record of his voicing any objection to the French clinics designed to serve the poor, such as the one manned by Mauchamp in Marrakesh. According to the explorer Segonzac, who visited Marrakesh during an exploratory mission to the south of Morocco in 1904–1905, the idea of a European medical clinic originated with the sultan's viceroy and half brother Moulay Hafid.[16] Indeed, if one can judge from the relative success of Mauchamp's clinic and the number of patients routinely seen by other medical missionaries, it seems as if many Moroccans had no aversion at all to European medicine. Moroccan pilgrims returning through the coastal ports from Mecca would certainly have been familiar with the practice of quarantine.[17] And at least in theory, Moroccans who were vaccinated against smallpox by European doctors would have understood the practice as conceptually related to variolation, an indigenous form of inoculation.

Between 1885 and 1900 vaccination gained widespread use in the coastal cities, largely due to the efforts of Protestant missionaries. That it was efficacious was surely noted by Moroccans. In 1888 a smallpox epidemic carried off an estimated six thousand people in Marrakesh. Yet in Essaouira during the same year, according to the French consul there, the ravages of the disease were comparatively light, owing to the propensity of the city's inhabitants to have their children inoculated.[18]

Whether European medicine was in itself sufficient to win the hearts and minds of Moroccans to French policy, as Delcassé and later Lyautey both claimed, was a different matter. The willingness of Jews to receive vaccination from European physicians—and a corresponding reluctance by some members of the Rahamna and Haha tribes to receive vaccination—has led one scholar to argue that "those who accepted vaccination were close to the sultan" and that those who rejected it were engaging in a form of political protest.[19] In fact, for whatever reason, it seems that all through the nineteenth and early twentieth centuries Jews in North Africa were more readily inclined to try European remedies than their Muslim neighbors. A French doctor working to eradicate a cholera epidemic in the Tunisian city of Bizerte in 1867 noted the difference in response of the two communities: "Many Muslims want neither the doctor nor the medicine, but as for the Jews, they call the doctor right away."[20]

By any criterion, the doctor played an integral role in the process of colonial exploitation. As Frantz Fanon, a French-trained psychiatrist and the best-known critic of France's colonial régime in Algeria, would later argue, "The doctor always appears as a link in the colonialist network, as a spokesman for the occupying power."[21] Nevertheless, the marriage of medicine and colonialism was not simply one of imperialist opportunism or diplomatic expediency. Indeed, a persuasive argument can be made that nineteenth-century medicine and imperialism had an "elective affinity." "Both were driven by a global sense of man that emerged out of the Enlightenment. Both concerned the extension of 'rational' control over domains of nature that were vital and dangerous. . . . Medicine both informed and was informed by imperialism, in Africa and elsewhere. It gave the validity of science to the humanitarian claims of colonialism while finding confirmation for its own authority in the living laboratories enclosed by expanding imperial frontiers."[22]

A prime example of this connection between medicine and imperialism can be found in the Pasteur Institutes. Although the institutes themselves had no direct connection to the government, the far-flung research laboratories founded by Louis Pasteur and his disciples mirrored French colonial expansion. The institutes often consulted on behalf of colonial administrations. Indeed, as a scientific discipline, microbiology was in many ways a tangible beneficiary of imperialism. French expansion overseas not only provided the institutes' researchers with "new" diseases to "conquer," but it gave them the financial resources to carry out their activities as well. Not surprisingly, "pastorians"—who already maintained a quasi-religious reverence for their founding father Pasteur—saw themselves as exponents of France's civilizing mission. Nevertheless, researchers in the colonies did not enjoy the same prestige or acclaim as their counterparts in the *métropole*.

In this light it is interesting to compare Mauchamp's career with that of his contemporary Charles Nicolle (1866–1936). As an ambitious young microbiologist from Rouen, Nicolle became head of the Pasteur Institute in Tunis in 1902. In 1928 he won the Nobel Prize in Medicine for his discovery linking the louse to the transmission of typhus. In Tunis today, where few of the streets retain their French colonial names, the Avenue Charles Nicolle still bears his.

Nicolle was convinced that the humanitarian benefits of colonialism outweighed its detrimental aspects, and he maintained that France had a twin responsibility to disseminate "world culture" and "world health." But in arguing for humankind's interconnectedness, Nicolle also called for a division of labor that would allow areas on the periphery of the West to make their contribution to universal civilization. During his long tenure as head of the Pasteur Institute in Tunis, Nicolle sought—in the words of his biographer—to create a "Tunisian medical cosmos." Although he ultimately failed in his later efforts to remake the Pasteur Institute in Paris on the lines of his Tunisian institution, his many achievements were far from negligible. Not least, Nicolle was something of a visionary in recognizing that the colonies had the potential to make scientific contributions in their own right. As he imagined it, the civilizing mission could be multidirectional.[23]

During the second half of the nineteenth century the practice of

European medicine underwent enormous change. The discoveries of Pasteur and his German rival Koch resulted in a new understanding regarding the causes and treatment of disease. Theoretically, Mauchamp was the beneficiary of this collective experience. However, in at least one other area, Mauchamp's views were already anachronistic, and this was in the area of race. Unlike their counterparts in Britain and Germany, French naturalists were reluctant to adopt Darwinian ideas about natural selection and instead clung to variants of Lamarck's theory regarding the inheritance of acquired traits. Likewise, for French racial theorists, biological explanations of race never entirely supplanted cultural ones.[24]

In this vein, Mauchamp's *Sorcery in Morocco* is laced with neo-Lamarckian ideas about the effects of Islamic culture and the desert environment. These two factors seem to be the principal causes of the Moroccans' supposed moral and racial degeneracy for Mauchamp. However, like other nineteenth- and early-twentieth-century social theorists, Mauchamp speaks as if morality and race were synonymous. Mauchamp never examines the implications of the inherent ambiguity of the two terms. If morality had become an immutable part of a posited racial identity, then Moroccans were no longer susceptible to change through mere guidance and education. That left few alternatives for societal improvement and progress. Quite possibly, Mauchamp thought in terms of eugenics—puericulturists like Mauchamp were among the founding fathers of the eugenics movement in France—but Mauchamp himself never says as much, and the link between him and the eugenics movement is not explicit. What we do know is that on the face of it, Mauchamp paints a dismal portrait of Moroccans, offering them little hope of improvement except by de facto cultural annihilation.

Sorcery in Morocco

Among the scattered notes collected from Mauchamp's looted house, the only completed section of Mauchamp's book was the introduction. Entitled "The Humanitarian Reasons for European Intervention in Morocco," it offers a psychological profile of Morocco's Arabs and Jews. In the chapters that follow, Mauchamp defines sorcery in the broadest possible terms. Quite possibly the book's title was not Mauchamp's at all but that of his editor, Jules Bois, an authority on medieval European occult practices. In any event, *Sorcery in Morocco* presents an encyclopedic overview of all manner of Moroccan customs. The first chapter deals with rites related to marriage, divorce, birth, circumcision, and death, while the second chapter offers a potpourri ranging from the use of depilatories to dream interpretation. Other chapters deal with so-called social vices and aspects of popular religious practice. Only the second half of the book is devoted to witchcraft and sorcery per se. In particular, the two concluding chapters are a veritable recipe book of what is called "aggressive" and "defensive" magic. These include things such as love potions, rites performed by a woman to make her husband submit to her will, or the casting of a spell to make someone insane. Magic rites are always performed in secret. Incantations and rituals empower the powerless by symbolically linking the petitioner to unseen forces; they provide him or her with protection or make anonymous acts of retaliation possible. In this regard Moroccan magic, at least as Mauchamp presents it, stood in stark contrast to European medicine. Far from being secretive, European medicine, especially as practice in the colonies, represented an overt, even ostentatious, display of imperial and cultural power.

A great deal of material collected by Mauchamp in his book is a simple pharmacopoeia of an "eye of newt" sort. This meticulous attention to detail is exactly what one would expect of someone with Mauchamp's clinical training and particularly of someone with expertise in devising infant formula. The chapters on childbirth similarly show a clinician's eye. Again, much of what Mauchamp labels as sorcery was in many cases no more than simple Moroccan folk medicine. Nevertheless, it is also clear that Mauchamp is unwilling to embrace his Moroccan counterparts—whom he openly identifies as the enemy—as professional colleagues.

From the text itself it is difficult to gauge how much Arabic Mauchamp actually knew. Likewise, a century after its composition, one hesitates either to evaluate the reliability of its ethnographic material or to venture a comparison between Mauchamp's book and Edmond Doutté's *Magic and Religion in North Africa*, a more widely cited work that appeared at about the same time.[25] We know that to communicate with his medical patients in Marrakesh Mauchamp relied on a Moroccan translator. Yet despite this, his editor would have us believe that all of the information Mauchamp provides comes "straight from the horse's mouth." What we are asked to believe is that we are reading Mauchamp's unadulterated notes taken surreptitiously as he interviewed his Muslim and Jewish informants.

One useful gauge of the quality of Mauchamp's work is to compare it with a book by a modern-day Moroccan physician named

Mustapha Akhmisse. In its organization and pharmacological emphasis Akhmisse's book resembles Mauchamp's, even down to its title, *Medicine, Magic and Sorcery in Morocco*. In fact, Mauchamp's book is the source of Akhmisse's chapters on sexuality and sexual disorders. However, the differences in perspective are noteworthy. Beyond making a plea that much of traditional medicine has therapeutic value and is appropriate in the Moroccan context where European medicine is in short supply, Akhmisse sees what Mauchamp clearly could not, namely, the symbolic aspects of Moroccan medical practice.

Moroccan healers, according to Akhmisse, identify two sources of human suffering. One is positive or physical (for example, rheumatism is attributable to cold), but other disorders—largely psychological in nature—are "expiatory." These are the result of divine sanctions for misdeeds for which the intercession of saints or the mediation of sorcerers is indeed a culturally appropriate recourse. Mauchamp—despite his pretensions to being an authority on the Moroccan mentality—could conceive of medicine only somatically. Suffering from cultural myopia, Mauchamp comprehended the object of medicine to be the patient's body, not the patient's soul.[26]

Not surprisingly, the body on which Mauchamp focused was more often than not the female body. The nineteenth-century European imagination created febrile myths of black sexuality that intimately linked women with pathology and disease.[27] And despite the differences in Africanist and Orientalist discourses, one can argue that many of the same assumptions made about black women extended to Muslim women as well. Ironically, while sub-Saharan Africans did not wear enough clothing, North African Muslim women were chided for wearing too much. Their clothed bodies were indeed perceived as the physical embodiment of Islamic obscurantism. Significantly, Mauchamp set as a deliberate goal obtaining women patients from among the Muslim community. Their seeking treatment at his clinic represented for Mauchamp the measure of success in his one-man campaign against Moroccan ignorance.

Mauchamp was hardly exempt from the paternalistic, not to say misogynistic, discourse of his day. He castigates Moroccan Muslim women as the most superstitious and ignorant of all Moroccans. Denied a place in the public sphere, possessing no individuality whatsoever, these women are (according to Mauchamp) repositories of a kind of "pure animality." Islam consigned them to a life of passive bestiality. They can find emancipation, he writes, only by becoming prostitutes. And as if to demonstrate his expert knowledge regarding Islam, Mauchamp makes a point of comparing Moroccan women unfavorably to Turkish women, who, he argues, were consciously working to improve their plight.

Sequestered in their harems, Middle Eastern women were infamously the source of European male fantasy.[28] But Mauchamp seems to be immune to all the exotic allures of the East. As a writer Mauchamp is far removed from a Gerard de Nerval or a Pierre Loti, authors famous for concocting Middle Eastern fantasies. Instead, Mauchamp presents himself as a realist, and in resorting to a rhetoric of social hygiene, he reveals not a trace of romanticism. Readers of Mauchamp's *Sorcery in Morocco* are specifically forewarned in a prefatory note that they are about to be exposed to an unbelievably disgusting depiction of filth and moral degradation. Metropolitan readers of the book were to open its pages at their own risk.

Ultimately, to talk about the colonial body is to talk about the European body. Mauchamp, determined to keep his person untainted by Moroccan pollution, made a personal vow never to exchange his conspicuous European clothes for a Moroccan *jallaba*—even though many of his more timid European colleagues in Marrakesh did. Similarly, Mauchamp forsook the relative safety of the *mellah*, the walled Jewish quarter, where most of the city's minuscule European colony resided. Moroccan Jews were viewed—one might say, socially constructed—as mediating figures between Europeans and Arabs.[29] But for Mauchamp, there could be no halfway measures. Instead, he chose to locate his house and his clinic in the heart of the Muslim *madina*. He did this not for the purposes of "going native." On the contrary, he wanted to set himself up as an example to the Moroccans. He wanted them to see the possibilities of civilized European life. He furnished his house with European and Oriental objets d'art. In the evenings, the European colony repaired to his patio for games of tennis.

In death, Mauchamp was powerless to protect his body. Covered with wounds and dragged to an open clearing, his naked corpse was doused with oil in an attempt to set it on fire. Only the belated arrival of troops dispatched by the governor rescued Mauchamp's body from further damage. The Moroccan soldiers returned the dead Mauchamp to his clinic, which had escaped the looting, and solicitously clothed his corpse in a Moroccan robe—a final irony that could not pass without comment among Mauchamp's European friends.

It scarcely needs to be pointed out that the language of colonialism was also heavily gendered. The sexual connotations of a phrase such as "peaceful penetration" were not lost on French colonialists. And yet it is unlikely that Mauchamp himself ever envisioned Morocco as an inviting, seductive woman. Just the opposite. The source of Mauchamp's moral revulsion is what he perceives to be the rampant homosexuality of Morocco.

"Pederasty is a veritable national institution," he writes. Whereas it may occur in other countries as a secret vice, only in Morocco, he claims, is it openly avowed and public. Few boys, he asserts, grow up without having to submit to their neighbors, and he reports that some government officials owe their positions to the performance of sexual favors. He claims that homosexuality is more common among the Arabs of the plain and less prevalent among the Berbers of the mountain precisely because Berber women are not veiled. The public baths, despite Islamic admonishments against the wanton gaze, also encourage immorality.

The extent of Moroccan moral degeneracy extends to the drugging of young girls with kif and then raping them while asleep. Mauchamp writes that not infrequently "there are horrible tears of the perineum," even among children. Lesbianism is equally widespread and almost universal among women confined in the palace harem. In a footnote, Mauchamp comments knowingly on the techniques of female masturbation. The supposed deleterious health effects of masturbation were yet another preoccupation of early-twentieth-century medicine that Mauchamp transferred from the *métropole* to the colonial setting.[30]

Some of Mauchamp's more slanderous accusations can only be apocryphal. He claims that it is illegal for butchers to sell women the genitalia of a ram. For similarly obvious reasons especially big taproot vegetables such as beets and turnips have to be cut up into smaller pieces before they can be brought into the women's quarters of the palace. Last but not least he cites the widespread practice of bestiality. He claims that copulating with a she-ass is one of the requirements for becoming a sorcerer in Morocco. Copulation with she-asses is also prescribed as a cure for nervous irritability, although, Mauchamp adds, "cows, goats and ewes are not disdained either." All of these sexual anomalies are "weaknesses of the Arab." Just this once Mauchamp lets Jews off the hook.

And yet curiously—and despite Mauchamp's vociferous complaints about Moroccan hostility to anything Western—his dispensary never lacked for patients. He reported seeing upward of one hundred to two hundred patients a day. Indeed he spent his vacation in Paris lobbying for more financial and material support from the French government. As a consequence, we should not take Mauchamp at his word or be misled by the spin his admirers put on the official narrative of his death. There is in fact nothing in the Mauchamp episode to support the assertion that Moroccans either then or now were hostile to modern medicine. Indeed it would be interesting to know exactly which therapies were sought from the French doctor and which were disdained. It appears then that what Moroccans found objectionable was not European medicine but the imperialist politics of its practitioner Mauchamp.[31]

Medicine and Magic

Mauchamp bluntly states that his object in writing a book on Moroccan magic is so that his countrymen can know the enemy better. For this reason Mauchamp includes under the rubric of magic much that was simply indigenous medical practice. Mauchamp was not alone in drawing such an obdurate line between medicine and magic. His opinion typifies the hardening of the European attitude toward traditional healing that seems to have occurred everywhere by the end of the nineteenth century. Earlier European physicians were often far more accommodating toward indigenous practices and certainly not above learning from Muslim practitioners. Following an outbreak of the plague in Marseilles in 1720–1721, for example, one inquisitive French physician traveled to Tunis to see how his Muslim colleagues on the other side of the Mediterranean handled the contagion. At that point in time Europeans and Muslims still subscribed to roughly the same medical paradigm. As one historian reminds her reader, "The germ theory was not substantially developed until the second half of the nineteenth century. . . . Thus European and Muslim medicine embodied similar ideas concerning epidemics derived from empirical observation, the common Judaeo-Christian-Islamic heritage, and from Galenic (Greek) medicine. By 1800 the two systems of thought had only begun to diverge."[32]

With the imposition of colonial rule in North Africa, indigenous medical institutions slowly eroded. European physicians no longer made a distinction between the medical traditions of "high" Islam and those of popular "folk" medicine. Both were labeled magic. Dr. Mauran, inspector general of the Protectorate Health Service in Morocco in 1920, did not mince words:

Indigenous medicine, such as it is currently practiced in Morocco, springs from a kind of magico-medical formula in which religious *kitaba* (therapeutics), astrology, incantation, exorcism, properties of germs, therapeutics of simples, and some notions of chemistry and antisepsy, even organotherapy, are strangely mixed. . . . What one sees today is the preponderance of the magic or religious formula over the medicine . . . the grand science of the Middle Ages today has degraded to a base charlatanism.[33]

But if French doctors in Morocco saw themselves as waging war on superstition, many other European doctors elsewhere in Africa, especially those attached to religious missions, were not beyond representing their craft in terms of its alleged magical properties. Like their North African brethren, sub-Saharan Africans avidly sought injections of all kinds. They might not have understood germ theory, but they fully comprehended the prophylactic efficacy of a needle and thus accepted European biomedicine as much as they could in terms of their own understanding.[34]

In retrospect, Mauchamp's posthumous study might be considered a harmless compendium of exotic customs, the work of an ardent amateur rather than a trained anthropologist. Much of the book is *materia medica*. Nevertheless, Mauchamp conceived of "magic" broadly, and no aspect of Moroccan private or public life escaped his cognizance. At the risk of introducing an anachronism, Mauchamp sought to provide nothing less than an account of Moroccan *mentalité*. "How can one succeed in this work of public health, of physical as well as moral purification [*assainissement*], if one doesn't know, in detail, the forces of the order which one must combat and destroy?"[35]

Yet where Mauchamp felt disgust, other writers saw a certain charm in Morocco's decrepitude. Writing in 1889, the novelist and travel writer Pierre Loti typified the romantic and uncritical viewpoint of the many Europeans who viewed Morocco as a last preserve of a bygone past. "O somber Maghreb," Loti wrote, "remain walled for a long time more, impenetrable to new things, turn your back on Europe and immobilize yourself in things past. Sleep a good long time and continue your old dream, so that at least there will be one last country where men perform their prayers."[36]

But Loti's impression of Morocco's paralysis was entirely mistaken. Far from being a static society, forever lost in *son rêve immobile*, "its motionless dream," Morocco was caught up in a critical and unprecedented state of flux.[37] Like most of their contemporaries,

Loti the romantic and Mauchamp the realist both failed to see how developments in the world economy and in European politics had contributed to the economic crisis and political disequilibrium that plagued Morocco in the late nineteenth century.

Mauchamp in particular vehemently decried Morocco's backwardness and the Moroccans' alleged inability to evolve or adapt to new social conditions. Writing as a stern and impatient schoolmaster, he extolled the universal values of the Enlightenment. "It is not an oppression that we wish to impose but a contribution that we seek, a participation in the collective effort toward betterment. Solidarity is no longer national, it is human: With everyone profiting from the benefits of the common progress, no one has the right to dispense from contributing to it."[38]

Mauchamp's call for solidarity reflected prevailing intellectual trends within French republican circles, and it is hardly surprising then that he would make such an appeal. The term "solidarity" gained wide-prominence owing to its use by the sociologist Émile Durkheim in his 1893 book, *The Division of Labor*.[39] As one historian has observed, it "was the most talked about ideal of the nineties and the first decade of the twentieth century."[40] But for Mauchamp, who was an adherent of the older descriptive ethnography and merely an amateur anthropologist at best, the Moroccans' inability to advance to a supposedly higher level of social organization did not lie in their tribal structure. Instead, the problem was the human matériel presented by the Moroccans themselves. As he observed the Moroccans around him, Mauchamp keenly discerned their supposed grievous moral failings. Moroccan Jews were avaricious, with no sensual refinement or artistic imagination; Moroccan Arabs were voluptuaries, high-strung, proud, and impressionable. Both groups were mendacious. Only the Berbers fared better in comparison. In writing of them, Mauchamp repeated the stock sentiments of French ethnography that were long enshrined in a policy of divide-and-rule. Viewed as vigorous mountain folk and indifferent Muslims, the simple Berbers were held to be as different in character from the Arabs as the Scandinavians were from the "Latin" races.[41]

The tenor of Mauchamp's diatribe is illuminating because it makes clear what all the paeans to European progress and civilization obscure: for Moroccans to partake of the benefits of human progress, they must cease to be Moroccans. In formulating this view of Morocco's future, Mauchamp clung to an assimilationist ideal that was already becoming passé. Five years after Mauchamp's death, with the establishment of the Protectorate in 1912, the competing doctrine of association became—at least during Lyautey's residence—the hallmark of French administrative policy of indirect rule.[42]

In 1924, as he departed Morocco at the end of his career as resident general, Lyautey spoke of the benefits that France had putatively bestowed on Morocco. These included peace and order, business security and economic equipment. "But that which has brought us still more good will," he claimed, "is the fact that we have shown our esteem for this people by having respected all they respect, by assuring them the retention of their traditional institutions. In a word we have placed our hand in theirs."[43]

In stark contrast to the admiring Lyautey, the unsympathetic Mauchamp saw nothing redeemable in Moroccan society. Accordingly, he conceived of his *Sorcery in Morocco* as both an inventory of Morocco's outmoded customs, soon to be erased, and an attack on those who would defend them. "Before we can dream of rebuilding this society on the foundations of modern progress, one must first complete its demolition, disperse the obsolete materials, [and] make a clean sweep of a past without luster, without grandeur and without glory."[44]

Although denunciations of Muslim decadence and degeneration can be found in the writing of other colonialists, such an uncharitable view of humankind coming from a self-described humanitarian such as Mauchamp may seem surprising at first. No small part may be attributable to the doctor's own irritability and frustration. But perhaps there is another explanation for Mauchamp's vehemence. In *fin-de-siècle* France decadence had become an artistic byword in some circles, and even prior to World War I, an underlying pessimism had replaced the optimism with which the long nineteenth century had begun.[45] Is it reading too much into Mauchamp's denunciation of Moroccan culture to see in it a projection of his fears about the fate of his own civilization?

Again, Mauchamp was nothing if not contradictory. As an apostle of hygiene and infant formula, Mauchamp—much like the followers of Saint Simon who preceded him—espoused an abiding faith in science and human perfectibility. But there was also rancor in his words. He writes with despair about Moroccans living in a closed, hermetically sealed world, vegetating in a retrograde environment filled with outmoded ideas. Their supposed lassitude was a personal affront, and Mauchamp saw little hope that even the most Westernized Moroccans could ever attain the true attributes of full European personhood. Moroccans in trousers, the so-called *évolués* or "developed" natives, were to Mauchamp little more than joke. The native might change in his external appearance, but in his mental conception he was still caught in the vise of superstition. European condescension presented the assimilated native with a terrible dilemma. At best, he would forever be—in the words of one postcolonial theorist—a "mimic man," a simulacrum of a European, "almost the same but not quite."[46]

Despite European efforts to create clear lines of demarcation between colonizer and colonized, ambiguity was in fact everywhere in the colonial encounter. Writing of the colonial experience in the Dutch East Indies, one historian has described the legal as well as moral quandary posed to colonial authorities by *métissage,* or miscegenation. Were the mixed race progeny of Dutch men and Indonesian women Dutch or Indonesian? Colonial authorities everywhere feared the consequences of Europeans "going native," a possibility that offered an affront to the metropolitan order.[47] In the long history of European and North African interaction, there were many examples of Frenchmen "going native," but the temptation seems never to have enticed Mauchamp.

Peaceful Penetration

It was Mauchamp's own idea that he go to Morocco. According to Segonzac, Mauchamp first offered his services for his 1904 expedition to the country's south, but the expedition's sponsor, the Morocco Committee, already foresaw a role for Mauchamp in a projected clinic in Marrakesh.[48] Whatever the veracity of Segonzac's recollection, the ambitious doctor was still in Jerusalem when he contacted the foreign minister Théophile Delcassé to request a post in one of the new French clinics in Morocco. In January 1905, at the start of the new year, Delcassé wrote to the legation in Tangier to seek an appointment for Mauchamp should a vacancy arise. "Our consul general in Palestine offers the most favorable testimony of the services of this doctor whose professional capacities and intelligence seems particularly suited for a medical post in the country of your residence."

In offering Mauchamp's name, Delcassé was also responding to political pressures. He noted the "pressing recommendations" of both the deputy and the senator from Saône-et-Loire. "I would be happy," he concluded, "if it be possible for you, should the case arise, to assign him an advantageous place in the ranks of our new medical organization in Morocco."[49]

Independently, Mauchamp explored the possibility of a practice in Rabat. The proximity to the Makhzan, the royal court that occasionally resided in the coastal capital, held an obvious allure; undoubtedly Mauchamp thought to carve out for himself a role comparable to that of Linarès. Indeed, once in Marrakesh, Mauchamp sought to emulate Linarès in his efforts to ingratiate himself with the Makhzan's viceroy in the south, Moulay Hafid, a half brother of Abdelaziz and himself a future sultan.[50]

By June, however, Delcassé and Mauchamp had agreed upon a posting in Marrakesh. "Do you see any inconvenience in his nomination?" the Quai d'Orsay asked the French minister in Morocco, Saint-René Taillandier.[51] The latter wired back that normally he thought it prudent to put doctors in places where they could benefit from the close support of French consular authorities. However, he did not think it inconvenient to install in Marrakesh "a sure and tested physician like Dr. Mauchamp" prior to the creation of a vice-consulate in the city.[52] Owing to his experience in Jerusalem, Mauchamp was considered a particularly good candidate for the first of the French dispensaries to be established in the interior of Morocco.

With his appointment confirmed, Mauchamp, while still in Chalon-sur-Saône, set about doing his homework. On the back of a piece of Paris hotel stationery, Mauchamp wrote the names and capsule biographies of a dozen or so Frenchmen with experience in Morocco.[53] From his parent's home Mauchamp corresponded with Auguste Terrier, the secretary of the Morocco Committee.

The Morocco Committee was an organization formed the previous year in February 1904 by Eugène Étienne, the energetic deputy from Oran in Algeria and at the time the president of the chamber. An offshoot of the Committee for French Africa, the Morocco Committee was the last entry in a series of lobbying groups of a similar nature devoted to promoting French interests in Asia and Madagascar. In this sense the Morocco Committee was the final embodiment of the *parti colonial,* or colonial lobby. Not a political party per se, the colonial lobby was an amalgamation of politicians, soldiers, merchants, explorers, and missionaries united in their desire to see Morocco come under French control. To this end the committee used the money it raised from banks and other large commercial interests to wage an effective public relations campaign. Apart from publishing a newspaper and lobbying politicians over dinner (one wit jokingly referred to the Morocco Committee as the "committee that dines"), the group also financed exploration designed to aid in the eventual takeover of Morocco. Within two years of its existence, it awarded over a quarter million francs in the form of various grants.[54]

Étienne made no bones about his imperialist ambitions. "Morocco constitutes the last imperial chance which can remain for us," he wrote. As he reasoned, the best parts of the globe were already divided, and even China—if the opportunity for its exploitation arose—offered nothing more than the prospect of economic development. "Only in Morocco, that country which is complementary to the territories we already govern in North Africa, do we have the possibility of enlarging our ethnic, and above all our linguistic, domain. Here we can enlarge the area of our civilization; it is here where there is to be found our last chance of compensating, albeit inadequately, for the irreparable losses we suffered in North America."[55]

Mauchamp also queried Linarès, and he sent letters to the French legation in Tangier. Segonzac put Mauchamp in contact with Nissim Falcon, the Alliance Israélite Universelle schoolmaster in Marrakesh who would later become his close friend. From the tenor of Falcon's lengthy reply of August 2, 1905, we can see Mauchamp eagerly sizing up his competition and assessing his chances for success.[56]

There were already two doctors in Marrakesh, Falcon informed Mauchamp. One, Alan Lennox, was a Protestant missionary who doubled as the British vice-consul. Although he lacked a diploma, Lennox maintained a clinic in the *madina,* seeing Muslims and Jews from time to time and making house calls. The other, Judah Holzmann, was "of German or Austrian origin (no one knows for sure)"; Holzmann, who styled himself the viceroy Moulay Hafid's personal physician, would emerge as Mauchamp's principal rival in Marrakesh both professionally and politically. Following Mauchamp's murder, there was much speculation in the French press that this presumed German agent had somehow incited the mob against Mauchamp.

In Falcon's opinion neither Lennox nor Holzmann was much of a doctor. Falcon's low opinion of Holzmann's medical abilities was later seconded by another Frenchman, Christian Houel, who had had frequent conversations with Holzmann during the months he spent covering Moulay Hafid for the French paper *Le Matin* in late 1907. In his memoirs, the French journalist ridiculed the German-trained physician, describing him as unable even to lance a boil properly. According to Houel, no one in Moulay Hafid's *mahalla* ever consulted him. "Everyone preferred the Arab *toubibs*, the sorcerers, to him."[57]

To the Frenchmen who met him, Holzmann was an elusive and enigmatic figure, a Jew born of Russian or Polish parentage, raised in Jerusalem, and educated in Germany. His linguistic talents were impressive. While his command of Hebrew contributed to his prestige in the *mellah*, his knowledge of Arabic won him entry into the viceroy's palace.[58] Houel described Holzmann as "a curious individual, full of finesse, with a gentle appearance, but so withdrawn that I never knew his true thoughts."[59]

> He had arrived in Marrakesh well before Doctor Mauchamp and declared himself a doctor in medicine the way others declare themselves to be a dentist or a grocer. Speaking Syrian Arabic, a very refined language, as well as French, German and Italian fluently and a little English, his intelligence and smooth manners attracted to him a rich clientele, despite a reputation as a political agent that was confirmed by his reports to the German consul Mir [*sic,* Niehr].[60]

Holzmann, to whom Houel owed his introduction to Moulay Hafid, was an invaluable source of information. "He knew all the high-ranking individuals who surrounded us, their origins, their wealth, their vices and their intrigues."[61] But if Houel expected more from their relationship in the months they were together in the *mahalla,* he was disappointed.

> I imagined as well that he had a cultivated spirit and that in an idle moment we could depart from all the gossip about the qaids [the tribal and military commanders]. I was deceived. He hardly recognized Goethe. He knew nothing at all of Schopenhauer, Nietzsche or Hegel.
>
> I would have loved to know how this stateless person, converted to German doctrines, could reconcile the Hegelian future with Muslim fatalism. The doctor stripped himself of metaphysical digressions. He only extemporized so as to boast of German power, German genius, and German taste.[62]

In Marrakesh, Holzmann operated out of the *mellah,* the Jewish quarter, where he gave free consultations. Falcon suspected that

Holzmann, like Lennox, lacked a diploma, but he did not know for sure. In any case neither of Mauchamp's competitors made medicine his exclusive activity. "Holzmann in particular plays with the viceroy the same role that Maclean plays with the sultan; he looks after him bringing from Germany and France a pile of little machines."[63]

Falcon was referring to sultan Abdelaziz's well-known infatuation with European mechanical devices and toys of all kinds. Maclean was Harry Aubrey de Vere Maclean, variously styled in the sources Caïd Maclean and Sir Harry. As a young lieutenant in Gibraltar, the Scotsman found himself in either financial straits or romantic difficulties (accounts vary). In any event he resigned his British commission in 1876 to spend the next thirty-two years in the service of the Makhzan. There he trained the Moroccan infantry. He was especially close to the young sultan Abdelaziz, and in 1901 took part in a Moroccan diplomatic mission to the British court. Edward VII knighted him, and French observers naturally assumed that he was an agent working for the British. In Maclean's absence from Marrakesh, the British vice-consul Lennox and his family occupied the Scotsman's large house.

Meanwhile, Falcon warned Mauchamp not expect too great a clientele. The locals were not accustomed to paying good money to a doctor when they could have the services of "a bunch of nurses" (*une tas de bonnes femmes*) for pennies. More than in any other Arab country, Falcon warned, Mauchamp would have to arm himself with patience. As for Mauchamp being a Frenchman, the lower classes were indifferent to politics, he told Mauchamp. Accordingly, he should expect to be received much the same as any doctor of any nationality. "Your debut will be very difficult, I confess to you frankly; you will have to struggle against the fatalism of the Muslims and the parsimony of the Jews."[64]

Falcon encouraged Mauchamp to open two clinics, one in the *mellah*, the Jewish quarter, and the other in the *madina*, the Arab quarter, stressing that he would find the Jews more receptive to his practice. "Here all the vital force is concentrated in the *mellah*. As for the Arabs, where the Jews don't go, there's nothing to be done."

As there was no pharmacy ("not even a Moorish one") in Marrakesh, Falcon suggested that Mauchamp take one of his better French-reading and -writing students under his wing to train. Warning Mauchamp that he would find nothing with which to furnish his house or kitchen, Falcon also advised bringing with him whatever was absolutely necessary. And, given the poor likelihood that Mauchamp would find a cook locally to his taste, Falcon suggested hiring a Spanish housekeeper on his way through Tangier or Essaouira.

Falcon offered additional practical advice: Mauchamp should bring an English saddle with him and a pith helmet for the summer months. "Let me add parenthetically," Falcon added, "that you should know there's neither a tailor nor a shoemaker here."

As for the local Moroccan who represented France as the consular agent in the absence of any official French representative, Falcon was emphatic. "He is a native, completely unintelligent, very black, without authority or prestige." When Mauchamp went through Tangier, Falcon advised, he should obtain good letters of introduction to local Moroccan authorities because recourse to the consular agent would be useless. In conclusion, Falcon offered to provide Mauchamp with any and all details he could desire regarding life in Marrakesh.

Anticipating an early September departure for Marrakesh, Mauchamp made his preparations. Writing to the legation in Tangier, the doctor explained that although he already knew some Arabic, it was Palestinian dialect, not Moroccan, and he specifically requested the services of Si Muhammad al-Marrakshi Desaulty as a translator. It is not clear how Mauchamp became aware of this individual, whose services to the French legation included providing detailed intelligence reports from the south. In any case the legation was not willing to give up such a valuable employee. In the same letter Mauchamp pressed the diplomats in Morocco concerning housing for himself and his clinic, and he asked for a letter of introduction to the sharif of the *zawiya*, or shrine, at Wazzan, the venerated head of a Sufi order and a politically influential French protégé.[65]

September 1905 passed with Mauchamp still in France. Auguste Terrier, secretary general of the Morocco Committee and the "mainspring" of the organization, as one observer called him, asked the doctor about his plans. Terrier told Mauchamp that he had put at his disposal Ernest Vaffier-Pollet, his representative in Tangier and an agent of the Compagnie Marocaine. "He burns with envy to go to Marrakesh," Terrier wrote.[66] The Frenchman Vaffier—a longtime friend of Al-Madani al-Glawi, one of the Berber "lords of the Atlas"—would later forge a close relationship with Moulay Hafid, the future sultan.

As Mauchamp finally prepared his departure in October, he believed he had solved his biggest difficulty—where to locate his clinic in Marrakesh. In years gone by, Dr. Linarès had occupied a large house in Marrakesh, the "Dar Ould Bellah." That house, Mauchamp decided, would be his. There was, however, one problem: the Dar Ould Bellah was already claimed by the French military mission to Morocco. Naturally, the mission followed the sultan Abdelaziz when he changed his residence from Marrakesh to Fez in December 1901, but five years later it was reluctant to abandon its claim to the building. Not only that, but, as Mauchamp would soon learn, the Makhzan too claimed ownership of the building.

Mauchamp enlisted Terrier's help with the foreign ministry, but having gotten nowhere, Terrier advised Mauchamp to let the matter of Linarés's house drop. "I have the impression it would be best for you to get by on your own," he wrote. "Everything is already organized in Morocco. . . . In my opinion the best you could do is to go to Marrakesh and establish yourself as well and as quickly as you can." He tried to brace Mauchamp for what lay ahead. "Everyone has to manage for himself!" Terrier wrote. "That's the watchword!"[67]

But Terrier's words of advice and encouragement were penned too late. On that very day, Saturday, October 28, 1905, Mauchamp arrived in Marrakesh determined to follow his own plan. On the face of it, Mauchamp's efforts to acquire the Dar Ould Bellah house for his clinic may seem like a trivial incident, but viewed with hindsight, the episode serves as a perfect illustration of Mauchamp's character and methods. It also explains why in subsequent dealings his superiors at the French legation in Tangier strived to keep Mauchamp at arm's length.

Moroccan Real Estate

As Mauchamp took measure of his new surroundings, he initially stayed with Falcon and his wife in the *mellah*. Barely a week after his arrival, he wrote home, putting the best face on discouraging news. It was rumored, he wrote, "that I am not a doctor, but secretly sent by the French government to draw up maps, to study the topography and to spy in anticipation of a future invasion by the French."

Optimistically, Mauchamp believed he had disarmed these rumors by the theatrical gesture of opening his crates and displaying his medical gear in the street outside the building where he hoped to open his clinic the following week. Moreover, in full view of the bazaar, he had given a serious thrashing to someone who had maliciously yanked the reins of his mule. As a result, he said, "people were now laughing with me, not at me."

Only eight days after arriving in Marrakesh, people had already grown used to him, he wrote, welcoming him in the street as he made his rounds with his household servant and the Muslim consular agent Si Umar. "My current situation is a long way from the dangers of my arrival." The petty intrigues of petty people did not matter. "I have already succeeded in destroying them by my attitude alone," he wrote. "Once I begin my charitable mission, the rebuttal will be complete."[68]

A letter arrived from Dr. Linarès. Writing from his retirement in Dordogne, the former personal physician of the late sultan Moulay Hassan attested that the disputed house had been given to him by the late monarch, and he in turn bequeathed it to Mauchamp. But on the reverse side of the letter, Linarès added a pessimistic personal note. "The Muslim spirit in Morocco is, I believe, the worst in the Islamic world. Having lived twenty-five years in Morocco in various cities of the empire, I am obliged to confirm this very pessimistic opinion that the Moroccan (in general) is completely opposed to humanitarian and civilizing processes. . . . I fear that in a few years you will share my opinion."[69]

Mauchamp's commandeering of the military mission house did not go unnoticed. Within days the Moroccan foreign minister Abd al-Karim bin Sulayman lodged a complaint that the French doctor had illegally occupied a property belonging to the Makhzan.[70] From Tangier, the Comte de Saint-Aulaire, the chargé d'affaires at the French mission, wrote to Mauchamp explaining as diplomatically as he could the reasons why Mauchamp should vacate the premises. While Mauchamp may have been given promises by Paris that the Makhzan would furnish him with a house in Marrakesh, the chargé d'affaires wrote, this remained a future possibility. The Paris office could be excused for sometimes losing sight "of certain local contingencies." In the meantime, Mauchamp was to find *another* house on his own for his clinic. All his other medical colleagues had to fend for themselves.

Saint-Aulaire also dismissed claims made by Mauchamp that Moroccan officials in Essaouira and Marrakesh had been given inadequate official notice or had not been informed at all of his mission. While Mauchamp could seek additional support in this matter from the French minister in Fez, Saint-Aulaire pointed out that in his opinion any additional documentation was superfluous. Again, none of his other medical colleagues had had any problems.

Regarding Mauchamp's complaints that a smear campaign had been launched against him in Marrakesh, "you have too much experience in Muslim countries," Saint-Aulaire wrote, "not to appreciate its true worth." In time, the diplomat counseled the doctor, his situation would improve and he would gain the recognition he deserved.

Finally, in response to Mauchamp's charge that the legation was indifferent to the clinics, the diplomat acknowledged that there had been unfortunate gaps and omissions. These, he said, were due to the precipitous nature by which the medical service in Morocco had been established and to the extraordinary demands placed upon the French legation during this period, which coincided with the conference in Algeciras. The doctors' salaries, he assured Mauchamp, would be regularly paid starting in January.

No doubt Saint-Aulaire saw in the bourgeois doctor in Marrakesh a potential nuisance, and he concluded his letter with a postscript. "I don't have to tell you that this letter should conserve its entirely personal character." Mauchamp for his part disregarded the request entirely, making it no secret to friends and family alike that he had found an enemy in the aristocratic diplomat in Tangier.

Meanwhile, a flurry of telegrams and letters flew between the military commandant Fariau, the chargé d'affaires in Tangier, the vice-consul in Essaouira, and the Quai d'Orsay in Paris. The obstinate doctor would not abandon the house lent to the French military mission by the Makhzan. On December 19, Saint-Aulaire received a telegram from the foreign ministry in Paris: "Despite the mistake committed by Dr. Mauchamp, it is essential to safeguard the function to which he is entrusted. You must aid him in finding a sufficient installation." The telegram cautioned Saint-Aulaire to do this quickly, as the Quai d'Orsay did not want to compromise the person and function of Dr. Mauchamp vis-à-vis the Moroccan authorities and population.[71] The legation in Tangier sent Mauchamp another letter requesting that he vacate the military mission house.[72]

Mauchamp responded by letting blast both barrels. Writing a four-page reply in a minuscule hand to Jeannier, the vice-consul in Essaouira, he explained the circumstances by which he came to believe that the disputed house was his to occupy. The doctor denounced the "deception" that he felt had been perpetrated against him. He had received assurances from various officials in Paris that the house was at his disposal, including one from Paul Révoil, who had led the French delegation at the Algeciras conference. He had written to French officials in Tangier and Fez, informing them of his intention. He left France without having received a reply to his letters, "well convinced upon my passage to Tangier that I would find confirmation that the military house in Marrakesh was at my disposal."

Disingenuously, Mauchamp sought to give the impression that he learned that the military mission had the final say in the matter only when he met with the chargé d'affaires in Tangier. There, acting on Saint-Aulaire's instructions, he said he had written to Commandant Fariau on October 4. He informed the officer of his intention to occupy the house, and he offered to restore the house should the military mission return to Marrakesh.

Mauchamp said he awaited a reply from Fariau during his long layover in Essaouira. None arrived by the time of his departure on October 22. Thus, when he arrived in Marrakesh on October 28 and took the keys of the military mission house from Si Umar, the local French agent, Mauchamp said, he believed that there was no obstacle at all in his path.

The house in reality consisted of three separate lodgings, and Mauchamp describes how he allowed one of the displaced Arab tenants to remain with his family. This tenant was none other than the son-in-law of the Marrakesh governor, Hajj Abdeslam al-Warzazi. Meanwhile, Mauchamp energetically set about commissioning extensive repairs of the roof, floors, and doors, and he had the house painted throughout and replaced or repaired the locks and windows. All this cost more than twelve hundred francs, he wrote.

"I ordered this as quickly as possible in order to attend to patients without unnecessary delay." Moreover, close to the *madina,* the *mellah,* and the *qasba,* the house was ideally situated to serve as a clinic.

"The installation was thus complete," Mauchamp wrote, "when I received from Fez the response of Commandant Fariau on November 6, that is to say, a month after my letter from Tangier!" Fariau's letter, dated October 19, asserted that the house was not his to dispose in any case as it belonged to the Makhzan.[73] According to Mauchamp, this was the first he had heard of the Makhzan owning the property. Still he did not feel it presented any problems since he was on excellent terms with the governor of Marrakesh, members of whose family occupied the parts of the house he was not using. The last thing he expected, Mauchamp said, "was opposition from the French side."

Mauchamp claimed that he found it difficult to believe that the Makhzan's objection originated in Marrakesh. There, he claimed, he had instantly forged a bond with the local officials. He had even operated on one official the day before, an "unprecedented" event that only illustrated the "great confidence" enjoyed by the French doctor. "But that the *French* military mission protests against the occupation of a house by a doctor sent on mission by the French government, after having written to me to the effect that this house is not answerable to the military mission in any fashion, well, that seems singular!" (emphasis in the original).

If the house did not belong to the mission, Mauchamp asked, why then did the mission care if he occupied it? Moreover, the mission seemed indifferent to the fact that various Frenchmen and a host of Moroccans had occupied the house over the past four years. In any event, the military mission was now located in Fez. Mauchamp had already proposed restoring the house to it if it ever returned to Marrakesh. Finally, Dr. Mauran had similarly opened *his* clinic in Rabat in a house assigned to the French military mission.

Mauchamp then proceeded to explain how he had managed to open the clinic without any help whatsoever from the legation and that he was already seeing more than a hundred patients a day, every day, except Sunday. Seeking to explain the success of the clinic only six weeks after it opened, Mauchamp ventured that it was precisely owing to the fact that the building belonged to the Makhzan that the population had confidence in the clinic. His abandoning the building for another, the doctor argued, would ultimately damage French prestige and influence!

Mauchamp intimated that he would resign unless French authorities found a solution, and he introduced into his text excerpts from Linarès's letter that "bestowed" on him the house. Although the letter arrived after he was already installed, Mauchamp said that he presented it to Hajj Abdeslam al-Warzazi, the governor of Marrakesh. The governor, he claimed, then devoted considerable Makhzan resources to the building's repair.

Mauchamp reminded his correspondent that his was an official mission by the foreign ministry, which would not look kindly on obstacles being put in his path by the French authorities in Morocco. He would continue to treat patients at the military mission house, and he concluded in dramatic fashion: "The day I am chased from it, I will say to the people waiting for care that it was the French authorities who expelled me."

Finally, as a postscript, Mauchamp contrasted his case with another dispute involving a Makhzan-owned property. According to Mauchamp, an Algerian Jew and French subject named Ben Schimol was scandalizing local Muslims by operating a brothel and selling alcohol in an illegally occupied property that belonged to the Makhzan. Given the choice between a brothel and a medical clinic, the French legation naturally chose to investigate the clinic! Mauchamp laid the irony on thick. Nothing would surprise the locals more than to see the French doctor expelled from the Makhzan house and Ben Schimol's scandalous business continue to flourish.

In Paris the investigation continued with an inquiry to Dr. Linarès. The doctor related in detail the vicissitudes of the Dar Ould Bellah house and how it had been given to him by the sultan Moulay Hassan:

> Although purely verbal, this gift was, I am convinced, absolutely real in the spirit of the sultan and in the spirit of his entourage because, after the death of Moulay Hassan in 1894 and all during the duration of the Rahamna [tribal] insurrection in 1895, the governor of Marrakesh guarded with care this house which had become the "Doctor's House." On the return of the Makhzan to Marrakesh at the end of 1895 I installed myself in my house without seeking anyone's permission and without the least objection being made to me on the part of the regent Ba Ahmed.

Linarès later sought permission from the Makhzan to undertake repairs and was told by Moroccan authorities that it was his house to do what he saw fit. When he vacated the city in 1902, he left the house in the care of the governor. "Under these conditions, I believe that we have the right, following the customs of the country, to consider 'Dar Ould Bellah'—although not strictly French property—at the very least a building *conceded* to French functionaries, of the same title as the house of the French military mission."

For that reason, Linarès continued, he consigned the house to Mauchamp. "Although there were some repairs to do, I believe we would be wrong to renounce this building, one of the prettiest in Marrakesh."

Meanwhile, through his father's political connections, Mauchamp sought to bring pressure on the diplomats of the Quai d'Orsay. The minister of the interior, Dubief, carried the tale of Dar Ould Bellah to Rouvier, council president of the foreign ministry, who in turn wrote to Saint-René Taillandier, France's minister in Tangier.[74]

Rouvier included in his letter a copy of Linarès's statement, asking him to do what he could to smooth over the difficulties caused by Mauchamp's installation in the house. And at Dubief's request he requested that Mauchamp also be given more money. Setting up the house had required an outlay of five or six thousand francs. A supplementary sum of two thousand francs would be needed to pay for a nurse and a pharmacy aide. As Rouvier read the situation, "If Monsieur Mauchamp, without experience in things Moroccan and without authorized counsel, has brought upon himself to a certain extent the situation which he acquired in Marrakesh, we must still lend him our support and save the institution with which he has been charged."

A month later, reporting that Mauchamp was still occupying the disputed house, the French minister in Tangier requested more money for the Marrakesh clinic.[75]

Eventually Mauchamp relented. On March 25 the doctor wrote to Saint-René Taillandier to report that he had relocated the clinic and rented a different house in the *madina* for himself. The four thousand francs allocated by the ministry were not enough to cover expenses. Citing the 2,642 patients he said he had already seen over the previous three and a half months, he requested an additional one thousand francs.[76]

The controversy over Mauchamp's occupation of the Dar Ould Bellah was over, but it was a sure sign of further difficulties to come. The cantankerous Mauchamp was fast acquiring a reputation as a difficult employee. Over the course of the following year it would take all the skill that he could muster for Eugène Regnault—Saint-René Taillandier's replacement in Tangier—to mollify the frequently disgruntled doctor. But even Regnault's kind words and patient encouragement were not enough. After his murder, Mauchamp's family and supporters were quick to accuse the French administration of having abandoned their cherished son and friend in his hour of need.

3

Europeans and Jews

The European Colony of Marrakesh

At the turn of the century, explorers such as Segonzac and Doutté had visited Marrakesh and written accounts of the city, but apart from a handful of missionaries and commercial agents who represented European firms headquartered in Tangier, few Europeans had taken up residence there. This, of course, would all soon change. The 1906 Algeciras conference was a watershed event that opened Morocco's doors to French investment and permitted Europeans to purchase land beyond the perimeter of the coast.[1] In the six years that followed the conference, the European population of Morocco doubled from ten thousand (two-thirds of whom were Spanish) to twenty thousand. Estimates put the total Moroccan population at between four and four and a half million. Likewise, following the establishment of the French Protectorate in 1912, the European population of Marrakesh alone soon swelled into the thousands. In keeping with the urban planning policies of Resident-General Lyautey, an entirely separate French city, *la ville nouvelle,* would grow up alongside the old Arab and Jewish quarters. Travel writers, chief among them André Chevrillon, the Tharaud brothers, and Edith Wharton, would write romantic descriptions of the red-hued southern capital. By the 1920s Marrakesh was already on its way to becoming a popular "exotic" tourist destination.[2]

But in October 1905, when Mauchamp arrived on the scene, all this growth and change remained unimaginable. Barely twenty Europeans, counting wives and children, lived among Marrakesh's one hundred thousand inhabitants. This paltry number stood in contrast to Tangier, which housed an estimated 5,252 Europeans. In 1905

Essaouira alone, the closest coastal town to Marrakesh, counted twenty-six Frenchmen or French subjects among two hundred and fifty Europeans. The other ports along the coast—Safi, El-Jadida, Casablanca, Larache, Tetuan—all had European populations numbering in the hundreds. With its commercial development hampered by the lack of a decent harbor, Rabat-Salé was the notable exception among the coastal cities in that it lacked a sizable European population.[3] In 1907 *La Dépêche Marocaine* put the total French population of Morocco, excluding Algerians, at one thousand. Of these, six hundred lived in Tangier. "Although very inferior in number to the Spanish colony, [the French] surpass it in quality," the paper boasted, "because its representatives hold the great part of the capital, and they are the ones who have created most of the industrial enterprises."[4]

"The opening of Morocco to international commerce in the middle of the nineteenth century occurred," one expert on the Moroccan economy has written, "only after many false starts and difficult negotiations." Foreign trade was theoretically a monopoly of the Makhzan. "Commercial activities strictly defined—that is, the purchasing, packing and transporting of goods to ports of embarkation—were carried out by private individuals who had acquired temporary and revocable monopoly trade rights." But as foreign demand for Moroccan goods (grain, cattle, olive oil, wool, animal skins, etc.) grew, the Moroccan buyers who operated under Makhzan trade licenses were unable to supply the demand. This provided an opportunity for European businessmen, living for the most part in the coastal cities, to enter into the market. They did this initially by forming alliances with Moroccans, to whom they provided small sums of money. "The foreign businessmen then selected intermediaries at a higher level and progressively created alongside the trade administered by the Makhzen [*sic*] a private network that was strongly linked to foreign companies. Within twenty years, from 1880 to 1900, the bulk of trade passed into the hands of foreign businessmen."[5]

Meanwhile, so as to protect their Moroccan agents from the interference of the Makhzan and its functionaries, European businessmen pressed their consulates to extend consular protection to their local associates. In this manner, an ever-increasing number of Moroccans acquired immunity from taxation and the judicial control of the Makhzan. The 1880 Madrid Conference, called to restrain the excesses of the protégé system, failed miserably. The numbers of protégés continued to grow, a phenomenon that not only reduced the Makhzan's revenues but further eroded the nation's sovereignty. Those seeking to become protégés often included Makhzan officials themselves and tribal *qaid*s such as Al-Madani al-Glawi, a wealthy and powerful figure in southern Morocco, and his brother Thami, who would later become the pasha of Marrakesh.[6]

Inevitably, enterprising European merchants set up shop in the interior. Beginning in the 1880s, the German merchant von Maur, who had previously operated from Essaouira, started to do business in Marrakesh, although it was not until 1894 that his agent established himself there on a permanent basis. By 1896, there were three European commercial houses with European agents in the city—one German, one Swiss, and one French. As for the British in Marrakesh, apart from the sultan's military advisor, Maclean, the British presence can be said to begin in 1890 with the arrival of Presbyterian missionaries sent by the Southern Morocco Mission. As with other British missionary efforts in North Africa, their efforts were primarily directed at Jews, who were viewed as more likely candidates for conversion than Muslims.[7] The following year the sultan granted the Europeans permission to establish a cemetery. Prior to that, the bodies of deceased European merchants had to be sent to the coast for burial, a journey of five days.

Thus, slowly, the tiny European colony in Marrakesh came into being. According to one account from 1896, it could count among its members a French dentist, a veterinarian, an English doctor (no doubt the missionary Lennox), a watchmaker, and two Spanish photographers. By 1900 there were seventeen Europeans in all.[8]

French representation took a significant step forward in 1901 when the philanthropic Jewish organization the Alliance Israélite Universelle opened a school for children in the *mellah,* the crowded Jewish quarter. The following year, the Compagnie Marocaine sent its representative to Marrakesh to oversee its operations in the country's south.

Established in May 1902, the Compagnie Marocaine was the first French joint stock company to be set up in Morocco. It soon found itself in a rivalry with the Banque de Paris et des Pays-Bas (better known as Paribas), until then the main economic player in Morocco and the force behind the 1904 French loan to the Makhzan. When it looked like the rivalry between the two companies might threaten France's success in negotiating the loan (and consequently open the door to British or German initiatives), the French government

Figure 4. The French colony in Marrakesh. Rear from left to right: Firbach, Gentil, Lassallas, Bouvier, Falcon, and Boujo. Front row: Mme. Gentil, Si Umar bin Majjad, Mme. Falcon, and Mlle. Garzon. The two children are the daughters of Falcon and Gentil. Reproduced from *La Sorcellerie au Maroc.*

stepped in. Acceding to the arbitration of the French minister of finance, Maurice Rouvier, Paribas agreed to restrict its activities to banking, while leaving the commercial and industrial fields to the Compagnie Marocaine.[9] In Marrakesh, the firm's agent was Jean Denaut Lassallas, who—as we will soon discover—figured prominently in Mauchamp's story.

Isolated and feeling vulnerable, members of the little European colony in Marrakesh for the most part took shelter with the Jewish community behind the walls of the *mellah.* There they hoped that in times of crisis the Makhzan would be able to protect them. Developments stemming from Algeciras especially exacerbated relations with Moroccans, who were perturbed by the growing presence of Europeans and their influence in the country. Not surprisingly, the conference also created tensions among the Europeans themselves. Despite their small numbers, the Europeans of Marrakesh did not always enjoy one another's company. Just as their governments sought to profit from Morocco's tragic state of affairs, so too the handful of Germans, French, and English in Marrakesh similarly competed for influence. Each small group was unwilling to concede any advantage to its rivals.

Sometimes the game had comic overtones. According to his biographer Guillemin, Mauchamp had, upon his arrival in Marrakesh, contracted the services of a resident German woman as a housekeeper. Tongue-in-cheek, Guillemin writes that this was in lieu of purchasing a slave, an option still possible in Marrakesh in the days before the Protectorate, but certainly something Mauchamp would never have considered. "But *voilà*, such is the effect of civilization that [Mauchamp] himself, turning into a slave, had to renounce her authoritarian and insufficiently loyal services."[10]

The story may be apocryphal, but the pettiness of the Franco-German rivalry in Marrakesh mirrored antagonisms that could be found elsewhere in the country within the expatriate community. In the spring of 1907, just days before Mauchamp himself was fated to die, the Alliance Française in Tangier organized a charity bazaar to raise funds for the families of the victims of the battleship *Iéna* explosion. As the French minister Regnault eagerly reported to the French embassy in Berlin, the event was attended by all the European residents in Tangier *except* the Germans. They instead attended a picnic deliberately organized, he claimed, by the German minister so as to compete with the French charity bazaar.[11]

The Alliance Israélite Universelle

At the time of Mauchamp's arrival in Marrakesh, France's symbolic presence in the city could be found in the French-language school operated by the Alliance Israélite Universelle. The Parisian-based Jewish philanthropic organization, which had operated schools in Morocco since 1862, opened its primary school in Marrakesh in 1901.[12] Despite his antipathy to religion in general and his anti-Semitism in particular, the lack of alternative society drew Mauchamp into the social circle of the Alliance and its teachers. Indeed, because of the school's association with France, Mauchamp's fate and that of the city's Jews became entwined.

According to the Alliance's reckoning, Marrakesh's Jewish population in 1905 was 15,700. This made it the largest Jewish community in Morocco, followed by Essaouira and Fez, with Jewish populations put at 10,000 each; Tetuan with 6,500; Tangier with 6,000; Casablanca with 5,000; Sefrou with 3,000;[13] Rabat with

2,000; and Larache with 1,400. And yet despite the size of the Jewish population of Marrakesh, it was one of the last of the Moroccan cities to house an Alliance school. A variety of reasons contributed to the delay, chief among them the relative isolation of Marrakesh and the paucity of Europeans there compared to the coastal towns. But factors within the Marrakesh community itself also no doubt played a role in the Alliance's decision to hold back. In his 1920 history of the Alliance, Narcisse Leven, the organization's president, remarked on the dearth of strong communal institutions in Marrakesh. Lacking an "intellectual aristocracy, the rabbis are less numerous and less influential than in the north, the notables monopolize the direction of the community. For travelers who visited Tetuan and Fez, the absence of a hierarchy and organization is striking."[14] Although the Alliance was an instrument of European philanthropy, the success of its mission depended on mobilizing the support of the local community. In this vein it expected not only parents to pay tuition for their children but the community as a whole to offer financial support from its communal coffers.

The Alliance's interest in Marrakesh dated back to 1876, when the French Orientalist Joseph Halévy visited the community on the Alliance's behalf. Like other visitors before and after him, Halévy depicted the *mellah* as a place of desperate poverty and disease. Despite the protecting presence of the sultan in Marrakesh, which served as the ruler's primary residence through the 1890s, Jews were subjected both individually and communally to humiliating treatment and occasional persecution. In 1893 leaders of the Marrakesh community wrote to the Alliance in the hope that the European organization could put pressure on the Makhzan to address its complaints. Specifically, the letter told of an incident in which a Jewish woman and her children were seized by Makhzan soldiers after her husband had converted to Islam. The community's efforts to redeem the woman and her children had failed. In the same letter the correspondents reported that a Jew had been beaten to death by a Muslim.[15]

At the end of the nineteenth century and with the accession of the young sultan Abdelaziz, the Alliance deemed the time ripe for expanding its efforts to additional cities along the coast and in the interior. In July of 1896, the Alliance charged Abraham Ribbi, a veteran instructor in Morocco since 1880 and the head of the school in Tangier, to make contact with various communities and submit a detailed report on the possibilities for new schools. Ribbi made his initial contacts with the Jewish community in Marrakesh in 1899, but his subsequent recommendations were colored by an incident that occurred in Fez the following year in June.[16] The incident involved Marcus Azzagui, a Moroccan-born Jew and naturalized American citizen who managed the local affairs of the French commercial firm Braunschvig. While riding on horseback in a narrow street, Azzagui brushed against an Arab riding a mule. An altercation erupted, and Azzagui, brandishing a pistol, shot the Arab in the foot. Azzagui, who died in the ensuing riot, left behind a young widow and child. Ribbi complained of the weak response of the American diplomats, and as the perpetrators went unpunished, he foresaw future difficulties for the Marrakesh school.[17] Writing to his superiors in Paris, Ribbi introduced a theme that would continue to echo throughout the following decade in the correspondence of the Alliance's instructors in Marrakesh, namely the need for respect and security for the Alliance's staff and schools: "Our teacher in Marrakesh, our schools even, absolutely need the prestige of independence [*l'émancipation*]. It will only be assured them if an authorized voice—that of a representative of a great power—makes the Sharifian government understand that our teachers and our schools must be shielded from the fanaticism and rudeness of the natives."[18]

Even without the benefit of a French consul in Marrakesh, the Alliance was nevertheless determined to establish a school in Marrakesh, and it finally did so in 1901. Its first teachers were Moïse Lévy and Messody Coriat, who subsequently married.[19] Enrollments fluctuated, hovering initially around 116 boys, of whom 38 were paying students, and 61 girls, of whom 27 paid tuition.[20] In times of communal strife between Muslims and Jews, many parents would withdraw their students from the schools. At one point, in February 1904, Lévy contemplated closing the girls' school. Its enrollment had fallen to below a dozen. The few girl students took away resources from the boys' school.

While the Alliance's primary mission was education, the local Jews in Marrakesh quickly turned to the schools' director for political support. To his superiors in Paris, Lévy explained how the local Jews—ordered to go barefoot when they left the *mellah*—had called on him to confront the pasha of the *qasba*.

> In this country, it suffices to be called European or to be known as a protégé of some Western power to command a certain measure of respect on the part of the indigenous population. This is enough to

guarantee the security of a foreigner in Marrakesh. But by our title of Alliance teachers, we are called to the more humanitarian task of guaranteeing the security of the great majority of our fellow Jews, who find no favor with the pasha.[21]

Lacking a consular official to whom he could apply, Lévy appealed to the Alliance's Central Committee in Paris. The committee in turn wrote directly to Si Muhammad al-Turris, the sultan's representative in Tangier. This application of pressure from on high had the desired effect. The pasha rescinded his order and offered an apology for requiring that Jews remove their shoes on leaving the *mellah*.

Following a period of drought and monetary inflation, the situation again worsened for the Jewish community in Marrakesh. In January 1904 a protest by shoemakers over the introduction of new copper coins escalated into a violent attack on the Jewish quarter.[22] Many merchants, among them Jews, would not accept the cheaper coinage as payment. The ranks of the demonstrators in the Arab *madina* were supplemented by Berbers from the countryside. The mob then marched on the *mellah* armed with sticks and chanting, according to Lévy, "We'll eat the *mellah*." The *mellah* guards were able to shut the Jewish quarter's gates in time, but that did not prevent a panic from breaking out inside the *mellah* or stop the rioters from hurling stones into the *mellah* from outside.

The governor, Hajj Abdeslam al-Warzazi, made an unsuccessful attempt to restore order. Finally the sultan's viceroy and half brother, Moulay Hafid, came to the rescue at the head of troops called from the *qasba*, the city's military barracks. Guards were posted throughout the *madina* and around the *mellah*, and the ringleaders among the demonstrators were arrested. Lévy praised Moulay Hafid as "a man of remarkable intelligence, very learned, just and vigilant over all his subjects."[23] Four years later Moulay Hafid would supplant his brother Abdelaziz on the throne.

A catastrophe was thus averted, but nearly fifty Jews who had been working outside the *mellah* had been assaulted and wounded. During the course of the demonstration, the Christian cemetery was also desecrated, and the head of a young woman was disinterred and burned before the governor's residence. Lévy concluded his report by outlining the various costs that the community incurred in the wake of the riots, in particular payment for guards and assistance to those who were wounded, and he asked the Alliance's Central Community for additional funds.

As December 1904 came to an end, Lévy and his wife were transferred to Tetuan and replaced by Nissim Falcon. Falcon had corresponded with Mauchamp before the latter's arrival and was an important witness to the events that surrounded his death. Like most of the Alliance teachers, Falcon was a Sephardi Jew from the Ottoman empire. Born in Izmir in 1878, he received his higher education at the Alliance's training school in Auteuil outside of Paris, the École Normale Israélite Orientale. Within the Ottoman empire Jews of Spanish origin formed fairly homogeneous communities—the largest concentrations were in Salonika, Izmir, Edirne, and Istanbul—with smaller communities scattered throughout the Balkans and Western Asia Minor. The Alliance operated schools in the major Judeo-Spanish centers and eventually became the dominant force for cultural change in these communities. As a result of the Alliance's activities, Eastern Sephardi Jews were often bilingual in Judeo-Spanish and French, and many such as Falcon looked on "gallicization" as a means of upward mobility.[24]

Falcon began his long career with the Alliance in Tangier in 1901. Over the course of the next three decades, he held posts in Tetuan, Safi, Marrakesh, Essaouira, and Fez. Eventually he would find service under the French Protectorate in 1927 as director of the École Franco-Israélite Albert Sonsol in Fez. Despite his subsequent long career with the Alliance, Falcon's initial service record was not entirely without blemish. In Tetuan in May 1903, when the city was under siege and threatened with attack from revolting tribes in the Rif, Falcon, then the assistant to the director, joined the city's wealthier citizens and other Europeans in evacuating the city by sea. Elie Carmona, the head of the Alliance school, stayed behind. From the Alliance's Paris headquarters, the Alliance secretary, Jacques Bigart, wrote to the beleaguered Carmona, ordering him to stay in Tetuan to provide support to the poorer Jews who had not fled. "We consider the departure of Mr. Falcon," he wrote, "a desertion and a most serious breach of professional honor."[25]

Falcon's experience in Tetuan inevitably colored his perception of and reaction to events as they would unfold in Marrakesh. From the start, Marrakesh was not a happy assignment for Falcon. His letters to his superiors in Paris are filled with complaints about the inadequacy of his pay, the cost of setting up a household, and the recurrent health problems of him and his wife. "We suffer enough from a thousand little things in this somber land of misery," he wrote soon after his arrival. "And if the only consolation, that is, to have the esteem and confidence of our superiors, is refused, then we will consider ourselves among the worse servants of the Task [*l'Oeuvre*]."[26]

Louis Gentil, also destined to be an important actor in the Mauchamp drama, met Falcon for the first time when he visited the school in January 1905. At the time Gentil was taking part in the Segonzac scientific expedition to southern Morocco, and he expressed an interest in the affairs of Morocco's Jews. For the visitor's benefit, Falcon had his students give a recitation in Hebrew. Since Falcon had just arrived in Marrakesh, one can imagine that having them recite Hebrew seemed far less risky to the new schoolmaster than having them attempt French.[27] Nearly three years later, when Christian Houel visited Marrakesh in his capacity as reporter for the French paper *Le Matin,* one of Falcon's students recited with confidence from La Fontaine's fables. Houel recalled being overcome by emotion at the sight. "These sentences so simply spoken by this young boy in such a city where a hatred of everything French sweated from all its walls, had, in my depths, such a resonance that I felt my eyes fill with tears."[28]

During Falcon's tenure as headmaster, the school for boys enrolled 350 students, of whom only 24 paid tuition. The girls' school, under the direction of Falcon's wife, had 117 students, of whom 20 paid. A subvention from the Alliance accounted for some 93 percent of the budget, the rest coming from fees and the support from the local community.[29]

Apart from Falcon and his wife, there was also an adjunct director for the boys' school, a native Moroccan Jew, also educated at the École Normale in Auteuil, named Souessia. In 1906 Souessia took a position at Essaouira, where, becoming a correspondent of Mauchamp's, he entered into a lengthy exchange over efforts to hire Mauchamp a European cook.[30] His successor in Marrakesh was one Monsieur Boujo.[31] A Mademoiselle Garzon served as the adjunct director for girls. In addition, the staff included four Hebrew instructors, who were locally hired, two monitors, and two housekeepers. Despite the Westernizing mission of the school, much of the school's curriculum for boys remained consecrated to learning Hebrew so as to compete more effectively with Marrakesh's traditional yeshiva schools.

In March 1905, now settled into his position, Falcon sent off the first of his bimonthly reports to Paris. His sixteen-page letter was filled with despondency. While the students were generally in good health, he lamented the lack of hygiene. He described one student with a head crawling with vermin and eyes full of pus. "It's enough to know on my word," he wrote, "that the use of a washcloth is unknown even among the rich." The classroom, a narrow room packed with forty to fifty children and lacking sufficient light or air, gave off a disagreeable odor. Outside, the streets of the *mellah* were filled with blind people and others suffering from eye infections and running sores. Falcon claimed that he was unsuccessful in convincing a single student to bathe; parents were astonished that he should make this request. Lice or not, Falcon complained, one could not ask a religious father to cut his son's sidecurls.

Falcon said he was reluctant to devote the first hour or two of the school day to the children's *toilette* and that installing a small bathroom with towels and hot water represented another unanticipated expense. The students were intelligent but lazy. Moreover, they approached the study of French like they approached Hebrew, that is, as a dead language. The teachers were prone to corporal punishment. "I energetically forbid the use of these instruments of torture from a bygone age, but that doesn't prevent some professors from breaking the rules when I'm busy in my class."

The Alliance was in a tenuous position in Marrakesh. Older members of the community viewed the boys' and girls' schools with suspicion and saw them as a contaminating influence on the youth and even their fathers. Meanwhile, "everybody believes that the Alliance, after having obtained permission to open the schools, will take charge of supporting the *mellah*." Some, according to Falcon, anxiously worried that the Alliance would require them to pay dues.

More than outright hostility, what Falcon bemoaned, however, was the indifference. "*Voilà*, we've been here three months and not one notable has come to see the schools, to interest himself in what we do, to encourage us with a good word."

"If only the 'Marrakeschiotes' knew enough to interest themselves in something useful!" he complained. "In a large community like this there is no organization outside the burial society and some funds for the rabbis and for maintaining the tomb of some saint."

The Bikur Holim, the society for visiting the sick enthusiastically organized by Falcon's predecessor Lévy, had fallen apart. The Jews of Marrakesh, according to Falcon, excelled at only one thing, making a profit from the smallest transaction. "Incomparable quibblers [*chicaneurs*] . . . they appreciate only the power of the god Mammon and know how to use this power in their relationship with the Makhzan."[32]

In subsequent reports, Falcon describes the plight of the *mellah*'s Jews in increasingly desperate terms. In June 1905 famine again raged, the harvests were mediocre, and the price of wheat had doubled. The community chest was exhausted, unable to alleviate the general distress or see to the distribution of bread. Meanwhile bandits had infested the roads and were pillaging caravans. Camel drivers were selling their animals because they could no longer feed them. Communication with the cities of the coast had become difficult.[33]

By August, Falcon—like Lévy before him—was asking the Central Committee of the Alliance to provide aid. The demand of people seeking community assistance had tripled; the supplicants were no longer ordinary indigents, but now included workers. Falcon wrote:

> Everywhere the processions of the miserable, the paralyzed, everywhere beings with cadaverous faces with feverish and haggard eyes, half-naked, trailing their limbs, dry, all skin and bones, in the dust under an implacable sky; everywhere the lamentable cries, the women who tug on you to stop you by force to demand your offering. Our school is entirely invaded by beggars, and our students are attacked by the hungry who want to rob them of the morsel of bread we have for them.[34]

In this Hobbesian world of hunger and desperation, one Jew was the community's uncrowned king. This was Yashu'a Corcos, the *mellah*'s most powerful and richest man, president of the *maamad*, the community council, and banker to the viceroy, Moulay Hafid.[35] If the Alliance's efforts were to succeed in Marrakesh, they could do so only with the support of Corcos. Writing in the 1930s, one historian of the *mellah* attributed the establishment of the Alliance schools in Marrakesh to the "energetic intervention" of Corcos. The latter had broken through the barrier of resistance put up by the rabbis and the population as a whole, who "saw religious danger and no practical utility in profane education."[36]

While the relationship between the Alliance directors and the school's wealthy benefactor was not always smooth, Corcos nonetheless took evident personal pride in his own family's success at the school. As the first to enroll his children, Corcos set the example for the other notables of the community. The Frenchman Eugène Aubin describes a Shabbat dinner at the home of the wealthy banker in 1902: "The women, faithful to the ancient custom, did not appear at the meal. Only his youngest daughter, educated at the school of the Jewish Alliance, and dressed in European clothes, inaugurated the new *régime* by sitting down at the table."[37] Moreover, Corcos showed his support of the schools when it counted most. In the summer of 1907, when Falcon and the other European schoolteachers sought refuge on the coast, Corcos undertook a commitment to keep the schools open.[38] He later used his influence to secure from Moulay Hafid and his minister, Si Al-Madani al-Glawi, a pledge in 1908 to reopen the schools. The venerable Corcos died in 1929. In 1948 the Alliance converted his home into a school for boys.[39]

Even so, Corcos was not without his rivals for authority, particularly another wealthy notable of Marrakesh, Samuel Turjuman. Consequently the Alliance schools became a political football caught between the Corcos and Turjuman factions.

Amid the famine of 1905, Falcon reported an increase in prostitution in the *mellah* and *madina* owing to the desperate economic crisis. According to his lurid account, the community's chief rabbi had done nothing to remedy the situation and was even said to encourage it, being paid to maintain his silence. Youths from good families were profiting from the relaxation in morals and having relations with their maids. If the girl became pregnant, they had her accuse someone innocent. The accused was then brought before the rabbinic court. He was forced to either marry the girl and provide her with a dowry or swear his innocence upon the Torah scroll. Alternatively, those who refused to swear could pay the rabbis, and the girl would be sent back to her parents or even to prison.

Falcon learned of the system's corruption the hard way when a maid at the school, all of fourteen years old, became pregnant. Falcon's wife made inquiries and identified the father as a certain friend of the Turjuman and Rosilio families, both community notables. When, at Falcon's insistence, the community council met to render judgment, Corcos was absent, and those present made a peremptory ruling in only five minutes. The boy was found innocent, the girl condemned to prison. Falcon protested in vain. He brought charges against the girl in order to protect the school's good name, but he had expected that the young man would be punished as well. "Our words displeased these gentlemen and immediately they asked us to leave saying they had had enough of our schools, of our continual intervention in the communal affairs, etc. etc."[40]

The campaign against the Alliance schools continued into the autumn, this time with demands that Falcon fire his Moroccan-born assistant, Souessia. By taking the interests of the school to heart over that of the Jewish leadership of Marrakesh, Souessia had evidently displayed disloyalty to the notables. Turjuman had circulated a letter among the notables calling on them to withdraw their financial assistance to the school. Moreover, Turjuman had written to Benjamin Baruch Braunschvig to complain. An Alsatian Jew who established himself in Tangier in 1875, Braunschvig was Morocco's richest and most powerful foreign merchant.[41] Turjuman was Braunschvig's protégé.

The go-between in this squabble was Holzmann, the German-trained physician whom, Falcon wrote in a letter to Paris, "I had not seen up to that moment more than two or three times." Holzmann's report regarding communal dissatisfaction astonished Falcon, who had just come from a meeting with Yashu'a Corcos and other notables. All had reassured him that the schools were going well and providing a great service to the community. Taking up his pen, Falcon wrote to Braunschvig in an effort to set the record straight. He encouraged him to "counsel his friend and representative in Marrakesh to cease his hostilities." He asked, moreover, that Turjuman give him the satisfaction of enrolling his two children in the school. With the support of Corcos and Jacob Hazzan, the local director of the French postal service, Falcon stuck by his adjutant, and Souessia remained.[42]

Subsequent to Mauchamp's death, French reports cast Holzmann in the role of the French doctor's implacable enemy and the principal architect behind his murder. While the accounts of Holzmann's complicity in Mauchamp's murder are surely exaggerated, the rivalry between the two men was real. Holzmann had once provided valuable and much appreciated services to the Alliance schools and the wider Jewish community. Now his relationship with the Alliance had turned sour. With the arrival of Émile Mauchamp, Holzmann could see the writing on the wall and decided that it was time to choose sides.

As for Falcon, the arrival of a French government doctor was particularly welcome. He wrote approvingly to his superiors in Paris of Mauchamp and asked them to write a formal letter of gratitude. Although "all the doctors sent by the government have been ordered to attend in particular only to the Muslims," Falcon said that he successfully imposed on Mauchamp to admit poor Jews to the free consultations given thrice weekly. And, finding the Alliance students to be thin and sickly, Mauchamp also offered to examine and care for several students "without distinction to fortune" during the times of his paying consultations. At the moment, Mauchamp was concentrating on children with scalp infections. "We hope that with the aid of Dr. Mauchamp and with the student excursions that I've instituted that our students will present less suffering faces."[43]

In a city without French consular representation, Falcon also viewed the appearance of the French doctor as another tool in his effort to represent the Jews to the Makhzan. In mid-March 1906 a fracas broke out on the grounds of the Alliance school involving the school's janitor and two black slaves who belonged to the sultan's brothers. The Moroccan authorities failed to treat the incident seriously, and no punishment was meted out to the offending slaves. After a round of ineffectual meetings with the pasha of the *qasba*, Mauchamp and Falcon appealed to Jeannier, the French vice-consul in Essaouira, for help. Eventually the pressure on the pasha bore fruit and, from Falcon's vantage point, the story had a satisfactory ending. At the end of May, the two slaves were brought before the *qaid* of the *mellah*, the French consular agent, and all the students and staff of the school, where, in a public demonstration, they requested "pardon for their cowardly aggression."

The pasha, meanwhile, remained hostile to the schools. If the schools had not been authorized by the Makhzan, he told Falcon, "I would send twenty soldiers to close them down and expel all the personnel from Marrakesh."[44]

In June 1906, Mauchamp again became involved in representing the interests of the Alliance school before the Makhzan. In the midst of a typhus epidemic, the viceroy, Moulay Hafid, cut off water to the *mellah* in order to irrigate his adjacent gardens. With Mauchamp in tow, Falcon made a successful representation to Hajj Abdeslam Figuig, the *qaid* of the *madina*, who immediately went to the viceroy. As Mauchamp remonstrated, "should the *mellah* lack water, he would not be responsible for the spread of the epidemic."[45]

As 1906 came to an end, Falcon summed up his report to Paris by reflecting on the condition of the Jewish community in Marrakesh. He deemed the Alliance school a great success, and he spoke of plans to add a little museum that would display the range of human endeavor. Much, however, remained to be done within the Jewish community, and Falcon painted a dismal portrait.

The crisis of the preceding years has left profound traces of moral distress in the bosom of our community. The rich have become more egotistical, the authorities more greedy, the starving crowd freely supports itself by theft and debauchery. Some bands of thieves have organized themselves and all the houses submit to their assaults. They even resort to setting fire to the shops so as to profit from the confusion. The prisons are full, and excommunications rain upon the young girls, the women who traffic their bodies. Add to this that in the space of two months, three women, six young people (under eighteen years of age) and five adults, whether to escape justice or out of self interest, have abandoned their religion in order to embrace Islam, and you have a picture of the misery of the *mellah.* One no longer fears God or man.[46]

The miseries of the *mellah* as described by Falcon were hardly an exaggeration. Similar accounts had for decades been a staple of European writing about Morocco. Although the material and judicial plight of ordinary Moroccans was often hardly better, proponents of colonialism frequently cited the degradation of Jewish life in the Sharifian empire as justification for European intervention in Morocco's affairs. In particular, Europeans criticized the second-class legal status that Islamic law placed upon Jews as *dhimmis*—an officially tolerated but unequal minority. The European stance—apart from its hypocrisy in light of the recent Dreyfus affair—ignored the complexity of Jewish-Muslim community relations. Indeed, in many instances the traditional restrictions on Jews no longer applied or were honored only in the breach.[47]

With hindsight, historians point to the socioeconomic and political contradictions that resulted from colonial pressure as the principal cause for the increasing tension between Morocco's Jews and Muslims. The first decade of the twentieth century saw an acceleration of earlier disruptive trends in Moroccan society. These include the weakening of the economy, inflation, the breakdown of traditional markets, and the transformation of the rural-urban relationship owing to the increasing concentration of land in the hands of city dwellers. Morocco's cities grew swollen with the displaced people from the countryside (including rural Jews flocking to the *mellah*). An increasing number of people found themselves imprisoned because of real or imagined debts. In the context of growing lawlessness, urban dwellers also held Jews responsible for selling contraband weapons to surrounding tribes.

Not surprisingly, Jews also suffered to the extent that they were identified with the foreigners or had ties to unpopular representatives of the Makhzan. In particular, many Jewish merchants—together with their counterparts among the Muslim notables—benefited from and often abused their status as European protégés. On the other hand, in those instances in which the French refrained from direct involvement, Jews were just as often ignored. "Contrary to the image spread at the time in the papers of 'the Jews as the first victims of trouble,' most of the *mellah*s were in fact spared even during the most pointed phases of the agitation, not least where there was no intervention of foreign troops."[48] Indeed, Jewish opinion on the whole was far from uniform in its support of European intervention. In Marrakesh and elsewhere, the very Jews who looked upon the Alliance Israélite Universelle as an advocate for their community could still oppose the organization's assimilationist program aimed at turning Moroccan Jews into Jewish Frenchmen.[49]

In a letter to Narcisse Leven sent on September 2, 1907, Falcon cautioned the Alliance president not to be "taken in" by Moroccan Jewish fears over security. For all the noise he makes, Falcon wrote, "the Jew, as much as the Muslim, fears the intervention of Europe." With the installation of Europeans in the country, Falcon observed, the Jews would relinquish their traditional role as middlemen.[50]

While giving up their traditional social role was something Morocco's Jews might have been reluctant to do, the Alliance and its directors imagined they knew what was best for Morocco's Jews. Echoing Falcon's words, one observer wrote in the 1930s, "The directors of the Alliance forever cherish the dream of tearing away the Jew away from his eternal occupation of middleman, which condemns him to insolent fate or to extreme misery."[51]

For graduates of the Alliance, and particularly those from the impoverished community of Marrakesh, French penetration and the establishment of the Protectorate did in fact mean more and better jobs. "Only recently," the Alliance director in Marrakesh wrote in 1912, "the French consul in Marrakesh asked me to select qualified pupils to join French enterprises and the French administration. The parents of our pupils and graduates, who in the past displayed indifference toward the schools, are learning to regret this attitude in the wake of the new opportunities awaiting the youth."[52]

To a large extent the Alliance succeeded in its goal of providing new occupations and opportunities for the Jews of Morocco, but success also brought with it unanticipated social and political consequences. In 1955, on the eve of Moroccan independence, the eighty-three schools of the Alliance Israélite Universelle in Morocco enrolled thirty-three thousand Jewish children. This figure represented a far greater proportion of Jewish children attending school than Muslim children. Alliance enrollment also cut across a wide range of social classes. As a result, the schools' graduates, including those from humble origins, tended to identify for the most part with the European colonial elite. "The educational progress of the Jews before and after 1912, the social consequences of the cultural and educational diversity among Muslims and Jews, the policies of the colonial systems, and the activities of the AIU [*sic*] in all aspects of communal and educational activities, deepened the already existing divisions between these two peoples."[53] Zionism and the establishment of Israel would also have profound repercussions for Morocco's Jews, leading many to reexamine their national identity.[54]

At the start of the twentieth century Alliance teachers such as Moïse Lévy and Nissim Falcon entertained a vision of the future that was simultaneously down-to-earth and idealistically high-minded. For these Alliance teachers, the decades before the Protectorate were a time of great challenge and opportunity. As privileged outsiders, they time and again fought to improve the day-to-day lot of their fellow Jews in Marrakesh. All the while, they held tightly to the Alliance's ideal that Jews everywhere—including their coreligionists in Morocco—would participate in the modern world that was then emerging. The teachers did not seem to be aware that these goals were fraught with contradictions. Today, the Alliance schools in Morocco are closed, and Morocco's Jews—apart from a few thousand in Casablanca and Rabat—have long departed for Israel, France, Canada, and Spain. A century after Falcon first arrived in Marrakesh, what once seemed unimaginable has occurred: the *mellah* of Marrakesh today still teems with humanity (and tourists), but it no longer houses Jews.

4

A Doctor in Marrakesh

The Practice of Medicine

By December 1905, Mauchamp's clinic was up and running, at least for the time being, in the disputed but now remodeled Dar Ould Bellah house. Mauchamp wrote enthusiastic letters to all and sundry, extolling the immediate success of his practice. To the Morocco Committee he reported that he had between thirty and forty patients at a time waiting for a consultation. For the moment these were predominantly Jews, but he expected this eventually to change. Several Muslim notables, including two sharifs, or descendants of the Prophet Muhammad, had already come to his practice with their wives in tow. Treating women was, for Mauchamp, a particular triumph, "especially here, where the Arabs and Jews are very fanatical in what concerns their women."

In terms of his staff, Mauchamp now had an Arab translator, Si Muhammad, sent to him by the legation in Tangier. He was "more clever and better understood" than the Jewish translator, whom Mauchamp reassigned to duty in the pharmacy. The clinic employed two domestics as well, one a Berber and the other a Tunisian named Hajj Umar, a "hard worker" who had seen military service with the French as a drummer and who, along with the translator, could double as a nurse.[1]

Writing to his father on December 29, Mauchamp confided that he was waiting impatiently for the Algeciras conference to end so that that the diplomats in Tangier would be free. Then he would request permission to expand and hire a pharmacist. He boasted of already having a reputation of sorts as a miracle worker, especially for afflictions of the eyes. His practice was growing, he wrote, especially because of the notables who sought him out both as a doctor and as a friend. The *qadi*, or judge, of the *madina* sent him bananas from his own garden and received Mauchamp sumptuously at his home. There "some *négresses* saturated me with various perfumes from silver ewers, [and] some *négres* filled me with incense even under my clothes with pans of smoking wood from the mosque." He looked forward to an "indigestible" dinner with the sons of Si Muhammad Sibai, an important adviser to the sultan. The *qaid* of the Doukkala tribe, who had a garden near Mauchamp's residence, had invited him for dinner the following week. Meanwhile, half his patients, he reported to his father, both Jewish and Muslim, were now women.[2] A legation report sent from Tangier to Paris put Mauchamp's daily quota of patients at 150 and reported that the doctor already had plans for a hospital with eight to ten beds for native Moroccans.[3]

But if Mauchamp put on a good face for some, to others he complained vociferously. Early in January he wrote at length to the French consul in Essaouira, claiming that "Mister Holtzmann [*sic*], calling himself a German and a doctor," had launched a deliberate campaign to sabotage his practice. As the teachers Falcon and Souessia and "many Arab personalities" could all attest, Holzmann had spread rumors about him even before he had set foot in Marrakesh. "I was, he claimed, not a doctor but a French officer come here in disguise to draw up maps, conduct espionage, and lay the groundwork for a future French invasion."

Mauchamp said he ignored the reports, confident that the success of his clinic would dispel the rumors. In this he was encouraged by the patronage of many notables. Not least, the successful surgery he performed on the wife of one of them, a merchant named Si Ahmad bin Sami, contributed to his growing reputation.

Nevertheless, he complained that his Arab clients, especially among the notables, had recently dropped off; patients on whom he had only recently operated no longer wanted to see him. Mauchamp's translator made inquiries and reported that Holzmann allegedly was making statements linking Mauchamp to a "Franco-Christian Freemason conspiracy" designed to dispatch as many Muslims as possible. "Clever" physicians such as Mauchamp, Holzmann reportedly said, "care for the Arabs with a show of great kindness, heal them, whether by medicines or by operations of the maladies from which they suffer, draw to them the confidence of all and attract a great reputation, but at the same time, they make them take a subtle poison that only works two, three, four years later, and which surely makes them die."

Apropos of Holzmann's "extravagant fantasy," Mauchamp wrote that all that was needed was for someone who he had previously treated to contract a serious illness and die. Then the entire "credulous and superstitious" population would turn on him in a "deplorable outburst of fanaticism." He further warned that should this legend spread it would threaten the status of all French doctors in Morocco. For his own protection, he asked that the legation, which had a responsibility to protect him, take every precaution "to cut short these intrigues."[4]

Although Mauchamp's biographer Guillemin writes that the government did nothing in response to the doctor's complaint, Jeannier, the vice-consul in Essaouira, in fact forwarded the letter to Saint-Aulaire in Tangier and sent instructions to Si Umar bin Majjad, the French agent in Marrakesh, that he should reassure the viceroy Moulay Hafid about Mauchamp's humanitarian intentions. Moreover, Ibn Majjad was to advise the viceroy to ignore the comments of the Jerusalem-born Holzmann, who, as an Ottoman subject without diplomatic representation in Morocco, was prejudiced against Mauchamp.[5]

Meanwhile, in letters home to his father, Mauchamp painted a grim picture of life in Marrakesh and in the surrounding areas. The famine still reigned, and food prices remained high. Mauchamp reported that it cost as much to maintain his two "indispensable" mules as it did to nourish him and his staff. Outside the city walls villagers piled mounds of locusts. These they sold cooked at two pennies a dozen. Much of the population was reduced to eating roots. Merchants reportedly hoarded grain out of fear that if they opened their stores, the *qaid*s would confiscate them. Mauchamp put the daily death toll from hunger at twelve in the *mellah* and even higher in the Arab quarter. He requested aid from the consul in Essaouira and, while waiting for a response, began on his own to distribute soup to those in need.[6]

In April, typhus broke out, ravaging a population already severely malnourished by the famine. Mauchamp reported that he was barely able to get the governor to clean the town's dirtiest quarters. Mauchamp had a considerable number of patients to visit in town, and he often remained at his clinic until three o'clock in the afternoon. An Englishman from Gibraltar died. And along with typhus, smallpox was raging at the same time.[7]

In May Falcon surveyed the eighteen Jewish Talmud Torah schools, the traditional religious schools run by the community. He counted 376 students and made arrangements for the distribution of food. Rosilio, one of the Jewish notables, put at Falcon's disposal a small house to be used to distribute soup to children who roamed the streets during the day, too young to attend school. Corcos and Turjuman advanced Falcon money for the operation of this kitchen. The kitchen opened each morning at ten, and for the next two hours each day the street was mobbed with people seeking bread and soup.[8]

In June, as the arrival of the intense summer heat further enervated the population, Mauchamp cut back on making house calls so as to maximize the number of patients he could see at the clinic. He saw between seventy-five and a hundred people each day before stopping at 1:30 in the afternoon.[9]

Mauchamp protested that the rumors allegedly spread by Holzmann were cutting into his practice, but in fact his semiannual report submitted to the legation in Tangier at the end of June shows steady growth. Over the first six months of 1906 Mauchamp reported 6,164 patients. These included 2,956 Jews, of whom 985 were men, 1,071 were women, and 900 were children. Of these he vaccinated 487. Among Muslims, he saw 2,550, including 1,080 men, 1,065 women, and 405 children. Of these he vaccinated 171. From a start of 790 patients in January 1906, Mauchamp's monthly tally of patients rose to 1,238 patients in June as a result of the typhus epidemic.[10] In August he saw 1,774 patients.[11] Writing to the French minister Regnault in Tangier, he pleaded for an increase in his budget and commented on the lack of staff. He reported seeing 160 patients in a single day, turning away others after nine hours of work. Meanwhile his capable nurse had gone to Tangier.[12] In his mind's eye Mauchamp could already envision the creation of a hospital in which he would be seconded by an Arabic-speaking Tunisian doctor.[13]

In addition to his daily practice Mauchamp continued to collect data for what would ultimately be his posthumous book, *Sorcery in Morocco*. He also oversaw the preparation of Hebrew and vernacular Moroccan Arabic versions of his infant-healthcare brochure, although these were never published.[14] Finally, despite the press of his medical work, Mauchamp somehow found time to worry about his own health and well-being. Taking up a collection from other members of the French community, he raised six hundred francs to install a tennis court in his backyard. Mauchamp's home became the social center for Marrakesh's little French community.

153. MARRAKECH — *Arsa Moulay Moussa*

Félix Photo-éditeur Marrakech

Figure 5. Arsa Moulay Musa, the quarter where Mauchamp lived and died.
Reprinted from *Le Maroc en Cartes Postales, 1900–1920*.

The Pursuit of Politics

In November 1906, nearly a year after his arrival in Marrakesh, Mauchamp received an admiring letter from T. Guichard, a family friend from Chalon and president of the local Chamber of Commerce. Guichard had just come from visiting the doctor's family, where he learned of Mauchamp's "struggles" in Morocco. In his letter Guichard echoed the republican sentiments common among the provincial bourgeoisie:

> Everything that I've learned confirmed for me an opinion that I've held for a long time already, that which we call "the career," that is to say, diplomacy, is an anachronism in our democratic society. . . . What good is it to maintain at great cost a crowd of *messieurs* to go about and to dress in antediluvian costumes before some court or other? Their opinions, their traditions, are the born enemies of the Republic; the people whom they are assigned to frequent, I mean to say the kings, princes, even the bishops of Rome, are naturally the born enemies of the Republic; and we would be naïve to believe that this little world serves the Republic, as a good citizen ought![15]

The sentiments could well have been Mauchamp's. "They play polo in Tangier," Mauchamp concluded one letter to a friend in exasperation.[16]

With a republican distrust of diplomats and a firm belief in the righteousness of France's civilizing mission, Mauchamp undertook to promote as he saw fit the policy of "peaceful penetration" in southern Morocco. Despite what many would claim after his death, the young doctor was far from being an espionage agent sent by the Quai d'Orsay under the cloak of a humanitarian mission. Rather, it was Mauchamp's own meddlesome nature that drew him into the whirlwind of Moroccan politics. Unable to confine himself to his patients and his scholarly jottings, Mauchamp found the temptation to dabble in political intrigue too strong to resist.

The aristocratic chargé d'affaires in Tangier, August de Beaupoil, le Comte de Saint-Aulaire, had been right all along in harboring doubts about the doctor. Mauchamp was a loose cannon, sent to a city with no consular representation and consequently no one to hold his energetic and sometimes irksome personality in check. The controversy over the occupation of the Dar Ould Bellah house that marked Mauchamp's arrival in Marrakesh was just the beginning. Over the course of 1906 Mauchamp's list of complaints and demands grew, only confirming Saint-Aulaire's opinion of Mauchamp as a nuisance.

As one might expect, in his memoirs published nearly a half century after Mauchamp's murder, Saint-Aulaire offered a more kindly estimate of Émile Mauchamp. "In Marrakesh, the young and charming Doctor Mauchamp directed with much knowledge and devotion a clinic. During his passage in Tangier, I recommended to him extreme caution, which astonished him, [as] any act of hostility directed at a man devoting himself to the care of the sick seemed to him unthinkable."

With hindsight, the Comte de Saint-Aulaire wrote that he himself had looked askance at the idea of peaceful penetration and saw it as counterintuitive. A peaceful penetration that preceded a military conquest, rather than followed it, endangered its agents. The policy, in his view, was a dubious one foisted on the government by Jean Jaurès. According to Saint-Aulaire, the socialist leader's inclination to pacifism in the face of a mounting German threat only further endangered France.

Saint-Aulaire quoted the cynical Jaffary, the French doctor in Fez who ruefully quipped after Mauchamp's murder, "The lancet is a precious weapon for the conquest of Morocco, but in the sense that it supposes a surgical operation to cut out excesses incompatible with progress. This is not a simple question of hygiene. Besides, in massacring our doctors, the patient vomits out the herbal infusions we offer."

For his part, Saint-Aulaire approved of the approach offered by the French military attaché Fariau. "True peaceful penetration," the officer said, "consists of pitting a thousand men armed with cannon against a hundred louts with peashooters." Saint-Aulaire called this method a variation of the formula applied by Lyautey in the aftermath of Mauchamp's death: "One shows force so as to avoid using it."[17]

But not all of the diplomats shared the Comte de Saint-Aulaire's skepticism regarding Mauchamp's humanitarian mission. Eugène Regnault, the French minister in Tangier, saw in Mauchamp's ever-growing lists of patients and consultations confirmation of the foreign ministry's policy of peaceful penetration. By year's end Regnault had become Mauchamp's principal benefactor, energetic in his efforts to turn Mauchamp's clinic into a full-fledged hospital and to allocate money for the purchase of land.[18] In February 1907 he wrote to Charles Jonnart, the governor general of Algeria, hoping to identify a suitable Algerian Arab doctor who could second Mauchamp. In Paris, too, Mauchamp had his admirers, politicians from Mauchamp's native Saône-et-Loire department who lobbied for a Legion of Honor decoration on their countryman's behalf.

And finally, Mauchamp arrived in Marrakesh with the blessings of the Morocco Committee. Once there he entered into an active correspondence with Charles René-Leclerc, the committee's representative in Tangier and the author of several knowledgeable books on Morocco's economy and society. Mauchamp became the committee's man in Marrakesh, hosting the occasional French visitor to the city, such as the young Charmetant, a business student from Lyon on a tour to study commercial prospects in Morocco.[19]

In addition to answering René-Leclerc's queries about political activities in the south, Mauchamp on occasion submitted articles to be published anonymously in the committee's Moroccan mouthpieces, *La Dépêche Marocaine* and the Arabic-language *Al-Saada*. Mauchamp's articles (or at the very least, articles to which he contributed information) evidently had an alarmist air. At the end of July 1906, the French mission decided to send its trusty employee Muhammad al-Marrakshi Desaulty on a tour of the south to gather intelligence. As René-Leclerc wrote to Mauchamp, the diplomats thought that the reports appearing in *La Dépêche Marocaine* exaggerated the situation in the south.[20]

In his correspondence Mauchamp alleged that there was a growing threat of danger to the European colony in Marrakesh. Moreover, it was frequently rumored that supporters of Moulay Hafid, the viceroy of the south and the reigning sultan's brother, were on the verge of insurrection. In his dispatches Lennox, the English vice-consul in Marrakesh, repeatedly dismissed both allegations, and Jeannier, reporting from Essaouira, similarly played down the rumors that Moulay Hafid was about to proclaim himself sultan.[21] But if neither claim was necessarily true at the time they were made in the summer of 1906, they soon took on aspects of a self-fulfilling prophecy. Mauchamp's death the following spring provided the catalyst not only for Lyautey's military incursion into Morocco but for Moulay Hafid's successful rebellion against his brother, the reigning sultan Abdelaziz.

Mauchamp's work on behalf of the Morocco Committee was only one display of his sense of patriotic duty. In April 1906, he responded at length to a query from the Alliance Française in Lyon regarding the prospects of a French language school in Marrakesh.[22] The Alliance Française, which continues to operate throughout the world today, was founded in 1883 under the aegis of the Paul Cambon, the foreign minister, for the expressed purpose of promoting the French language overseas. Citing the Alliance Israélite's school in the *mellah*, and the obstacles that attending the Jewish school posed for Muslims who might want a French education, Mauchamp came out wholeheartedly in support of the idea. He designed an entire curriculum in his mind: French language, arithmetic ("this last subject . . . will serve as the draw for the other"), Arabic, and Koran. The first subjects should be taught by an Algerian, but Mauchamp recommended that the religious subjects be taught by a Moroccan of unimpeachable orthodoxy. Mauchamp's recommendation in this regard reflected a widespread perception that Algerians were poorly educated in their own religion.[23] He advised that the school be open only three days a week at the start.

Mauchamp staked his own reputation on its success. He would find an acceptably observant schoolmaster for the school. "The notables here have a certain confidence in me, and as I've always made efforts to convince them of my respect and even my sympathy for their religious faith, they know that I require of all my employees the observance of the Moroccan practices."

Mauchamp thought it unlikely that he could find locally in Morocco a qualified Tunisian or Algerian to run the school. He recommended that his correspondent apply directly to Jonnart, the governor general of Algeria, for help. Mauchamp held out little hope for aid from the French legation in Tangier. "The legation seems to me very detached from practical questions of French influence and having little desire at present to favor initiations of this type."[24]

Meanwhile, Mauchamp's personal initiatives in the name of peaceful penetration could sometimes take on a comic quality. In conversation with the Algerian-born secretary of the Essaouira consulate, Mauchamp learned that the local *qaid* of the Abda tribe, Si Aissa bin Umar, fancied a pair of Arabian falcons. Writing in July 1906 to his father, Mauchamp says that several Frenchmen, among them the explorer Segonzac and the geologist Gentil, had promised to provide the *qaid* with the birds but had failed to deliver. Without ever having met the *qaid* himself, Mauchamp nonetheless undertook to safeguard his nation's honor and demonstrate that a Frenchman's word could be trusted. Through the intermediary of a Dominican priest in Jerusalem and Bedouin friends in Arabia, Mauchamp arranged to send two falcons to the *qaid*. Traveling via the Persian Gulf, the poor birds were in transit for more than four months, but evidently arrived in full health. As Mauchamp wrote his father, the consular secretary conveyed to him Si Aissa's "enthusiastic thanks."[25]

The secretary may have overstated the *qaid*'s gratitude. In any case, the matter was far from over. Among Mauchamp's later correspondence two letters written from Safi make allusions to Si Aissa and his birds. The last letter puts it bluntly: "From my personal inquiry regarding your affair, it seems that Si Aissa didn't recognize in your falcons [authentic] birds of the country [Arabia], but a quality very inferior to these falcons."[26]

Like so many other supposedly selfless gestures of the French, Mauchamp's gift had failed to achieve its desired results. And indeed, like other Frenchmen, Mauchamp could misconstrue the courteous nature of Moroccans as a gesture of reciprocity and genuine acceptance. In late March 1906 Mauchamp visited one of the rural notables, the sharif of Tamesloht. Telling Mauchamp that he cared for him like a son, the sharif sent him an armed escort for the three-hour journey from Marrakesh. An enthusiastic Mauchamp wrote to his father how his arrival at the sharif's *zawiya,* or shrine, coincided with the onset of the spring rains. Flattering Mauchamp, the sharif told the Frenchman that the rains were a sign of his divine *baraka,* or grace, and he refused to let him depart until all his fields were watered.

"The rain stopped as soon as I got in the saddle, and there hasn't been any rain since. Not a few people to whom we've recounted this marvel seriously believe in my *baraka* and two delegations came asking me to return!!!" Unable to forgo a jibe at the expense of the Moroccan government, Mauchamp told his beseechers "that I would only return when the Makhzan reestablished security."

The *zawiya* of Tamesloht was a thriving commercial and agricultural center, and Mauchamp's close relations with its sharif rankled British observers. It now appeared that the sharif, who was already a British protégé, was about to change sides. "Our friend in Tamesloht," the British consul in Casablanca reported, "is making love to the French now."[27]

Mauchamp's visit was a success from another standpoint. "I earned a superb copper-chestnut stallion that the sharif of Tamesloht offered me in recognition of the fertility I brought on his fields!"

While Mauchamp took the gift of a horse as a special mark of distinction, the giving of a horse was in fact a common expression

of hospitality among Moroccan notables. According to Felix Weisgerber, Si Aissa bin Umar, the *qaid* of the Abda, seldom if ever let a
European leave his house without first offering a horse. Walter Harris, the longtime British journalist and resident of Morocco, went so
far as to bemoan the unnecessary expense that came as a result of
his accumulating one gift horse after another.[28]

In the absence of a consul in Marrakesh, it required only a small
leap on the part of Mauchamp, as an employee of the foreign ministry, to imagine himself to be the ranking French representative in
the city. In his response to a friend's inquiry about his mission in Morocco midway through the first year of his assignment, Mauchamp's
remarks are revealing in their pretentiousness.

> You ask me what I'm doing in Morocco where they offered me the
> most delicate, the most difficult, post, assuring me all the while with
> flattery that if I did not accept, they would not send anyone else.
> . . . Yes, they found it necessary to establish in this very xenophobic
> southern capital of Morocco a center of French influence; a lone
> doctor could succeed there and we did not dare send a consul; be-
> sides it required that the doctor know the Muslim soul well, that he
> understand how not to disturb it and to support it without loving it.
> I believe that I have finally succeeded in this. This was not without
> pain and without obstacles. . . . This [required] a struggle in many
> forms against the native element and against the German intrigues
> that have gone very far. I was the first Frenchman in Marrakesh.

The self-important Mauchamp could not let his pompous declaration end there. He accused the French government of neglect—a
theme that would return to haunt French officials after Mauchamp's
death.

> Let me add that at the time of these difficult conjunctures, which
> coincided with [the conference at] Algeciras, I was completely
> abandoned by the French legation and I had to hold up by my own
> means against the hostility intentionally waged by the natives and
> the Makhzan.
>
> All that is over. I made myself difficult and now everything is
> straightened out. My clinic is bursting and I've asked for reinforce-
> ments. *Voilà*, that's what I'm doing among these savage Berbers and
> Arabs.[29]

Given his strident defense of French interests, others around
Mauchamp naturally tended to cast him in the role of consul. It soon
became known that Mauchamp gathered information. A Monsieur
Castro (in Morocco, a Jewish name) sent Mauchamp a list of local

sharifs, the genealogical descendants of the Prophet who formed a kind of nobility in Morocco. To this he appended a plea for employment, saying he received a small stipend from the Makhzan, but had no responsibilities. It would be a "philanthropic act," he wrote, for Mauchamp to employ him.[30] Whether Mauchamp used Castro's services is not known.

We have already seen how Falcon, the Alliance Israélite headmaster, often turned to Mauchamp for support with Makhzan officials. The handful of French businessmen in Marrakesh also looked to Mauchamp to represent their interests. The merchant Firbach wrote to Mauchamp to complain that the governor of Marrakesh had sent soldiers to his house and that they had interfered with his employees. In another scrawled note, Firbach called for Mauchamp to come immediately to care for his workers whom the governor had imprisoned and to prepare certificates regarding their condition to send to the legation.[31]

Mauchamp became involved in extending protection to Moroccans and defending the interest of French protégés. To his parents he wrote proudly of his success in obtaining the release of a protégé from Essaouira. The farmer, he said, had been unjustly imprisoned and his flocks seized by the *qaid* of the Menabha. Not only that, Mauchamp boasted, but after his intervention, the *qaid* asked to be his friend and proposed that he put his own relations under Mauchamp's protection.[32]

In a similar vein, Mauchamp received a desperate note from an Algerian imprisoned for some offense in Marrakesh. Identifying himself as someone who had attended school in Constantine in Algeria, he scrawled in French that he was an "Arab by race but a Frenchman at heart." The letter, addressed to "Monsieur le Docteur Français," had been forwarded by Marie Nicolet, a Swiss missionary in Marrakesh, who wrote, "I sense that even if he is guilty, he is in a terrible position."

The unfortunate Algerian pleaded with Mauchamp in a second letter to post his bond. Sent just days before Mauchamp's death, this pathetic plea arrived too late to do any good.[33] Indeed, as it turned out, the cocky French doctor could do little to save himself.

International Diplomacy and Local Intrigue

Mauchamp arrived in Morocco's southern capital at a critical moment in the nation's history. In mid-1904 France and England signed the Entente Cordiale. In exchange for France's recognizing British control of Egypt, the new agreement gave France the upper hand in Morocco. With Britain, its most serious rival for influence, now out of the way, France was able to successfully negotiate with the Makhzan a major new loan. The loan agreement consolidated the country's huge debt and gave France direct control over Morocco's finances, with 60 percent of the customs revenues earmarked as collateral.[34] It also encouraged France to dictate a complete package of political and economic reforms. In late 1904 Abdelaziz assembled a Council of Notables to debate how best to withstand French demands, and he warily dismissed French military advisers. Nevertheless, the young sultan's efforts at resisting the French seemed inadequate to many. Goaded into action by the Sufi shaykh Muhammad bin Abd al-Kabir al-Kattani, the Fez ulama began to oppose Abdelaziz and his policies, which they saw as endangering Moroccan independence.[35] The eventual beneficiary of this mounting opposition to Abdelaziz would be his brother Moulay Hafid, the southern viceroy in Marrakesh. In 1908, presenting himself as the leader of a jihad, or holy war, in defense of Moroccan sovereignty, he supplanted his brother on the throne despite French opposition. Nonetheless, he proved as incapable as Abdelaziz of resisting French intervention in Moroccan affairs. In 1912 he signed the protectorate agreement, only in turn to be forced to abdicate by the French in favor of a younger brother, Youssef.

Meanwhile, beginning in 1905, Germany's unanticipated intervention in Morocco's affairs temporarily thwarted French colonial ambitions. In return for a variety of economic and commercial concessions, Germany offered itself as a defender of Moroccan independence. The so-called First Moroccan Crisis, instigated by Kaiser Wilhelm's celebrated visit to Tangier in March 1905, set the stage for the international conference at Algeciras the following year. Moroccan diplomats "anticipated that by placing the reform question in an international context it would be possible to ward off French claims to predominance."[36]

The Moroccan strategy backfired. Germany did not strongly defend Moroccan interests. Instead, the reforms proposed by the Act of Algeciras merely confirmed French policy and extended French control. In early June the dean of the Tangier diplomatic community, the Italian minister Malmusi, went to Fez to make a formal presentation of the Act of Algeciras to Abdelaziz. "The mission was received cordially enough by the Moorish authorities," one observer wrote, but with "no kind of enthusiasm."

As the diplomats made their way to the palace, the animals they passed looked ragged and slack, the guards haggard. The Europeans held their nose against a dead mule carcass that lay prominently in the path. The reception of the mission reflected the hard, dispirited mood of the times. In a gesture that delighted Abdelaziz, the Arabic-speaking Malmusi "departed from custom" and did without the services of an interpreter.[37] But even this token of accommodation and respect could not soften the unpleasantness of his message. Abdelaziz's ratification of the Act of Algeciras on June 18, 1906, "consummated the break between the sultan and those Moroccans who favored continued resistance to France."[38]

In March 1906, reading in *La Dépêche Marocaine* the accounts of the conference then underway in the sleepy Spanish fishing town, Mauchamp anticipated that the Germans would be the ultimate beneficiaries.[39] A month later, he was only slightly more optimistic. "The excellent moral result of Algeciras is only for our European situation; as for the Moroccans, they know that they can create all sorts of obstacles for us, put us in all the possible corners, without us daring to have the energy to impose ourselves."[40]

The French vice-consul Jeannier in Essaouira sized up Moroccan public opinion by saying that the "few natives" who had heard of Algeciras "believe it would not have any result: the Europeans, they say, want to hide a greyhound under a sieve and seize Morocco by ruse, but it is by a ruse that Morocco will escape them."[41] Jeannier did not say on what basis this confidence felt by his informants was warranted.

While the conference of Algeciras was under way, Mauchamp's rivalry with the pro-German Dr. Holzmann heated further. Already at the end of February Mauchamp wrote,

> I am in the process of *working* [emphasis in the original] Moulay Hafid . . . so as to distance him from Holzmann and make him call on me. I have on my side the brother-in-law of the sultan, his friend the *qadi* [judge], who put himself under my protection, and the *qaid* [Al-Madani] al-Glawi as well, who is the most powerful supporter of the viceroy. It seems that Moulay Hafid is intelligent, decent, and learned. I think I will be able to attach him to us.[42]

A week later, Mauchamp sized up his rival. "Holzmann remains quiet and from time to time sends to me someone to protest that he has good intentions in my regard. I wait for visible proofs before acknowledging his offerings of devotion. All the more as I know at present that he is indeed a German agent, openly and under the responsibility of the German consul [Niehr] despite his denials."[43]

Not many weeks after Mauchamp's death, Nissim Falcon

summed up Mauchamp's political efforts vis-à-vis Moulay Hafid. At the moment the doctor arrived on the scene in Marrakesh, Moulay Hafid, whom Falcon rightly described as having neither an army nor a treasury at his disposal but who long entertained ambitions of seizing the throne, was caught in a balancing act between the three powerful *qaid*s who controlled southern Morocco: Glawi, Goundafi, and Mtouggi.[44] When Holzmann was unable to deliver on promised German support, Moulay Hafid then approached Mauchamp.[45] The doctor encouraged the viceroy to reconcile the three rival *qaid*s, and in exchange for French protection and support, Moulay Hafid would open the southern part of Morocco to exclusive French economic penetration.

According to Falcon, even Mauchamp was amazed by his own success as a "diplomat." On his return to Marrakesh from his trip to Paris, he brought expensive presents from the French government for Moulay Hafid and, supposedly, the promise from the foreign minister Pichon that a patent of protection for the viceroy would soon follow. Moreover, by "winning" Moulay Hafid over to the French side, Falcon claimed Mauchamp had "scooped" another Frenchman, the geologist Brives, who arrived in Marrakesh in early spring, allegedly sent by Regnault in Tangier on a covert diplomatic mission to secure Moulay Hafid for France.

But all came to naught. "The death of the poor doctor," Falcon concluded in May 1907, "has cast these beautiful dreams into the abyss. Moulay Hafid has fallen again under the evil influence of his courtiers. His ambitions remain the same as always; but he searches today for allies among the tribes in revolt."[46]

Beautiful dreams, indeed. The ambitious super-patriot Mauchamp could campaign all he might on behalf of Moulay Hafid, but French policymakers at the Quai d'Orsay had no intention of abandoning sultan Abdelaziz for his brother. Still, the suspicion lingered that the foreign ministry had indeed charged Mauchamp to conduct secret diplomatic negotiations. A year after Mauchamp's death, as France became ever more deeply entangled militarily in Morocco and as Moulay Hafid's ascendance to the throne seemed imminent, Jean Jaurès rose in the chamber with a blistering allegation. Citing three letters written by Mauchamp, Jaurès accused the foreign minister Pichon of double-dealing, backing Moulay Hafid in secret while openly supporting Abdelaziz.

It was an accusation that Pichon staunchly denied . . . but we are getting ahead of our story.

5

False Starts and False Reports

Holzmann and Rumors

To many observers southern Morocco seemed primed to explode in the second half of 1906. Throughout the summer rumors circulated that Moulay Hafid was about to proclaim himself sultan in Marrakesh. In nearby Essaouira an inexplicable panic seized the Jewish quarter as it anticipated coming under attack, first from neighboring tribesmen and then from Tuareg followers of Ma al-Aynayn, the so-called *hommes bleus,* or blue men, who were then passing through the port city. The leader of the Saharan resistance to the French was returning south from a visit to the court in Fez. The sultan had promised him support, much to the chagrin of the French, who were determined to take over neighboring Mauritania. Meanwhile, in separate incidents throughout the country, Frenchmen, among them a friend of Mauchamp's named Lassallas, came under attack.

In Tangier, French diplomats downplayed the possibility of Moulay Hafid mounting a challenge to his half-brother Abdelaziz for the throne. To the extent that the diplomats of the Quai d'Orsay had a policy toward Morocco, it depended on bolstering the existing Makhzan, both financially and militarily. French policymakers saw no reason to abandon their commitment to Abdelaziz. The young sultan was a known entity and amenable—or so it seemed—to French plans for reform. Moreover, France had already committed itself to helping Abdelaziz defend his throne from rival claimants.

Chief among these was the Rogui, or "Pretender," also known as Abu Himara, the "Man on the She-Donkey." Born Jilani bin Idris al-Zarhuni, this clever fraud had succeeded in convincing his fol-

lowers that he was Moulay Muhammad, the older brother of Abdelaziz, allegedly escaped from imprisonment. For nearly a decade
Abu Himara ruled over his own little kingdom, first in a portion of
eastern Morocco, and later in the Rif to the north. In 1906 he had
still eluded capture.[1]

Abu Himara's antics were merely a diversion. But, as the diplomats well understood—and evidently Mauchamp did not—a bid for
power by the sultan's half-brother Moulay Hafid posed a genuine
threat to French interests. Learned in Islamic law and an accomplished scholar, the viceroy of the south possessed the royal bearing
and respect for tradition that his younger half-brother, the reigning
Abdelaziz, seemed to lack. At the head of a jihad, Moulay Hafid was
at least in theory capable of uniting Morocco's disparate tribes and
mounting a stiff resistance to French ambitions. All that he required
to be the legitimate ruler of Morocco was for the ulama to give him
the requisite *baya*, or oath of loyalty. Adhering to Islamic tradition,
the sultan as the "leader of the faithful" essentially entered into a
contractual relationship with his subjects, in this case represented
by the learned scholars of the community. But the oath of loyalty
was not so easily obtained. However much they might oppose European intervention in Moroccan affairs, the ulama in Fez—with the
notable exception of the controversial and charismatic Muhammad
bin Abd al-Kabir al-Kattani—remained docilely loyal to the reigning
sultan Abdelaziz.

A revivalist leader and the head of the Kattaniyya mystical brotherhood, Muhammad al-Kattani was at one time himself suspected
of seeking the throne. Moreover, in 1897, the ulama of Fez tried
to have him executed for heresy, accusing him of doctrinal excess.
He was saved through the intervention of the Mauritanian Sufi
shaykh Ma al-Aynayn, and for the next seven years, somewhat
ironically considering later events, he enjoyed the support of the
sultan Abdelaziz. In 1903 al-Kattani made the pilgrimage to Mecca
at Abdelaziz's expense, only to become the sultan's staunchest critic
upon his return the following year. While al-Kattani openly expressed the anti-French sentiments that many educated Moroccans
no doubt thought, even he was reticent about declaring a change of
loyalty. Instead, he and some other ulama in Fez cautiously waited
till Abdelaziz and his army departed Fez in September 1907 before
coming out for Moulay Hafid.[2]

Not all Frenchmen shared the Quai d'Orsay's aversion to Moulay Hafid. For example, Vaffier-Pollet, an agent for the Companie

Marocaine and a representative of the Morocco Committee, actively promoted Moulay Hafid's cause. Vaffier-Pollet was especially close to Si Al-Madani al-Glawi, Moulay Hafid's principal supporter. It was most likely due to Vaffier-Pollet's influence that Mauchamp became an eager convert to the Hafidist cause. Mauchamp was evidently indifferent to the difficulties that such a stance might pose for French diplomats committed to supporting Abdelaziz, who, for all his faults, remained the country's legitimate ruler.

From Mauchamp's perspective, Moulay Hafid's accession to the throne was already inevitable. And if that were the case, then the real task was to draw him away from the Germans and into the French camp. It was a task that Mauchamp would undertake for himself whether he had direct orders to do so or not. Meanwhile, anticipating that Moulay Hafid would soon make his move, Mauchamp and other local observers in the south subjected Holzmann's every move to the closest scrutiny. The pro-German adviser and physician to Moulay Hafid had become the canary in the mineshaft.

As it turned out, the political reality in 1906 was more complicated than Mauchamp imagined. Without an army of his own or the financial resources to buy influence among the tribes, Moulay Hafid was reluctant to make a move. If he were to launch a military campaign against his brother Abdelaziz, he would be dependent on the great *qaid*s of the south, the so-called Lords of the Atlas. That dependence posed risks of its own, and so Moulay Hafid, fearful of becoming hostage to Si Al-Madani al-Glawi's ambitions, hesitated to make a move.

Throughout it all, Alan Lennox, the missionary who doubled as the British vice-consul in Marrakesh, remained skeptical that Moulay Hafid entertained ambitions of becoming sultan. Drawing on his five years of close friendship with Moulay Hafid, Lennox labored to convince his superiors that Moulay Hafid had no immediate intention of revolting against his brother. Moulay Hafid's position, he wrote, was "very difficult, and almost anything he does for the pacifying of the Southern tribes is put down for ulterior motives. . . . At present he has no force in hand to put a stop to the plundering of farms and villages around the city, but by giving presents to the chiefs of Rehamna [*sic*] he is trying to will them over to suppress these robberies and keep the tribes tranquil. To this he is said to be buying them over to enable him to rise against his brother."[3]

The Rahamna, who were the most important tribe of the Marrakesh region, occupied some seventy-five hundred square kilometers of the sparsely populated Haouz region to the north and east of the city. In addition, members of the Rahamna tribe comprised perhaps a third of the city's population. Mostly concentrated in the northern part of the city near the *zawiya* of Sidi bel Abbas, these included some well-to-do families but also many "poor people who had lost rights to flocks or pastureland in their area of origin."[4] Some Rahamna *qaids* also spent part of the year in the city, where they conducted business or engaged in politics. Because the Makhzan tried to assert control over the tribe and collect taxes from it, the Rahamna often found themselves in competition with the leaders of Marrakesh for control of the region. Moreover, the tribe had played a central role in the various succession crises that plagued the Moroccan monarchy. In 1894, upon the death of Moulay Hassan, the Rahamna opposed the accession of Abdelaziz and were brutally suppressed by the regent Ba Ahmad. Memories of the 1894 revolt and Abdelaziz's increasing involvement with Europeans would eventually lead the Rahamna to rally to Moulay Hafid's cause.[5]

According to Lennox, Moulay Hafid was intensely anti-French and much perturbed by Abdelaziz's mismanagement of Morocco's affairs. Nonetheless he remained loyal to his brother. First, he lacked sufficient troops to raise a revolt. Secondly, the cautious Moulay Hafid would not "trust himself to sit between such two uncertain stools" as Mtouggi and Glawi.[6]

Writing from his post in Essaouira, the French vice-consul Jeannier also reported the recurrence of separatist rumors throughout the month of August. Like his English counterpart in Marrakesh, Jeannier discounted them. He pointed to the "German pseudo-doctor Holzmann" as their source and dismissed reports of an agitated south as being exaggerated.

"I insist on the word 'rumors,'" Jeannier wrote to Regnault in Tangier on August 19, 1906, "because up till now all this makes more noise than harm: the region appears especially troubled in the newspapers; the caravans that want to go pay arbitrary taxes, it is true, but the taxes are paid, there's nothing abnormal to say there."

Reviewing the ever-shifting alliances between Moulay Hafid and the various *qaids* of the Mtougga, the Haha, the Goundafa, the Glawa and the Rahamna tribes, Jeannier placed blame squarely on Holzmann and German meddling. Moulay Hafid's "commercial factotum, Doctor Holzmann, an ambitious and greedy Ottoman Jew, has truly exploited this situation, allowing him to understand that

the true believers, discontented with Abdelaziz following his acceptance of the Algeciras reforms, would readily call for another Filali
[dynasty] sultan—and what Filali is better qualified than Moulay
Hafid to replace Abdelaziz?"

Like Lennox, Jeannier did not think Moulay Hafid's proclamation was imminent. The powerful *qaid* Al-Madani al-Glawi, Moulay
Hafid's principal backer, "will be, let us say, very shaken," having
just learned that "Doctor Holzmann is only an Ottoman Jew." Meanwhile, Holzmann would lobby Si Aissa bin Umar, the *qaid* of the
Abda (and the recipient of Mauchamp's falcons). However, he was
unlikely to betray Abdelaziz, "as he contributed more than anyone
else to have him proclaimed [sultan]."

What was required, Jeannier suggested, was pulling in the reins
on Holzmann. "If Doctor Holzmann, a foreigner without consular
representation in Morocco were invited, under pain of expulsion,
to cease these agitations which no one would dare support, without fire, none of these separatist tendencies of Moulay Hafid would
continue any longer."[7]

The appearance of Holzmann, traveling in the company of a
soldier provided by Moulay Hafid and horsemen furnished by the
governor of Marrakesh, attracted attention on the coast. Souessia,
formerly the Alliance schoolteacher in Marrakesh, added a postscript
to his usual correspondence with Mauchamp about the difficulty of
finding good help and availability of cooks who only spoke Spanish.
"I almost forgot to tell you," he wrote, "that I saw Holzmann himself
walking about with two Germans; they always dress Arab-style. I
don't know anything else about what he came here for."[8]

A communiqué from the French consulate in Safi dated August
21 also credited Holzmann and an unnamed Italian (undoubtedly
Mauchamp's friend Berrino) with spreading anti-French propaganda
in Marrakesh and offered further speculation on the suspicious doctor's visit. Armed with a letter of recommendation from a merchant
in Marrakesh, Holzmann lodged in Safi with a local Jew and made
visits to the Germans. The "native chiefs," whom Holzmann did not
visit, "seem to ignore his presence."

> The general opinion among the Europeans of Marrakesh and Safi is
> that the individual under consideration is an official German agent
> and that he receives subsidies from the [German] legation in Tangier,
> but we cannot confirm this fact in any certain fashion. What is unde-
> niable is his anti-French zeal and the place which he occupies in the
> spirit of Moulay Hafid who does nothing without consulting him.[9]

Holzmann had given out that he left Marrakesh to seek shelter from the epidemic raging there ("a reason little excusable for a doctor," the report commented), but the real aim of his mission was to recruit support for Moulay Hafid. To do so, Holzmann offered his services as an arbiter between Anflus al-Miknasi, the *qaid* of the Haha, and the *qaid* of the Chiadma, who had been quarreling. Moulay Hafid reportedly sent other emissaries from Marrakesh to the *qaid*s of the Mtougga and the Sous.

The flurry of correspondence and the surveillance of Holzmann continued. On August 24, Jeannier again wrote to Regnault, tallying the scorecard of who would be for and who would be against a proclamation by Moulay Hafid. He predicted that Holzmann would have little success with Si Aissa bin Umar. As for the others *qaid*s,

> they only await the return from Fez of the shaykh Ma al-Aynayn [the Saharan anti-French leader was then visiting the court] for them to declare Moulay Hafid sultan. The Glawi is the warmest partisan of the latter, but given that Marrakesh, half of the Rahamna, the shaykh [sharif] of Tamesloht, the Doukkala, the Abda and the Ras el-Oued are against him, his chances of success are weak. Holzmann can't always be on the lookout.[10]

A final communiqué from Safi dated August 29 reported that before departing Safi on the 27th for Marrakesh, Holzmann made a brief roundtrip voyage to Essaouira on a German steamer. The nature of this brief mission was uncertain, but the consul commented that on his return Holzmann paid long visits to several Germans, including one Hans Richter, singled out by name because his older brother had converted to Islam a few months earlier. And finally, the consul speculated that Holzmann might prolong his return to Marrakesh with a detour to the north to press Moulay Hafid's case further with Si Aissa bin Umar.[11]

Meanwhile, back in Marrakesh, Mauchamp reckoned that he had all but vanquished his rival Holzmann. Writing home on October 7, he spoke of the current warmth of his relations with the viceroy Moulay Hafid. In particular, Mauchamp noted that Moulay Hafid held him in high regard and seemed pleased by his "dignified" attitude, "which is a change from the base courtesy of Holzmann and some other adventurers who hung around him not so long ago. . . . Instead of making me wait like his viziers and familiars, he comes to meet me and returns with me almost to the exterior door of the palace. The people, soldiers and beggars who swarm about there don't believe their eyes and say that never has a *qaid* had an equal honor."

Mauchamp anticipated Moulay Hafid's making an "opening" toward the French. Mauchamp gloated that if this were case, he would have succeeded without the benefit of a consulate, without any aid from the legation, and "solely by the prestige of my persevering and dignified attitude."[12]

Calling Moulay Hafid the inevitable successor to the sultan Abdelaziz, Mauchamp wrote the following month to Regnault in Tangier. He told him of his expectation that he would soon dislodge and replace Holzmann as Moulay Hafid's physician. Moreover, he reported that Moulay Hafid wanted him to speak on his behalf to the French minister. Tactfully, Mauchamp said he told Moulay Hafid that he would have to consult Regnault, his superior. Two weeks later, an impatient Mauchamp again asked permission to carry a message from the viceroy. Regnault replied in a letter that crossed paths that he would be happy to talk with Mauchamp when he came through Tangier.[13] From all appearances, it seems that the always cordial Regnault was cool to the idea of entrusting the physician with a diplomatic mission. Least of all, he was not about to change the course of French policy toward the reigning monarch of Morocco simply on the basis of Mauchamp's whim.

The doctor remained undeterred. Writing to a friend at about the same time, Mauchamp displayed less restraint. With more than a bit of exaggeration, he described himself as the only Frenchman among one hundred thousand natives, beset by German secret agents and adventurers who managed to monopolize the viceroy Moulay Hafid and "who made the law in this capital." Despite all adversity, he nonetheless claimed success. "I have become the sole confidant of the viceroy whom I have completed turned to our side. Thus all goes well. I am a bit exhausted and overworked, but it will all turn out all right. . . . This life of agitation and struggle pleases me and the days pass with a vertiginous rapidity."[14]

"Anarchy"

With Holzmann's departure from the coast, the attention of French diplomats in Safi and Essaouira quickly turned to more "routine" disruptions, in this instance, the appearance in Essaouira of the *qaid* Anflus al-Miknasi and some three hundred of his men. This *qaid*, routinely described in the Tangier papers as a "boor," threatened to uproot Jews who were living in the Arab *madina* of Essaouira instead of the two *mellah*s, old and new, reserved for them.[15] Moreover, his men went around removing by force the shoes of Jews who walked past the *zawiya* of the local Sufi brotherhood. According to the vice-consul Jeannier, this trivial incident became greatly exaggerated as it was spread from mouth to mouth. As a consequence, a "strange panic" broke out among the Jews, who locked themselves behind the *mellah* gates. "Encouraged by this puerile fear, two or three *chleuh* [Berbers] from Miknasi's entourage and the Arab street urchins of the town hurled stones through the windows of the houses of the *mellah* on Safi Street."

Reportedly profiting from Anflus men's encampment, Essaouira's governor Abd al-Rahman Bargash did nothing to control the situation despite protests from the European diplomatic corps. According to Jeannier, similar incidents occurred when Ma al-Aynayn and his Saharan followers came through town, and it was feared that when they returned from Fez, they would unite with Anflus's armed men. In the end the appearance of the French cruiser *Galilée* in the port of Essaouira temporarily restored order.[16] A few months later Anflus's men would be back again, attempting for a second time to confine Essaouira's Jews to the *mellah* on the pretext that some among them had established bars and brothels in the Arab quarter.[17]

The episode with the *qaid* Anflus in Essaouira, what Jeannier described as "a strange panic . . . that followed a very exaggerated and trivial incident," turned out to be a harbinger of unforeseen things to come. Only a year later, when events spiraled out of control in Casablanca after a fatal attack on European quarry workers there, Arab tribesman used the occasion to attack the Jewish quarter there, and the *Galilée* was again called into action. This second time, however, the French captain was eager to make a genuine show of force. In July 1907, the *Galilée*'s guns virtually flattened Casablanca. The subsequent effort to restore order in the Shawiya region obliged the French military to occupy ever greater amounts of Moroccan soil and guaranteed the uprising of Moulay Hafid upon which diplomats had only speculated in the summer of 1906.

French politicians forever railed against the "anarchic" state of Morocco, but they were blind to their own contributions to this self-fulfilling prophecy. In the wake of the Algeciras conference, as European and especially French influence in Morocco rose, so too did attacks on Europeans by Moroccans. Nevertheless, uncertain about German aims in Morocco and concerned about the risk of war in Europe, the French policymakers who succeeded Delcassé remained committed to the policy of peaceful penetration.

French influence manifested itself in the creation of a port police and, following the establishment of the Debt Commission in 1904, the installation of European agents to supervise the customs administration, a move bitterly opposed by Moroccan customs inspectors. France continued to expand its medical missionary service, and in 1906 the French military mission to Fez resumed after a year and a half hiatus. Meanwhile, French and other European business firms flocked to Morocco in 1906 and 1907 in "the expectation of a dramatic increase in trade possibilities."[18]

Prior to 1906, Morocco witnessed a number of spectacular but isolated incidents involving the assault or kidnapping of Europeans. In October 1902, David J. Cooper, a British missionary, was killed by an incensed Moroccan tribesman after he inattentively wandered past the shrine of the patron saint of Fez, Moulay Idris. The murderer took sanctuary in the shrine and agreed to appear before the sultan Abdelaziz only when he was assured that he still enjoyed the saint's protection. However, responding to European demands that he set an example, the sultan ordered the man executed. Abdelaziz's flagrant disregard for the sanctity of the Moulay Idris shrine provoked a public outcry and provided the pretext for the Rogui's revolt.[19]

Six months later, the government unsuccessfully tried to suppress Ahmad bin Muhammad al-Raisuli, a sharif who enjoyed great prestige among the Bani Arus and other tribes near Tangier. In retaliation for the capture of five of his men, al-Raisuli held for ransom Walter Harris, the *Times* of London correspondent. The move proved so successful that he next targeted the wealthiest man in Tangier's expatriate community, Ion Perdicaris, a Greek-born naturalized American citizen, and his son-in-law. Apart from receiving a large ransom, his negotiations with the Makhzan led to his appointment as governor of Tangier province and assured his reputation among some anti-French elements in Fez as a Moroccan patriot.[20] Al-Raisuli revived his career as a kidnapper again in 1908, when he took the sultan's British military adviser, Maclean, hostage. He continued to play a role in Moroccan affairs when during the Rif War he emerged as a rival to the rebel leader Abd al-Karim al-Khattabi.

French nationals also became the object of attacks. On May 27, 1906, a young French bank employee named Charbonnier was murdered by supporters of al-Raisuli while horseback riding on the beach outside Tangier. The French government responded by sending warships in a display of force and presenting demands that included finding and executing the murderers, a full apology to the French minister, payment of an indemnity of one hundred thousand francs to Charbonnier's family, and granting a plot of land on which would be erected a monument to the victim.[21]

Lastly, in September of the same year, a French commercial agent with the Compagnie Marocaine was shot and wounded in the vicinity of Marrakesh. The agent, Jean Denaut Lassallas, was a friend of Mauchamp, who now moved into high gear. Characteristically, he directed his ire at the legation in Tangier, irritated by the diplomats' alleged indifference to the safety of the little French colony in the south.

The Lassallas Affair

The so-called Lassallas affair was yet another entry in the growing list of grievances Mauchamp had against his government's legation in Tangier. Not long after his controversy over the Dar Ould Bellah house, Mauchamp became embroiled in a dispute with the French postal service. The latter maintained a *rakkas*, or foot courier, service linking Marrakesh to the coastal city of El-Jadida and from there to Casablanca. In early June 1906, a courier was robbed on the highway between El-Jadida and Azemmour. Among the stolen mail were three scientific papers that Mauchamp had posted to the Academy of Medicine in Paris. One was a paper destined for the section on infant hygiene, another for the vaccine service, and a third—considered by Mauchamp to be his most important—for the epidemiology department. In letters to Regnault and the postal service minister in Paris, Mauchamp protested the theft and demanded that those responsible for the loss of the articles be punished. The articles, he wrote, represented three years of work and were to be submitted for academic prizes worth, he said, between three and six thousand francs. Of course it was not the lost money but the inability to be represented for the prize that troubled him.[22]

Mauchamp wrote to his father in July:

> As for the legation, it continues to be mute and I have not received any response to my various letters dating from over one to three months in regards to: (1) reimbursement for the clinic's expenses, (2) a proposal for an information brochure analogous to the one I had distributed in Palestine, *Advice to Mothers for Rearing their Children,* (3) a request to authorize sending picric acid which I've lacked the past three months at the clinic, (4) my claim in regard to theft of my manuscripts. Besides, for the past two months I have not received the monthly [diplomatic] report.[23]

Regnault eventually arranged to have the picric acid sent from a military hospital, but the loss of Mauchamp's academic papers generated no sympathy whatsoever from French officials.[24] Indeed, they must have scratched their heads at why anyone would have been so foolish as to entrust valuable documents to the Moroccan post without first making copies. Nevertheless, Mauchamp tenaciously continued his campaign for compensation. Among other irritations, the attacks on the foot couriers interrupted his subscription to *Le Matin*.[25] During his brief furlough in France in January 1907, Mauchamp even went so far as to meet with the director of the French overseas post, to whom he offered proposals for reforming the postal system in Morocco.[26] Based on these experiences, Mauchamp anticipated an attitude of indifference from the legation when he reported that his friend Lassallas had been shot in the thigh. The story of the attack was full of drama, and both Lassallas and Mauchamp exploited it for all it was worth.

On September 18, 1906, while traveling between Essaouira and Marrakesh, Lassallas passed the night at the *zawiya* of Bel Lahouel, about thirty-five miles from Marrakesh, in territory belonging to the Tekna tribe. Earlier that year Lassallas had had some success establishing agricultural operations in the south and the vicinity of Essaouira. He now used the visit with the *zawiya*'s head Si Mahjub bin Makki to either lease or possibly purchase land.[27] The deal was concluded, and the following morning, Lassallas went out hunting with the head of the *zawiya*. Some fifteen men, hidden in the bushes, fired upon them, but the attack was without any consequence, and Lassallas and his companions galloped back to the *zawiya*. There they came under fire again, this time by some fifteen to twenty men on horseback. Up until then Lassallas had escaped harm, but waiting for his servant to catch up, he received a severe wound in the thigh.

Soon after, the *qaid* of Tekna appeared and ordered Lassallas carried back to his house. There Lassallas was kept captive until he agreed to swear before notaries that the shots had not come from the *qaid*'s men but rather from the direction of the *zawiya*. Lassallas thus secured his release, but in his place the *qaid* imprisoned Lassallas' host, Si Mahjub.[28]

As to the motive for the attack, Jeannier, the French vice-consul in Essaouira, told his British counterpart Madden, that "personally he was of the opinion that this was not a simple act of ill will towards a Christian, but rather that the motive must be looked for in the invitation the Frenchman received to pass the night in the Zawia al-Raisuli [sic]."[29] Later Jeannier advanced a theory that Lassallas had been proceeding to Tekna with a Moroccan from the area who already was or was about to become a French protégé. As Jeannier explained, "the Tribe of Tekna will not allow one of their numbers to accept protection, and they further alleged that this Moor in particular was implicated in a murder case in Tekna."[30] The Moroccan, it was alleged, had not been heard from since the attack.

Jeannier dutifully launched an investigation, sending at once the consulate's Algerian-born chancellor, Allal Abdi, to Marrakesh to inquire.[31] Mauchamp took Abdi's arrival as an encouraging sign. "This is a veritable summons for the Makhzan. This is the first time that we have displayed an energetic attitude; it has to make us happy to have been furnished, finally, with an occasion to prove that we do not intend to let ourselves be eaten alive."[32]

Nevertheless, the investigation got off to a rocky start. At first, the authorities in Marrakesh would not allow Abdi to interview the *qaid* of Tekna and his men, who happened to be in the city at the same time. Then they presented someone whom they said to have been the *qaid*'s deputy but who turned out to be a simple Makhzani soldier. "Even this man was not allowed to give his version of the affair."

At the end of the day, Moulay Hafid weighed in on the side of the French, seeing it to his advantage to imprison the *qaid* of Tekna and the other men who were implicated in the attack. On the other hand, Abdeslam al-Warzazi, the pasha of Marrakesh, earned the enmity of the French for his obstructions. According to the British consul, Madden, who observed the affair from afar in Essaouira, al-Warzazi "obstructed the French demands for investigation in every conceivable way, treating M. Allal el Abdi [sic] . . . with scant courtesy; he had refused any inquiry, and had simply stated to M. Lassalas [sic] that he was shot at by mistake for a German, M. Nier [sic] . . . who had bought or wished to buy land belonging to the Zawia in the Tekna."[33]

The Lassallas affair led Mauchamp and his compatriots in Marrakesh to believe, not without reason, that their position in the southern city was precarious and that their very lives were threatened. A mining engineer from the École Supérieure de Paris, Louis Peffau-Garavini, took it upon himself to report on the danger when he passed through Tangier in mid-October 1906. Earlier that year

Peffau-Garavini, in the company of Vaffier-Pollet , had spent several months with the *qaid* Si Al-Madani al-Glawi, visiting him at his mountain fortress at Telouet. He would later write of his experience in the French weekly *L'Illustration*. On his return he also spent nearly two months in Marrakesh and was thus the source of several of the pictures of Mauchamp published in the newspapers after his murder.

"My countrymen are desperate," he wrote in a hastily penned letter to Regnault on stationery from Tangier's Grand Café and Ice Cream Parlour. "They consider themselves abandoned and sacrificed by those who ought to protect them, and have asked me to inform you, in particular, of what is happening there." The French colony in Marrakesh, he reported, feared that the legation in Tangier thought that they were exaggerating and that it considered the Lassallas affair to be negligible. Writing to Mauchamp later in the month, the Morocco Committee representative, René-Leclerc, reported these same sentiments. In particular he remarked that the chargé d'affaires, Saint-Aulaire, was accusing Mauchamp of exaggeration.[34]

The controversy hinged on whether Lassallas was wearing native clothing or not. Saint-Aulaire reportedly thought that Lassallas was shot owing to mistaken identity. In holding this opinion he echoed the view of the British consul in Essaouira, namely, that the attackers mistook Lassallas for Niehr, the German consul in Marrakesh. Nevertheless, both Mauchamp and Peffau-Garavini insisted that Lassallas was dressed in European clothing. While Lassallas sometime wore "Arab" costume in the city, they insisted that he never wore it on his rounds outside the city.

Mauchamp was beginning to feel edgy, but perhaps he was entitled. After all, he was the one who had dug the bullet out of Lassallas's leg. But the legation's response, or lack of one, failed to placate Mauchamp and his friends in Marrakesh. In November, Mauchamp, Lassallas, the businessman Firbach, and others penned a letter again calling for the French legation to pressure the Makhzan to provide greater security for them in Marrakesh. Undoubtedly hoping to embarrass the legation, they had the letter published in *La Dépêche Marocaine* in Tangier. Meanwhile, Lassallas's firm had also put pressure on the French government. The Companie Marocaine evidently was convinced that the situation was safe enough. In the weeks preceding Mauchamp's death, Lassallas's employers sent word authorizing him to increase his investment in sheep and grain.[35]

Ma al-Aynayn: The Saharan "Sorcerer"

To the south of Morocco in the Sahara, the Moroccan government had a longstanding policy of supporting Mauritanian rebels against the French. There Xavier Coppolani, the French administrator and the co-author of a widely circulated book on Sufi brotherhoods, was murdered in May 1905. The assassination does not seem to have been unanticipated. In the words of one British diplomat, Coppolani was "extraordinarily brutal toward the natives."[36]

Moroccan sultans periodically played host to the Mauritanians' leader, the charismatic Sufi shaykh Ma al-Aynayn.[37] Many members of the Makhzan also joined lodges of the Aynayniyya Sufi order that had opened at Marrakesh and Fez.[38] Born in 1831, Ma al-Aynayn was first received by the Moroccan sultan Abd al-Rahman in 1858, and during the course of his long career, Morocco's subsequent rulers turned to Ma al-Aynayn in an effort to repel European incursions along the coast. From the sultan Abdelaziz's perspective, Moroccan support for Ma al-Aynayn made sense. For one thing, it bolstered his legitimacy as the protector of the faithful. For another, it gave him some leverage to use against the French and their constant barrage of demands. Beyond moral support, the Makhzan also provided the rebels with smuggled arms. Often as not these weapons never reached their destination but ended up for sale in Essaouira.[39]

In June 1906 the Mauritanian shaykh and some three hundred of his men encamped near Essaouira on their way to Fez. Among his entourage were said to be ten representatives from a number of Saharan tribes bearing a proclamation of allegiance to the Moroccan sultan. "These tribes have never before acknowledged the Shereefian [*sic*] Authority," the British consul wrote.[40]

In Fez, Ma al-Aynayn was received with great ceremony by the sultan, lodged at government expense, and supplied weapons from Makhzan stores. Meanwhile, over the protests of the French government, an uncle of the sultan, Moulay Idris, was sent as the Makhzan representative to the Wadi Dra [Adrar] region, thus providing "at least the façade of Moroccan sovereignty in the extreme South."[41]

As the shaykh and his followers returned south in order to board ship, a number of incidents broke out between his followers and Europeans in Casablanca, Marrakesh, and Essaouira.[42] One of the clashes involved Mauchamp. On September 25 the doctor wrote angrily and at length to Regnault in Tangier, describing his encounter the previous evening with a group of Ma al-Aynayn's Tuareg blue men. According to Mauchamp, he came across the blue men as he was riding home after seeing patients. One of his servants was accompanying him on foot. As Mauchamp approached the men—all armed with new rifles provided by the Moroccan government—a "Sudanese" loaded a cartridge into his rifle and took aim. At this the French doctor pulled out his own revolver, pressed his mount forward as fast he could in the direction of the men, and took aim at his would-be attacker. The Tuareg tribesman backed down, taking the cartridge out of the bolt and letting Mauchamp pass. Mauchamp then ordered his would-be assailants to back off, which they did momentarily, and he resumed his way. A moment later, however, another of the tribesmen lifted his rifle to his shoulder. Again, according to Mauchamp, he showed his revolver and the men dispersed. Meanwhile, "a number of Arabs were indifferent witnesses to this incident."

In high dudgeon, Mauchamp sent his translator and Si Umar, the French consular agent, to the governor of the *madina*, Hajj Abdeslam al-Warzazi. They demanded that the pasha protect the city's Europeans from the "dangerous whims of these wild fanatics." But on their return, they reported that al-Warzazi, to the contrary, refused to take any measure "against these friends of the sultan of whom he received an order to treat with the greatest regard and 'let them do whatever they pleased.'"

Outraged, Mauchamp dispatched Si Umar again, this time demanding that the governor receive Mauchamp in person. Claiming to be ill, Hajj Abdeslam refused. Two more times the irate Mauchamp sent Si Umar with the demand that the governor provide security for the Europeans. If not, Mauchamp threatened to lodge a complaint against him with the French legation. To this, the governor replied that "I could write all I want to the legation, which will do nothing and that, moreover, between a *great saint* like Ma al-Aynayn and me there were no two ways about it" (emphasis in original).

Mauchamp says he had earlier proposed to the governor that he confine the blue men to the quarter of the city that contained their mosque. The governor promised to do so, but evidently did nothing. As a consequence, Mauchamp was now lodging a formal complaint against Hajj Abdeslam al-Warzazi, holding him responsible not only for this most recent incident, but for those that preceded it. In particular, he cited the governor's inattention to the Lassallas affair and to another incident that took place a few days later involving a German national. Meanwhile, the *qaid* of Tekna, who was culpable for the attack on Lassallas, was (at the time Mauchamp wrote) still free in the city.[43]

Further contributing to the insecurity of the Europeans, Mauchamp argued, was the incompetence of Si Umar. The French consular agent was "too timid, too old, and lacking prestige." Communications with the consulates at the coast were too slow. The French community in Marrakesh deserved to be represented by a full-fledged consul.

Mauchamp added to his litany of complaints against Hajj Abdeslam one final allegation. The governor, he claimed, had turned a blind eye to the criminal activities of his brother-in-law. According to Mauchamp, the latter was one of Marrakesh's principal counterfeiters, who illicitly minted coins in a building adjacent to Mauchamp's clinic. The building, like the one that housed the clinic, was owned by Hajj Abdeslam himself. When Mauchamp complained to the governor, the governor told him that he authorized his brother-in-law's mint and that he would not chase his brother-in-law from the city.

Ironically, Mauchamp reported that when he paid his seventeen *douros* in rent to the governor, the governor complained that one and a half *douros* were in false coins. "I refused to take them back saying that the day when the governor decides to prevent the fabrication of counterfeit money by his family, there will no longer circulate counterfeit coins. He offered the reply that he would chase me from his house if I paid him in counterfeit money again."

Mauchamp concluded his letter with a complaint that life would no longer be possible for Frenchmen in Marrakesh without the energetic intervention of the legation. The merchants Bouvier and Lassallas, he told Regnault, were already contemplating moving their activities to the coast.[44]

While Mauchamp struck a note of desperation writing to the minister in Tangier, he adopted a more jaunty tone with his father. *Ici, pas mal de choses intéressantes* (There's no lack of interesting things here), he wrote. Among the many interesting things was Lassallas's condition. Before it entered his thigh, the bullet shattered the keys in the Frenchman's pocket, so that it lodged metal fragments in his flesh. Mauchamp's friend would recover despite the seriousness of the wound.

Meanwhile Ma al-Aynayn's blue men appeared to have the run of the city. "Perhaps the newspapers will inform you that I was attacked by them; I made a rush on the group when one of them took aim at me, but the quickness of my revolver prevented him from firing on me. . . . Don't fear for me," he wrote his parents. "Besides, I never go out without my translator, armed with a repeating rifle and my stable boy, furnished with a stout truncheon."[45]

Ma al-Aynayn and his men stayed on in Marrakesh until late October before moving on to Essaouira, where they were received in state by the governor there. Eventually, in mid-November, the party boarded the *Cartagena,* a Spanish steamer especially chartered by the Moroccan government for the shaykh's homeward journey. The shaykh had never traveled by sea before, but it had been rumored that he had been forewarned of an attack on his richly loaded caravan by enemies in or about Wad Nun.

The British consul also noted that the Saharans' weapons, sold by many of them to Jewish merchants in Essaouira, "will doubtless be resold to tribesmen."[46]

The Legion of Honor

As December 1906 approached, Mauchamp prepared to leave Marrakesh for what would be his first and only leave in France. Although the chargé d'affaires, Saint-Aulaire, had written to the doctor to defend the legation against the charge of official indifference to the medical clinics, Mauchamp continued to find the legation's response to his various complaints disappointing.[47] As a result, Mauchamp and his friends took their campaign to the French press. Initially, this move resulted in a series of claims and counterclaims about the plight of Europeans in Marrakesh. Who, the articles asked, were more responsible for the growing insecurity in Morocco, the Germans or the French? The Tangier correspondent of the German *Gazette de Cologne* accused the French in Marrakesh of fabricating rumors. To this, Mauchamp's friend Louis Peffau-Garavini responded in *L'Echo de Paris* with a truculent denial:

> During my stay in Marrakesh, the German consular agent was thrown from his mule and beaten with sticks twice in the space of two weeks. Witnesses to this fact, besides me, are Doctor Mauchamp, Monsieur Bouvier and Monsieur Lanallas [sic]. I learned, on arriving in Mogador [Essaouira], that the brother of the consular agent denies the fact and that the *Gazette de Cologne* lied about it. This proves indeed that the Germans, like everyone else, have reason to complain of the Moroccan anarchy. Do they know this in Berlin and do they want to explain?[48]

Peffau-Garavini also endeavored, on Mauchamp's behalf, to expose publicly Saint-Aulaire's alleged negligence and indifference. But smearing a French diplomat was no doubt more difficult than attacking nameless Germans. *L'Echo de Paris* did not want to print what it considered a polemic against Saint-Aulaire. *Le Matin* told Peffau the same thing, "which is to say that they [the newspaper] often act on orders from the government." Unable to go public, the engineer wrote to Mauchamp that he informed Pichon, the foreign minister, that Saint-Aulaire had developed a personal animosity toward the doctor.

The controversy continued to revolve around the question of whether Lassallas was dressed like an Arab when he was shot and whether the legation took the matter seriously. The controversy pitted Mauchamp's word against Saint-Aulaire's. A few days later Peffau wrote to Mauchamp in triumph. *L'Éclair* would run his exposé.[49]

Mauchamp's father, too, saw Saint-Aulaire as an impediment to his son's well-being. Exploiting his political connections, Pierre Mauchamp wrote to Sarrien, the former council president, to complain about the diplomat in Tangier. Saint-Aulaire, he wrote, was not taking the plight of the French community in Marrakesh seriously enough. Over and over the diplomat dismissed the son as a nuisance. "[Saint-Aulaire's] opinion concerning Doctor Mauchamp is this: Doctor Mauchamp—with his dispensary, his story about the blue men, his complaint about lost documents in the mail—passes his time with hot air, boasting, and publicity [*d'esbroufe, de la réclame, du battage*]."

The elder Mauchamp accused Saint-Aulaire of passing on to Regnault the most deplorable information about the French in Marrakesh in general, and his son in particular. He reminded his reader of his son's devotion to his mission, his friendship with Moulay Hafid, and his efforts to seek punishment for those involved in the Lassallas affair. Complaining that it was simply not right that someone so dedicated to France be so unappreciated, he asked Sarrien to support his son's receiving the cross of the Legion of Honor the coming January 1.[50]

Sarrien forwarded the letter at once to Pichon, the foreign minister. The latter in turn wrote to Regnault seeking letters of support of Mauchamp's nomination. Mauchamp himself contributed to the campaign to bestow the cross on him. Writing to Doctor F.

Dubief, a former minister of the interior and the present deputy from Mâcon, he complained about the government's indifference to his efforts. The senators and deputies from Saône-et-Loire joined in the campaign for the decoration—which would be awarded only posthumously.[51]

On December 14, 1906, Mauchamp wrote his father "a few quick lines" to confirm his departure from Marrakesh the following day. He planned to set out for El-Jadida in the company of his three servants, four soldiers handpicked by Moulay Hafid, an escort of Oulad Sidi Cheikh tribesmen, and some ex-*goumiers,* former Algerian soldiers, two of whom would accompany him the entire way to Tangier, where Mauchamp would meet with Regnault. On the eve of his departure, Mauchamp wrote a self-aggrandizing account of his role in Marrakesh:

> All the French protégés are sorry at my departure because they fear that the governor, Hajj Abdeslam, will treat them badly in my absence. It is even predicted that one of them will be imprisoned as soon as I depart! I put them all under the protection of Moulay Hafid, to whom I presented them yesterday, inasmuch as our pseudo-consular agent Si Umar was afraid for himself. It seems that my landlord [the governor Hajj Abdeslam al-Warzazi] is only restrained by the terror that I inspire in him, because he hates every European and European accomplice. Two Germans even came to me yesterday to tell me their fantasies concerning the governor and to ask me to recommend the Germans to the sharif [Moulay Hafid]! That tops everything and is amusing.[52]

Chalon Interlude

Departing Marrakesh on December 15 for his vacation in France, Mauchamp stopped in Tangier to discuss with Regnault the state of affairs vis-à-vis Moulay Hafid. "Doctor Mauchamp," Regnault wrote to Paris on January 2, 1907, "believes that it would not be impossible, by means of certain kindnesses, to remove the anti-French influences which [Moulay Hafid] has exclusively followed till now and that the bestowal of a gift would make an excellent impression on his mind." Mauchamp suggested "a rug, of the carpet type with large flowers." In Paris, the Ministry of Foreign Affairs approved the purchase, charging to the legation's "special funds" 750 francs for the purchase of two rugs and 140 for a tea service to be given to one of Moulay Hafid's advisers.[53]

Back in France, Mauchamp stayed with his family in Chalon-sur-Saône until February 10. There, apart from occasional trips to Paris to lobby support for his clinic, he occupied himself with his collection of archeological artifacts, objets d'art, and oriental rugs that he was to bring with him on his return to Marrakesh.

Morocco, however, was never far from his mind. His tennis partners and fellow colonists in Marrakesh—Lassallas, Bouvier, Falcon—wrote frequent, gossipy letters. His Italian friend Berrino sent advice on what size rug would make a suitable gift for Moulay Hafid.[54] Meanwhile, to Regnault in Tangier he offered an impatient disquisition on the difference between civilian and military doctors. In particular, Mauchamp objected to an impending inspection of the clinics by the military doctor Foubert.[55] Regnault sought to allay the concerns of his touchy subordinate. He accused him of misrepresenting Foubert and offered his assurances that the inspection would not in any way infringe on Mauchamp's independence of action. He hoped that Mauchamp "like all your other colleagues" would understand the ministry's need to assert some control over its clinics.

More importantly, during Mauchamp's absence the anthropologist Edmond Doutté and Allal Abdi, the Algerian-born chancellor from Essaouira, made a reconnaissance tour of the Haouz district in southern Morocco. Besides reporting on the Rahamna tribe, they attempted to meet with Al-Madani al-Glawi in an effort to discover Moulay Hafid's real intentions.[56] According to Mauchamp's friend Bouvier they were poorly received and even chased away on the pretext that they did not carry a letter from the Makhzan—this in spite of the fact that they carried a letter of introduction from Vaffier-Pollet, who, along with Peffau-Garavini, had spent several weeks with the *qaid* the previous year.

Bouvier gloated over Doutté's failure. Just days after Doutté was sent packing back to Essaouira, Bouvier visited Al-Madani al-Glawi in the company of the Sibai brothers, sons of an important adviser to the sultan. They were admirably received. "One couldn't do better," he reported. The *qaid* Al-Madani told Bouvier he looked forward to continuing their relation in Marrakesh and gave him a pretty horse as a present. Bouvier also paid a visit to Moulay Brahim, the deputy of the *qaid* of the Chiadma, who accorded him an escort of twenty horsemen.

In Mauchamp's absence, another French explorer, a geology professor from Algiers named Brives, also arrived in town. Bouvier said he planned to check out Brives's report that Moulay Hafid was seeking French protection. More generally, Bouvier reported that the country was "perfectly calm" and that there was enough water to permit the hope of a good harvest.

And yet, despite Bouvier's optimism, not all the news from Marrakesh was positive. "Since his return [from a trip to the coast] M. Falcon is struck by the anti-French spirit that reigns in the *mellah* and that Holzmann has profited from your absence to regain lost ground, and that he would do this with surprising ease."[57] As Mauchamp would discover when he returned to Marrakesh in March, Falcon was indeed correct in his estimate of Moroccan public opinion. The climate had indeed suddenly changed for the worse.

On March 6, just days prior to Mauchamp's setting out from El-Jadida on his return to Marrakesh, a French tourist named Gironcourt was attacked in Fez. Gironcourt had stopped to photograph some women and children in the street when he was pelted with stones. Two Makhzan soldiers happened to pass by in time to rescue him.

"Amongst certain foreigners here," the British consul MacLeod wrote in reporting the event, "M. de Gironcourt is blamed and the Makhzan is held excused in the matter, because M. de Gironcourt was going about without a native attendant or soldier."

Three weeks after the attack Gironcourt still suffered from giddiness and had not yet regained control of one of his hands and one of his legs.[58] It is unlikely that Mauchamp learned of the attack on Gironcourt. Had he known, he might have comported himself differently on his return to Marrakesh.

Or then again, possibly not.

6

March 19, 1907

"Perfectly Calm"

At the start of February 1907, with his furlough in France at an end, Mauchamp left Chalon for the long journey to Marrakesh. In Tangier he joined up with the geologist Louis Gentil, who was traveling with his wife and their six-year-old daughter, Suzanne. With funding from the Geographic Society of Paris and the Morocco Committee and working under the auspices of the Ministry of Public Instruction, Gentil was returning to Marrakesh to complete his geological survey of the Atlas Mountains. He had previously accompanied the Marquis de Segonzac on an earlier scientific mission to Morocco. *La Dépêche Marocaine* heralded his return as an outstanding example of the "scientific penetration" that complemented French political action in the country.[1]

Born in Algeria in 1868, Gentil was for most of his illustrious career a member of the faculty of the Sorbonne. In the words of one historian, his numerous publications were "dull, primitive, and pretentious although comparable to those of many among his Parisian colleagues." But that did not matter. "It was in his role as an enthusiastic apologist for French imperialism that he won the hearts and minds of the metropolitan educational bureaucracy."[2] Looking back on his life in science in 1922, Gentil was unabashed in describing his aims:

> My entire career was transformed by this desire: to traverse and know Morocco, and perhaps to contribute to the best of my ability to French expansion up to the Atlantic. . . . Without waiting for the French penetration that our policies had us glimpse, I set off across

the Maghreb, resolved to work with all at my disposal toward a scientific understanding of this country and to begin there the work of peaceful conquest that France would be led to undertake.[3]

Later, when France cast aside its policy of peaceful penetration for direct military intervention, Gentil had no difficulty adapting. He consulted with the French military in the field (as a geologist he helped locate waterholes), advised the minister of war back in Paris, and published a useful descriptive geography of Morocco, *Le Maroc physique* (Physical Morocco). In 1912, soon after the establishment of the Protectorate, Lyautey appointed Gentil as his scientific adviser. Yet despite his prominence, Gentil was never admitted into the prestigious Academy of Sciences. "He solved no burning scientific issues, formulated no general propositions, and made use of no great body of existing knowledge." The academy recognized his accomplishments in any case, awarding him a prize in 1917 for his "first-rate role in the *scientific conquest of Morocco*."[4]

Gentil's "pragmatic" approach to Morocco—and to a similar extent that of Mauchamp as well—typifies a change in attitude that had emerged almost imperceptibly as the nineteenth century gave way to the twentieth. For much of the nineteenth century Morocco was seen as a "sort of China on the doorsteps of Europe" and a "true paleontological museum of Islam."[5] In the nineteenth century it was the exoticism of Morocco—and not much more—that excited public interest in France. Emphasizing the "unknown" and "picturesque" aspects of Moroccan life and culture, European writers promoted an image of Morocco as a religiously fanatical and impenetrable country.

But by the start of the twentieth century, the propaganda of the colonial lobby had paid off. The acquisition of Morocco, whether by peaceful means or otherwise, and its expropriation for utilitarian purposes had taken on an aspect of inevitability. French science went to work in the interest of this North African version of Manifest Destiny. Exploration became systematic, and the multitalented amateur explorer such as Charles de Foucauld or the Marquis de Segonzac was soon replaced by the academic specialist.

The new presumption that exploration required professional scientific expertise did not necessarily mean that its practitioners were dispassionate, disinterested or, least of all, collegial toward one another. Like everything else associated with Morocco, scientific exploration became a political football. In addition to the Morocco

Committee, which financed the explorations of Segonzac and Gentil, a rival institution emerged in Paris as a sponsor of scientific inquiry into all things Moroccan. This was the Mission Scientifique au Maroc (Scientific Mission in Morocco), the brainchild of Alfred le Chatelier, a former Native Affairs officer in Algeria and a politically ambitious explorer. In 1902 Le Chatelier was appointed to the newly created and government-funded "Chair of Muslim Sociology and Sociography" at the Collège de France. Both the creation of the chair, with its modern-sounding name, and Le Chatelier's appointment to it were controversial. Le Chatelier had none of the requisite university degrees. But what Le Chatelier lacked in academic credentials was amply compensated by his having powerful friends such as the colonialist Eugène Étienne and Paul Révoil, the latter a one-time French minister in Tangier and later governor general of Algeria. While Le Chatelier's principal ambition of creating an institute devoted to Moroccan studies foundered, he was able to create the Scientific Mission. Its somewhat vaguely conceived aim was to encourage scholars to produce ethnographic studies—later published as the many-volume series *Archives marocaines*—that would aid the French legation in its work in Morocco.[6]

Several factors led the Quai d'Orsay to support the creation of a new, government-sponsored Scientific Mission. First, the centralization of research under one umbrella has always had a certain bureaucratic appeal. Second, the legation in Tangier, which was concerned about the safety of French nationals in Morocco, took a dim view of "unauthorized" explorers setting off into areas in which the Makhzan had limited control. Third and perhaps most important, the diplomats were concerned that many of the researchers in Morocco were in fact *too* politically zealous. Not surprisingly, these were most often French scholars and scientists from neighboring Algeria such as Edmond Doutté and Louis Gentil. Their impatient demands for direct military action (the so-called tribal policy that called for encroaching into Morocco from the Algerian border) contradicted—or at the least threatened to compromise—the Quai d'Orsay's gradualist policy of working through the Makhzan to achieve its aim of peaceful penetration. At least initially the French legation in Tangier used its support for the Scientific Mission as justification for denying permits and diplomatic support to explorers from Algeria, and this further fueled resentment between academic factions.[7]

The conflict between the Scientific Mission and its opponents, known collectively as the School of Algiers, was more than a simple battle over turf. By identifying themselves with the new discipline of sociology, Le Chatelier and his colleagues represented themselves as being on the cutting edge of scholarship. The Algerian school, steeped in the traditions of French ethnography, was in contrast made to look provincial and anachronistic.[8] And if institutional rivalries and differences in political strategy and intellectual approach were not enough to cause tension between the two groups, there were inevitably personal resentments at work. It did not help matters that in 1895 Le Chatelier killed in a duel Harry Alis (a.k.a. Hippolyte Percher), a journalist and the head of the Comité d'Afrique Française (French Africa Committee), the parent organization of the Morocco Committee. Le Chatelier and Alis had been friends, but when Le Chatelier made the allegation that Alis had improperly benefited from railway concessions in the Congo, the two men were obliged by convention to stage a duel. Neither was supposed to suffer serious harm. The newspapers reported that Alis seemed calm the morning of the combat as he drank his customary chocolate with his wife. But in the heat of the moment Le Chatelier seems to have gotten carried away, and he ran Alis through with his sword.[9]

It should come as no surprise that, united in their mistrust of the legation in Tangier and suspicious of the diplomats in Paris, Mauchamp and Gentil—both pugnacious polymaths and political dabblers—should hit it off. And so they made their plans to travel together. As they judged the road from Essaouira to Marrakesh to be unsafe, they set sail instead for El-Jadida. There they spent a fortnight, and Mauchamp had an opportunity to visit Dr. Guichard, his medical counterpart sent by the ministry of foreign affairs. When Guichard next encountered Mauchamp again a few weeks later, it would be to examine his corpse.

From El-Jadida Mauchamp wrote his old schoolmaster Henri Guillemin in Chalon. Mauchamp thanked his acquaintance for the warm toast he made on his behalf at a banquet held by the Natural Sciences Society of Saône-et-Loire, and he promised that he would send an article to the society's *Bulletin* once he was settled in again in Marrakesh. This was not to be. Barely a year later, it was Guillemin who would publish a biography of Mauchamp in the very same *Bulletin*.[10]

On March 6, on the eve of his departure from El-Jadida, Mauchamp wrote his father to assure him about the security precautions they were taking. He described in detail the stops they would make on the six-day overland journey. Rather than go by way of Safi, Mauchamp and Gentil arranged to take a northerly route in small stages. They would travel in the company of armed soldiers; the *qaid*s through whose territory they would travel had guaranteed their safety. The detour would allow Mauchamp to meet at last the *qaid* Si Aissa bin Umar al-Abdi, to whom he had earlier sent the falcons, and it would permit Gentil to make scientific observations along the Oum er-Rebia river. All along the way, they would be met by Moroccan protégés of Mauchamp's European friends.[11] The final night they would spend with one of Mauchamp's own protégés. The journey itself, while not long, required lengthy negotiations and preparations. Did it dawn on Mauchamp that their itinerary turned the notion of protection on its head? The so-called European protectors were clearly at the mercy of their Moroccan clients.

Mauchamp insisted to his father that he had put the lengthy stay over in El-Jadida to profitable use. Asserting that he was well-received by everyone—French, English, German, and Italian—Mauchamp viewed the maintenance of good political relations with other Europeans as necessary if he was to establish a hospital in Marrakesh. "I have presented myself as firm and energetic; they have seen that I can be without pity. I now want to force myself to earn the sympathy of everyone who could lend themselves to it and who will be encouraged in it by their friends and their bosses in the firms in El-Jadida; most of all it's the German side I especially want to work."[12]

Six days later Mauchamp arrived in Marrakesh, and two days after that, on the 14th, he penned a long letter to his father. Full of optimism and expectation, this final letter home arrived in Chalon-sur-Saône on March 27, more than week after Mauchamp's death. "Thanks to the introductions that I told you about," he wrote, "we were passed from brigand to brigand, attentively protected by them, fed and sheltered royally, and in full security." The trip was, in his words, "delicious." Their route took them through a mountainous region that was filled with flowers and more picturesque than Mauchamp had anticipated. "The rains of the preceding weeks produced a treasure of vegetation that hasn't been seen here for years; where it's been planted, they expect superb harvests."

Mauchamp reported that he and Gentil had succeeded in meeting up with other Frenchmen and Europeans at various stages along the way. The mining engineer Quinson and his associate Martel joined up with them on the road at Smira where they regained the main

route from El-Jadida. When they entered Menabha territory, Lassallas and Berrino were there to meet them. And two hours outside
Marrakesh, more friends, both Moroccan and European, joined
them, the crowd growing as they crossed the Tensift bridge and
approached the city gates. Describing the scene, the doctor allowed
himself a rare foray into sentiment:

> I never saw anything more beautiful than the immense oasis of Mar-
> rakesh, flooded in this season in greenery and flowers, sitting at the
> foot of the Atlas, glistening with snow. It was fairylike at the outlet
> of the Djibelet; I confess that all this light, this color, this warmth has
> rendered very agreeable this return *home* [here Mauchamp used the
> English word], where everything was in order, my staff waiting there
> for me, having prepared everything as I ordered. I am still installing
> myself and not till Monday will I open the clinic. All our friends gave
> us a very warm reception; everyone is well.

Mauchamp discussed his plans to purchase land for his hospital
and concluded his letter without any presentiment of the future.
"The region of Marrakesh is perfectly calm," he wrote, "and the
people very tranquil."

The day before he died, Mauchamp penned his final letter to a
friend. It included a request for a handful of books. Among the titles
were Raynaud's *Medicine in Morocco*, Brault's *Pathology and Hygiene
among the Muslim Natives of Algeria*, Dercle's *On the Practice of Medicine
among the Arabs: A French-Arabic Vocabulary*, a brochure on Fez by
his friend René-Leclerc, and Gustave Wolfrom's *Morocco, What One
Should Know About It*, a new title just published by the Morocco Committee in the wake of the Algeciras conference.[13]

The Wireless Telegraph

On an ordinary day, Mauchamp would have arrived early at his
clinic to begin work, but the morning of March 19, the day on which
the French doctor died, was not ordinary. On that day Mauchamp
arrived late, detained by a visit from Gentil, who left him a little
before ten.[14] Nonetheless, one can imagine that he was in a good
mood. He had been in Marrakesh only a week after his long vacation, and he had just put into effect that morning what he thought
of as *une inoffensive plaisanterie*, "an innocent practical joke." This was
the phrase Gentil later used to describe it in the report he filed with
the foreign ministry.[15] But of course this was not how the Moroccans took it, nor was it the way the newspapers or French officials

reported it. The published version of Gentil's report and subsequent newspaper reports in fact say nothing about a joke, an important detail that lay buried in the archives for nearly eighty years.[16] After all, no Frenchman should die on account of a joke, least of all a dignified and normally serious physician in the employ of the ministry of foreign affairs.

The crux of the joke consisted of nothing more than a pole about twenty feet long with some string dangling from it.[17] Mauchamp planted the pole on the roof of his house to give the impression of a wireless telegraph antenna. Why?

Mauchamp had returned to Morocco at precisely the moment when a kind of hysteria over wireless telegraphy was sweeping the country. In his report on Mauchamp's murder, filed a month after the event, Gentil accused Niehr, the German consul of Marrakesh, of first raising the alarm against Mauchamp. Gentil insisted that Niehr had persuaded the governor, Hajj Abdeslam, that the French doctor had surreptitiously imported telegraph equipment. What especially aroused the suspicions, he alleged, was a narrow wooden box about four meters long brought by Mauchamp from France. The box held a rug intended as a gift for Moulay Hafid, but people in Marrakesh suspected that the box in fact contained telegraph equipment.

In making his accusation Gentil had only circumstantial evidence at his disposal. "Niehr's trembling after the murder of Mauchamp," he wrote, "confirmed what I already knew." According to Gentil, Mauchamp was "so convinced" that accusations were being made against him by Niehr "that he wanted to see how far the Germans would push their protestations."

To this end, Mauchamp had his translator purchase the poles, which he then lashed together to create the poor simulacra of a wireless telegraph antenna. Gentil does not say whether he was actually present when Mauchamp put the pole on the roof, nor does he say anything about the role of Quinson, the French engineer who was staying with Mauchamp. However, in his version of the event, the British vice-consul, Alan Lennox, suggests that one of the recently arrived Frenchmen helped install the pole.

The joke backfired on Mauchamp in more ways than one. First, no one in Marrakesh had any idea what a telegraph antenna should look like. Moroccan officials thought that he had placed a flag of some sort on his roof. Lennox also subscribed to this interpretation. As for French accounts of the incident, they tried to dignify the simple reed pole by describing it as scientific equipment used in connection with Gentil's investigations.

In the end, the dispute over the nature of the object has served to obscure the actual picture of Mauchamp's role in Marrakesh. Unwilling to credit official French denials, some historians have come to the erroneous conclusion that the French doctor had actually conveyed wireless apparatus to Marrakesh.[18] For others, French denials only confirmed their conviction that Mauchamp's primary task was indeed espionage, not medicine.[19] And at least one historian, speculating that Mauchamp and Gentil had attempted to rig a means of communication between the *madina* and the *mellah,* sees in Gentil's version of events an effort by the scientist to deflect responsibility for his own role in the affair.[20]

The seeds of the wireless telegraph hysteria—and Mauchamp's eventual demise—were first planted in the autumn of 1906. In an effort to distance himself from the French after signing the Act of Algeciras, the Moroccan sultan Abdelaziz hosted a German military mission to Fez led by two cavalry officers, Wolff and von Tschudi. The presence of Major von Tschudi, whose previous military experience included command of a wireless telegraph company, naturally led to speculation that he was sent to Fez "with a view to the Sultan being enabled later on to establish wireless telegraph stations in this country without having to put the work out to public order."[21] Nothing came of it.

In late February 1907, however, reports circulated that a French businessman named Victor Bopp and his son Henri were importing telegraph apparatus and buying parcels of land as sites for transmitters. The surreptitious and unauthorized action by a French citizen (albeit reportedly of Romanian origin) clearly violated the provisions of the recently concluded Algeciras treaty. The English minister in Tangier linked Bopp's efforts to create a telegraph network to an earlier, unsuccessful 1903 attempt by the British to establish a wireless telegraph at Cape Spartel near Tangier. This was where Lloyd's already operated a signal station.[22] Efforts at that time fell through owing to German objections, and Morocco adopted the position that the Powers would have to concur before any action was taken. In the words of the British minister, "It is clear that a private wireless telegraphic system in the possession of one Power to the exclusion of others, existing along the coast would be of immense value to that Power, and His Majesty's Government seems always to have implied that the permission of the Sovereign Power would have to be obtained."[23]

The Casablanca correspondent of the English paper *Al-Moghreb al-Aksa* echoed the diplomat's point of view. "It is rather astonishing to find now that the project which was forbidden to respectable men of the different nationalities in this country is now being carried out apparently by surprise, and by one nationality alone!"[24]

Nevertheless, reports of unauthorized activities in the coastal towns of El-Jadida, Casablanca, Safi, and Essaouira soon filtered into the Makhzan. In Tangier, Muhammad al-Turris, the sultan's representative to the foreign legations, garnered support for the Moroccan position from Dr. Rosen, the German ambassador. Rosen concurred that the independent French initiative violated Article 105 of the Act of Algeciras. That article stipulated that the telegraph was a public service and should be subject to competition by public tender. Moreover, the Makhzan could not offer any concession without the approval of the diplomatic representatives of the Powers in Tangier. Rosen also furnished al-Turris with a copy of an international agreement on wireless telegraphy that had been recently concluded in Berlin.[25]

Meanwhile, Makhzan officials in both Fez and Tangier dispatched a flurry of correspondence, first to customs officials and functionaries along the coast and then to the pasha of Marrakesh.[26] In one letter, sultan Abdelaziz ordered customs agents in Tetuan to post spies and lookouts along the coastline. They were to prevent the importation of a radio antenna or mechanical equipment of any type.[27] The sultan cautioned care. His agents were to confiscate the material only in a way that did not give rise to incident or furnish the European merchants with a pretext to claim an indemnity. Moreover, they were at once to inform the local governor, whose responsibility it was to notify the appropriate consul.

In Tangier, responding to the sultan's command, customs officials diligently reported that they had posted surveillance in the Sawani garden district, where they suspected the French of attempting to erect a building.[28] While the agents in the field turned up nothing, zealous customs officials in Tangier confiscated the microscope of one Mademoiselle Fol, a young zoology student from the Sorbonne.[29]

Likewise, further to the south, the governor of Essaouira, Abd al-Rahman Bargash, informed al-Turris in Tangier and the sultan Abdelaziz in Fez that a Monsieur Boule, the local agent of the French steamship company, had purchased from a Jew there a small garden plot outside the Doukkala gate.[30] The governor had posted a guard, but that had not deterred Boule from starting construction of a suspicious building with the help of the local Spanish teacher.

In Marrakesh, three days before Mauchamp's murder, Hajj Abdeslam al-Warzazi assembled the headmen of the city's various quarters and warned them to be on the lookout for suspicious activity among the Europeans. In particular, they were to keep an eye out for exterior construction of any kind. As it turns out, Gentil's suspicions of a German provocation against Mauchamp may not have been warranted. Al-Warzazi already had his orders from the Makhzan to be on the alert. Ironically, it seems that Gentil—and not Mauchamp—was the object of the Makhzan's suspicions. In a letter dated February 14, 1907, the sultan alerted al-Warzazi that Gentil was arriving in Marrakesh with plans to install a wireless telegraph that would communicate with another telegraph post in El-Jadida. The governor was to monitor the situation and take all possible measures not to provoke a disorder of any kind.[31]

Initially, the French-language *La Dépêche Marocaine* dismissed the wireless telegraph story as mere gossip. "Could it be true?" the newspaper asked its readers. "Could Morocco, the least civilized country in the world, know of this perfection so new that old Europe has barely yet put it in practice?"[32]

But the following week, the newspaper conceded that a French company was buying land in all the port cities as sites for antennae. The paper anticipated that installation would be completed within three months. In justification of the French effort, the paper noted that there was no single telegraph or post office monopoly in Morocco and that each of the Powers maintained its own network of communication.

When the rumors first broke in late February, the French minister in Tangier was coy. Questioned by his German and British counterparts, Regnault initially claimed that the buildings were stations for pumping water. The British minister reported him as having said that Bopp "had recently applied to him for introductions in connection with certain agricultural and industrial enterprises in this country, and had mentioned some pumping apparatus which he had intended to install. Until quite recently he had heard nothing more about the man until the stir came about the wireless telegraphy installation."

Nonetheless, once he admitted to having discovered Bopp's true intentions, Regnault defended them. The telegraph, the French minister argued, was a legitimate private enterprise that did not infringe upon any article of the Algeciras agreement. "Every one was at liberty to establish similar stations," Regnault maintained.[33]

The English-language paper *Al-Moghreb al-Aksa* followed the emerging story of the telegraph rumors closely. A suspicious building was under construction on the beach northwest of Casablanca. In Safi a scuffle broke out at the customs house when materials allegedly destined for the construction of a telegraph post were unloaded from the French steamer *Arménie*. The paper's correspondent in Essaouira further anticipated "trouble" at the hands of the district *qaid,* the reputedly volatile Hamad Anflus, against whom the paper enjoyed railing frequently. "He is quite capable of waiting until building operations are well under way and then—some fine evening—coming down and raiding the whole show."[34]

On March 23, in the same edition that carried the initial report of Mauchamp's murder in Marrakesh, *Al-Moghreb al-Aksa* warned about potential disturbances in Casablanca. "A certain unrest is observed among the country people in this neighbourhood regarding the installation of wireless telegraphy outside of town." The paper then censured the French for jeopardizing the entire European community: "If a serious disturbance takes place none but the French will have to be blamed, as before the Moors thought, or attempted to say anything against the establishment of the wireless apparatuses, it were the French who openly expressed the fear that the installation might be attacked and pulled down by the natives. And the fear is rapidly spreading, for no one can say where the threatening disturbance, once started, may end."

Arsa Moulay Musa

On the morning of March 19, 1907, the aged and ailing Hajj Abdeslam al-Warzazi lay immobile in bed as an endless stream of visitors came to his house near the famed Kutubiyya minaret.[35] With each visitor the news only worsened. The parade began with Larbi bin Sahil, the headman of Arsa Moulay Musa, where Mauchamp had his home and clinic. The quarter, with its twisting, narrow streets, lay on the other side of the vast space that was the Jma el-Fna, Marrakesh's large open square. Larbi bin Sahil had already had a dispute earlier in the week with Mauchamp. The French doctor had installed a door to his clinic that opened in front of one of Ibn Sahil's property.[36] And now the doctor and his European friends were making trouble again. "They have raised a flag," he reported to the governor.[37]

In making his report, Ibn Sahil was only doing what the governor had asked him to do—keep an eye on foreigners. The recent letters the governor had received from the Makhzan had made it clear: Frenchmen were attempting to erect wireless telegraph posts all over the country without the permission of the Moroccan government.

But a flag? This was not the first time Hajj Abdeslam had heard rumors that the doctor had raised a flag in the courtyard of his house. The house, incidentally, belonged to the governor. There was nothing to it. If in fact the doctor had put up a flag, he would simply have the doctor take it down.

The governor sent word to Si Umar bin Majjad for him to talk to Mauchamp. But Si Umar, the agent for the French consul in Essaouira, could not be found. He was out in the country and would not return till later in the day. Hajj Abdeslam then had his son summon Muhammad Sghir, the business agent who had rented the governor's house to Mauchamp in the first place.[38] The governor's friend and a British protégé, Muhammad Sghir had frequent dealings with the Europeans. Every month he collected Mauchamp's rent and gave the doctor Hajj Abdeslam al-Warzazi's receipt in exchange.

This morning the governor's son, the *qaid* Si Muhammad, reproached his father's friend for having installed a Frenchman in the house in Arsa Moulay Musa. He recounted the news of the pole on the roof and the agitated state of the neighborhood. In no uncertain terms the governor's son made it clear that the responsibility for the pole's removal lay squarely on Muhammad Sghir's shoulders. Muhammad Sghir set out immediately.

When Muhammad Sghir arrived at the door, asking for Mauchamp and his interpreter, the doctor and his helpers were busy making preparations for the following day's public consultations. Mauchamp had been the last to arrive that morning, delayed by his little prank of putting a pole on the roof. Moreover, his friend Gentil had stopped by at the house and kept him there past ten o'clock. Mauchamp's interpreter, Muhammad Hassani Zailachi from Asilah in the north, was the first to arrive.[39] While waiting for his boss, he occupied himself with the usual tasks of cleaning instruments and preparing medicines. He was joined by Jacob, the Jewish pharmacy

aide and interpreter, and the servant Ali bin Ibrahim, a man in his
forties, who busied himself boiling water. By the time Mauchamp
arrived at the clinic, which was only a few hundred meters from his
home, the daily chores seemed in fact well in hand. There was only
some sublimate left for him to prepare. Mauchamp was seated in the
pharmacy section of the clinic attending to this task when Muhammad Sghir arrived at the door, asking to see him.

Ali bin Ibrahim let the visitor in, although later he recalled how
in the course of his visit Muhammad Sghir had stepped outside into
the street for a few minutes. "Don't lock the door," Ali heard him
say. Ali later reported that he thought this detail suspicious.[40]

Muhammad Sghir stayed in the clinic only long enough to explain his mission. "The governor asks you to take down whatever is
on your roof because there are some Arabs who are unhappy."

Mauchamp said he had no problem with the request. The pole
was "nothing." "It did not matter." He set out (unarmed, as several
later accounts noted) with Muhammad Sghir and the interpreter.
Meanwhile, Jacob closed up the pharmacy and took off. Ali alone
remained another quarter of an hour to clean the clinic and to feed
the doctor's horses in the courtyard.

The clinic was only two hundred yards from Mauchamp's house,
but the three men—Mauchamp, Muhammad Sghir, and the interpreter, Muhammad Hassani—had not walked far when they found
their passage blocked. The interpreter recognized the man at the
head of the group standing in their way.

"*Muqaddim,*" he said to Larbi bin Sahil, "Headman, what's the
meaning of this? You have come for the pole. We are going to take
it down."

Armed with a saber, Ibn Sahil seemed furious. "Yes," he answered, "it's you that we're going to begin by killing first." At that
instant Muhammad Hassani felt himself being hit by rifle butts. A
blow on the side of his head knocked off his turban. Reaching down
to pick it up, he heard the doctor say, "Look, be calm, we're going
to take down the pole."

Mauchamp's interpreter took flight. At first, a woman let Muhammad Hassani into her house and hid him behind some sacks.
"I'm going to protect you because you're a Muslim," she said, but a
moment later, hearing the ear-piercing ululating of the women in
the crowd, she changed her mind. "Get out of my house. They just
killed a Christian and I don't want you killed in my house."

Finding refuge in another house nearby, Muhammad Hassani

AU MAROC

Assassinat du Docteur MAUCHAMP, à Marakech

Figure 6. A contemporary artist's rendition of Mauchamp's murder.
Illustration courtesy of C. R. Pennell.

hid for the next four hours. He came out only when a neighbor
announced the arrival of Moulay Hafid's soldiers, who would take
him to safety at the Dar Makhzan, the viceroy's palace. As for Mauchamp, who was struck by a club and a dagger, he too tried to flee
as the crowd pressed in on him. He succeeded only as far as the narrow alley that lay opposite his house. There, at the end of the alley,

the house was empty except for the maid, a young Jewish woman. Had she opened the door, she might have hid the French doctor, but Mauchamp did not have enough time to knock.

Years later, Brahim bin Muhammad Touggani, a moneychanger in the Arsa Moulay Musa quarter, recalled the events of that morning.[41] The two headmen of the district, he recalled, went through their neighborhood telling shopkeepers to close their stores and to arm themselves. They were under orders from the Makhzan, they said, to attack the "Rumi." Taking his rifle, Brahim joined the growing crowd in the street outside Mauchamp's house.

Outside the doctor's house an official named Si Driss Khunishish, the majordomo of the viceroy's palace, pleaded with the crowd not to attack the doctor or his house, but to no avail. When the headmen of the quarter gave the order, people were quick to respond. Brahim Touggani, the moneychanger, thought it was a black man who struck the first blow with a dagger, but others too claimed that honor. The moneychanger recognized a man named Muhammad Gebit, a grocer from the neighborhood, who was holding a heavy club in his hand. He turned to Brahim and asked for confirmation, "Did not I hit him first?" Brahim also remembered a deaf-mute gesticulating with joy at his role in spilling the blood of a Christian. And in the crowd, looking on until the completion of the crime and then disappearing, Brahim thought he saw the governor's son Abd al-Majid.

As for Ali bin Ibrahim, Mauchamp's servant in the dispensary, he just missed being a witness to the actual murder. After he had fed and watered the doctor's animals, he took off across an empty lot in the direction of the doctor's house. From there he could see a crowd forming, and he heard the loud chant, "God's blessing upon you, O Messenger of God."

Ali crossed paths with the fleeing Muhammad Sghir. "What's going on? Where are the doctor and the interpreter?" the servant asked. The governor's agent was pale and trembling. Someone had slashed his robe with a dagger, just missing his flesh.

"I haven't seen them, I don't know," Muhammad Sghir replied. "Just let them kill them." Sghir and the soldier who accompanied him took off in the direction of the governor's house near the Kutubiyya mosque. Arriving at the governor's house, Muhammad Sghir informed them of what he had seen. Later he recalled that the old man let out cries of despair, while the governor's son, Muhammad, who had berated him earlier for renting the house to the French doctor, received the news with indifference.

Ali bin Ibrahim recalled that by the time he arrived at the doctor's house, the crowd was hurling stones and crying, "The Christian is dead." Some unarmed soldiers tried to prevent the crowd from breaking down the door of Mauchamp's house, but they were pelted with stones. Ali ran to the Dar Makhzan. Later, when asked why he did not go to the house of the governor, Hajj Abdeslam, instead, Ali replied that he knew the doctor was on unfriendly terms with the governor.

At the door of the Dar Makhzan Ali told one of the viceroy's servants what he had just seen. Ali was admitted into the palace, where he recalled Moulay Hafid coming halfway across the courtyard to meet him. Ali leaned forward to kiss the noble sharif's shoulder, but Moulay Hafid pushed the servant back with a quick gesture. "And the doctor," he asked, "is he dead?"

The servant recounted what he knew—that Muhammad Sghir had come for the doctor, that the doctor was then assaulted by the crowd in front of his house, and that the doctor had received blows to the head.

"And you know for sure that he is dead?" Moulay Hafid asked again, as if uncertain of what he had just heard.

Moulay Hafid ordered his black soldiers to see if Mauchamp was still alive and to prevent anyone from entering the house. More than fifty of them, unarmed, set out, but the first to arrive on the scene soon returned, saying that the crowd was too large and that they would need weapons.

At the same time that Mauchamp was being assaulted in Arsa Moulay Musa, one of the governor's soldiers summoned Alan Lennox, the British vice-consul. The Englishman and his family were staying in a large house adjacent to the Jma el-Fna.[42] The house belonged to Maclean, the sultan's British military adviser, who had graciously lent it to Lennox during his absence from Marrakesh.

The soldier was clearly excited. As they approached the governor's house, he explained that the French doctor had placed a white flag on his roof. Despite the day being cloudy and still, Lennox too thought he could make out a white flag in the distance and people standing on rooftops. Although all members of the French community with whom Lennox later spoke adamantly denied that Mauchamp had hoisted a flag of any kind, Lennox would stick to his assertion that there was at least a white cloth of some kind hanging from the pole.

At the governor's house Hajj Abdeslam and his two sons told him about the excitement over the flag. They discussed how best to handle the affair. Someone recalled a similar episode in Fez. In 1892 the British minister there had hoisted a British flag over the consulate. The Makhzan then staged a demonstration that accomplished its removal without any serious consequence.

Lennox insisted that they find Mauchamp's body and guard the house. Si Muhammad, the governor's oldest son, set out at the head of twenty-five to thirty unarmed soldiers to rescue the doctor but soon returned after being pummeled with stones.

Now it was the turn of the younger son, Si Abd al-Majid. Gathering all the armed troops he could muster, Si Abd al-Majid set out to find Mauchamp's body. Meanwhile, Lennox urged them to remove the flag that had provoked the incident in the first place, but the soldiers refused, saying they were afraid to enter the Frenchman's house. The discussion turned to which Frenchman they should contact. Just then Umar bin Majjad, the local French consular agent whom they had failed to locate earlier, arrived, but he too refused to enter Mauchamp's house, fearful of the crowd that was gathered outside, and claiming that only the government had the authority to enter.

Throughout the day, the doctor's maid, Aisha, witnessed the events that took place outside Mauchamp's house.[43] She was occupied in the kitchen that morning when the French doctor left for his clinic. The other servant, a boy whom they called Little Muhammad, took off a bit later, leaving the maid alone in the house. Scarcely was the boy gone than Aisha heard cries from the street. Curious, she tried to open the door, but she quickly closed it when she saw rifle butts thrust in her direction. She took refuge on the roof, but the crowd spotted her and started to throw stones, breaking the windows in the process. From across the roof, a neighbor tried to calm her. "This is nothing," he called. "There's nothing bad." The maid hid on the roof, listening to the shouts insulting the Christians.

From her perch Aisha noted the arrival in succession of the governor's son Si Abd al-Majid and his soldiers. The governor's son argued with the crowd. "The Christian is not there. Don't attack his house. Go search elsewhere." In vain, he tried to explain that the house belonged to the governor, his father.

The crowd did, in fact, begin to break up, and there was a moment of calm. But then Aisha heard the entire quarter rejoice as the women began to ululate. "The Christian is dead," went up the cry. "The Rumi is dead." The crowd again took to throwing stones. Si Abd al-Majid made an effort to prevent people from entering the house, but they entered anyway. At this, Aisha let herself down to the roof of the neighboring house. It was deserted. Out of fear that their house, too, would be looted, the neighbors had quickly gathered their belongings and their mattresses and fled. The looting, Aisha recalled, took place around the afternoon prayers. Aisha remained alone in the neighbors' empty house until nightfall, when they returned. There had been talk of murdering the doctor for the past three days, they told her, and they reproached her for not stealing the Frenchman's money when she had the chance. This assertion of premeditation raised the obvious and perplexing question as to who lay behind the assault.

By 1:30 the issue of the flag became moot. The news arrived that the mob had broken into the house and already had torn the pole down on its own. At this point, Alan Lennox, the British vice-consul, urged the governor to occupy the house at any cost. With great reluctance Si Abd al-Majid, this time with soldiers armed with European rifles, went to the house. There he was met by mounted troops sent by Moulay Hafid and commanded by the *qaid* Driss bin Minu. The house and the street were cleared, but not before shots were fired. Years later Ibn Minu, who himself eventually became governor of Marrakesh for a short time, would recall that he specifically gave orders not to fire on the crowd directly. Nevertheless, he acknowledged reports that many were injured in the press of the throng as it dispersed.[44]

Ali bin Ibrahim, Mauchamp's servant, left the viceroy's palace at the same time the armed troops set out with Driss bin Minu. Passing by the gate of the *mellah,* someone who recognized him urged him to take cover. "The people gathered in front of the doctor's house are looking for his friends to kill."

Ali then changed paths and headed home, taking a route that led past the clinic. There he saw the governor's son Si Abd al-Majid on horseback, his brother Si Muhammad, and a group of the governor's soldiers. Some soldiers carried Mauchamp by the arms and legs. Si Muhammad had removed some of his own clothes to throw over the doctor's naked body.[45] All the while the crowd pelted them with stones and cried insults regarding the governor. "Cursed be the father of Hajj Abdeslam the Christian."

In addition to stabbing Mauchamp repeatedly, even after he was dead, the crowd stripped the corpse of its clothes—it was the women who did this, according to some reports—and tied a length of rope around the ankles. While some of the attackers dragged the dead man to the nearby empty lot, others went off in search of petrol with which to set the body ablaze. It was at this moment that Si Abd al-Majid and his men arrived, dispersed the crowd, and carried Mauchamp's corpse to his clinic.[46] Remarkably, the clinic had escaped the notice of the looters bent on plunder.

Behind the Barricades

Paul Bouvier, a French merchant of longstanding in Marrakesh, could see from the window of his office the street that led to Mauchamp's house some three hundred yards away.[47] At 10:35 he and Firbach, another French businessman, who had only just arrived at Bouvier's house minutes before, heard a clamor in the street. Climbing to the roof for a better look, Bouvier saw armed men whom he could not identify. He immediately descended and readied his own weapons.

Thinking that the demonstration might well be directed against the doctor, Bouvier then sent Ibrahim, a black youth in his service, to see if it were possible for them to go check on Mauchamp. He remembered thinking that Mauchamp would be with Muhammad Hassani, his interpreter, and Quinson, the young French civil engineer of mines then visiting Marrakesh.

Suddenly they heard an immense cry. "May God bless you, O Messenger of God." Just then Ibrahim returned with the terrible news. The doctor had just been killed in front of his house, and now the crowd was intent on killing all the Europeans in Marrakesh. In anticipation of an onslaught Bouvier and Firbach barricaded the door. They would only dare to open it two hours later to admit Si Abdallah, one of Bouvier's Moroccan employees. Passing before the doctor's house, Si Abdallah had been recognized and thrown from his mule by the menacing crowd.

Then at two o'clock a local official, the *qaid* Jilani, came to Bouvier's house to warn him of further danger. Seeing the crowd now growing outside the Frenchman's door, Jilani summoned Bouvier's neighbors, and together they convinced the crowd to disperse. Fifteen minutes later they heard again an enormous cry from the street. For a second time, Bouvier sent Ibrahim to reconnoiter. Ibrahim returned to report he saw no sign of the engineer nor the doctor and his interpreter. The crowd, which earlier had seemed to calm down, had just now broken down the door of Mauchamp's house.

Finally, at around 3:00 PM, the *qaid* Driss bin Minu, Moulay Hafid's right-hand man, arrived with fifty of the viceroy's black troops. With them was the doctor's interpreter, Muhammad Hassani. And at the same moment Si Abd al-Majid also arrived at the head of soldiers belonging to his father. The besieged Frenchmen were led to safety at the Dar Makhzan, while the governor's soldiers remained to stand guard over the house. For Bouvier and Firbach their ordeal was over.

In the Mellah

News of the disturbances in Arsa Moulay Musa reached the Europeans living in the *mellah,* the Jewish quarter, soon after the events occurred. At eleven o'clock that morning Louis Gentil was standing on the roof of Nissim Falcon's house. Unable to rent a house of his own upon his arrival in Marrakesh (an inconvenience he attributed to the Makhzan-incited hostility toward the French), Gentil and his family were staying with the schoolmaster at the Alliance Israélite school in the *mellah.*

With Quinson's help, Gentil busied himself with his work. On this particular morning he was attempting to determine the hour by observations of the sun. He heard a commotion in the city below, and it was his first thought that his own scientific work, "however inoffensive," had been the cause of the agitation. The *qaid* of the *mellah* gate came to inquire whether Gentil had hoisted a flag. A Muslim neighbor, reputed to be the son of a great sharif, climbed to the roof of a neighboring house to see for himself what was going on. Gentil allowed him to examine his instruments—his theodolite and the chronometers—and the man departed reassured.[48]

But the activity in the street below did not calm down, and Falcon sent a guard from the school to find out what was happening. The news was disquieting. At first they heard that Mauchamp had been wounded by his own revolver. A later report said he was attacked at his house. Fearing for their friend, Quinson and Gentil attempted to reach Mauchamp, but the *mellah* gates were locked and guarded. A little later, Berrino, the Italian merchant, arrived. He too had attempted to leave the *mellah,* but found his departure blocked.

Then Lassallas, the Frenchman who had been attacked six months earlier on the road from Tekna, came by. He too was upset. It was decided that he, dressed in Moroccan clothing, as was his habit, stood a better chance than the others of getting through for help. Taking a seldom-used route, he managed to reach the Dar Makhzan, the viceroy Moulay Hafid's palace. As for the others—Quinson, the Gentil family, and the personnel of the Alliance school, Falcon and his wife, Monsieur Boujo, and Mademoiselle Garzon—they waited, powerless to come to the aid of their friend.

Each new bit of news confirmed their worst fears. Around 1:30 PM a Muslim came to their door offering to sell them a book and a tennis racket that had belonged to Mauchamp. "It was material proof that the house was pillaged. I understood only at this moment that our lives were endangered," Gentil would write a month later in his report to the French foreign minister. And so he readied his four rifles and unpacked the two hundred or so cartridges that he had with him.

The women of the Jewish quarter expected an assault on the *mellah* at any minute and raised a cry of alarm. After panic broke out among the fifty or so schoolgirls in the courtyard of the school below, Gentil had Falcon send the frightened girls home to their families.

Throughout that long afternoon, Hajj Abdeslam al-Warzazi kept Alan Lennox, the British vice-consul, by his side. While they waited, Lennox took the opportunity to send a letter to Robert Spinney, the British vice-consul in El-Jadida, by special courier. Spinney, in turn, chartered the steamship *Djebel-Kebir* to inform the British vice-consul, Madden, in Casablanca. Through these means, the first word of the French doctor's murder reached Tangier late Saturday night, four days after the event.[49]

Meanwhile, throughout the day, snippets of rumor filtered into the governor's house. It was said that Mauchamp had rejected warnings by both his interpreter and a friend in the street to turn back. Lennox later maintained that "had he only remained in the clinic and sent his servant to remove the pole, the whole thing would have died down and the people would have gone away." Similarly, it was rumored that Mauchamp had pulled out his revolver but was cut down before he could use it, that he had hurled invectives at Moroccans and the government, and that he agreed only reluctantly to take the pole down. And finally, it was said that two or three Frenchmen had stood on the roof of the Jewish school in the *mellah* with a tripod and other equipment and watches in their hand, directing their attention toward the pole on Mauchamp's roof.

The governor puzzled over what to do with the corpse. Ibn Majjad, the French consular agent, had already cleared out. A messenger was sent to find Lassallas but could not to find him. Finally, Lennox said he would go talk to the French colony. The key to the small European cemetery, which he thought they would need, was in his possession.

Having taken his leave of the governor, Lennox stopped home to talk to his wife. It was now five o'clock and outside, in the broad expanse of the Jma el-Fna, a crowd was forming. Some boys threw stones at the house, and only with difficulty were the governor's soldiers who had accompanied him able to close the doors. The soldiers fired a couple of shots from the house. Soon Si Muhammad arrived with some more soldiers, and the crowd dispersed.

"In a few minutes the whole thing was over," Lennox noted drily in his report to the British consul in Casablanca. One of the demonstrators, a boy, was wounded, and Lennox's servant Umar lost part of a finger when his rifle exploded. It was quite unfortunate, Lennox wrote apologetically, that there had to be a row at Harry Maclean's house.[50]

News of an attack on Lennox's house in the Jma el-Fna caused only further alarm for the Frenchmen gathered in the *mellah*. Gentil was especially agitated. If the English community gathered in Caïd Maclean's house could be massacred, he fearfully reasoned, then what would be the fate of the other Europeans? In his report, Gentil later put the casualty figure *chez* Lennox at two dead and one wounded. "It was by this energetic riposte that Lennox and his family, Nairn, an English missionary, and a female missionary were saved."

A Monsieur Edhery, a Moroccan Jew and the president of the local Alliance alumni association, stopped by the school. He offered to conceal the members of the French colony among the Jewish households of the *mellah,* where, he thought, they could be better protected. Gentil turned down the offer, fearing that it would only expose Edhery and their protectors to greater risks.

Finally, accompanied by an escort of Moulay Hafid's men, the merchants Bouvier and Firbach arrived. Through them Gentil sent word to Moulay Hafid that he was concerned about Brives, a French geographer from Algeria, and his wife, who had arrived in Marrakesh two weeks before. The two, he thought, might be locked up in the *madina.* In fact, the couple had left the city the night before. Anticipating trouble, Moulay Hafid sent word to them in Djibelet to skirt Marrakesh on their way to Essaouira.

As Gentil later noted, Moulay Hafid took great pains to protect the Europeans in Marrakesh that day, sending slaves from his personal guard to the German and English colonies and to the one Spaniard and two Gibraltarians who also lived in the city. The viceroy also sent troops to the German consul, Niehr, who was in Tamesloht, to escort him back to the city. "Because of him," Gentil affirmed, "the foreigners in Marrakesh were not massacred."

With the French community assembled in Falcon's house, a decision was reached. They would not bury Mauchamp in Marrakesh, where, they feared, his grave would be dug up and his body set afire. Instead, they would transport the corpse the two hundred kilometers to the coast, from where it would be transported back to his family in France. At once Gentil set a Muslim carpenter to the task of building a coffin. Just that morning Gentil had instructed the carpenter to cut up a cedar trunk. He had wanted to use the planks to build a small meteorological observatory. The boards were now put to a more dismal use. A Jewish tinsmith was called in to fashion a tin lining to fit in the coffin, a measure required for the long trip the corpse would make on the back of a mule.

Five days later Mauchamp's body arrived at the coast, where Doctors Herzen and Guichard in El-Jadida would perform an autopsy. By then it was in a state of advanced putrefaction and much swollen by gas. The doctors concluded that the crushing blows to his forehead and the deep stab wound just at the point of his heart were the cause of death. Death was immediate, but they noted that given sufficient time to hemorrhage, the more than twenty other stab wounds that covered the trunk and limbs, too, would have killed the doctor. The autopsy report noted that the penis and scrotum were left intact.[51]

The Scene of the Crime

At six on the evening of the murder, a small party—made up of Gentil, Lassallas, Umar bin Majjad, and Hajj Abdeslam's two sons—visited the scene of the crime. The door had been forced open, and Mauchamp's empty house lay sacked. Only some broken furniture remained, most of it thrown about in the garden that Mauchamp had laid out with such care. Papers and torn books were everywhere, strewn with mud and blood. Gentil concluded that the plunderers had battled each other over the booty. Mauchamp's collection of paintings, his carpets, and his many objets d'art had all disappeared.

Gentil had the papers and scraps of books gathered in sacks. They weighed more than three hundred kilograms. Later he would send them, assembled in forty sealed packets, via the vice-consul in El-Jadida to the French minister in Tangier.

The group made its way from the victim's house to the clinic. There in a small room they found Mauchamp's body, laid out by soldiers on a bed of fresh straw and clothed in a shirt and white *jallaba*. The head, which was frighteningly crushed, was covered by a turban. They left the body, without the satisfaction of a wake, to be recovered the following day.

Before they left, Si Muhammad, acting as his father's deputy, claimed that Mauchamp had concealed women of ill-repute, singing girls, in the clinic. They were there still, he insisted, hiding. "To convince those present of the inanity of this malevolent insinuation," Gentil wrote, the party then made a visit to every corner of the clinic. The clinic was empty.

On concluding their inspection Gentil, Lassallas and Ibn Majjad drew up the first of many depositions pertaining to the murder of the unfortunate doctor. Indeed, that night and the next nearly everyone involved in the day's events wrote a letter. Bouvier and Gentil each wrote separately to Regnault, the French minister in Tangier. Falcon wrote to his superiors at the Alliance in Paris.[52] Lennox wrote to Madden, the British consul in Casablanca, and again to Spinney in El-Jadida. And lastly Hajj Abdeslam, dictating to his secretary, wrote to Muhammad al-Turris, the sultan's diplomatic representative in Tangier.[53]

The French geographer Brives, for whose safety Gentil had expressed concern, first learned of the murder while he was still in Misfiwa, in the foothills of the Atlas mountains, meeting with the *qaid* Al-Madani al-Glawi. There it was rumored that Mauchamp had raised the French tricolor on his roof. Although he had been nowhere near the scene of the attack on Mauchamp, Brives, within four days of the murder, confidently sent to the French minister in Tangier yet another version of what happened, complete with piquant details. According to Brives, Ahmad al-Misluhi, an associate of Hajj Abdeslam, was heard to remark after the doctor fell, "One dog is dead, another will take his place." And Brives could challenge Gentil and Bouvier's assertion that they had not used any flags. "I affirm," he wrote, "that everyone here saw the flags in the *mellah* and on the house of the doctor."[54]

In his letter to the sultan's representative in Tangier, Hajj Abdeslam al-Warzazi was eager to dispel the notion that he had in any way been negligent or harbored any particular animosity toward Mauchamp.[55] The doctor, he declared, had put a flag on his roof. He also noted that it was widely believed that Mauchamp had installed a wireless telegraph with which to communicate with the Frenchmen living in the *mellah*. In any event, the governor said that Mauchamp refused to remove the flag when he was approached and instead began verbally to abuse the Moroccans gathered around him. Hajj Abdeslam sent his son with some men to protect the doctor, but they arrived too late. Mauchamp was dead and the house already plundered; the most significant item stolen was Mauchamp's saddle. And as the governor was quick to point out, the house was in fact his own property. He had let it to Mauchamp in consideration of the doctor's medical care of him, and he had borne the French doctor no ill will.

Hajj Abdeslam then explained how his sons dispersed the crowd with gunfire, killing two and wounding three. Without this action, the toll in property and lives would have been higher. They had also taken care to rescue and guard the body, which the French colony now proposed to send to El-Jadida. And finally, he argued that, in accordance with the sultan's order, he had been vigilant in monitoring the activities of the foreigners residing in Marrakesh. If anything, the fault lay with the doctor, who had failed to notify either him or the viceroy, Moulay Hafid, of his intentions. Had the doctor done so, he would not have given him permission. The governor knew what feelings the doctor's actions would arouse among the "riffraff," as he called the rioters.

Two weeks later, in another letter to al-Turris, Hajj Abdeslam reiterated the notion that Mauchamp's death was unavoidable. Calling it "a celestial matter," he claimed that he had not stinted in his effort to prevent the doctor's death. But he also implied again that ultimate responsibility for inciting the crowd lay with Mauchamp himself. The doctor had been "attentive to women" in a way that could only incite the ire of the populace. Whether this was an allusion to his medical practice or to extracurricular activities outside the clinic remains hard to say.[56]

Whatever the governor might say in his personal defense, the French community in Marrakesh was unanimous in its vilification of him. Writing to his superior in Paris the day after the murder, Falcon echoed the opinion of his compatriots. "It is almost certain that the governor of the city, Hajj Abdeslam, is solely responsible for this sad event and the riot which followed and almost cost the lives of all the Europeans residing here. The governor is the personal enemy of the doctor and a rabid xenophobe."[57]

And as if Mauchamp himself had returned from the dead to pronounce sentence on his alleged murderer, *La Dépêche Marocaine* in Tangier published an excerpt from a letter it had received earlier from Mauchamp in which he too complained about Hajj Abdeslam al-Warzazi. "This fantastic governor," he wrote, "does nothing to remedy the troubled situation. [Our] exasperation increases. One doesn't leave the city, or even go about the city itself unless armed."[58] As the paper suggested, it seems as if the doctor foresaw his tragic end.

The Day After

The Europeans of Marrakesh were on edge the day after the murder. When they met among themselves they traded items of news, trying to gauge the climate of opinion among the Moroccans. Utting, a German merchant, had found his route cut by a band of Moroccans that was dispersed only by some Makhzan soldiers. Lassallas too was menaced on the road, as were the three German employees of the Casablanca-based merchant Carl Ficke who later that evening helped put Mauchamp in his coffin.[59] Crossing the Jma el-Fna, they were forced to take refuge at about 5:30 in Lennox's house.

With impunity Arab merchants throughout the city offered items pillaged from the doctor's house. Throughout the day, Moroccans arrived at Falcon's house at the Alliance school. They offered for sale to the Frenchmen who gathered there books and objects that had only the day before belonged to the ill-fated friend. Gentil, writing to Tangier, lambasted Hajj Abdeslam al-Warzazi for his inertia. He hoped that Moulay Hafid would do what was necessary to restore order and protect the Europeans. "Security can only return," he wrote, "after a model repression [*une repression exemplaire*]."[60]

Lennox arrived at Falcon's house with a letter of condolence and an offer to help prepare Mauchamp's remains. Despite the vehement denials of all the Frenchmen assembled, Lennox held fast to his assertion that Mauchamp had put a white flag or cloth on his roof. Gentil in particular felt that he was being impugned for his role in Mauchamp's murder. In the European press it was later widely reported that Mauchamp and Gentil had been on the rooftops undertaking a survey of the city, a report Gentil denied.[61]

The time of the murder was also hotly debated. It was an important question, for the adequacy of the governor's response hinged on ascertaining at exactly what point he dispatched troops. Gentil and Lennox had been conversing in Arabic when Gentil realized that he made a linguistic mistake. Wanting to say "between eleven and eleven-thirty," he had said instead, "between twelve and twelve-thirty." But before he could correct himself, Lennox seized the point "with vivacity."

"You see, M. Lassallas," Lennox exclaimed turning to the French merchant, "it was later than you said and the governor had sent immediately soldiers to protect the doctor."[62]

Privately, Lennox admitted that Hajj Abdeslam handled the affair ineptly. Nonetheless, he did not share the Frenchmen's antipathy for the governor. The fault, if anything, lay with Mauchamp himself.

"I asked Lassallas," he wrote to Madden, "why the doctor left [his clinic] when he heard the noise, and he answered that the doctor was a novice in Morocco who did not know Arabic and who was energetic and intrepid."

Although he could never convince the French, the British vice-consul—who was a long-time resident in Marrakesh—held fast to his assertion that "the Marrakchis were the most peaceable people, but one must not excite them."[63]

Together with Lennox and the German merchant Utting, a party of Frenchmen set out again for a second visit to the scene of the crime. Now, for the first time, they climbed to the roof of Mauchamp's house to see the pole that had been the object of recent discussion. It lay intact on the roof, having been taken down by the pillagers, two or three reeds bound together, some five and a half yards long, with two small cross-pieces near the top. Some strings were attached at the end, but if the pole had ever born a white cloth or flag, there was none there now. Lennox, still unconvinced, maintained that someone could have removed it.

They next went to the clinic, where Mauchamp's body lay. Lennox, who had had some medical training and who operated a missionary clinic of his own, examined the body. He decided to inject it with an antiseptic to prepare it for its transport to the coast, and in the pharmacy found a syringe and some *formol*. While Lennox and Lassallas busied themselves with the injections, Gentil prepared the winding sheet. Utting went off to find some of his German compatriots, and at four o'clock, the appointed hour, they all met to place Mauchamp in his coffin. They covered the body with fifty pounds of charcoal, soldered tightly the tinplate lining, and nailed the coffin shut.[64]

Figure 7. Mauchamp's
body being lowered into
a coffin. Reprinted from
L'Illustration, April 20, 1907.

That night the convoy to the coast was readied. Gentil at first thought he would accompany the body, but then, fearing that the situation in Marrakesh might deteriorate, elected to stay behind. Quinson and Berrino went in his place, accompanied by an escort of twenty-five men on horseback provided by Moulay Hafid. The convoy set out before dawn. In the meantime Gentil sought a *rak-kas,* a foot courier, to carry his letter to Huytèza, the vice-consul in El-Jadida. The courier, who set off at four in the morning, arrived in El-Jadida two days before the body.

A Protest

To the Europeans in Marrakesh, the situation over the course of the next week looked grave. On his return from Tamesloht, the German consul Niehr instructed his countrymen to remain indoors. Lennox and the English colony likewise stayed off the streets, and when the Frenchmen Lassallas and Gentil went out, they did so armed—a fact that Gentil did not conceal—or in the company of armed men. On the street, someone threatened Lassallas, "Your turn will come soon." One of Bouvier's servants was thrown off a mule and cursed as a "Christian's dog."

Figure 8. Mauchamp's coffin being carried across the desert a few miles outside of El-Jadida. Reprinted from *L'Illustration,* April 13, 1907.

On the morning of March 21, Lennox offered to draft a letter in Arabic to Hajj Abdeslam al-Warzazi, to be signed by delegates of the foreign community. The letter would energetically demand that the governor assure their security. To Gentil's chagrin, however, Lennox did not deem it necessary for the Europeans to meet *before* he drafted the letter.

Lennox set to his task. The following day, accompanied by Niehr and a German merchant named Daum, who had a good command of French, Lennox presented the small French colony with the letter that he had drafted. Neither Gentil nor Lassallas thought the letter was worded strongly enough. Nevertheless, as it would take Lennox another twenty-four hours to draft a new letter, the Europeans finally agreed that they should send the letter already in hand. In the letter—signed by Lennox, Niehr, Daum, Gentil, Lassallas, Bouvier, Firbach, and Falcon—the Europeans expressed concern for their safety. They accused the governor of demonstrating weakness and demanded that he punish those responsible for the attacks in order to set an example to others. Meanwhile, among themselves the Europeans debated whether they should leave at once for the coast. The French argued in favor of an immediate withdrawal. The two Germans said they could not leave without specific instructions from their employers on the coast. Lennox urged staying put. "Considering that the people had become quiet and the Government had proved themselves [*sic*] equal to quell the excitement, we would not be justified in complicating matters by a general exodus."[65]

Upon receiving the letter, Hajj Abdeslam told Lennox that he would transmit it to Moulay Hafid and wait for the latter's response. Moulay Hafid, in turn, told Lassallas that security in the city was Hajj Abdeslam's responsibility. In short, neither Lassallas nor Gentil entertained great hopes when they were summoned to the governor's house that Sunday evening, March 24.

The private rooms where Hajj Abdeslam al-Warzazi received the delegates of the foreign community were richly lit with candles. Si Muhammad, his son and deputy, bustled about in an ostentatious show of hospitality. The French representatives were surprised to learn that Lennox had already spent part of the afternoon in the company of Hajj Abdeslam. This relationship seemed too cozy for the Frenchmen. The most astonishing thing, however, was to see the German and English consular agents remove their boots. Moroccan custom or not, the French delegates thought it beneath the dignity of a European diplomatic representative to approach any authority of the Makhzan in his stocking feet.

The boot incident quickly appeared as an item in the Tangier French newspapers, but the English-language *Al-Moghreb al-Aksa* was able to turn the issue to advantage. In an article written by Lennox himself, the paper ridiculed the indignant pose struck by Lassallas and Gentil. In wearing their mud-stained boots in the private rooms of the governor, the Frenchmen displayed the kind of insensitivity to local custom that had garnered them the hostility of the Moroccan public in the first place.

> One marvels at the French who are famous for their courtesy not extending it towards the Moors. It would greatly help them in their pacific penetration if they considered the feelings of the natives in these and other things. When one has observed this custom for so many years to all it becomes habitual and binding so that he would no more think of keeping his hat on in an English drawing room than his boots on a fine Moorish carpet & richly draped mattress.[66]

In the presence of Hajj Abdeslam, the Europeans lodged their protest. The authorities, they claimed, had done nothing to prevent the disorder and were doing nothing to provide for the security of the Europeans. Si Muhammad replied on his father's behalf.

"There's nothing wrong," he told them. "Marrakesh is calm. If there was the least danger we'd protect you. I will accompany you myself if you are in peril."

In Gentil's account of the meeting, Lennox and Niehr remained silent while he continued his protest. He turned to the Englishman and the German for support, but Lennox disappointed him.

"We wrote a letter," he recalled the British vice-consul as saying. "We desired a response. What is past is past. We ask only for guarantees for the future."[67]

Lennox, for his part, reported the exchange differently. As he recalled, his speech followed that of Lassallas and Niehr, and he used the strongest terms possible to encourage the governor to establish his authority and take immediate action. "The others applauded me and approved of my statements."[68]

Having listening patiently to the Europeans, Si Muhammad said they would wait for orders from Fez. Meanwhile, his father remarked that it was not his practice to apply pressure to people and that in any case he lacked sufficient troops.

Gentil continued his demand that the authorities take positive steps to provide security. In the end Hajj Abdeslam relented, saying that he would establish a two-hundred-man guard.

"What will this guard's function be?" Gentil demanded to know.

The question bemused Hajj Abdeslam.

"I only thought about it just now," Gentil recalls him as saying.

With the decision to post guards on the street settled, the atmosphere relaxed, and Moroccan hospitality prevailed once more.

"The tension which had been rather great up to this point was now relieved," recalled Lennox, "the Frenchmen became quite jovial, and we all thawed somewhat. A most sumptuous meal was served and partaken by us all."[69]

The next day, as even Gentil had to admit, a ragtag posse of two hundred men was pressed into service on the streets of Marrakesh. Yet despite Gentil's criticisms, Hajj Abdeslam was not as inert as Gentil accused him of being. On the very day of their meeting, he had written the sultan's deputy Muhammad al-Turris in Tangier, enclosing a copy of Lennox's letter. Adopting the bureaucratic style of the Makhzan, he was characteristically vague. "A Nasrani [Christian] of the nationality of the three Powers living in Marrakesh," he noted, "wrote us."

As Hajj Abdeslam explained to al-Turris, he did not have enough troops at the time of the murder to contain the rioters, and he deliberately did not arrest the perpetrators of the murder for fear of provoking a greater riot. Now that calm had returned, he had set about picking up suspects. Already, "God judged that one of them should testify against himself about striking the victim and he testified against another Misfiwa man." Hajj Abdeslam already had depositions in his hand. "With God's help," he concluded, "we will continue to pursue suspects."

Hajj Abdeslam also said that he wrote a conciliatory letter to the Europeans, assuring them that they would continue to enjoy the security and freedom of circulation that they had long enjoyed in Marrakesh. "To assure your safety, I've renounced sleep," he asserted.

As for the doctor's unfortunate death, the governor of Marrakesh ascribed it to God's will. "It occurred because of the doctor's intrigues which troubled the spirit of the population." He defended the measures he had taken to prevent the situation from becoming worse.[70]

The Frenchmen remained unsatisfied. A few days later they wrote to their minister in Tangier, Regnault, still complaining of Hajj Abdeslam's "inertia." Referring to the many complaints they had lodged individually over recent months, they claimed that the governor had "ceaselessly excited the population against the Europeans." Thus the removal of Hajj Abdeslam joined the long list of other demands by the French in the wake of Mauchamp's death.

In letters to his British colleagues, Lennox summarized the various positions regarding Hajj Abdeslam's culpability.

> The French and Moulay-el-Hafeed [sic] put all blame on Hajj Abdslam [sic], who had never been on friendly terms with the doctor; but Moulay-el-Hafeed has been on bad terms with Hajj Abdslam for several months. The people so far as I can learn blame Moulay-el-Hafeed. There has been a good deal of excitement about the French for a few days, and no doubt Hajj Abdslam was on the alert and the people too. . . . Had the people not been in a nervous condition, the presence of a reed on a house would not have raised them.[71]

But the following day, Lennox wrote to Madden, the British vice-consul in Casablanca, to say that local opinion now accused Hajj Abdeslam of instigating the murder. In the company of Lassallas and

Figure 9. A crowd accompanies Mauchamp's coffin in El-Jadida before it is loaded on ship. Reprinted from *L'Illustration*, April 13, 1907.

Berrino, he went to meet with Moulay Hafid. The viceroy and the others were all convinced that the governor, learning from the Germans that the French were going to introduce wireless telegraphy in Marrakesh, had ordered the headmen of the various quarters to be on the lookout and to prevent Europeans from renting houses.

> They argue that the Mukaddanim [*sic*] must have created an anti-French feeling among their householders and the people, and that it only required the hoisting of a reed on the doctor's house to gather the mob, who, knowing that they had the sympathy of the Governor, were bold and daring. This is putting their argument in the mildest form, as they all declared at first that the Governor made the plot, raised the mob, and sent the doctor to his house in order that he might be murdered; and this will be the report that has been sent to Fez and Tangier.

Lennox knew that his friend Hajj Abdeslam was being set up. Moulay Hafid himself admitted that he had no firm proof against Hajj Abdeslam other than that he had told the local headmen to be on the alert. According to Lennox,

Figure 10. An honor guard stands watch over Mauchamp's coffin aboard the *Lalande*. Reprinted from *L'Illustration,* April 13, 1907.

The Governor [Hajj Abdeslam] had no share in the origin of the row any further than I have stated, nor did he send the doctor to the house to remove the flag, nor was he in sympathy with the mob. . . . The only thing that can be said against the Governor was his slackness and cowardice in not dispersing the mob at once and placing an armed guard in front of the house, and raising all the force he has to quell the disturbance. Such helplessness, such fear and indecision, you cannot conceive when they sent for me. They did not know what to do; they said they were afraid to use force lest the whole town should rise. The Governor himself is an old man, has been ill for several months, and is incapable of the office. His mental forces have failed very much, and he is weak and frail. Some two months ago a letter came from the Sultan appointing his eldest son, a learned "Fiki," to act for his father. He is a quiet man, a student, and acted as Cadi [judge] for nine months during the absence of the Chief Cadi; but he is not at all suited for the post of Governor, and quite incapable of taking the firm hand that this large city requires. Had we had a strong, resourceful man, this affair would never have taken place.[72]

As for Gentil, he had had enough of Marrakesh, and he wanted to convey in person to Regnault his concerns about the safety of his compatriots. On Thursday, March 28, little more than two weeks after their arrival, he and his wife and daughter set out for El-Jadida with an escort provided by Moulay Hafid. About thirty kilometers from their destination, they found themselves outnumbered by a hundred mounted and armed men from the Oulad Bou Aziz tribe. After first demanding fifteen hundred francs for safe passage, the men settled for the few gold pieces that Gentil had in his vest pocket.[73] To his relief, Gentil arrived in El-Jadida just as Mauchamp's body was being loaded on the cruiser *Lalande*. He would accompany his friend first to Tangier and later would stand at his graveside at Mauchamp's funeral in his native Chalon-sur-Saône.

Part 2. Death

7

In Morocco, No One Dies without a Reason

The Wireless Telegraph

In the aftermath of Mauchamp's death a controversy immediately arose. What was it exactly on the doctor's roof that had incited his Moroccan neighbors to violence? The official Moroccan version—disseminated throughout the country in a letter from the sultan—held that Mauchamp had placed a flag of some kind on his roof.[1]

For the most part, published press reports, too, chose to represent the offending object as a flag. Just what kind depended upon the paper one read. Mauchamp had hoisted either the French tricolor, or a white flag used as a marker for triangulation in Gentil's topographic observations, or even a Red Cross flag intended to mark the location of Mauchamp's clinic. Mauchamp's obituary in the *British Medical Journal* managed to conflate all possible versions of the pole story into one:

> [Mauchamp's] professional work among the natives was doing much to extend French influence in Morocco. He was extremely popular, and his murder appears to have been due to a misapprehension on the part of the natives. He had put a pole, bearing a flag, on the top of his house intended, it is said, to serve as a landmark in some triangulation work that is being carried out by a French scientific mission. The Moors thought this was part of an apparatus of wireless telegraphy which they thought would lead somehow to increased taxation. An angry crowd gathered outside the house, and Dr. Mauchamp coming out, it is believed with the intention of explaining the situation, was stoned to death.[2]

The scientific nature of the alleged equipment on the roof seemed especially plausible to those Frenchmen who wanted to imbue their countryman's death with a noble purpose.[3] This wish persisted in spite of the fact that Gentil himself vigorously denied that the alleged pole played any role in his observations. As he pointed out, if he needed a point to calibrate his instruments, the 280-foot Kutubiyya minaret would have served perfectly well.

In its account of the murder and the subsequent events, *Al-Saada*—a Tangier-based Arabic-language paper published with French financial support—faithfully repeated the sentiments of the Moroccan French press. However, on the question of the flag, it added a salient although probably apocryphal anecdote. Some six years earlier, it reported, a European astronomer had similarly put a white cloth on the roof of a house adjacent to the Jma al-Fna. The matter was referred to the governor at the time, who first scolded the complainant, presumably for being alarmist. He then ordered Moroccan scholars to confer with the European as to whether the white flag was really necessary for his work. Once informed that the raising of flags was a prerogative of the government, the European agreed to desist. The moral which the paper drew was not that Mauchamp had erred in raising his flag, but that the current governor, Hajj Abdeslam al-Warzazi, was negligent in not handling this affair in a manner similar to his predecessor.[4]

A few reports emphasized Mauchamp's alleged role as a French espionage agent, an interpretation subsequently adopted by historians skeptical of official French explanations.[5] These reports claimed that the pole was indeed an antenna and that Mauchamp had in fact established a wireless telegraph post on his roof. At the other extreme, some interpreters put forth a more banal explanation: the *roseau* or *poteau*, as it was styled in French, was nothing more than a clothesline prop.[6] Similarly, in his memoirs Christian Houel writes that he personally had stones hurled at him when he ventured onto a rooftop in Marrakesh. This indiscretion—which exposed Muslim women to the scrutiny of Westerners (a familiar trope in the literature)—was enough in Houel's view to put Mauchamp in mortal danger.[7]

The official French account of the murder appeared in the *Documents Diplomatiques: Affaires du Maroc* in the form of Louis Gentil's report to the foreign minister. Here, too, the object on Mauchamp's roof was represented as a flag, but this published report was a deliberate falsification. Evidently hoping to offer a more emphatic rebuttal to the charge that Mauchamp had indeed introduced a telegraph into Marrakesh, the Quai d'Orsay printed only a truncated and heavily edited version of Gentil's report. This official version of the report is the one subsequently quoted by Mauchamp's biographer, Guillemin. Meanwhile, the full text of the report lay buried in the diplomatic archives, undisturbed for eighty years. To reveal the true reasons for Mauchamp's death would undoubtedly have exposed the martyred Mauchamp—and French officials—to ridicule.

Lennox, the British vice-consul, reported to his superiors what Lassallas and the other Frenchmen had told him about the pole being a joke, but he remained skeptical. Under ordinary circumstances, he claimed, putting a pole on the roof would not have provoked the mob. However, "for several days there had been a strong feeling of resentment against the French caused by wild reports." He claimed that not long before, some of the French "had a large picnic in one of the gardens attended by a number of native women, so that the people were in a nervous condition watching events, and the erection of a reed would lead them to conclude all sorts of things."[8]

Allegations concerning allegedly immoral behavior by the Frenchmen of Marrakesh soon appeared in the Tangier paper, *Al-Moghreb al-Aksa*. Purported to be an interview with a Moroccan named "Abd-el-Kadder," the article has all the markings of having been penned by Lennox:

> You are not ignorant of what has been done in the last year in the City and its vicinity. How the *Franceses* have come to live here, how their protégés and friends have opened houses of ill-fame and filled them with Moorish girls and Jewesses. *Hashak* [shame]!

According to Abd-el-Kadder these women sat out of doors in the open eating during the fasting month of Ramadan. People complained to the governor, who was powerless against the *Franceses*.

> Then comes this *tabeeb* [doctor] with other *nassara* [Christians] and there were many rumours spread of what they were going to do. We heard of his going to erect a flag, a national flag, which to the ignorant implies possession of the country; we heard too of some kind of telegraph being introduced, and machines for this purpose landed at Saffi [*sic*]. The authorities too were on the alert, jealous for the integrity of the Empire and the peace of the community.
>
> It was known all over the city that orders had been given to the *m'kaddem* [chief man] of each district and to the heads of the building and carpenter trades to be on the watch for any new building

or anything new in or on the houses of the *nassara*. One day these *nassara* had two picnics attended by numbers of native women of bad repute.

Now you know at this time of the year when flowers deck the land, we, Marrakshees, like to go out to the gardens for picnics, and there were many out that day; but the pleasure was sadly marred by the presence of these *nassara* with native women.

You can understand, my friend, how the people were agitated against the *Franceses,* and it only need a reed with a white flag to be put on the roof of the doctor's house to raise a huge clamouring mob, who imagined all sorts of impossible things about this flag. When the doctor appeared there was nothing but certain death from this raving mad pack of hounds. You cannot believe how sorry we are over the terrible end of the *tabeeb* . . . but it was a dispensation from God, and who can withstand Him?

. . . If those *Franceses* would come among us and live quietly as other foreigners have done all these years, they would not get into trouble. How is it that other *nassara* have lived so long in our midst with their wives and children who are dear to us and to our women? Well, you know it is because they have some respect for our feelings; they don't want to trample us under their feet; they never make rows or get into trouble, like those new-comers, who are continually having rows.[9]

Of the allegedly obstreperous and ill-behaved Frenchmen who lived in Marrakesh, none fit the description better than Ernest Vaffier-Pollet. A former navy lieutenant, Vaffier-Pollet represented the Morocco Committee and was an agent for the Compagnie Marocaine. Although he was absent from Marrakesh at the time of Mauchamp's death, he was there again six months later. Christian Houel met him when he arrived to cover Moulay Hafid's accession to the throne for the Paris paper *Le Matin*. The former junior officer and the journalist became close friends. Vaffier-Pollet lived in a house that belonged to Al-Madani al-Glawi, alongside whom Vaffier-Pollet had fought against the rebel Abu Amama a half-dozen years earlier.[10]

Vaffier-Pollet was that rare being, a Frenchman completely assimilated to the Moroccan lifestyle. In this he was the exact opposite of the rigid Mauchamp.

"I was charmed by his extensive knowledge and especially by his perfect adaptation to the Muslim existence," Houel recalled. "He followed all the rituals and thus gained the trust of his Moroccan visitors. Sometimes, for their benefit, he would hire violinists and dancers. Songs and music filled his home."[11]

Vaffier-Pollet also became a great friend and champion of Moulay Hafid, and he worked hard to create a progressive image on the latter's behalf that would be palatable to the French. In collaboration with a Syrian Christian named Niamet Allah Dahdah, Vaffier-Pollet published a pro-Hafid Arabic newspaper called *Al-Fajr* (The Dawn). Begun in December 1908 in Fez, the project was abandoned after two numbers for lack of funds.[12] Houel later saw Moulay Hafid in 1912, and he claimed that the sultan's eyes misted at the mention of "Ouaffi" (Vaffier). The French adventurer had by then returned to his family in Cluny.

Whether the statements of Abd-el-Kadder were authentic or not, similar anti-French sentiments could be heard throughout Morocco. The German journalist Graf Sternberg was in Fez shortly after Mauchamp's death. In his infelicitously titled 1908 book, *The Barbarians of Morocco,* Sternberg relates at length a conversation he had in Fez with a high-placed but unnamed Moroccan.[13] A staunch Anglophile (his traveling companion was the book's illustrator, the English artist Douglas Fox-Pitt), Sternberg did not hesitate to put words of utter contempt toward the French in the mouth of his Moroccan informant. According to Sternberg's informant, the crimes of the French were manifold. "As he related to me the attempts of the French men to get possession of the Moorish wives and maidens," Sternberg writes, "the flush of anger overspread the features of this usually unruffled fatalist."

> The French are not satisfied with putting our people to shame, condemning them to poverty and slavery in Tunis and Algiers alone, but desire to visit the same fate on Morocco, on the last refuge of our race. Though they do not hold the country, they give themselves untold liberties. They called us barbarians because we killed Dr. Marchand [*sic*]. But what had he done? He hoisted the white flag of the Prophet on his house, and long before that he had shamelessly provoked and insulted the most peaceful people you could anywhere find. . . . Dr. Marchand knew the country and its customs. Why did he not respect them? Because the French tread us under their feet in Algiers, we need not suffer it here. Did not M. Gironcourt also brutally provoke our peace-loving people? The mosque he photographed is the sacred shrine of women. No one would have interfered had he chosen any day but Friday, when the women were assembled there; neither did he do it quietly, but very

ostentatiously, with a large camera on a stand. When he was asked to desist he insulted the people. How otherwise shall we protect our holy places against these barbarians?[14]

The austere Sternberg reports that his British traveling companion Fox-Pitt heard these remarks and similarly voiced approval. But it's clear from his account that Sternberg, who admired the colonial policies of the English ("the only people that know how to treat coloured races"), obviously did not understand their humor. He quotes without comment Fox-Pitt as saying, "From everything I have heard, I should not be surprised to be some day murdered by the Arabs, but I forgive them beforehand."

An English adventure writer and long-term observer of the Moroccan scene, R. B. Cunningham Grahame made the first public intimations that Mauchamp was the unwitting agent of his own demise.[15] In an article later reprinted in the English-language newspaper *Al-Moghreb al-Aksa*, Cunningham Grahame explained to the readers of the London paper *The Daily Chronicle* that the telegraph was a sensitive subject in Morocco. It was not the case that the Moroccans by and large superstitiously looked on wireless telegraphy "as a magic and a malign artifice." Rather the Moroccan objections could not be more rational.

First, it was widely known that the sultan had not offered a telegraph concession to any of the European powers. Second, merchants on the coast feared that "the introduction of such a system would enable foreign merchants to raise or lower the price of grain and wool up and down the coast over their heads without their being able to defend themselves."[16]

While French newspapers such as *Le Journal* in Paris could make knowing statements about "the Muslim horror of all modern inventions," Cunningham Grahame's assessment was indeed closer to the mark. Moroccans—and the Makzhan in particular—had no objections to the use of the telegraph *in principle*. The existing undersea cable to Europe allowed the Moroccan government to communicate with its envoys to Europe. Likewise, the conventional telegraph lines that ran east to Algiers put the Makhzan in touch with Oujda and its Eastern frontier. Anything would be an improvement over the *rakkas*, the couriers that crisscrossed the country on foot.

The furor over Bopp's efforts to install wireless telegraphy in Morocco contributed directly to Mauchamp's untimely death. Nevertheless, what roused the ire of the Makhzan was not the idea of the telegraph itself but the possibility that it would be under exclusive French control. Looking to exert countervailing pressure, the sultan advised his representative in Tangier to consult with the German minister. Dr. Rosen concurred that the telegraph was, under the recently signed Algeciras agreement, a public utility analogous to the railroad and therefore subject to international supervision. The British seconded the opinion. In April, meetings were held to negotiate a telegraph concession that would give all the Powers a stake. The agreement gave the British, Germans, and Moroccans a say in the management of the new telegraph company, but rewarded the French for being first in the field. The director of the new telegraph company was none other than Bopp. In the event of his death—which coincidentally came the following year—it was determined in advance that the directorship would turn to his son.[17]

The Press

News of Mauchamp's death filtered back to Tangier and Europe. The English-language Tangier paper *Al-Moghreb al-Aksa* ran its first account of the murder in its Saturday, March 23 issue, and, echoing a recurring theme within the European colony, quickly assigned blame. "Probably the indifference of the authorities is the cause of the lamentable murder committed by the mob at Marrakesh, as is generally the case with disturbances throughout the country." A few weeks later, after his return to France, Louis Gentil would write bluntly in the *Bulletin du Comité de l'Afrique Française,* "How does one explain such an atrocity? Very simply, like all the others, by the instigation of the Makhzan."[18]

The coverage of the murder soon assumed a partisan character that reflected the ongoing rivalry between the European powers in Morocco. The following week, when *Al-Moghreb al-Aksa* offered a fuller account of the events—including an account of the attack on Lennox's house—the paper actually defended the actions of the authorities in Marrakesh.

"Unfortunately," the article said, "the murder of Doctor Mauchamp took place at the beginning of the outbreak, when the gathering of the mob was hardly known, and had the Doctor adopted any precautionary measure of prudence, the lamented outrage could have been avoided, as undoubtedly the authorities did what they could from the moment they heard of the disturbances."

A common theme throughout the reporting of the English *Al-*

Moghreb al-Aksa was the tactlessness of the French in their dealings with the Moroccans. Mauchamp's death was a perfect example. "It requires great circumspection to live and move about in this part of the country at the present time, which unfortunately, has not been observed, and hence the lamented end of the French Doctor."

Rubbing salt into the wounds of hurt French pride, the paper's editors chose at this time to run alongside its report of Mauchamp's death a long, front-page feature entitled, "A Visit to Marrakesh." The anonymous series emphasized the cordiality of the "Marrakshis" and enthusiastically described Marrakesh as an ideal tourist destination.

> The southern metropolis of the Moorish Empire, with its busy main streets, fondaks [inns] and market places, beside the fact that one is compelled to walk side by side with the most fanatical Mohammedans in Africa—Moors, Berbers, Fillela, Sussies [*sic*], Sudanese, and many other types, possesses a wonderful and curious enchantment for the majority of Europeans. The hospitality exhibited and offered so freely by all classes to their Christian guests is astonishing, and we notice there less antipathy than is often experienced at the ports.[19]

Finally, in its April 13 issue, the paper reprinted the opinions of Cunningham Grahame as they appeared in the *Daily Chronicle*. Cunningham Grahame's remarks could only serve to goad the French colony in Morocco. "Frenchmen go about Morocco as if it were a conquered country, brow-beating native officials, disregarding native opinion upon every point, and endeavoring by all means—and here, I think, is a definite instance of how they break the spirit of the [Algeciras] Conference—to obtain an exclusive hold over the country."

Cunningham Grahame questioned the humanitarian motives of Mauchamp's missionary work. "I believe he was simply an advance agent of France, placed in Morocco City [i.e., Marrakesh] in order to extend French influence." The Moroccans themselves, he noted, could not have been unaware of "the ulterior motive of his presence."

Lastly, he noted that most of the recent attacks on Europeans were directed almost exclusively at French citizens. The Englishman Lennox, in contrast, had been able to live for years in Marrakesh without incident. "The truth is that the French have been intolerably overbearing and haughty in their conduct in Morocco, perhaps not intentionally so, but possibly because of their position as conquerors amongst an almost similar race in Algeria."

While by no means condoning the attacks on French citizens and calling for their perpetrators to be brought to justice, Cunningham Grahame called it "no wonder that the Moors, a free people for the last thousand years and more, should resent treating their country as if it were a conquered land."

Newspapers in Germany, too, could not help but observe that French nationals, far more than other Europeans, were the victims of attacks in Morocco. In contrast, French papers were preoccupied with two themes: the nobility of the French doctor's mission and the perfidy of the Makhzan officials and their alleged German accomplices. Naturally the German press and German officials denied the charge. Meanwhile, in metropolitan France, the doctor's death jostled for attention in papers crowded with equally tragic news. Two especially dolorous events had occurred that week to throw the French nation into a state of deep mourning. The first was the catastrophic explosion of the French destroyer *Iéna* in port in Toulon that left scores sailors dead and wounded. The second was the solemn installation of Berthelot and his wife in the Pantheon in Paris. The famous chemist and his wife had separately died of natural causes within the space of twenty-four hours.

In Tangier, Rober-Raynaud, the editor of *La Dépêche Marocaine*, ran a black-bordered elegy for Mauchamp on the front page. Papers in France such as the mass-circulation Parisian daily *L'Éclair* published Rober-Raynaud's words verbatim.

> Doctor Mauchamp had the vigorous and ardent nature that inspires esteem and affection. The loyalty of his gaze, the openness of his word, the generosity of his deeds marked his personality. He loved his career as doctor because he drew from it the means to help. No country in the world has as many ills to cure, or wounds to dress, as Morocco; thus to Morocco he came. His education, his family, his fortunate circumstances would have assured him in France an easy and golden existence, to which he preferred the rude work reserved for him here, the care of a clinic, a hostel for leprosy and typhus.

Speaking in the vaguest terms, Rober-Raynaud blamed the hostility of the mob on Mauchamp's unnamed rival—"a merchant of throat-lozenges," "an amulet-maker"—who claimed to be a doctor and who, "before the arrival of Doctor Mauchamp, had the privilege of tending without healing." That latter would not admit that a truly learned and generous doctor had opened his doors to offer free care to the suffering masses.[20]

The so-called doctor to whom the editor alluded was none other than Holzmann, with whom Mauchamp had often tangled during his months in Marrakesh. French commentators increasingly vilified him as a German agent determined to subvert Mauchamp's humanitarian mission. Under the heading, "A Mysterious Person," *L'Express de Lyon* ran an article attributed to the *Correspondencia de Espana* that set the tone of the campaign against Holzmann. The paper claimed that he was already Mauchamp's rival during the latter's sojourn in Palestine.[21] The alleged German agent was depicted as some kind of master spy, a "redoubtable adversary" who knew Arabic perfectly and spoke twelve languages: "In Syria, he was a rabbi; in Marrakesh, he converted to Mohammedanism, his conversion took place with great pomp in the great mosque of Marrakesh. From this day on he knew to create powerful sympathies. The sultan's brother made him his doctor and his most intimate confidant; the notables would take their orders at the home of the new convert." The appearance in Marrakesh of Mauchamp ("someone who was really a doctor and whose treatments earned him a large enough popularity") undercut Holzmann's position. Holzmann, the paper implied, took advantage of Mauchamp's absence in Paris to propagate the rumor that he was there to acquire equipment with which to communicate with France daily on the affairs of Morocco.

Meanwhile, the German press was quick to deny the allegations that Holzmann was a German agent. The British ambassador to Berlin cited a paragraph in the *Kölnische Zeitung* to the effect "that Dr. Holtzmann [sic] is neither a German subject nor under German protection, but was born in Palestine, and is therefore a Turkish subject. The fact that he bears a German name, has studied in Germany, and therefore speaks the language fluently, is presumed to be the cause of the error."[22]

The report in the German press was in fact not far from the truth. While German officials were aware of Holzmann's role as an adviser to Moulay Hafid, they clearly viewed him as a Turk and not as a German.[23] French commentators, nevertheless, remained unconvinced of Holzmann's neutrality. The British author Gavin Maxwell writing in 1966 even went so far as to place Holzmann at the crime scene, inciting the mob to violence.[24]

But Christian Houel, who knew Holzmann well from the months he spent covering Moulay Hafid in the fall of 1907, found the case against the German-trained Syrian-born doctor unconvincing. In his memoirs written almost a half century later, he describes Holzmann as an unprepossessing, bespectacled man about forty years of age with a sparse beard and "small eyes with looks full of malice."[25] He recalled their first meeting, at which time he repeated to Holzmann the accusations that had been made against him, namely, that he provoked Mauchamp's murder and that he was anti-French. Holzmann replied, "Sir, I know all that. But since you are here, you can easily find out for yourself. Interrogate the people around you who know all the circumstances of the drama. I had no involvement. You reproach me for being anti-French. Do I reproach you for being anti-German? I love Germany because I owe to it everything that I am. You love your country France for the same reasons, and you don't disdain to serve it."[26]

Some thirty years after the event, Driss bin Minu, the Makhzan officer who broke up the crowd outside Mauchamp's house, also subscribed to the theory that Holzmann incited the attack. According to his recollection, the German doctor had spread the rumor that Mauchamp had raised the French national flag on his roof. Not knowing the difference between the French flag and the white flag that Ibn Minu said Mauchamp had hoisted—a flag that signified simply the presence of a doctor's office—the crowd in its ignorance attacked Mauchamp "as was their wont in those days toward all things foreign."

The Moroccan historian Al-Mukhtar al-Susi, who recorded this conversation with Ibn Minu, cited it as example of yet another instance where European press reports had deviated from the truth. Accordingly, the real culprit of Mauchamp's murder was not the "fanaticism" of the Moroccan crowd, but "foreign intrigue." In reality, however, Ibn Minu's version, in blaming Holzmann, conforms closely to the dominant strain of European reporting of the event.[27]

La Dépêche Marocaine also reprinted another article about Mauchamp that originally had appeared in the *La Courrier du Maroc*, a rival paper launched just weeks earlier. In it Daniel Saurin, *La Courrier*'s editor and a friend of the late doctor, argued that while the murder was not an isolated crime, it was unparalleled in its atrociousness.[28] He heatedly refuted the suggestion that Mauchamp's political activities had somehow contributed to his murder. "This was not an enemy against whom [the mob] set itself, or a spy or a suspected representative of a threatening, armed civilization; the victim, Doctor Mauchamp, was one of the most peaceful soldiers of a beneficial civilization; he represented the science that protects and heals."

In its Wednesday, April 10 issue, *La Dépêche Marocaine* published a short note received from Mauchamp's father. Thanking Rober-Raynaud and Saurin for their words of tribute to his son, the elder Mauchamp echoed their sentiments regarding the nobility of France's civilizing mission in Morocco: "What softens our sufferings is the hope that his blood will not have been spilled in vain, that a French work be founded in Marrakesh and that one day when civilization has penetrated this country, the descendants of those who brutally murdered him will revere his name."

Even Mauchamp posthumously contributed to the creation of his own myth. The Parisian paper *L'Éclair* offered an excerpt of a letter that the doctor had written to his friends about his life in Marrakesh:

> It's a heavy load for a solitary doctor, without a pharmacist, that the government has confided to me in this capital of 100,000 inhabitants. You know perhaps that I arrived there as the first doctor and the first Frenchman, and, apart from my clinic, I had to face a formidable typhus epidemic that, in the aftermath of a murderous famine, killed in five months more than five thousand persons. It's for you to say that I don't have time to get bored here. I am, moreover, very pleased with the result of my mission because, despite first a population charged with hostility and the ill will that I encounter on all sides, especially on the part of the local authorities, I've come to the point where I close the doors of my clinic each morning on a clientele of one hundred to one hundred and fifty patients and I'm obliged to leave shivering at the door a crowd of people whom I can't admit because there are limits to human strength, and I could only obtain them sending me one assistant.[29]

Paris

News of Mauchamp's murder arrived in Paris on March 23, 1907. In addition to dispatching the warships *Lalande* and *Jeanne d'Arc* to Tangier, the cabinet ministers ordered French troops to cross the Algerian border and occupy the Moroccan town of Oujda. To justify this action—in a place far removed from Marrakesh—the council of ministers issued a communiqué. It cited the alleged persistent refusal of the Makhzan to abide by the accords controlling the frontier negotiated in 1901 and 1902 as well as its refusal to repress and indemnify the crimes committed against the French on Moroccan soil.

The occupation of Oujda—to which the Moroccan garrison of the border town acceded without offering the least gesture of defi-

Figure 11. Mauchamp on horseback on the cover of the French weekly *L'Illustration*. Sir Harry Maclean's house in the Jma al-Fna is seen in the top photograph. Reprinted from *L'Illustration*, March 30, 1907.

ance—arguably signaled a definitive change in French policy. For years, the so-called "colonial party" had demanded that France take a more "forward" policy toward Morocco that did not preclude military intervention. Nevertheless, despite the vigor of its response in the wake of Mauchamp's death, the government came under attack in a heated March 26 session of the Chamber. Truculent deputies on the left, including several who knew Mauchamp or his father personally, demanded to know why the government had sent the doctor to Marrakesh with—as they saw it—only minimal support. Why was Mauchamp put in jeopardy in the first place? Other deputies, especially those from the Algerian departments, lambasted the government for what they saw as a dilatory attitude in the face of repeated challenges by both Morocco itself and France's European rivals.

Speaking first, M. Chaussier accused the government of negligence, asserting that it was well-informed in advance of the alleged hostile attitude of Marrakesh's pasha. He was followed by César Trouin, the representative of the Algerian department of Oran that bordered Morocco. Trouin denounced the policy of peaceful penetration and relative restraint that the French government had heretofore demonstrated. "But in acting in this manner, we have committed an act of weakness in the eyes of the natives because the natives recognize neither good will nor generosity. Each time a criminal act is not immediately repressed, it passes for being weak and soft."

Taking the lectern, Ferdinand Dubief, the representative from Mauchamp's own department of Saône-et-Loire, returned to the theme of governmental neglect. To the repeated exclamations of his audience, he read verbatim a long letter he had received from Mauchamp. Writing on October 28, 1906, the doctor had complained in equal measure of the Tangier legation's lack of material support and the hostility of the local Marrakesh authorities, in particular Hajj Abdeslam al-Warzazi. Mauchamp accused the legation of dismissing his complaints as "bluff." In his letter to the politician, Mauchamp had written with prescience and in heroic terms of his own trials and tribulations. "I know well, as Monsieur Clemenceau [the prime minister] said in his recent speech, 'that man, like iron, needs to be forged,' but there is a limit to the tests, and bitterness sickens one in the end. I don't deserve this treatment; my energy and my patience are at an end, however much I tell you that I have both a well-tempered character and will."

Reiterating the theme of the Quai d'Orsay's abandonment of Mauchamp in hostile foreign territory, Dubief spoke of the unsuccessful effort by him and colleagues in the Senate to obtain for Mauchamp a cross of the Legion of Honor. The effort had begun as early as 1902 in the aftermath of Mauchamp's service in Jerusalem. Hearing this, one deputy from the extreme left interjected acidly, "They prefer to decorate cabinet aides and the sons of ministers."

Refusing to blame either Regnault, the current French minister in Tangier, or his subordinates, Dubief condemned the foreign ministry for a pattern of repeated negligence. On four separate occasions in the first quarter of 1906 he had written on Mauchamp's behalf to the foreign ministry and the council of ministers. Moreover, he had—over a period five or six years, beginning with Mauchamp's career in Jerusalem—frequently brought Mauchamp's concerns to the ministry.

His efforts came to naught. The foreign ministry, whose personnel the radical deputy wanted to "republicanize," was allegedly prejudiced against someone like Mauchamp. In his words, Mauchamp was "too much a republican" not to encounter hostility from the Quai d'Orsay.

Against these accusations the foreign minister Stephen Pichon defended himself and the Quai d'Orsay. First, he objected, the charges leveled by Dubief took place before he assumed his appointment, and second, in reviewing Mauchamp's dossier, he maintained that the ministry had indeed been conscientious in its duties, replying to his letters and giving him the utmost consideration.

Pichon read from a letter written a year earlier, on April 7, 1906, by his predecessor in the ministry, Léon Bourgeois. The letter referred to the contretemps Mauchamp experienced on arriving in Marrakesh that concerned the house earmarked for the French military mission. Bourgeois wrote that he had directed the legation to aid Mauchamp in finding other suitable housing. The letter also made mention that—despite the fact that Mauchamp did not take up his post till November of the preceding year—he began receiving his salary from the first of June, when he first received his appointment. Bourgeois concluded his letter by attesting to the high opinion his department and its agents in Morocco held of the doctor.

Pichon added that in January, as part of an aid appropriation of six hundred thousand francs, Regnault had applied for substantial credits to expand Mauchamp's clinic into a hospital. Pichon said he had authorized the credits at once and that he had approved an order for additional matériel as well. Finally, Pichon said that on December 26, at the request of Deputy Ferdinand Sarrien, he had instructed Regnault to examine Mauchamp's record with an eye to his candidacy for the cross of the Legion of Honor. The previous foreign minister, Bourgeois, had ordered the same at the request of Senator Gillot and Deputy Dubief.

Pichon blamed Mauchamp's death on the failure of the governor of Marrakesh to send in troops in a timely manner, and he reminded his listeners that this attack was only one in a series of humiliations suffered by France in the course of the preceding year. His long litany included the murder in February 1906 of two French customs agents along the Moroccan-Algerian frontier, the harassment of Algerian subjects in Oujda by authorities there, and the wounding of a Frenchman in May of 1906. He cited various infractions of the 1901 accords: some tribal groups had attempted to cut off movement between Algeria and Morocco, while the Oulad Djérir tribe, accorded to France under the accords, had moved far from their allotted territories. In October the minister in Tangier lodged a series of formal protests that, Pichon insisted, were ignored. "Our ultimatums, which only followed purely defensive measures on our part, had no other result but to increase the insolence of the Makhzan in our regard." The more serious incidents, Pichon insisted, were the recent attacks on French nationals. He cited the murder of Charbonnier in Tangier in May 1906 and the attack on Lassallas the previous fall.

From the bench, a deputy shouted, "You should take a lesson from the history of the government of Charles X." The allusion needed no explanation. In an altercation with the French minister, the Turkish ruler of Algiers had struck the diplomat with a flywhisk. The 1830 invasion of Algeria by the French was intended, ostensibly, to redress the insult.

Pichon continued his "enumeration of griefs" against the Moroccan government. Members of a hydrographic research mission organized by the Morocco Committee were fired upon by tribesmen from the Bani Hassem. The consul from Rabat was menaced by Moroccan soldiers and turned away from the town of Mehebya. The researcher Edmond Doutté was allegedly harassed by the governor of Marrakesh and denied permission to enter territory controlled by the *qaid* Al-Madani al-Glawi. Added to these slights to French honor was Makhzan support for the Mauritanian rebel leader Ma al-Aynayn.

Pichon conceded that earlier protests to the Makhzan had borne few results. Hence the rationale for a more robust policy. The occupation of Oujda would be maintained indefinitely until all of the French government's demands were met. And these demands were numerous. They not just included indemnification for Mauchamp's death and the attacks on the other French nationals but took into consideration a whole list of alleged claims and abuses going back for years. The frontier accords of 1901 and 1902 were to be put into effect at once. The police and customs were to be reorganized in accordance with the agreements of the Algeciras conference. Moreover, the French demanded that Moroccan support for the armed struggle against the French in Mauritania and Adrar province be withdrawn.

The occupation of Oujda indisputably represented a new tactic on the part of the French. Nevertheless, Pichon—in deference to the deputies on the extreme left—argued that it did not reflect a change in French policy. This was a "policy absolutely free from any idea of conquering Morocco, a policy resolutely hostile to territorial encroachment," but a policy that nonetheless would protect the life and rights of French nationals. "I cannot repeat it enough: the occupation of Oujda is in essence provisional; it will last up to the day we have obtained satisfaction and the reparations which we have the right to demand."[30]

In calling for unity behind the government's policy, Pichon resorted to the lofty rhetoric of the Third Republic and concluded by evoking Mauchamp's memory. "Thus our unfortunate compatriot will have rendered a final service in sacrificing his noble life—after already having dedicated it—to a cause which ought to unite us all, that of peace, the union of the races, civilization and brotherhood."

The foreign minister was followed in the tribune by Alexandre Ribot, the leader of the Progressists, as the moderate Republicans were called. Though the policy of peaceful penetration commended itself as a policy to everyone, he argued that at a moment when "fanaticism" was aroused in Morocco, it was hardly the time to undertake "a peaceful conquest by an imprudent penetration."[31] He furthermore criticized the measure taken by the government in sending Dr. Mauchamp to a city where there was no French consular officer and where he could not be adequately protected. And yet despite these criticisms, Ribot urged his colleagues to support a resolution backing the government's policy. The order of the day in support of the government's policy in Morocco passed unanimously.

Notably silent in this particular debate was the socialist leader Jean Jaurès. Although staunchly opposed to unilateral French action in Morocco, Jaurès understood that Mauchamp's tragic murder posed a risk of dividing his followers.[32]

Meanwhile, the French ambassador in Tangier, Regnault, cleverly sought to disarm whatever socialist opposition there might have been to the French government's action in Oujda. He did this by first orchestrating and then advertising a demonstration of solidarity on behalf of the government's policy by the incipient French labor movement in Morocco. On the morning of March 26, he wrote to the minister of foreign affairs that the "Union of French Workers in Morocco, which counts more than one hundred members, presented itself en masse to the legation this morning to protest the attacks committed against the French in Morocco and which remained unpunished."[33] Later, Pichon would cite in the chamber a motion passed on August 3 by the same union calling for French intervention in Morocco. What he neglected to tell his listeners was that the text of the resolution was dictated by Saint-Aulaire, the French chargé d'affaires in Tangier.[34]

Adieu to Morocco

In Tangier, on the afternoon of April 2, 1907, a small crowd gathered on the wharf for Mauchamp's final obsequies on Moroccan soil. As they watched from shore, a detail of thirty officers and seamen ceremoniously transferred Mauchamp's remains from the *Lalande* to its landing boat. This boat in turn was towed to shore by a steam-powered launch sent out from the destroyer *Jeanne d'Arc*. Finally, set on the wharf in a wagon, the coffin was soon engulfed in a mound of floral wreaths presented by the different delegations, all topped by a large tricolor band. A detail of French marines from the *Jeanne d'Arc* as well as fifty soldiers of the Makhzan stood guard.

On learning of Mauchamp's death two weeks earlier, Regnault had dispatched the cruiser *Lalande* to Mazagan to transport his remains to Tangier. Draped in a French flag, the coffin occupied a place of honor on the bow of the French warship. Set beneath an impromptu chapel decorated with the French tricolors, it was guarded by an honor guard of four marines.

Regnault and members of the French legation, members of the medical community, and other representatives of the French colony arrived at 3:30 PM. The sultan's deputy in Tangier, the elderly Muhammad al-Turris, did not attend but sent in his place as official representatives his son Ahmad and an aide. "It is to be remarked

Figure 12. The French minister to Morocco, Eugène Regnault, delivering a dockside eulogy for Mauchamp in Tangier. Reprinted from *L'Illustration,* April 13, 1907.

that, as at Mazagan so at Tangier, the Moorish authorities did their utmost to mark their sense of the gravity of the situation," the British minister noted, "the approaches to the wharf being lined by a considerable body of infantry."[35]

In light of the efforts exerted by the Makhzan to honor the dead Frenchman, one can only wonder at what Ahmad al-Turris and the other Moroccan officials made of the French minister's remarks.[36] After praising the young doctor's humanitarian efforts in Morocco and recounting his career up to the moment of his death, Regnault asked rhetorically why the people of Marrakesh, "giddy with fanaticism" and "obeying a sort of savage instinct," should have struck out against someone whose only crime was to know how to ease their sufferings. In attacking Mauchamp, the people of Marrakesh were no doubt attempting to "destroy the civilization of which he was in their eyes the living symbol." Regnault went on to explain:

We know, Messieurs, that the evolution of peoples cannot be accomplished without setbacks nor without victims. Among men, it is the best, the most useful, who merit distinction and who mark themselves for the blow of the barbarians. Without a doubt it is costly to lose a productive and beneficial intelligence like that of Mauchamp, but sacrifices, even the most cruel, never cause ideas to retreat.

Instead of pursuing a tranquil life at home, Mauchamp preferred the dangers of life abroad, "dominated by a noble ambition to serve his country in serving humanity." Regnault recounted for his audience the French claims that had been made to the Moroccan government, and he emphasized the French determination that a hospital commemorating Mauchamp be built in Marrakesh. Beyond recalling the crime, the hospital would "affirm our persistent and strong desire to introduce civilization into this barbaric land."

Following Regnault, the businessman Benjamin Braunschvig, described as the dean of the French colony in Morocco, spoke. Standing before Mauchamp's coffin, he recalled the death of Charbonnier, the young Frenchman who had been murdered while riding on the beach just outside of Tangier the previous year. In contrast to the earlier murder, which took place in an isolated spot, the most recent crime took place in full view, in the midst of the country's southern capital, in the very neighborhood where the victim lived. Citing mounting insecurity and the growing number of attacks, especially those directed against Frenchmen, Braunschvig expressed his conviction that the French government would take energetic measures to ensure the safety of its nationals. He used the occasion of Mauchamp's death to appeal to all nationalities in Morocco to put aside their rivalries. All were equally exposed to the dangers of fanaticism. "In the end, may this precious French blood yet again spilled so prematurely sow on Moroccan soil the beneficial work of civilization."

Following Braunschvig and speaking last as the representative of the medical corps was Dr. Spivacoff. Again reviewing Mauchamp's record of service, he noted with tragic irony: "The matériel for the native hospital obtained by Mauchamp is en route for Marrakesh, and Mauchamp, alas, a cadaver, is en route for France."

Placed on the launch of the *Jeanne d'Arc*, Mauchamp's coffin was delivered to the *Moulouya* for the voyage to Marseille. Fifteen cannon shots sounded from the *Jeanne d'Arc* in the harbor. The battery of the Tangier customs house replied with seventeen shots. In the words of *La Dépêche Marocaine*, "Moroccan soil salutes in its turn the remains of one who died in the service of Morocco."

8
Negotiations

Tangier

A quarter century after his departure, Georges Saint-René Taillandier wrote a memoir of his five years as France's minister to Morocco.[1] Saint-René Taillandier left Morocco in 1906, soon after Mauchamp's arrival. His tenure coincided with such notable events as the granting of major French loans to Morocco, the visit of the German kaiser Wilhelm II to Tangier, and the fateful Algeciras conference.

In his memoirs Saint-René Taillandier recalled with fondness the Moroccans with whom he dealt. First of all, there was the foreign minister, Abd al-Karim bin Sulayman. His quaint-sounding Moroccan title, "the minister of the sea," stemmed from the earlier corsair era, when negotiations with the European powers invariably dealt with the exchange of captives. Ibn Sulayman was a man in his fifties with a serious, expressive face. "His character, his simple and courtly dignity, his good grace quick to smile, worked in his favor from the start." Ibn Sulayman descended from an old Andalusian family and had a reputation for Islamic learning and knowledge of the Koran. Thus his approach to foreign affairs, described by Saint-René Taillandier as fanaticism, came as no surprise. "At its root, his policy was inspired by a constant idea: to withhold Moroccan Islam from the menacing grasp of the infidel, who was equally detestable no matter what the particular name of his nation."[2]

Working alongside Ibn Sulayman were his two aides, Ibn Nasir Ghannam and Muhammad al-Ghibbas. As Saint-René Taillandier could not refrain from commenting, both were "of pure white race." Ghannam was distinguished by his commanding presence and good appearance as well as "the impassiveness of his face with its large, regular features." Al-Ghibbas had a "keenly strong intelligence."

Saint-René Taillandier neglected to mention that al-Ghibbas was also educated in England, sent as a young man to study at the Royal School of Military Engineering in Chatham.[3]

Most European diplomats, however, had little personal contact with Ibn Sulayman, the Moroccan foreign minister, for the simple reason that the foreign minister resided in Fez as a member of the sultan's court. Instead, Saint-René Taillandier, along with all the other foreign envoys to the sultan, lived in Tangier, where, for more than a century, the Makhzan required foreign ambassadors to reside.[4] Styled the Dar al-Niaba in Arabic, or the House of Delegates, Tangier was Morocco's de facto diplomatic capital. But the advantage of the city's proximity to Europe, just across the Straits of Gibraltar, was offset by its distance from Fez, Marrakesh, or wherever else the sultan happened to be. A further source of frustration for European diplomats was the fact that the sultan's representative in Tangier with whom they routinely interacted had no authority to make policy. As the quintessential intermediary, the *naib*, or delegate, had only one responsibility—to convey information.

For decades that delegate was Si Muhammad al-Turris. From a prominent family in Tetuan, al-Turris began his career as a customs official and eventually became governor of Casablanca. As a young boy he had, uniquely for a Muslim, attended the Alliance Israélite school and as a consequence had at the least the rudiments of a Western education.[5] By the time Saint-René Taillandier and his successor Regnault arrived in Morocco, al-Turris was already in his eighties. His house, where he received the members of the diplomatic corps, was known—like the city itself—as the Dar al-Niaba. Located on a crowded, steep *madina* street, sandwiched between the Friday mosque and a Catholic parish maintained by Spanish Capuchin monks, the building can be easily overlooked. Today, the former seat of diplomacy serves less gloriously as a neighborhood office of the municipal government.

Saint-René Taillandier remembered his first visit. "Having been led by a *makhzani* into a miniscule room decorated with mosaics, furnished with divans, always opened onto a small patio full of silence, we soon saw arrive a small, elderly gent leaning on a long cane. The beautiful arrangement of his white linen robes, the whiteness of his long beard, the plump freshness of his hue wherein two small black eyes burned, made one think of a jolly Santa Claus from our childhood stories."[6]

Moroccan diplomats such as Abd al-Karim bin Sulayman and Muhammad al-Turris were at a perpetual disadvantage in their dealings with European diplomats. Over the second half of the nineteenth century a succession of treaties and conferences had opened Morocco to international trade. They also extended the pernicious protection system, thereby eroding Moroccan sovereignty and drastically reducing state revenues. Morocco's rulers had little alternative but to accede to European demands. And, as if the disastrous wars against France in 1844 and Spain in 1860 were not reminders enough, the European powers and the United States frequently sent naval squadrons to Tangier and other harbors to refresh the Moroccan memory.[7] If Turkey was the "sick man of Europe," Morocco was the "sick man of the Western Mediterranean," holding on to its last shred of dignity largely because the European states could not decide which one of them would deliver the coup de grace.

Over time, the real seat of power was no longer Marrakech or Fez but Tangier. There, as one Moroccan historian has observed with no small amount of bitterness, the foreign "legations would dictate their demands, burden the courts, demand the recall of governors and even judges hostile to foreigners and their protégés, demand expeditions against the tribes that were blamed and collectively held responsible for the interception of caravans, couriers, etc."[8] In Tangier, the foreign ministers acted as if they were founding veritable "states within the state." The Europeans worked through the Moroccan government, and thus the Moroccan government became an instrument of its own enslavement.

The Makhzan sought to mitigate the imbalance of power, but its efforts had unintended consequences. Confining diplomats to Tangier was designed to keep the Europeans at a distance and in theory to allow the Makhzan control over the flow of information. But the lack of clear channels of communication and the differences in protocol in fact meant that a few individual Europeans had privileged access to and inordinate influence over the sultan. Moreover, the Makhzan never set up permanent embassies in any of the European capitals. Instead, it preferred, much like the Ottoman court through most of its long history, to send special envoys to Europe whenever there were treaties or loans to be negotiated.

Without prompt access to accurate information, the Moroccans time and again found themselves caught off guard by events. Mauchamp's death is a case in point. On March 19, the night of

Mauchamp's death, the governor of Marrakesh dispatched a letter to Tangier. Unfortunately for Muhammad al-Turris, the letter failed to arrive before a meeting of the diplomatic representatives scheduled for Sunday morning, March 24, took place. Thus al-Turris learned of the death of the French doctor only when Regnault, the French minister, failed to attend the routine meeting.[9] Al-Turris then sent his deputies, his son Hajj Ahmad and Ibn Nasir Ghannam, to Regnault, ostensibly to offer condolences for "the incident" (as the Moroccan authorities quickly took to calling the murder) but also to seek additional details. Regnault had little to offer. He had just learned of the event himself from the French vice-consul in El-Jadida.

All this was dutifully reported to the Moroccan foreign minister in Fez, Abd al-Karim bin Sulayman, but it is clear from the minister's response written on March 27 that he too had little information to add. He simply noted that the sultan had ordered Moulay Hafid and Hajj Abdeslam al-Warzazi to conduct an investigation. They were to be especially attentive to the reasons, both "hidden" and "apparent," for Mauchamp's death.[10]

On the very day that Ibn Sulayman wrote to al-Turris, al-Turris dispatched to Ibn Sulayman an urgent letter. Telegrams had just arrived in Tangier with word that the French president had ordered the governor in Algiers to send troops to occupy Oujda until all the demands made in regard to the Mauchamp case be met. This was "mind-boggling" news, al-Turris wrote, and he sent his deputies to seek additional information from the German ambassador. The latter indeed confirmed the news, based on what the Austrian ambassador had heard from the French ambassador.[11] Meanwhile, on Friday, March 29, Ibn Sulayman wrote to inform al-Turris of what was now rumored in Fez—that the French had ordered the occupation of Oujda.[12]

The occupation of Oujda was only one of many rumors circulating in Fez. Indeed, to the Makhzan a French action against the town on the Algerian border seemed less likely than an attempted occupation of the coastal port of Essaouira. This was, after all, the closest coastal city to Marrakesh. The sultan Abdelaziz wrote a detailed letter to the governor of Essaouira, Abd al-Rahman Bargash, to warn him that French warships had been outfitted and were heading in his direction. In response, the governor was to make contact with the *qaid*s of the various tribes in the vicinity of the city and to assemble their men outside the city to mount a resistance against the

French if required. Having so many unruly tribesman assembled in one place in itself posed a risk, and the sultan elaborated steps to be taken to protect Essaouira's *madina* and *mellah*.[13]

The potential of Essaouira being sacked by tribesmen actually frightened the governor far more than the prospect of a French landing. In a long letter to Tangier, Bargash recounted in detail the gory sacking of Essaouira some sixty years earlier.The following week, certainly to the governor's relief, the order to assemble the tribes was rescinded.[14]

In the end, the French chose to occupy Oujda not out of concern for Moroccan sensibilities but because of European politics. "The temporary occupation of Oujda," a French official told the British ambassador in Paris, was "the course the least likely to entangle them in complications with other Powers, the town in question being at a safe distance from any European Colonies." A bombardment of Essaouira, on the other hand, would only result in European claims of damage.[15]

Al-Turris monitored developments as best he could from Tangier. On March 29 the translator in the German embassy informed him that his embassy had received a telegram from the German consul in Oran saying that French troops from Tilimsan had set out for Oujda. The translator also denied a report in *La Dépêche Marocaine* that Germany backed the French action. Germany's response, he claimed, was to acknowledge France's right and to say that Morocco's sultan would not prevent what was France's due. Similarly, the source asserted that England was not in agreement with France.[16]

Perhaps al-Turris took comfort in the views expressed by the German embassy's translator, believing that Germany and England would protect Morocco from any outright military aggression from France. French troops, after all, had crossed the border before, in 1901, and more or less occupied Oujda in support of the Makhzan's efforts to defeat the rebel Abu Amama.[17] Was there any reason to expect that this occupation was not a temporary affair, as indeed the French insisted?

For his part, Ibn Sulayman, the foreign minister, wrote from Fez giving his assurances. The occupation of Oujda was a special case and would end soon. He instructed al-Turris to send a telegram to *qaid* Abd al-Rahman bin Abd al-Sadiq and the officers of the small garrison of Moroccan troops stationed in Oujda. They were to remain steady and calm.

Oujda

Sitting in distant Fez, it was easy for Ibn Sulayman to counsel caution and patience. The view from Oujda itself was another story. Writing urgently to Tangier on March 28, the unsuspecting governor of Oujda, Ahmad bin Karrum al-Jaburi, noted the strange behavior of the Europeans living in the city's *qasba*. Led by Captain Mougin of the frontier section of the French military mission, the Europeans, both men and women, had all mounted their horses the previous day and departed the city without a word. The captain was later spotted, along with another French soldier, galloping on horseback at a fast clip. Neither had any baggage with him except for a box in the French captain's possession. What puzzled Ibn Karrum most was that the French officer normally informed the governor of his destination and schedule whenever he set out. And what caused further anxiety among the city's populace were rumors that across the border in Algeria, the French governor of Muqniyya had—for reasons still unknown to Ibn Karrum—gathered the Arab tribesmen of his region into a *mahalla*. This was the term Moroccans used to describe an impromptu and overwhelmingly large army, in most cases an expeditionary force assembled by the sultan as a goad to collecting taxes, but here meaning something just as ominous.

But before he could send his letter to al-Turris, more news came. In a hastily scribbled postscript Ibn Karrum added that he had just learned of the French intention to enter Oujda. He dutifully informed the town's notables. Later, in a second note scribbled in the margin, Ibn Karrum says that the French had sent the *qaid* of the Bani Bu Said tribe to inform him that they were entering Oujda on account of the European killed in Marrakesh. He was told that the French army would camp outside the city, where it would remain until the sultan negotiated the matter. "If we meet them with gunpowder," Ibn Karrum wrote, "they will flatten the city."[18]

Ibn Karrum had fallen for the French bluff. From Paris, Reginald Lister, the British ambassador, reported that "it had been decided to employ a considerable force in the occupation of Oujda, in order to obviate any possible mishap, and to impress the Arab mind."[19] The next day, March 29, Ibn Karrum rode out at dawn to greet Colonel Félineau at the head of his troops. Resigned to the "inevitable," Ibn Karrum assured the French colonel that, despite the differences between their two governments, he would cooperate fully with French authorities.

General Lyautey, who oversaw the operation, did not arrive till later that afternoon. As he put it in a telegram to Paris the following day, "the population, assured in advance of our intentions . . . had no impulse to resist."[20] In reporting to his superiors in Paris, the French general emphasized the fact that Ibn Karrum personally led the delegation that came out to meet the advancing troops. This was a sign, he wrote, of the Moroccan commander's alleged dissatisfaction with the Makhzan.[21] As the Tangier English-language paper *Al-Moghreb al-Aksa* later noted drily, the Moroccan soldiers' salaries were in arrears, and the Oujda garrison was already depleted from desertions.[22]

Ibn Karrum was not, as Lyautey imagined, disloyal to the sultan. He was merely being pragmatic. Later that day, Ibn Karrum sent a despondent note to his brother Qasim. "The French forces overwhelmed us so much so that there was no end to it, on the order of one hundred and fifty infantry and one hundred and twenty cavalry, with artillery and staff. . . . Right now they are in command of the city and our hopes have narrowed."[23]

From the very moment Muhammad al-Turris in Tangier learned on March 27 of the French resolution to occupy Oujda, the impoverished state of the eastern city's garrison weighed heavily on his mind. In a flurry of letters to various Makhzan military and financial officials, al-Turris sought to expedite sending to Oujda the 40,810 riyals and the supplies of semolina that had been earmarked for the garrison even before the emergence of the present crisis.[24] The problem, he wrote four days later to the foreign minister in Fez, was that the seas were too rough to entrust the shipment by boat. As a consequence, he still had not sent the money when news of the catastrophe in Oujda arrived. Now he feared that the Oujda garrison might have dispersed. He inquired as to the sultan's orders. In the interim, the money remained with him. And lastly, he had dispatched a message by steamship to the military authorities in the Oujda region.[25]

On April 2, an impatient Ibn Sulayman wrote back to al-Turris, saying that the sultan had already written to him once and there had been no reply. He ordered al-Turris to send a telegram to the government forces if he had not already done so. He was to assure the troops that their provisions and salaries were on the way and that the French occupation would soon come to an end. Finally, Ibn Sulayman stressed the importance of keeping Fez up-to-date on the status of the Oujda garrison.[26]

Writing to Ibn Sulayman on April 8, al-Turris was at last able to report that the long-promised provisions and payroll had been sent to Oujda by the Makhzan's steamer *Al-Saidi*. As soon as the steamer returned to port, he would forward to the minister news about the garrison.[27] Nevertheless, there were no grounds for optimism. Exasperated and unnamed Moroccan officers in Oujda wrote to the minister of war, complaining about the dire state of the garrison.[28] They noted that upon entering Oujda the French had summoned all the officials and leading men of the city to inquire about their function and rank. Despite orders not to divulge information, many Moroccan soldiers had met with the French invaders. Dejectedly, the officers noted that even these interrogations were not necessary as the French already had this intelligence from their spies.

Only one artillery officer, someone named Si Abd al-Salam al-Qarqur, complied with the Makhzan's order and held back the men under his command. The French gave the unit a couple of days' respite and then returned with threats to withhold rations from the Moroccans if they did not surrender to French command. The French expectation was that the local customs house, which served as the military bursar as well as the customs, would swindle the Moroccan troops from their ration. Out of desperation and hunger, the French authorities reasoned, the Moroccan troops would have nowhere else to turn.

Al-Qarqur's unit still refused, the men saying they needed nothing and that they would not accept a single dirham from the French except upon the order of the sultan. Biding their time, the French left al-Qarqur in charge of the hundred or so men that remained in the garrison. Not long after, the French quarrelled with him, and eventually they took over the daily distribution of rations from the customs house. "That's what led to the command of our army by them, and we had not enough strength to prevent it," the officers concluded.

The officers struck a plaintive note. Unless steps were taken, perhaps every soldier in the army would enter into French service. The French had other means of coercion as well. Another officer, al-Hajj Ali al-Bamrani, was threatened with imprisonment unless he turned his thirteen soldiers over to al-Qarqur's command.

The officers called on the minister of war to take direct control of the customs house and supervise the distribution of rations. They further recommended withdrawing the Moroccan forces from Oujda, removing them to the other side of the wadi outside the city, and taking the necessary steps to ensure future provisioning on a regular basis. The customs house, they said, had continued since the arrival of the French to collect import duties but had neglected its other responsibilities vis-à-vis the army. In fact, the customs officers were sitting on the money deposited with it. They asked that the minister bring this state of affairs to the attention of the sultan.

In their letter of complaint the officers implied that customs officials were in active collusion with the French occupiers. This was not universally the case. One customs agent wrote to Muhammad al-Turris to complain that the French had assigned a French supervisor to the customs house who interfered with its work, permitting the entrance of some taxable items and excluding others.[29]

Only weeks later did the sultan Abdelaziz finally respond to the officers' lament. Writing to Muhammad al-Turris in mid-May, he noted that the French commander in Oujda was interrogating his troops, distributing rations and salaries, and promoting officers. He instructed Muhammad al-Turris to take the matter up with the French minister in Tangier and have the French commander desist from interfering with the Moroccan army.[30]

The sultan and his officials were justifiably upset. Local administration of Oujda and the surrounding countryside came increasingly under French control. Nevertheless, the Makhzan was in no position to do anything other than have the elderly Muhammad al-Turris in Tangier recite his politely worded protests. The local garrison was already exhausted. The Makhzan troops were incapable of mounting any credible display of force. They had already demonstrated this in their long, inconclusive struggle against Abu Amama, a supporter of the pretender Abu Himara, the so-called Rogui. Indeed, the flimsy military apparatus of the Makhzan would be further strained later that year as Casablanca too came under French occupation and Moulay Hafid mounted his challenge to the throne.

Meanwhile, in Oujda itself, Moroccan officials believed the assurances disingenuously provided by Lyautey—and reinforced by the Makhzan—that the French occupation would be temporary. Thus, only a day after the arrival of the French, a "secret" society of neighborhood headmen and local Makhzan officials met to assess the situation. In the presence of the local notaries they affirmed their loyalty to the sultan and patriotically agreed to keep the wheels of government turning until the time, as they believed, that the Germans would come to their aid and expel the French. They anticipated it would be only a matter of weeks or months at most.

For his part, the French minister of war had ordered Lyautey to avoid, as much as possible, substituting his authority for that of local officials.[31] Nevertheless, a wide array of municipal services—chief among them public safety, the levying of duties, sanitation, water distribution, and regulation of newly installed lighting—quickly came under French military control. Each morning at the customs house, Martinot, the French translator, briefed the Moroccans on the tasks of the day. The governor, Ibn Karrum, meanwhile, continued to write despairingly to Muhammad al-Turris in Tangier.[32]

The citizens of Oujda grew resigned to the growing French presence. Lyautey, meanwhile, eagerly looked for an excuse to extend his authority beyond the city limits—in spite of instructions to the contrary from the foreign ministry. He soon found it. In the mountains beyond the city, the Bani Snassen tribesmen began to mount a credible resistance. In April, French forces seized the Moroccan post at Ajrud (Qasba al-Saidiyya) on the pretext that the Makhzan troops, whose orders were to fight the Rogui, were in fact giving support to the Bani Snassen. Within three months, the Bani Snassen were subdued, and by the end of the year the entire region of Oujda was under French control.[33]

Left in charge of Oujda, Colonel Félineau routinely wired reports of his progress to Lyautey, who remained installed across the Algerian border in Oran. Lyautey in turn represented the begrudging cooperation provided by the local Makhzan officials in Oujda as vindication of his policy of association. In the future French Protectorate, of which Lyautey would be the first resident general and principal architect, a Moroccan veneer would mask the French colonial apparatus. The occupation of Oujda was the harbinger of things to come.

The Sultan's Warning

On April 2, while Mauchamp's coffin was being loaded aboard the *Moulouya* for the journey to the other side of the Mediterranean, the sultan Abdelaziz set his scribes in Fez the task of copying out a letter to be dispatched to governors and tribal *qaids* throughout the country.[34] Somewhere between two and three thousand people also heard the letter read publicly the next day in the Qarawiyyin mosque in Fez. Almost all were "of the less respectable class," the British consul in Fez observed, "the quietest inhabitants keeping away, in case of a disturbance. There was a good deal of jeering at the Moorish Government, and, in regard to the occupation of Oujdah [*sic*], mutterings to the effect that such things did not happen in Mulai-al-Hassan's [*sic*] time were to be heard very generally."[35]

The sultan's letter laid out the details—as the Makhzan understood them at that moment—of Mauchamp's murder and the French retaliatory action in Oujda.

> A French doctor who was residing in Marrakesh hoisted a flag on his residence, thus inciting the rabble and they killed him. Prior to this another Frenchman was wounded in Tekna; similarly in Tangier another leading Frenchman was killed; and in Fez another was wounded. When this news reached the French government, it became agitated and furious on account of these incidents perpetrated by the recklessness of the rabble which neither recognizes the virtue of peace and tranquility nor considers the consequences of strife.

The sultan further accused the "rabble" of not recognizing the benefits of his undertaking truce negotiations and pursuing a policy of defense vis-à-vis the French. By recourse to just means, he asserted, the Makhzan was capable of lifting whatever created the confusion without causing further harm. Meanwhile, in their exasperation the French had occupied Oujda militarily as a means of securing justice in the cases cited above as well as in other areas where they had rights and claims. The French had tied their withdrawal from Oujda to the execution of these conditions; their occupation was temporary, intended only for the purpose of seeking indemnities.

"Therefore," the sultan explained, "we are being painstaking in our performance of the terms, doing whatever renders what is correct in this matter, and we are striving to arrange a solution releasing us from this so that their army will depart Oujda with God's aid."

The sultan explained that he was going to the utmost lengths to avoid further embroilments, and he affirmed that he was taking steps to resolve matters in the most peaceful and least arbitrary manner. He concluded his pronouncement with a warning to his subjects: "Do not lay a hand on anyone, no matter what the situation. And do not let fear grab hold of you and anxiety frighten you. For indeed, with God's help, we are striving in this matter and are arriving at a remedy so that they will leave in peace. Therefore, cease your worry and put your mind at ease because we are not sparing any of our money or men in striving for your protection and defense."[36]

Intended for Moroccan public consumption, Abdelaziz's proclamation could not fail to catch the attention of the Europeans. The British ambassador garnered his initial account of the letter from a variety of sources, including an oral version given by the sultan himself to his personal physician Dr. Verdon and then transmitted by the British doctor to the embassy in confidence. However, efforts by the British to obtain a copy of the official text from the Makhzan were thwarted. In his report, the British ambassador noted the Makhzan's "evasions" and commented on the "shifty language" of Ibn Sulayman and the grand vizier Gharnit.

It is difficult to see any reason for Ibn Sulayman's alleged evasiveness in this regard, but tactically it was a mistake for the foreign minister not to release the actual text of the letter. The French version, which appeared the following week in *La Dépêche Marocaine,* and subsequently in other newspapers, significantly deviated from the Arabic text.[37] Instead of blaming the "rabble" for Mauchamp's death, the French version had Abdelaziz single out the people of Marrakesh. The recent events, the paper had the sultan say, were the "fault" of the people who had not followed his orders.[38] Editorially, the paper commented that the Makhzan made abundant promises in the matter of reparations, but predicted that these would be "very slight in reality."

On the day the sultan's letter was read in the Qarawiyyin mosque in Fez, an unidentified member of the court there ("My name is not hidden from you," he signed his letter) wrote in secret to the sultan's brother Moulay Hafid in Marrakesh. His brief report was pessimistic. The French had occupied Oujda and had anchored twelve warships, he said, in the harbor of Tangier. The sultan's letter explained the reality of the situation. The Makhzan was constrained from any positive action until the French left Oujda. Meanwhile, he wrote, the people in Fez were increasingly agitated and displeased.[39]

Initially, Moroccans in Fez were afraid that the occupation of Oujda might be a prelude to a French march on their city. When this fear proved unwarranted, the occupation had a different effect, at least according to Henri Gaillard, the French consul. Writing three weeks after the occupation, he noted that the merchants of Fez had received only positive news regarding the French occupation of Oujda. "Not only have the inhabitants of Oujda not suffered any violence, but the French occupation, in giving a new boost to commerce, has inaugurated a period of prosperity and security. They make much of the fact that, having put aside the Makhzan officials, the French governor has paid them as well as the soldiers back wages."

Gaillard contrasted this state of affairs with the local situation in Fez, in which tradesmen and soldiers had gone without pay for weeks.[40] Other consular reports indicate that most Moroccans, to the extent that they knew of the occupation, seemed to take the news calmly. The British minister in Tangier, Gerard Lowther, wrote that obviously "the fact that a Moorish town is now in the hands of the French cannot be a pleasing fact to Moors at large." However, he reckoned that "the ill-feeling is directed rather against the Makhzan, and especially against the Tazzi group [*sic*], for their mismanagement of the affairs of the Government in general than against foreigners."[41] British officials had long maintained that the Tazi brothers, who held key financial posts in the Makhzan, were hostile to Britain and therefore pro-France.

At a minimum the sultan's letter succeeded in placating some Makhzan functionaries. One *qaid*, Muhammad al-Buzgawi, had earlier written to al-Turris on April 4 to offer his hypothesis regarding the French military action. France's real intent, he maintained, was to cut off the garrison's provisions as a prelude to the permanent annexation of Oujda. Using metaphorical language, he advised Muhammad al-Turris to warn the sultan. "It's no secret to you, o lover, that the cause of our expulsion from our lands is the encounter with the seductive adulterer, may God destroy him."[42] And yet three weeks later, the very same *qaid* wrote to Abdelaziz to acknowledge receipt of his circular letter and to say how the sultan's words had allayed his fears.[43] Another group of notables from the Zakrawi tribe similarly wrote to the sultan, expressing in the most profuse terms their confidence in his judgment.[44]

Not everyone shared the Makhzan's nervous and unwarranted optimism. One popular poet published a long poem in Fez later that year, at a time when armed resistance to the French was mounting in various corners of Morocco. He encouraged his readers to remember the events in Oujda: "O Islam, weep upon the intrusion in Oujda, taken as booty by the enemy without a fight, learn the lesson."[45] And another anonymous poet wrote a formal elegy for the fallen city:

> Woe upon Oujda, that surrendered impatiently
> Without a sword, without a death, without a fight.
> Woe upon the lions of Islam who failed,
> Overcome by the outrages of Rome, most amazing.[46]

A Free Press

The Moroccan government was not insensitive to public opinion. On April 2, Abd al-Karim bin Sulayman, the Moroccan foreign minister, assembled the consular representatives in Fez. Explaining the Moroccan position vis-à-vis the French occupation of Oujda, he advised the consuls that their nationals show caution and prudence. He predicted that the sultan's letter, to be read publicly the following day, was likely to stir up a temporary commotion. And he concluded his talk by waving a copy of *La Dépêche Marocaine*, complaining that the account of the occupation of Oujda that the paper had printed in Arabic as well as in French "would be very apt to inflame Moorish feeling hereabouts, and especially would tend to enrage natives against the Government."[47] As it was a French paper, the French representative said he would do his best to restrict the paper's circulation among Moroccans.

A month later Muhammad al-Turris in Tangier would complain again to Regnault about the French press. The version of Mauchamp's death and the occupation of Oujda that appeared in the French newspapers, he charged, ran counter to the facts. To this charge, the French ambassador simply replied "that the newspapers have freedom of speech." Al-Turris reported this answer without elaboration to Abdelaziz.[48]

In turn, al-Turris charged his aide Muhammad al-Muqri with the task of asking the British minister, Lowther, to restrain the English press. As he explained it, according to Lowther, "His Majesty [Abdelaziz] was much concerned the adverse criticism which appeared in the English Press of himself and his Government and these being reproduced in local Arabic papers and believed by the ignorant natives, added very much to his difficulty in governing at a moment when he required all the support he could obtain."

Like Regnault, Lowther lectured al-Muqri on the virtues of a free press. "All interference on my part with the Press was out of the question and he should explain to His Majesty, if this was necessary, that the Press in Great Britain had full liberty to criticize not only foreign Governments but our own as well."

In particular, al-Muqri complained of the coverage in the London *Times*. Since al-Muqri knew the *Times* correspondent Walter Harris personally, Lowther suggested that al-Muqri ask Harris himself to "insert a correction." And noting that the local English paper, *Al-Moghreb al-Aksa*, "usually commented in a very favourable manner" toward the Makhzan, "the Moorish Government could perhaps put these articles in their Arabic papers as an antidote to the *Times* reports."

What al-Muqri, al-Turris, or Abdelaziz thought of this principle of "freedom of the press" we can only imagine. In any event it appeared to Lowther that al-Muqri "merely desired of being able to report to his master that he had carried out his instructions and did not expect his Mission to bear fruit."[49]

Gerard Lowther, the British minister in Tangier, seconded the prevailing view that the French occupation of Oujda could only weaken the position of the sultan, who was seen as being under the influence of his courtiers and in particular the brothers Muhammad and Umar al-Tazi. For whatever reason, he observed, Ibn Sulayman and other Moroccan officials pretended to treat the matter "merely as a case or claim, to be settled in the usual course of things."[50]

Lowther informed al-Turris that the British government agreed with the French demands in respect to Mauchamp and hoped that the Moroccan government "would concede them with a good grace." Al-Turris replied that the Moroccan government had no choice but to comply with French demands and that in his opinion Mauchamp had brought this fate upon himself "by the inconsiderate way in which he aroused the fury of the mob."

The Europeans should look on the bright side, al-Turris told Lowther. "It was a matter for congratulation that the matter was not much more serious, as for fully seven years past the Makhzan has been most feeble, and would have been quite unable to maintain order had the necessity ever arisen for a show of authority, and that it was only due to the common sense of the people that other incidents had not arisen."[51]

Shuffle Diplomacy

In announcing the action in Oujda to the deputies in the French chamber on March 26, the foreign minister, Stephen Pichon, alluded to the claims being brought against the Moroccan government. Two days later Regnault, the French minister in Tangier, met with Muhammad al-Turris. In the presence of the commanders of the *Jeanne-d'Arc* and the *Lalande*, which lay in harbor ostensibly to protect French nationals, Regnault instructed his interpreter, Si Kaddour ben Ghabrit, to inform the sultan's delegate in Tangier of the French demands.[52]

The name of Regnault's dragoman or interpreter, Ben Ghabrit, appears frequently in accounts of the time. Always a controversial figure, he was both despised and admired by the Frenchmen who met him.[53] Although he often claimed Tlemcen as his place of origin, Ben Ghabrit was born in 1873 in Sidi bel Abbès, a colonial town near to Oran in Algeria. Quite possibly his father was a government employee.[54] Alternatively Ben Ghabrit may have been one of the many Algerian-born Muslims who had taken refuge from the French in Morocco.[55] What led Ben Ghabrit to have a change of heart toward Algeria's colonial occupiers—if this is indeed the case—is not clear, but eventually he found employment as an interpreter for the French legation in Tangier.

Gaining the confidence of his French employers, he assumed increasingly more important diplomatic duties.[56] A turning point seems to have been when he accompanied the chargé d'affaires at the time, le Comte de Saint-Aulaire, on his mission to Fez to negotiate the 1904 French loan. "Our Benjamin in age," the French diplomat Saint-Aulaire later wrote of the younger man, "he was our Nestor in wisdom and in his profound knowledge of things Moroccan. An incomparable liaison with the Makhzan as well as the administrative and religious authorities of the country, he performed tasks far above his grade."[57]

Among his other accomplishments Ben Ghabrit earned a footnote in the history of Francophone literature by being the first North African to write plays in French to be performed in Morocco.[58] He also opened a Franco-Arabic school for Muslim students in Tangier—to the minor consternation of the Alliance Israélite Universelle director there, who saw the new school as a potential competitor.[59] In 1906 he was part of the French delegation to the multilateral Algeciras conference that played an important role in deciding Morocco's fate. Over the next decade he was constantly on the move between Fez and Paris, helping to conduct the negotiations that surrounded the establishment of the French Protectorate over Morocco.

Saint-Aulaire describes the excitement that swept through the Tangier legation when Ben Ghabrit, in his white flowing *jallaba* and turban, entered the building: "We quit our files to group around him and learn the latest news. I don't know how: he knew the mysteries of the Makhzan as well as any minister; he knew them better. . . . I called him my 'trumpcard'; Madame Saint-René Taillandier called him our 'passkey.' He opened for us all doors, with the least indiscretion."[60]

Saint-Aulaire and others also marveled at the fluidity with which Ben Ghabrit could move between two cultures. Madame Saint-René Taillandier spoke of him as being "bicephalous," two-headed, equally at ease among French diplomats and Muslim clerics. In her memoirs, the former ambassador's wife writes that she once asked Ben Ghabit how he managed to "pull it off," having "one head to think 'French,' the other to think 'Islam' and to translate between the one and the other."

"He laughed," she writes, "'Whatever you might think, *que voulez-vous*, Madame, I was born Algerian and French; for me, there's only one.'"[61]

Ben Ghabrit's devotion to France was well rewarded. During the early years of the Protectorate Ben Ghabrit formed close ties with the resident general, Lyautey, who appointed him director of protocol to the sultan Moulay Youssef. Ben Ghabrit also played an important role in the 1916 French mission to the Hijaz, where he represented France in discussions with Sharif Husayn of Mecca.[62] Renowned as "the most Parisian of Muslims," he later served for three decades until his death in 1954 as the rector of the Paris mosque that he helped create. During World War II he helped French Jews escape German-occupied Paris by allowing them to access the Parisian sewers through the mosque grounds, an episode celebrated in Derri Berkani's French documentary, *A Forgotten Resistance: The Paris Mosque, 1940–44.*[63]

The message Ben Ghabrit delivered to the elderly al-Turris on March 28 was forwarded in a strongly worded and more detailed written version to the Moroccan foreign minister Ibn Sulayman in Fez.[64] The list included nine items in all and reflected a potpourri of demands, of which half had nothing to do at all with Mauchamp's murder. By these means the French government showed its determination to assert its will in Morocco, and as with the demands the Austrian government presented to the Serbs on the death of the Archduke Franz Ferdinand, one suspects that there was never any expectation or even desire that the demands be fulfilled.

1. The French demanded the dismissal of the pasha of Marrakesh, Hajj Abdeslam al-Warzazi. The demand had originally been made six months earlier after the attack on Lassallas. This time, however, the French called for the governor's imprisonment in Tangier pending an investigation into his role in inciting the crowd against Mauchamp.

2. The new French consul in Essaouira, Nooman Kouri, was charged with conducting an investigation in Marrakesh "to discover the authors of the crime and establish the role of the authorities." The Makhzan was to provide aid to Kouri in his mission, including a military escort.

3. The individuals guilty in the attack on Mauchamp were to be punished. "My government," the French minister wrote, "reserves for itself, moreover, the right to set the punishments."

4. The French demanded indemnities for Mauchamp's family and—as the late doctor had been charged with an official mission—to the French government. The exact sums were to be determined later, but they would be used for the establishment of a hospital in Mauchamp's memory in Marrakesh. The French communication observed that the "shameful crime commited against a benefactor" by the population of Marrakesh followed other incidents, namely the murder of Charbonnier in Tangier the preceding year and the attack on Lassallas. The bullying language of Regnault's letter left no doubt that the French held the Makhzan accountable: "The blamable inertia of the authorities demonstrates the state of anarchy which exists in the country and the dangerous excitations spread in the native milieux. . . . [France] will no longer tolerate the tergiversations and endless delays used to hold off the execution of reforms to which His Majesty has agreed."

5. The French minister accused the Makhzan of delaying discussions for the reorganization of the port police, one of the reforms specified by the Act of Algerciras. This was despite the fact that the Moroccan minister of war—supposedly delegated with the power to conduct these negotiations—was at present in Tangier.

6. The French demanded the full enactment of the 1901 and 1902 accords on the Algerian frontier, specifically the establishment of a force to police the border. Having failed to receive a satisfactory response to letters that he had written back in October, Regnault said that the French government had decided to act on its own.[65]

7. The French accused the Moroccans of supporting an armed rebellion against the French in Mauritania and the Adrar region of the Sahara. Regnault demanded that Mawlay Idris, an uncle of the sultan Abdelaziz, be recalled from his mission to the insurgents and officially disavowed.

8. The French called on the Makhzan to stop supplying the Mauritanian shaykh Ma al-Aynayn with weapons to fight the French.

9. Regnault referred to a detailed list of outstanding French claims submitted earlier to the Makhzan by the French consul in Fez, called for their settlement, and blamed the Moroccan authorites for creating a climate hostile to French citizens. Unwilling to tolerate the situation any longer, Regnault concluded, the French troops would continue to occupy the city of Oujda until such time as all reparations were fulfilled and the police were organized in conformity with the treaty agreements.

Eager to see an end to the occupation of Oujda, Ibn Sulayman responded quickly. First he communicated in person to the French consul, Gaillard, in Fez the Makhzan's intent to comply fully with the French demands. Later he wrote to Regnault. In his letter, Ibn Sulayman took pains to explain the Moroccan perception of the state of affairs. The sultan, he said, was greatly aggrieved by the event in Marrakesh and had, even before receiving Regnault's letter, given orders for the arrest of those responsible and for the removal of the governor of Marrakesh ("even though," he added, "no reason has yet been established against him for relieving him"). He then outlined to Regnault the version of events as relayed to him by the governor, Hajj Abdeslam al-Warzazi, saying that the governor's actions had prevented the matter from becoming even more grave. As al-Warzazi was ill, the sultan had instructed his son to come in his place to Tangier.[66]

Ibn Sulayman then struck a poignant note when he observed that the French decision to occupy Oujda, taken without notice and before any claims for indemnification had been made, had come as a complete surprise to the sultan. It was entirely unexpected that the French government seize Oujda *before* presenting its claims.[67] Moreover, he reminded the French government that its action could only increase the instability in the interior of the country and make increasingly difficult the application of the commitments undertaken at the Algeciras conference.

Ibn Sulayman's pleas garnered no sympathy from the French. Writing to Pichon on April 9, Regnault recounted his understanding of the events in Marrakesh. Whereas he blamed al-Warzazi in particular for inadequately protecting Mauchamp, he held the Makhzan accountable for fomenting a climate hostile to Europeans in Morocco. During the previous past two years, Regnault claimed, the Makhzan encouraged "troublemakers" and "deeply tainted the prestige which Europeans enjoyed in Morocco until now." He continued: "The scandalous impunity accorded all the fanatics who have attacked our compatriots nearly daily has done the rest. Supposing itself sheltered from all reprisals on our part, the Makhzan believed itself invulnerable. The energetic attitude of the government of the Republic will reestablish respect for French name in Morocco."[68]

Having made their demands, the French would brook no compromise. When a delegation consisting of Muhammad al-Turris and his aides Ghannam and al-Muqri called on Regnault on April 9, the French minister rebuffed them. There was nothing to talk about, he told them, until he received a letter from Ibn Sulayman accepting all the French demands.[69]

Another long letter from Ibn Sulayman, dated April 20, 1907, addressed each of the demands set out by the French. Full of remonstrations of the Makhzan's good intentions, the letter did little to placate Regnault. Specifically, Regnault took exception with a Moroccan plan to send its own troops under Moroccan command to police the Algerian frontier. The Moroccans saw this move simply as a means of putting into effect existing agreements and belatedly reasserting its sovereignty over the border following the French occupation of Oujda. The French argued that this was a new development not provided for by the border agreement worked out between the two countries in 1901–1902.

The Makhzan proposal called for sending to Oujda the palace chamberlain and former governor of Oujda, Driss bin Ya'ish, to discuss with a French representative questions of border security. According to MacLeod, the British consul in Fez, Ibn Ya'ish was implacably anti-French and the chief architect of the policy of supporting Ma al-Aynayn's resistance in the Sahara.

In diplomatic exchanges with the French the Makhzan insisted that Ibn Ya'ish have a military escort befitting his rank as the Moroccan representative. In making this demand the foreign minister Ibn Sulayman understood fully well the symbolic importance of having Moroccan troops ride into the occupied city. However, Ibn Ya'ish was himself reluctant to take up his new assignment. From his perspective he saw it as a tactic by the rival Tazi faction at court to have him removed from Fez.[70] As troubles in the south of Morocco increased that spring, Ibn Ya'ish successfully thwarted the Tazi efforts to push him out of the way, and his mission to Oujda was abandoned. Considered the principal intermediary between the sultan and the tribal *qaid*s, Ibn Ya'ish would be indispensable should Abdelaziz decide to mount a campaign in the south.[71]

The second issue concerned a Moroccan proposal to establish a joint commission to determine the border in the southern Adrar region and to decide which tribes came under French jurisdiction and which came under Moroccan. As Regnault noted, "This is the first time that the Makhzan officially claimed right to the tribes neighboring our possessions in western Africa."

As for the Mauchamp affair, Ibn Sulayman again refused to send the ailing Hajj Abdeslam al-Warzazi, the ailing governor of Marrakesh, to Tangier. Instead he offered to send in his place the governor's son, along with the prisoners already arrested. In conversation with Gaillard, the French consul in Fez, Ibn Sulayman explained this as a "question of humanity," and he suggested that the French send a doctor to determine whether al-Warzazi could indeed make the trip to Tangier.[72]

While Ibn Sulayman accepted the proposal for an investigation by the French consul in Essaouira, this seemed unlikely to take place any time soon given the present circumstances. Meanwhile, Regnault wrote to Pichon, "According to my information, the real culprits have not been disturbed." Assessing the text of the Moroccan response, which he deemed deliberately confusing, Regnault concluded that "the Makhzan is showing itself to be less intransigent, but still without giving formal adherence to all the points we demanded."[73]

Finally, despite Ibn Sulayman's denials that the Makhzan was furnishing contraband to the Mauritanian rebels, the French consul in Essaouira reported that weapons ultimately destined for Ma al-Aynayn had arrived on a German freighter and had been transferred, on April 14, to the Spanish ship *Rosario* for transit to the Moroccan post at Cape Juby. The cruiser *Lalande,* fresh from its mission of carrying Mauchamp's corpse to Tangier, was ordered to station itself at Cape Juby to intercept, if possible, any additional arms shipments on Moroccan vessels. In response to a French request, Madrid sent its own cruiser as well, the *Don Alvaro de Bazán,* to intercept any arms shipped on Spanish vessels.[74]

Thus, despite Ibn Sulayman's stated willingness to meet with French demands, Regnault gave Pichon a grim assessment of Moroccan intentions. "The most recent facts of the importation of arms proves that the Makhzan hasn't paid any regard to our protests."[75]

Pichon agreed with Regnault's pessimistic assessment, again affirming that no negotiations would take place until the Makhzan complied with all the demands. He instructed Regnault to be blunt with Ibn Sulayman, telling him that before authorizing the Makhzan's envoy to enter Oujda with an escort, the French were to have copies of the instructions that he carried in order to verify that he was given powers to apply all the protocols established. Moreover, the French rejected the proposition of a joint commission to settle the claims regarding the Adrar region. Finally, Pichon chastised the Moroccans for the alleged shipment of arms at Cape Juby.[76]

English observers such as Gerard Lowther, the British minister in Tangier, offered a more generous interpretation of the Moroccan response. "You will observe that in principle the Makhzan agrees to all the French demands, though it is certain that there will be much delay in carrying them out."[77]

The European powers tended to see in Morocco's dilatory execution of agreements a habitual and deliberate recourse to delay. As preliminary talks over the French claims dragged on, the London *Times* resorted to racial stereotypes, explaining to its readers that "the shifting and temporizing diplomacy of the Orientals has to be reckoned with, even when any of the Great Powers is concerned."[78] A commission meeting at precisely the same time in Tangier to settle the question of the port police as outlined by the Act of Algeciras held twenty-two sessions before arriving at an agreement, a delay attributed to "the vacillating attitude of the Moroccan war minister."[79] And when Ibn Nasir Ghannam, one of the Moroccan representatives assigned to negotiate the claims arising from the Mauchamp affair, resigned his post in June 1907, *Al-Moghreb al-Aksa* noted with tongue-in-cheek that he was "generally admired as one of the ablest circumlocutionists among the local officials, and as a diligent opposer to every useful project which had to go through the Moorish Foreign Office."[80]

Nevertheless, stalling was not always a deliberate tactic by the Makhzan. It could just as well reflect the lassitude of individual officials. Thus, writing a letter to Muhammad al-Turris on April 2 in which he reviewed the French demands, the foreign minister Ibn Sulayman himself expressed dismay that the murderers responsible for Charbonnier's death were still at large a year after the crime. Rumors that the perpetrators came and went freely in Tangier had reached the sultan, and Ibn Sulayman strongly chastised the sultan's representative in Tangier. Given the seriousness of the case, the in-

terest the Makhzan had in solving it, and the agitation it continued
to cause the French, how, the incredulous Ibn Sulayman asked al-
Turris, could he have possibly neglected this matter?[81]

On April 3, the sultan himself dispatched additional instructions
to al-Turris for negotiating with Regnault. While he emphasized that
French demands had to be met in their entirety as a condition for
the French evacuation of Oujda, it was clear that the Makhzan's traditional worry—money—continued to be uppermost in Abdelaziz's
mind. He instructed al-Turris to seek yet another loan from the
French along the lines of earlier loans. Moreover, al-Turris was to
seek the advice of the German minister and make an appeal for
some kind of third-party intervention regarding both the question of
Oujda and the new issue of a loan. In pursuing a new loan, he cautioned al-Turris not to make any concessions that would lengthen
the French occupation of Oujda. He left to the elderly statesman
in Tangier the option to pursue whatever option he thought more
obtainable.[82]

Regnault's intransigence resulted in a third, detailed letter from
Ibn Sulayman in early May with even more remonstrations of the
Makhzan's good faith.[83] Finally, on Tuesday afternoon, May 28, *a full
two months* after the French occupation of Oujda, Regnault held his
first conference with the Moroccan delegates, al-Muqri and Ghannam. The meeting lasted three hours. The French minister at last
acknowledged the Moroccan expression of willingness to comply
with France's demands. This admission is ironic. Indeed, the letters
written by Ibn Sulayman to Regnault since the occupation of Oujda
demonstrate that very little, if anything, had changed in the Moroccan position throughout the entire period.

The Substance of Negotiations

Regnault's report of the May 28 meeting to Pichon was relatively
brief. In marked contrast, the two Moroccan negotiators prepared
for al-Turris what was, by Moroccan standards, an unusually detailed summary. Going systematically through each of the French
demands in the order that they were discussed, al-Muqri and Ghannam made certain to indicate where an agreement had been reached
in favor of the Makhzan's position and where a decision had been
deferred to a later session.

Despite its relative length, the tone of the Moroccan document
was businesslike and perfunctory. Regnault's account of the meeting,
on the other hand, shows that he lectured the Moroccans sternly.

Calling for al-Warzazi's immediate replacement, he told the Moroccans they were not to pursue a policy of delay or to use the same "ruse" that he alleged the Makhzan had used earlier in the year in delaying action against the brigand al-Raisuli. Specifically, he insisted that the Makhzan bring al-Warzazi to one of the coastal ports for a doctor's examination and subsequent treatment if he were unable to be transferred to Tangier.

As to al-Warzazi's replacement, both sides agreed upon Kaddour bel Ghazi. Considered a strong man by the Makhzan, Bel Ghazi concurrently held the post of governor of both Tangier and Tetuan. Despite a "reputation of being fanatical and ill-disposed toward foreigners," he had a track record of imposing law-and-order on lawless tribes.[84]

Regarding the Mauchamp affair specifically, the negotiators discussed in passing the question of erecting and financing a hospital in Mauchamp's memory as a means of indemnifying the French government. Regnault was still waiting to hear from Mauchamp's mother, the Moroccans reported, regarding the amount of the indemnity owed the doctor's family.[85] By the time negotiations were finally completed, the sultan Abdelaziz had agreed to the French proposal to build a hospital in lieu of an indemnity. The indemnity (the Moroccans used the word *diya,* or blood money) was set at one hundred thousand francs for the doctor's life, with an additional forty thousand francs for property damage. The Moroccan government also agreed to finance its operation with fifteen thousand francs to be paid annually by the Makhzan or derived from *hubus,* or specially earmarked religious foundation funds.[86] The importance attached to Mauchamp's person can be gauged by the fact that the indemnity in the death of Charbonnier, the young bank employee murdered in Tangier, was set at forty thousand francs. Dead Frenchman did not come cheap: the indemnity demanded for Mauchamp was a hundred times the amount typically paid by Moroccan Berbers in the case of murder.[87]

In addition to the indemnity, Regnault insisted that Mauchamp's murderer, once in custody, be put to death. Specifically, Regnault held the headman of the Arsa Moulay Musa quarter responsible and blamed al-Warzazi for allowing him to flee the city. Regnault also initially demanded the death penalty for the two black slaves charged with being the principal attackers of Gironcourt in Fez. The Moroccans in their turn asked for a five-year prison term. The parties finally agreed to ten-year sentences for the slaves, with a possibility of parole at the end of three. Moreover, the French minister demanded that the convicted men be publicly chastised in the name of the sultan in the presence of the *qaid* of the palace, the local governor, the French consul, and the chiefs and notables of the various quarters of Fez. Regnault first demanded the public chastisement be held in the sultan's palace itself.[88] Here too a compromise was reached. The Makhzan argued for a lesser venue, the palace of Abu Ali al-Muhdar, to which Regnault agreed only on the condition that the palace *qaid* himself be in attendance.

The Moroccan negotiators disagreed with Regnault in the case of the Charbonnier murder as well. Apart from demanding that the Moroccans underwrite the erection of a bronze statue in Tangier of the murdered bank clerk, Regnault called for the execution of five Moroccans whom he held responsible for the murder. Al-Muqri and Ghannam insisted there were only two murderers, one of whom was already in custody and the other of whom they expected to capture soon. The Moroccans agreed to underwrite Charbonnier's statue and also acceded to Regnault's request that the French legation's interpreter, Ben Ghabrit, be present during the second prisoner's interrogation.

The Makhzan's concern for the fate of the prisoners in the Gironcourt and Lassallas attacks typified the dilemma that the Moroccans faced in negotiating with the French. On the one hand, they sought to resist efforts by the French to dictate the fate of Moroccan subjects. On the other hand, they felt compelled to satisfy French demands for justice as quickly as possible, taking France's assurances at face value that their troops would soon vacate Oujda.

In wanting to believe that the French would indeed vacate Oujda, the Makhzan officials were not alone. The British ambassador to Berlin, F. C. Lascelles, similarly expressed confidence in the French policy. Soon after the French entered Oujda, he told Heinrich von Tschirschky, the German foreign minister, that he "did not see any reason to doubt the assurance which the French Government had given that the occupation of Ujda [*sic*] would be merely temporary. It surely could not be to the interests of France to create a situation in Morocco which might lead to complications with other countries."[89]

As Regnault finally sat down to talk with al-Turris, more than two months after Lyautey's troops entered Oujda, the London *Times* likewise expressed optimism in regard to the French policy. "The patience and tact which have characterized the treatment on the part of France of the Marrakesh incident have met with their reward," its Paris correspondent wrote. "Even the Sultan of Morocco has shown his appreciation of French forbearance."[90]

On June 4, Ibn Sulayman penned yet another letter to Regnault, this time expressing gratitude that the French had finally agreed to commence negotiations necessary for the evacuation of troops from Oujda. Again he insisted that the Makhzan had every intention of satisfying the French demands. Even Saint-Aulaire, who wrote the cover letter to Pichon in Regnault's absence, was forced to concede that "the delays which we will have to submit are from now on less imputable to bad will than to the powerlessness of the Moroccan government."[91]

Honor and Vengeance

The protracted negotiations over reparations and the putative withdrawal of French forces from Oujda reflect the enormously difficult and strained relationship that existed between the French diplomats and the Moroccans. The French held all the cards. All that was left for al-Muqri and Ghannam to negotiate were the terms of Makhzan compliance.

European observers naturally blamed the Moroccan negotiators for frequent delays and temporizing. A century after the event, the temptation is strong to reinterpret the drawn-out talks as a deliberate subterfuge by the Moroccans, the kind of *passive resistance* that colonized peoples have engaged in historically throughout the world.[92] But the evidence suggests otherwise. Far from obstructing progress, the Moroccans quickly and repeatedly conceded to French demands. Indeed, the pragmatic Ibn Sulayman, characterized by Saint-René Taillandier as "fanatically" Muslim in his approach, was gracious to a fault. Regnault, on the other hand, displayed a biblical "hardening of the heart" and scarcely budged.

As the Oujda negotiations demonstrated, the overwhelming disparity in power between the French and the Moroccans was obvious to everyone. Nevertheless, in the context of their interactions as a whole, each side faced the other convinced of its own moral superiority. Moroccans were buoyed by their religious identity as Muslims, recipients of the Lord's final dispensation. French diplomats, meanwhile, adhered to the positivist dogmas of the early twentieth century. Their faith in Western civilization and Europe's forward march into the future was not yet shaken by the slaughter of the impending Great War.

Cultural misapprehension accompanied the French colonial adventure from the start. In the case of Mauchamp, despite his five years in Jerusalem and his alleged expertise in the Moroccan mentality, the ill-fated French doctor showed virtually no appreciation for Muslim sensibilities. Six months after the event, Christian Houel visited the scene of Mauchamp's death in Marrakesh. There a score of people recounted the same story. "Everyone agreed in attributing the reasons [for the murder] to a curious tendency in Mauchamp's character to defy or fail to recognize the susceptibilities of the populace."[93]

Conspicuous in Marrakesh in his European attire, Mauchamp suffered one final indignity after his death when the soldiers sent by Moulay Hafid solicitously clothed his mutilated corpse in a *jallaba*. For Mauchamp his Western costume was a point of honor, a symbol of his identity as a European. In this regard, it is instructive to contrast the French depiction of Mauchamp with that of his rival Holzmann. The French portrayal of Holzmann hinges on the malleability of the latter's identity. Simultaneously a Jew, a Syrian, a German, a "so-called doctor," a convert to Islam, and a renegade, the chameleon-like Holzmann was by definition Mauchamp's inferior—and hence, not a man of honor.

In the context of the Mauchamp affair, the French obsession with honor was played out on many levels, both public and private. In its dealings with the Makhzan, France maintained that the satisfaction of its demands was a point of honor. Honor also played a role in France's rivalry with the other European powers as they jostled for influence in Morocco. In the French chamber, deputies debated the question of whether France should "internationalize" the response to Mauchamp's death (in accordance with the Act of Algeciras) or reserve the right to act independently. This was as much a debate over how one redresses a slight as a discussion of foreign policy.[94]

Whose rules applied? Those of the French or those of the Moroccans? At the 1905 Algeciras conference the Makhzan tried to play by France's rules and to give at least an outward adherence to European codes of honor. Given the unfavorable outcome of the conference from the Moroccan standpoint, Morocco's effort to be recognized as an "equal" obviously backfired. Yet despite this failure, one can credit the Act of Algeciras with at least giving Morocco "a special status" that ultimately preserved the germ of national sovereignty.[95]

Meanwhile, the French search for "honorable" interlocutors operated at several levels simultaneously. Despite his avowed republicanism, Mauchamp deliberately courted the local elite in Marrakesh, whom he believed to be models for social emulation by the lower classes. Perhaps unconsciously, Mauchamp anticipated that Moroccan society would adhere to the pattern of nineteenth-century Europe. There a rising bourgeoisie adopted the "chivalrous" manners of the aristocrats whom they sought to replace. If the European model held true, ordinary Moroccans would eventually emulate their social superiors. Thus, if the *qaids* brought their wives to Mauchamp for treatment, he reasoned, sooner or later the ordinary Moroccan would, too.

Mauchamp, of course, was not alone in gravitating toward the powerful *qaids*. The subsequent policy of Lyautey, for example, gave a prominent role to the grand *seigneurs* of the south such as Thami al-Glawi, who served as governor of Marrakesh throughout the length of the Protectorate. While one can interpret Lyautey's approach as an expression of the resident general's aristocratic sensibilities, the structure of nineteenth- and early-twentieth-century Moroccan society in fact offered French policymakers few alternatives. On the lookout for intermediaries through which to rule, the French naturally settled on the existing notables, whether they were tribal *qaids* or the bureaucrats of the Makhzan.

In more ways than one, Mauchamp's experience embodied the homogenizing and universalist impulse at the heart of the French civilizing mission. On the one hand, Moroccans had to play by European rules. On the other hand, one sees time and again Mauchamp's own inability to accommodate to Moroccan culture. His few attempts to negotiate local cultural byways are staggeringly awkward. Consider Mauchamp's importation of an Arabian hunting falcon for a Berber *qaid* and later the Beauvais rug intended for Moulay Hafid. On the surface, the innocent gift-giving might seem to be an accommodation to North African customs, but the very choice of items belies Mauchamp's prejudices: Given its provenance, an Arabian falcon is inherently superior to any indigenous variety, while the rug demonstrates that even at the level of "local" handicrafts French products are superior. The falcon, Mauchamp wrote to his father, had been promised to the *qaid* Aissa bin Umar al-Abdi by earlier French travelers in the area. Mauchamp undertook the task of acquiring the birds as a point of honor to demonstrate that one could trust the word of a Frenchman.[96]

What gave Mauchamp the keenest sense of affront was his belief that the Moroccans had rebuffed his greatest "gift," his medicine;

hence his resentment against the sorcerer's magic, which he saw as the antithesis of his own science. While Mauchamp correctly characterizes some Moroccan magic as "aggressive," his preoccupation with its technique blinds him to its underlying conceptual basis. The notion of the *'ar* curse, which arguably had the same force in contemporary Morocco as the code of honor had among the bourgeoisie in France prior to World War I, escaped him entirely. "The word *'ar* literally means 'shame,'" according to his Finnish contemporary, the groundbreaking anthropologist Edward Westermarck, "but in Morocco it is used to denote an act which intrinsically implies the transference of a conditional curse for the purpose of compelling somebody to grant a request." In practical terms, the *'ar* worked much as a contract, stipulating conditions and specifying consequences in the absence of their fulfilment.[97]

As much as a demand for the satisfaction of French honor, French conditions for the retreat from Oujda could well be interpreted as a European variety of *'ar* or, better yet, an *'ar* in reverse. Moroccans typically invoked the *'ar* from a position of weakness and not, as in the case here of the French, from strength. Shame after all is the flipside of honor. One appeals to another's sense of shame when that person exhibits disrespect. Ibn Sulayman's response to Regnault must be seen in this light when he pointed out how unexpected it was that the French government would first seize Oujda and only later present its claims. In other words, from the Moroccan perspective, the French government had not played by the rules when it acted preemptively.

Perceived by his contemporaries as a weak sultan, Abdelaziz found himself in an increasingly paradoxical position. His dependence on European military and financial support eventually undermined his legitimacy in the eyes of the Moroccan population. The standard argument that Abdelaziz acceded to French claims following Mauchamp's death simply because he had no alternative is largely true. Nevertheless, one can also argue that the sultan acceded to French demands from a sense of moral obligation. Makhzan correspondence routinely uses the word *diya,* or blood money, to refer to the indemnity demanded by the French. Similarly, Moroccan documents describe French efforts to redress their grievances as seeking *insaf,* justice. In short, the French appeal to honor did not fall on deaf ears, and Abdelaziz responded with the *noblesse* expected of him.

The French reciprocated in kind. In October 1907, after presenting his credentials in Rabat as the French ambassador, Eugène Regnault bestowed on the sultan Abdelaziz the *grand cordon* of the Legion of Honor. As one might imagine, Moroccans had no notion of European decorations. Among his uncomprehending Muslim subjects, the rumor circulated that the sultan had in fact been baptized.[98]

The question of honor—that is, the competing and differing self-representations of the French and the Moroccans—suggests that a more complex range of cultural relations existed during the colonial period than is often assumed. Considered from the French side, we see honor's multidirectional trajectory, its recapitulation from the individual (someone like Mauchamp) through the group (in this case, the professional collectivity of French physicians) and a class (the provincial *bonne bourgeoisie*) to the Third Republic as a whole.[99]

In the end, Abdelaziz's efforts to deal with the death of the French doctor Mauchamp encountered little sympathy among the bulk of his countrymen. To them the sultan's "honorable" response of agreeing to French demands for *insaf,* justice, was only further proof of just how weak and malleable he was in the face of European pressure.

9

The Crisis of the Month

The Usual Suspects

While Moroccan negotiators in Tangier engaged in "tergiversation," as Regnault put it, justice spun its wheels in Marrakesh. Under pressure to arrest Mauchamp's murderers, Hajj Abdeslam al-Warzazi, first apprehended two men. One, identified as being from the Misfiwa tribe, admitted to hitting Mauchamp in the head; another was accused of striking the doctor "left and right" with an iron implement. Their affidavits and additional inquiries in turn implicated eight others for either the assault or the looting of the French doctor's house.[1] The names of these ten men, with the notable exception of an unfamiliar deaf-mute, were duly recorded.[2]

Although it renders the names somewhat differently, a French list compiled after the arrival of the prisoners in Tangier on June 30, 1907, provides additional information about the individuals' origins and occupations. Two were listed as sellers of vegetable, charcoal, and wood, two as grain weighers, two as carpenters, one as a bread seller, and another simply as a worker. One prisoner, who protested his innocence, described himself as a farmer and water carrier who happened to be in Marrakesh that day purchasing seeds. The deaf mute, whose identify remained unknown, was apprehended while engaged working with sheepskins.[3] None of the subsequent official correspondence, however, indicates which of the ten were the two men formally accused of committing the murder. And, as French diplomats noted, conspicuously missing from the list of those apprehended was the headman of the Arsa Moulay Musa quarter whom they held responsible for instigating the crowd.

Observing the case from afar in Tangier, Europeans soon concluded that the prisoners were mere scapegoats who were rounded up "while [the] real culprits have been allowed to go free." In either case, as the British minister Gerard Lowther noted, the Makhzan faced disagreeable alternatives: "It would have an equally bad effect if innocent persons were punished for the murder of a Frenchman, or if prisoners declared by the Makhzan authorities to be the criminals were allowed to go free."[4]

Under attack for his alleged role in the crime, the governor, Hajj Abdeslam al-Warzazi, washed his hands of the case and transferred the ten prisoners to Moulay Hafid, the sultan's brother and viceroy. In the interim Abdclaziz issued orders in early April for the prisoners to be shipped by way of El-Jadida to Tangier. There Muhammad al-Turris was to make the case for life imprisonment should the French demand the death penalty. If the French were unwilling to compromise, then the two considered to be the actual murderers were to be hanged—but only in Tangier, where, presumably, the execution would create less of a stir.[5]

In Marrakesh, however, the arrest of the prisoners had already created a ruckus. Most of the ten prisoners were members of the Rahamna tribe. The rioters' rural origin is a point worth noting. As in the shoemakers' revolt that had threatened the *mellah* in 1904 or the "strange panic" that had seized Essaouira's Jews in 1906 or Mauchamp's passing encounter with the blue men, the principal actors were not "real" city dwellers. In terms of its perpetrators urban violence was not exclusively or even characteristically urban. When violence got out of hand, the urban bourgeoisie stood the most to lose.

On April 28, the same day al-Warzazi handed the prisoners to Moulay Hafid, the governor received a letter from the Rahamna tribesmen—many of whom were in town for the *mawlid,* or birthday of the Prophet Muhammad.[6] The tribesmen threatened to attack the town if their demands were not met. Besides the release of the prisoners, they demanded the expulsion of all foreigners and the enforcement of a variety of restrictions on Jews. Jews were not to ride saddled donkeys or wear shoes when passing Muslims in the street, regulations that had existed in the past but were now tacitly ignored. A letter stating similar demands was sent to Moulay Hafid.[7]

The English-paper *Al-Moghreb al-Aksa* reported that the Rahamna and other tribes of the Haouz region surrounding Marrakesh were also demanding that al-Warzazi be retained in office. Significantly, the physically ill and politically beleaguered governor himself makes no mention of this in his correspondence to the sultan. "They say," the paper also reported, seizing the point to goad the French, "that Kaid Warzazi [sic], being one of the few honest officials in the country, must be retained in his post for the convenience of the people."

Writing to Paris to say that he and his colleagues were now afraid to remain in Marrakesh, the Alliance director Falcon noted that the Rahamna demands also included forbidding the French consul from coming to Marrakesh, ending all duties paid on goods brought in from the countryside, and suppressing the city guard.[8] For his part al-Warzazi would have none of the Rahamna demands, replying point blank that "he had never heard such stupidity." He would inform the sultan of their disloyalty, he told them. Intimidated by al-Warzazi's threat, some of the Rahamna contritely appeared before him to pronounce their loyalty to the sultan. A decade earlier Abdelaziz (or rather, his regent Ba Ahmad) had brutally repressed a Rahamna revolt, and the memory was still fresh. Undaunted, yet another group decided to press their case with Moulay Hafid.

Moulay Hafid dealt carefully with the Rahamna at a late-night meeting attended by many of the city's notables, including the market inspector, several of the customs agents, and al-Warzazi's two sons. The city's notables took the easy way out. They would take no responsibility in the matter, arguing that it was the sultan, not they, who had given the foreigners permission to live in Marrakesh.[9]

Moulay Hafid sought to placate and divide the Rahamna by acquiescing to some demands and temporizing on others. He agreed to the restrictions on the Jews and sent word to Hajj Abdeslam al-Warzazi to disband the two-hundred-man auxiliary police force that the governor had established two weeks earlier. However, on the central question of the prisoners' release, Moulay Hafid refused to capitulate. Instead he dispersed fifteen thousand riyals from the treasury to secure the loyalty of the Rahamna.[10]

Writing to his brother Abdelaziz, the sultan, Moulay Hafid said that the payments only partially worked. Most of the Rahamna left the city, and the fear of an attack had subsided. However, a small, intransigent group of the Rahamna leadership remained, and Moulay Hafid claimed that an unnamed group of notables continued to provoke them by paying them dirhams and offering to aid them in the release of the prisoners. These leaders of the Rahamna, he said, refused further negotiations until Moulay Hafid released the prisoners. For his part, the viceroy assured his brother that he would not give in to their demand. Unless he received an order otherwise, he promised to resist to the point of death. The letter concluded with assurances that everyone was doing what he could to carry out the sultan's intentions.[11]

It was a curious letter, especially coming from a man whom everyone suspected of plotting the overthrow of his brother. "It is thought," wrote Lennox, the British vice-consul in Marrakesh, "that [Moulay Hafid] has instructed the Rehamna [sic] how to act, either with the view of keeping Bel Ghazi from coming or to test the Government in Fez whether they have any authority and can leave Fez, or to prove to the Government how faithful he is and how hard he is working on their behalf." In any event, Lennox interpreted the actions of Moulay Hafid and the Rahamna as being directed solely against the French. "He told them plainly that if they were successful in their plans, they cannot dispense with the Germans and English."[12]

The following day Lennox met with Moulay Hafid, who reported that the crisis was over. Again affirming his loyalty to his brother, Moulay Hafid assured him that he did not oppose Bel Ghazi's coming to replace al-Warzazi as governor, and he blamed the Europeans for spreading rumors that he wanted to be sultan.[13]

For the time being, British officials remained convinced that Moulay Hafid did not entertain ambitions for the throne.[14] Likewise, the weekly *L'Illustration* informed its readers in France that it was thought unlikely that Moulay Hafid sought to depose his brother. Rather, it was claimed that Hajj Abdeslam al-Warzazi's friends had circulated these audacious rumors in the hope that they would fore-stall the arrival of his replacement, Bel Ghazi.[15]

Nevertheless, the disturbances in southern Morocco were now being reported in the London *Times* and had even become the subject of British parliamentary debate. Reluctantly, and with some concern over whether they could obtain an adequate escort from Moulay Hafid, Lennox and most of the remaining European residents abandoned Marrakesh for the coast.[16] "The feeling against Europeans is so strong," Lennox wrote to Casablanca on May 6, "that if any Europeans were killed in any row in the streets a general rising would be made against all, and it would only be in hiding that we could have any chance of escape."[17]

To his superiors in Paris, Falcon wrote that Corcos, the leader of the Jewish community, had encouraged the French schoolteachers to leave. The continued presence of Europeans endangered the entire *mellah*. In the interim a committee of local Jewish leaders would endeavor to keep the school open. Meanwhile, Hajj Abdeslam al-Warzazi responded to all who came to complain about the lack of security that he was "no longer" the pasha.[18]

Later that summer Falcon would write despairingly from Safi that al-Warzazi was still pasha and that, short of a miracle, nothing seemed likely to change in Marrakesh. Reluctant to leave his school forever in "inexpert hands," Falcon asked the Alliance's central committee to consider closing the school. In his own defense he repeated "that we did not leave Marrakesh out of fear, but solely in the interest of the Task [*l'Oeuvre*] and our coreligionists. I hope that our attitude and my steps before the French minister [Regnault] will—once calm is reestablished in Morocco—have happy results."[19]

On May 7, the Europeans living in Marrakesh met with Moulay Hafid who tried to assure them that everything was again calm. Accepting responsibility for the countryside but not the town, the viceroy nonetheless offered the Europeans guards for their homes and businesses. This offer they turned down. "He says," Lennox reported, "that if we wish to go to the coast for a change it is all right, he will give us an escort, but there is no need to leave for any other cause. He blames Europeans for causing all this by spreading the report that he wishes to become Sultan."[20]

Anxious about their businesses, the Germans, six in all, remained, waiting till they received orders to leave. But their position was by no means secure either. The German merchant Utting had barely escaped being shot a few days earlier. Nonetheless, as Lennox's correspondence circulated around the Foreign Office, a functionary could not help but note on the folder, "It is curious that the Germans should stay on when other foreigners are leaving. They evidently feel confident that the movement, whatever its character or origin, is not directed against them—which is not without significance."[21]

And Holzmann? Having converted to Islam, he assumed the name Si Uthman. With nothing to fear, Mauchamp's erstwhile rival remained in Marrakesh, where he continued on as a member of Moulay Hafid's entourage, much to the chagrin of the French, ever leery of German support for Moulay Hafid.

The journalist Christian Houel, newly arrived in Morocco, first met Holzmann late in 1907 when covering Moulay Hafid's campaign in the south for the Parisian paper *Le Matin*. Years later, in 1912, he encountered the doctor by chance on the street in Fez soon after French troops had occupied the capital. Holzmann, he recalled, was gloating. "What did I tell you . . . that Moulay Hafid would be recognized by the Powers?"

"That's true," Houel replied. "But what you didn't tell me was that the French would also be here."

This was the last time Houel saw Moulay Hafid's physician.[22] Meanwhile, the French government never abandoned its suspicions that Holzmann had complicity in Mauchamp's murder. In this regard Houel himself was questioned in 1914 while serving in the army in France. Houel says he was unconvinced of Holzmann's guilt. Both he and Paul Bouvier, who had been in Marrakesh at the time of Mauchamp's death, gave testimony in Holzmann's favor. Houel speculated that Holzmann, like other suspicious Germans in Morocco, had been arrested, brought to France, and then repatriated to Germany, "serving without doubt, as money of exchange."[23]

A more likely alternative is that Holzmann simply disappeared on his own. Lyautey undertook an investigation into the "pseudo-doctor" in January 1915, and an effort was made in July of that year to track down Mauchamp's former interpreter in Asilah. The available documents do not indicate whether Holzmann was actually in custody or not. In any event, the investigation seems to have failed to establish anything concrete.[24]

The Sideshow in Safi

On May 8, 1907, Bel Ghazi, the former pasha of Tangier and al-Warzazi's designated replacement, disembarked the British ship *Gibel Musa* in the port of Safi with a ragtag force of 350 troops destined for Marrakesh. He was also accompanied by his wives, one of whom gave birth to a baby boy in the course of the short voyage from Tangier. Many observers assumed that his real orders were to arrest Moulay Hafid. Hunot, the British vice-consul in Safi, reported rumors that Moulay Hafid had intercepted letters precisely to that effect.[25]

The Bel Ghazi mission was especially ill-conceived and ill-fated. Writing to Muhammad al-Turris soon after his arrival, Bel Ghazi complained that no provisions had been sent ahead from Tangier for his troops. These would, in any case, be wholly inadequate if he were to meet opposition on his march on Marrakesh.[26] Alarmed at the prospect of having to combat tribesmen all the way to the southern capital, Bel Ghazi dispatched messengers with letters from Abdelaziz to the *qaid* of Safi, Aissa bin Umar al-Abdi, in the hope that Aissa could somehow placate the other unruly tribes. In Tangier,

Al-Moghreb al-Aksa optimistically reported that Bel Ghazi was "preparing a more benevolent feeling among the tribes around Morocco City [i.e., Marrakesh], before venturing there, and it is believed he will succeed now that the effervescence of the first moments is past."[27]

But even Aissa, one the last of the southern *qaids* to remain loyal to Abdelaziz, would soon succumb to the attraction of Moulay Hafid. Barely a month after their arrival in Safi, Bel Ghazi disbanded his tiny, demoralized force. The 350 men on whom the sultan Abdelaziz pinned his hopes boarded ship and returned to Tangier.[28] Bel Ghazi himself meanwhile lingered on till September 11, when, despite efforts by local authorities in the Hafidist camp to prevent it, he and his family boarded the French destroyer *Galilée* for the return trip to Tangier.[29]

The British Assessment

The British assessment of the situation in the south changed materially as spring turned to summer. At first reluctant to believe that Moulay Hafid entertained plans to challenge his brother's hold on the throne, British officials eventually came to see Moulay Hafid's bid to seize the throne as inevitable. Lennox, temporarily taking leave of Marrakesh, arrived in Tangier and met with his superior, Lowther, the British minister. "[Lennox] does not anticipate anything serious in the district until after the harvest, that is in July," Lowther reported to London on May 29, "but that he is convinced in his own mind that nothing can then arrest a very serious movement, unless the Sultan moves from Fez to Rabat and employs the usual methods of showing his authority, namely devastating the country of disloyal tribes."

Lennox offered Lowther an assessment of Moulay Hafid's character and motives that bears repetition at length:

> Although unwilling to believe in Mulai Hafid's [*sic*] disloyalty, as he has always been his friend, Mr. Lennox is now brought to the belief that he is playing for his own hand, and that if the Sultan [Abdelaziz] remains at Fez there can be no doubt of Mulai Hafid's success. Mr. Lennox is convinced that there is no leader amongst the Rehamna [*sic*], and that that tribe, who are not even united, never would have dared to make a movement unless they had received encouragement from the Viceroy. Indeed there seems reason to believe that Mulai Hafid has had a share in the proceeds of the numerous caravan robberies, &tc.

Mulai Hafid has always been considered here as a mild man, fond of reading and of mild pursuits and endowed with no character or energy. Mr. Lennox holds a quite different view of him, and says he is a man of some thirty-five years of age, full of ambition and vigour, and whose one idea is that nothing can be done without fighting. He says he has always declared himself as very anti-French, but has lately received some presents from the French Government for services rendered, and Mr. Lennox does not know what his real feelings may now be. He has probably not yet decided into which channel to direct these feelings. Mr. Lennox attributes the murder of Doctor Mauchamp and the subsequent troubles to the want of energy of the Governor, Hadj Absalom-el-Warzazi [sic]. He described him as a man absolutely loyal, intelligent, and learned, but completely broken down in health and now devoid of all energy; and his son, whom he named as his deputy, seems to lack all the qualities necessary to deal with a turbulent population. The fact that the viceroy [Moulay Hafid] and the Governor [al-Warzazi] were never in accord, Mr. Lennox attributes to the loyalty of the Governor to his Sovereign.[30]

Moulay Hafid, in the meantime, danced gingerly around the Rahamna and the other tribesmen of the Haouz. On June 5, Muhammad bin Abu Bakr Ghanjawi wrote from Marrakesh to Lowther. Abu Bakr was a wealthy and somewhat controversial British protégé. While the French press campaigned violently against him as a British agent, he also managed to earn the mistrust of his English sponsors owing to his reputation as one of Morocco's principal slave traffickers.[31] Despite his faults, he remained a valuable source of information. To MacLeod he reported that about eight hundred Rahamna tribesmen and others were camped in a garden about a half hour from town. Their delegates to Moulay Hafid reiterated earlier demands that "the prisons be emptied of the prisoners, then that the Europeans leave the city, that Jews remove their slippers and not go through the town riding." To these they added a new demand that the townspeople in Marrakesh vacate houses they inhabited that formerly belonged to the tribe.

Abu Bakr judged matters to be "very difficult for Mulai Hafid [sic] and for the townspeople." Having already received his letter of dismissal from the sultan, al-Warzazi reportedly told Moulay Hafid not to expect any cooperation from him: he was merely waiting to turn the keys of the town and the prison over to Bel Ghazi on his arrival. "The townspeople are in great straits," Abu Bakr continued, "as there is no one here to deal with the people—a Governor or any one to take charge of matters—and the Jews and the people of the Foreign Powers are in a difficult position."

Abu Bakr reported that many Muslims, especially the protégés of the European powers, and the Jews would flee Marrakesh if they could. The common people, he reported, said they could no longer support a sultan who dealt with the Europeans. The wealthy Abu Bakr saw this as "merely a pretext to get into the town to pillage." The merchant anticipated unprecedented violence. "Affairs are in God's hand, and there is no one here to be relied upon. . . . The people thought that only Rehamna [sic] was in this, but now they find all the tribes are in concert with them."[32]

According to *Al-Moghreb al-Aksa*, the viceroy met with a delegation of the Rahamna in his palace on the morning of June 9, but the meeting was canceled when one of his daughters fell ill and subsequently died that evening. Chiefs of the various factions met again in Marrakesh two days later but were unable to come to an agreement among themselves. A few days later, Moulay Hafid rode out of Marrakesh to meet with delegates of factions of the Rahamna, Saraghna, Zemran, and other tribes. There they presented him with a written request that he proclaim himself sultan, a request that he declined, but not before the tribesman, threatening to raid the *mellah*, managed to extort the equivalent of $1,200 from the viceroy.[33]

The paper further reported that Moulay Hafid had written to his brother, informing him of the Rahamna's defection and encouraging the sultan to set out from Fez for Marrakesh at once. Meanwhile, the leading *qaid*s of the South, Aissa bin Umar of Safi, Mtouggi, and Goundafi, had warned Moulay Hafid not to intrigue against his brother.

Lowther, the British minister, assessed the situation from his vantage point in Tangier. After dispersing the funds, Moulay Hafid invited the tribes to reassemble fifteen days later. Rahamna support for Moulay Hafid's bid as sultan still seemed tentative. Not all the tribal leaders were united behind the viceroy, and given that they were practically independent at the moment it was "not easy to see what the Viceroy could offer to the tribes in return for their support." Moulay Hafid, meanwhile, was waiting to see if his brother, the sultan Abdelaziz, would leave Fez to mount a campaign in the south. "If he does, Marrakesh will probably remain quiet. If he does not Mulai Hafid [sic] may make a move. In the meanwhile, he will probably periodically have to pay the tribes to keep them quiet."[34]

In June, while Moulay Hafid dealt with the fractious Rahamna in Marrakesh, his brother Abdelaziz ordered his tent to be pitched outside of Fez. Erecting his tent outside the city was an exercise in royal theater and nothing more, a symbolic demonstration that he was planning to set out personally to chastise the unruly southern tribes. Meanwhile, throughout June and July, the two royal brothers engaged in an elaborate charade in which they mutually proclaimed their fidelity to one another. Just as Moulay Hafid eagerly displayed his loyalty to the brother he would soon seek to overthrow, so Abdelaziz, in his correspondence to Moulay Hafid, called his older brother his "chief support."[35] Abdelaziz elaborately proclaimed his gratitude for his attentive handling of the prisoners.[36] He also sent a reassuring letter to Hajj Abdeslam al-Warzazi, praising him for his role in the handling of the Rahamna and ordering that he lock the gates against their return.[37]

Nonetheless, even with the threat of a raid by the Rahamna temporarily gone, fresh reports of general lawlessness in Marrakesh now reached Abdelaziz's ears in Fez. The sultan dispatched a flurry of letters to Moulay Hafid, al-Warzazi, and Ibn Kabbur, the pasha of the *qasba*, demanding that the officials crackdown on crime.[38] Meanwhile, preparations were made for the visit of the French consul, Kouri, to Marrakesh. The sultan seemed anxious to satisfy French demands that the consul conduct an investigation, and he gave detailed instructions to his brother Moulay Hafid regarding which palace in Marrakesh would be suitable for the visiting dignitary.[39]

As for Moulay Hafid, he arranged for the transport of the prisoners to Essaouira on June 15. His assumption was that the consul would come to Marrakesh when Driss bin Minu and the horsemen who had escorted the prisoners to Essaouira returned. This was not the case. Kouri postponed the trip indefinitely, saying it had not yet been approved by his superiors. The agitation of the Rahamna made the roads unsafe. With Abdelaziz unwilling to risk another incident, the foreign minister, Ibn Sulayman, requested that the consul's trip to Marrakesh be delayed.[40]

From his safe distance in Essaouira, Kouri continued his correspondence with Moulay Hafid. As Kouri assured Regnault in Tangier, his relations with Moulay Hafid had always been strongly cordial. There existed a strong foundation of trust, he said, despite the machinations of Holzmann, "who does everything possible to detach him from us."[41] Indeed, Moulay Hafid claimed to admire the Lebanese-born Kouri, going so far as to dedicate a number of his poems to him, and he inquired why Kouri, rather than Regnault, was not appointed French minister to Morocco.[42]

The Transfer of the Prisoners

On June 15, as a further sign of his loyalty to his brother, Moulay Hafid sent the ten prisoners in his custody to Essaouira. Originally ordered to send them to El-Jadida, Moulay Hafid changed the destination on the supposition that Nooman Kouri, now assigned the task of investigating Mauchamp's murder, would want to interrogate the prisoners before transporting them to Tangier.

The prisoners arrived on June 17 in Essaouira, where they had the distinction of being the last prisoners to be lodged in the prison/lazaret on the island in the harbor.[43] Under orders from Moulay Hafid to transfer the prisoners to Tangier on the first available ship, the Essaouira governor, Abd al-Rahman Bargash, then loaded the prisoners on the Spanish vessel *Cartagena* on June 23.[44] A week later they arrived in Tangier. *Al-Moghreb al-Aksa* ruefully observed, "It is to be hoped that the prisoners will be properly tried according to law and justice, and that they will not be condemned to any punishment unless they are found guilty."[45]

Moulay Hafid assumed that the prisoners would be kept in custody in Tangier. However, Driss bin Minu, who accompanied the prisoners to Essaouira, informed him that the French minister in Tangier intended to release the prisoners. At least that is what Nooman Kouri had led Driss bin Minu to believe. Moulay Hafid immediately wrote to the consul in Essaouira that he had transferred the prisoners to Essaouira only with the greatest difficulty because he thought that he urgently needed to question the prisoners as part of his investigation. Moulay Hafid told Kouri to write to the minister to have the prisoners returned to Essaouira.[46]

Moulay Hafid had not exaggerated when he recounted the effort required to bring the prisoners to Essaouira. The transport of the prisoners required considerable subterfuge. Thami al-Glawi, the younger brother of *qaid* Al-Madani al-Glawi, was put in charge of the escort. Thami and his prisoners departed Marrakesh at night with twenty-four of his own horsemen and eight of Moulay Hafid's, including Driss bin Minu. Learning of the transport, the aggrieved Rahamna tribesmen felt betrayed. Thami had given them assurances that he was not removing the prisoners. The Rahamna now threatened to attack the city.

At Moulay Hafid's order, al-Warzazi once again dispersed a force of two hundred men to every quarter of the city to provide internal security. His strongest men, armed with good weapons, were posted to the city gates.[47] To move the Rahamna further from the city, Moulay Hafid then dispatched his cousin Muhammad bin Abd al-Salam bin Ath to the tribal *qaid*s with an order allegedly from Abdelaziz that they pack up at once and regroup where Ibn Ath commanded them.

The way the entire drama had played itself out filled Moulay Hafid with evident disgust. At the end of the day, "a worthless individual" who "shouted with the grunts of the wild Anflus" spread the rumor that the prisoners had been released.[48] Finally, calm was restored.

In the weeks that followed, the French legation in Tangier proposed returning the prisoners, who were now held in Tangier, to Essaouira and releasing them on bail. But at this point Ibn Sulayman, the Moroccan foreign minister, objected to the idea, arguing that those culpable for Mauchamp's murder were indeed the very ones under arrest. The Makhzan wanted to comply with French demands, but if it released the men, the Moroccan government could no longer assume responsibility for them.[49] Moulay Hafid, meanwhile, continued his correspondence with the French consul Kouri in Essaouira. Kouri, for his part, thought that the prisoners should be returned to Marrakesh. There, he argued, they were known, and rather than keep them in prison, Moulay Hafid could supervise their release on bail.

On August 17, the sultan Abdelaziz wrote letters to Muhammad al-Turris in Tangier and Abd al-Rahman Bargash of Essaouira, authorizing the transfer of the prisoners back to Essaouira.[50] Nonetheless, the transfer order soon became a moot point when news arrived in Fez that Moulay Hafid had proclaimed himself sultan. As a consequence of the political turmoil that ensued, the prisoners remained in Tangier. Indeed, three years later, by which point Moulay Hafid had long since succeeded in displacing Abdelaziz as sultan, French and Moroccan officials were again corresponding over their transfer to Essaouira.[51] And not until the summer of 1910 did Nooman Kouri venture forth to Marrakesh to conduct his investigation. By then, he had radically altered his opinion of Moulay Hafid.

For the time being, however, a semblance of calm was restored once again to Marrakesh. In June Lennox and the other Europeans again returned to their homes in Marrakesh. In July, the Austrian government, evidently undeterred by the disturbances that had plagued the city that past spring, announced to the Makhzan its intention of sending a vice-consul to the city.[52] Commenting on the improved state of affairs, *Al-Moghreb al-Aksa* noted that "the power of the Government is again quite evident. How this change has come about is something of a mystery, but all the same it is satisfactory to record."[53]

The Bombardment of Casablanca

The calm that settled momentarily over Marrakesh and much of Morocco in the middle of June 1907 was misleading. Further to the north, in Tangier, the Moroccan delegates al-Muqri and Ghannam continued to meet with the French chargé d'affaires Saint-Aulaire. The minister Regnault was in France on vacation. Throughout the early summer, their slow-motion negotiations, intended to bring about the French evacuation of Oujda, led nowhere. Elsewhere in Tangier, Moroccans and Europeans discussed the reorganization of the state bank in accordance with the Algeciras program. The occupation of Oujda, European diplomats optimistically told themselves, had "sobered" the Makhzan. But if they thought that a chastened Morocco was now at last set on the course of stability, the diplomats were wrong. By July, the government of sultan Abdelaziz entered the "crisis of the month" phase from which it would never recover. A series of calamities, culminating with the tragic and needlessly destructive bombardment of Casablanca by the French, would push Morocco beyond the point of no return into the hands of France.

Abdelaziz's woes began when the Makhzan's British-born military adviser Harry Maclean fell captive to Ahmad al-Raisuli and was held for ransom. As we saw earlier, the infamous brigand and erstwhile governor of Tangier and its countryside had much experience as a kidnapper. In two earlier incidents al-Raisuli held for ransom first the British journalist Walter Harris and then a wealthy Greek-American resident of Tangier, Ion Perdicaris, and his English son-in-law. Harris was released in exchange for some of al-Raisuli's men held in a Moroccan prison. In the case of Perdicaris, Teddy Roosevelt rushed warships to Tangier. There the American minister helped the president's 1904 reelection by delivering the famous message, "This government wants Perdicaris alive or Raisuli dead." Ultimately, the Makhzan capitulated to al-Raisuli's demand to be made a *qaid,* and Perdicaris was set free.[54]

Like the others, Sir Harry would also be released, but only after seven months of protracted negotiations and payment of a £20,000 ransom. The tough old Scotsman bore his captivity with good-humored stoicism. Permitted to write to Lowther in September, he acknowledged receipt of the cigars Lowther had sent him, and he described his ordeal. For eighteen days, until al-Raisuli himself intervened, he had been confined to a pit where rubbish and ashes were thrown just behind his head. Despite improvements, he had not been able to wash properly in over two months and, except for one day, had slept entirely on the floor. "I was, and still am, quite ready to be killed, but to be bullied for eight weeks out of the nearly eleven weeks I have been here was hard." He was reconciled to a long captivity "as Raisuli's demands are preposterous at first, but as long as I am fairly treated I do not mind."[55]

Far more catastrophic was the murder of nine European laborers—three Frenchmen, three Italians and three Spaniards—on July 30 in Casablanca.[56] The men were involved in quarrying stone for harbor construction at a site adjacent to a cemetery beyond the city walls. Their attackers, tribesmen from the surrounding Shawiya district, believed that the railroad line leading from the quarry to the quai desecrated the cemetery through which it ran.

Reporting the incident, the British consul Madden noted that a sudden change of mood had precipitated the attack. That morning a mounted tribesman attracted attention in town by denouncing the Europeans and threatening that anyone who brought provisions to town would be robbed. A Portuguese man was wounded "by a nigger in the crowd." In another incident Moroccans threw stones at a shop owned by a British subject. Madden's protests to the local *qaid* were at first ignored. Then, that afternoon, the *qaid* summoned the consular corps to a meeting. "He explained to us the demands of the tribesmen for the removal of the French railway, and the French control of the Custom House: to which he had replied that it was a matter for the Makhzan entirely, a reply that was not accepted by the tribesmen."

Not long afterward the first report arrived that two Frenchmen working on the quarry railway had been killed. "A scene of great excitement at once began, and the Governor ordered the soldiers of the Tangier regiment to go out. There was a further delay as the men had no cartridges, and these had to be obtained."[57]

In a postscript to his report and in a subsequent letter that same day, Madden stressed the anti-French nature of the attack. He speculated that the "[Moroccan] workers employed actually by the French company were disloyal, as they have many men at work, and they ought to have been able to defend the European workers." And he added that, "when the Arab horsemen came along looting, we heard them say, 'stop, stop': that is, the English house, and were not interfered with in the least." Madden further noted that the tribal leaders only consented to the evacuation by ship of French subjects, "thus making a clear distinction between the Nationalities." "I have heard it stated that the workers on the engine, and at the quarries were told to stop work, and that had they not refused and given way at once, the killing might not have happened at all."

As tribesmen threatened the *mellah,* Jewish and European refugees fled to Tangier aboard the British steamship *Demetian.* Those French residents who remained took refuge in the French consulate, where they awaited the arrival of the frigate *Galilée.*[58] Meanwhile, responding to pleas from the British consul, the sultan's viceroy Moulay al-Amin replaced the ineffectual *qaid* Abu Bakr with a reportedly stronger leader, the *qaid* Wold Hadj Hamu.

Madden was confident that Moulay al-Amin and his men would soon restore order, but aboard the French frigate *Galilée* Captain Ollivier entertained a different notion. Over the British consul's objection that a hasty French action might endanger all of Casablanca's Europeans—a view incidentally also held by the French vice-consul Maigret—Ollivier deemed it absolutely necessary that he land a detachment of marines. To Moroccan officials, he announced that his limited goal was to secure the French consulate. Given that they had no choice, the Makhzan officials assured the French captain that the landing party would not meet with resistance. But to his superiors, Ollivier spoke of the greater opportunities at hand.

"We cannot rest there," he wrote in regard to safeguarding the consulate. He recounted the necessity of reestablishing the works of the port, reasserting French control of the customs, and vigorously pursuing and punishing the murderers. "All of this ought to be done under the protection of our marines. Only a naval division capable of landing on its arrival a force of three or four hundred men to occupy the city can obtain these results which are important to achieve without any delay."[59] Ollivier could not conceal his impatience and landed his small marine detachment without waiting for the arrival of the rest of the fleet.

When the smoke and dust had finally cleared, the outcome was disastrous beyond what anyone could anticipate. The English firm of Murdoch, Butler, and Company wrote to Lloyd's, its insurance brokers in London, offering a "condensed report of recent occurrences." According to Messrs. Murdoch and Butler, recent French projects such as the wireless telegraphy, the port expansion, and the appointment of a French controller in the customs house had met with widespread disapproval among both the townsmen and the Arabs of the surrounding tribes. Representatives of these groups were voicing their complaints to the local viceroy Moulay al-Amin when the attack on the quarry workers took place.

The French frigate *Galilée* arrived on August 1. Four days later a landing party of sixty-six men commanded by Enseigne Ballande disembarked at 5:30 AM to protect the French consulate, "for which step," according to Messers. Murdoch and Butler, "there was no immediate necessity." At the Bab al-Marsa (Marine Gate) the party met with resistance and thus began to fight its way along the remaining two hundred and fifty meters to the French consulate. Two quartermasters and a sailor were wounded. Upon a signal from the French consulate the ship began its bombardment.

At this point townspeople commenced to loot Casablanca's shops, banks, and customs house stores. They were soon joined by tribesmen from the countryside, who had battered in the city gates. While the rioting went on unimpeded, the Spanish cruiser *Don Alvaro de Bazán* and the French cruiser *Du Chayla* arrived to aid the *Galilée*. A Spanish landing party of forty men joined the earlier French contingent. The French bombardment continued sporadically for three days, reaching a crescendo on August 7 with the arrival of four additional French battleships. After three hours of unrelenting bombardment, some twelve hundred troops—Senegalese *tirailleurs* and French Legionnaires—were landed. Assuming the offensive, French troops cleared the streets by shooting everyone in sight.

The English observers judged the French action "very precipitate." "Had the *Galilée* only awaited the arrival of the fleet on the seventh, it is most probable that the town would have been occupied without a shot fired, or any loss of life or property."[60]

Writing to Tangier on August 7, Moulay al-Amin, the regional viceroy, provided a desperate account of events to the sultan's deputy, Muhammad al-Turris, and the minister of war, al-Ghibbas. The viceroy had been unable to bring troops into the city in time to stop the rioting Arabs, he said. He described the horrifying scene that ensued: the indiscriminant shooting by the French troops, the wanton destruction of businesses by the Arabs, the carrying off of women, and the terrifying naval bombardment. In desperation he pleaded with al-Turris and al-Ghibbas to rescue him.

They died who died, and the rest fled into the desert, including our own family, my retainers, my animals and all that I possess. And now I'm left alone and at wit's end. I don't know what to do and now I beseech you. You must speak to the French headman there that he write to those responsible that they leave us and that they send a steamship to us to take us to you in Tangier because I no longer know what to do or say. I beseech you that you spare no pains on our behalf and that you hurry sending a steamship. As for the city, may the French release her and her fortress, and you must see to our deliverance.[61]

While the European community was saved from a nonexistent danger, the cost to the native Muslim and Jewish populations was enormous. Exact figures remain unknown, but one contemporary source claims that "before order was restored nearly every inhabitant had been killed or wounded or had fled; the dead alone numbered in the thousands."[62] Five days after the French landing, *Al-Moghreb al-Aksa* put the casualties conservatively at one hundred Jews and five hundred Arabs killed in town, two thousand Moroccans killed outside town by the warships and the troops, and one hundred Jewish and three hundred Muslim girls abducted.[63]

Although shops owned by Muslim merchants were also attacked, the *mellah* was particularly hard hit by rioting that took place simultaneously with the French bombardment. According to the head of the Alliance Israélite school in Casablanca, the *mellah* was invaded the moment the *Galilée* fired its first shot. It was "as if the Arabs were waiting for the signal," he wrote. Thousands of looters, including soldiers from the Makhzan, rampaged through the Jewish quarter. According to this account, no household was spared, and only five or six households that had taken refuge in the consulates remained intact. The Kaiseria, the Jewish commercial district that had housed more than five hundred stores, was set on fire. All the schools and synagogues were destroyed.

After three days of rioting, Pisa, the Alliance teacher, put the Jewish dead at thirty with some sixty wounded, among them twenty seriously. He also cited innumerable instances of rape and said that more than two hundred and fifty young women and children had been carried off. Of Casablanca's six thousand Jews, an estimated one thousand had departed for Ceuta, Gibraltar, and Tangier. Another fifteen hundred to two thousand dispersed in the countryside. The city was almost deserted. The three to four thousand Jews that remained had neither belongings nor shelter and were merely wandering among the soldiers in the otherwise empty streets. The Arab population had either been killed or fled, he wrote.[64]

In France, *L'Illustration* departed from its usual fare showing French soldiers chatting amiably with Moroccans in Oujda. Instead, it provided its readers with a gruesome cover photo of dead humans and animals lying among ruins in a Casablanca alley.[65] A shocking sight, the photograph serves as a kind of parallel image to the earlier one the magazine displayed of Mauchamp laid out in his coffin.

Nearly a century after the events, the tragic ironies of the French policy in Morocco are only all too apparent. Having first declared their own intentions peaceful, French diplomats loudly protested the outrages committed in Marrakesh. In the aftermath of Mauchamp's death, they called for the removal of the governor, Hajj Abdeslam al-Warzazi, who was viewed as inept and ineffective. Evidence of anarchy was everywhere, French officials claimed, and they called for the establishment of law and order. On the other hand, when faced with an opportunity to act unimpeded, as in Casablanca, France showed no evidence of the restraint it demanded from others. Claiming to have been lenient in Marrakesh, France exacted a harsh revenge in Casablanca. Certainly, there were critics of France's precipitous action in Casablanca, Frenchmen among them, but French official-dom quickly covered its tracks. Despite his imprudence and even insubordination by taking action before the rest of the fleet arrived, Ollivier, the captain of the *Galilée*, received commendations and a promotion. For his part, Maigret, the young vice-consul who wisely advised caution, was made the scapegoat. Because he bravely and humanely resisted the use of force, subsequent accounts of the misadventure were quick to impugn his patriotism.[66]

The Turning Point

For the French, the bombardment of Casablanca and the landing of several thousand French troops to secure the surrounding Shawiya was a turning point. Over the next five years, a period that culminated in the establishment of the French Protectorate over Morocco in 1912, the initiative over French Moroccan policy passed in fits and starts from the diplomats to the soldiers. The Quai d'Orsay had pursued a gradualist approach devised to secure the favor of the Makhzan and subordinate it to French goals. However, the diplomats found themselves outmaneuvered by the military, who advocated a "forward" policy. Backed by a vocal colonial party and French interests in Algeria, the military advocated a "tribes" approach to Morocco. This policy called for subduing the countryside and establishing direct French control on the ground. This was the method of General Lyautey, who, having crossed the border from Algeria, never once entertained a thought of relinquishing Oujda.

Lyautey further demonstrated the success of his approach in January 1908 by provoking and then subduing the neighboring Bani Snassen tribe. The metaphor Lyautey used to describe the French military tactic was *une tache d'huile,* a spot of oil. The spreading French military presence was accompanied by medical missions, public works, and the creation of regional markets—all measures designed to win the hearts and minds of Moroccans in the countryside. Once the Protectorate was finally established, it was Lyautey, the military man, and not his civilian rival, the diplomat Eugène Regnault, who was named France's first resident general. Lyautey's approach, euphemistically called "pacification," thus replaced the Quai d'Orsay's earlier program of "peaceful penetration." Nevertheless, rural resistance to French rule, especially in the Berber regions of the Atlas Mountains, continued till 1934. Only then was it checked once and for all and pacification declared a success.

For the Moroccans, the French campaign in the Shawiya emerged as a turning point as well. Under orders not to pursue attacking Moroccan tribesmen more than fifteen miles from his base, General D'Amade, the French commander of the Shawiya, held his men back. This initial reluctance of the French to engage the Moroccans, as well as the unsuitability of D'Amade's static tactics, encouraged the Moroccan attackers to believe that they were in fact winning against the French. The success of the tribesmen was illusory. Eventually French forces in the region would swell to fifteen thousand, and by June 1908 quiet in the Shawiya would be restored. Nonetheless, in the summer of 1907 the tribes of the Shawiya were buoyed by appearances of an easy victory, and the call to jihad against the French presence resonated far and wide.

In Marrakesh, where his intentions had been the object of speculation for years, Moulay Hafid could wait no longer. Al-Madani al-Glawi brought five hundred horsemen into Marrakesh. They were joined by five hundred Rahamna horsemen. Goundafi contributed two hundred more. When the horsemen occupied half the city, Moulay Hafid asked the city's principal people to assemble in the Friday mosque on August 16 at eight in the morning.[67] There, in a ceremony attended by various notables, he received the *baya,* or oath of loyalty, from the ulama of Marrakesh. In declaring their al-

legiance to Moulay Hafid as sultan, the religious scholars offered the
rationale that his brother Abdelaziz had abdicated his responsibility
in leading the jihad against the French.[68] In reality, the city's ulama
were initially reluctant to take the drastic step of deposing Abdelaziz.
According to later reports, the first scholar to sign the oath did so
only when Al-Madani al-Glawi threatened to shoot him with a pistol. The other notables then fell in line.[69]

Over the next weeks and months the notables of other cities too
published declarations of allegiance to Moulay Hafid. The movement
culminated in January 4, 1908, with the *baya* signed by the ulama
of Fez. Here too coercion played a role. During the preceding month
Fez had been rocked by riots as artisans, peasants, and the urban
poor protested the imposition of a market tax. On the day the oath
was signed, some forty thousand people waited impatiently outside
the Qarawiyyin mosque to where the ulama had been escorted
earlier. Under these circumstances, the Fez ulama readily acceded
to the mob's demands.[70]

While this oath of loyalty virtually confirmed Moulay Hafid's
success, it carried a number of stipulations that severely limited the
aspiring sultan's ability to maneuver. Among other terms, the oath
called for Moulay Hafid to abrogate the Act of Algeciras, repudiate
all debts incurred by his brother Abdelaziz, and undertake no agreements with foreigners "except with the approval of the people."[71]

The Fez *baya*—which Moulay Hafid would later reject, demanding in its place one with no attached conditions—exemplifies the
dilemma faced by Moulay Hafid.[72] On the one hand, his claim to
legitimacy depended upon his ability to lead a jihad against the
French. On the other, Moulay Hafid was fully aware that by antago-
nizing France he risked provoking a military conflict that he could
not win. Consequently, in territories under his control, Moulay
Hafid went to great lengths to see that Europeans were not harmed.
Shortly after his proclamation, he wrote conciliatory letters to the
European ministers in Tangier and went so far as to write to al-Raisuli, pressuring him to release Maclean.[73] Strapped for cash to pay
his troops, Moulay Hafid sent representatives, including Holzmann,
to Europe to seek financial support for his cause.[74] Moulay Hafid
knew all along that even should he succeed in deposing his brother,
Morocco would still have to walk a difficult tightrope were it to fend
off French designs.

"The war between the two Sultans was tedious and uninterest-
ing," the long-time Moroccan observer Walter B. Harris pronounced
wryly fifteen years after the fact.

The principal object of both seemed to be how to avoid an encounter, and they contented themselves by issuing edicts of mutual excommunication, and, in order to obtain money, by pillaging the tribes, regardless of their political opinions. When either Sultan had funds he had also soldiers; failing resources, the armies alternately dwindled away almost to the point of disappearance. In fact, both were dependent for troops on deserters from each other's forces.[75]

Described as a "cold war" between the two brothers, the most outstanding feature of the conflict was the exchange of capitals between the sultans, the premise being that to secure his throne, each claimant had to undermine the other's base of support. On July 12, 1908, Abdelaziz, who had earlier moved his court from Fez to Rabat, began an advance on the south with a *mahalla* of four thousand men. All proceeded well until August 19, when the *mahalla* arrived at a place called Abu Ajiba. There, in the midst of a battle against forces loyal to Moulay Hafid, Abdelaziz's tribal auxiliaries defected. The sultan beat a hasty retreat to Casablanca, where, arriving on August 21, he abdicated his throne. In the meantime, Moulay Hafid had entered Fez on June 7, having taken the difficult interior route from Marrakesh through Meknes.[76]

Jean Jaurès and the Ghost of Mauchamp

Among Moroccans, Moulay Hafid derived popular support from his role as the leader of jihad against the European invaders. Nevertheless, "in his dealings with the powers he consistently sought to allay fears that he was a sanguinary fanatic."[77] Writing on January 29, 1908, to Herbert White, the British chargé d'affaires at Tangier, Moulay Hafid asserted that "as regards to any reports which may have reached you of the proclaiming of the Holy War, we merely employed that as a stratagem to tranquillize the excitement of the people on seeing their land occupied by force, the slaughter of their kin on their own territory, and their being prevented from ruling in their own country."[78]

A half year later, Moulay Hafid sent a letter to King Edward VII of Britain, defending his claim to the throne and again rebutting the assertion that he was waging a holy war against Europe. Citing the mismanagement of the country during the reign of his brother Abdelaziz, Moulay Hafid said he had come to the throne so as to bring security and order to Morocco once again. "We restrained the tribes and the soldiers, and prevented them from being impetuous in all places, in order that untruthful complaints should not be made about them in the same way as they were reported about me, that I have declared a 'jehad' [sic]." Finally, Moulay Hafid asserted his willingness to comply with all of Morocco's treaty obligations, including the Act of Algeciras.[79]

Moulay Hafid could make all the assertions he wanted about his reasonableness, but these had little effect on French public opinion, which focused on Moulay Hafid's alleged xenophobia. Despite an official policy of neutrality, France continued to back Abdelaziz during the struggle between the two brothers. Indeed, even when Moulay Hafid was clearly the victor, seeing an opportunity to gain leverage over the new sultan, both France and Spain withheld recognition till January 5, 1909.[80]

As the war dragged on throughout the second half of 1907 and the first half of 1908, deputies in the French chamber debated the future of Morocco. In the chamber of deputies and in the press, Jean Jaurès railed against the government's interventionist policy, which he said threatened the sovereignty of Morocco. Querying the government on January 24, 1908, the socialist leader and longtime opponent of French military involvement in Morocco accused the government of playing a double-game. According to Jaurès, the Quai d'Orsay had hedged its bets by having secretly backed Moulay Hafid, whom it now despised and sought to discredit.

In this one instance, the usually perceptive Jaurès had in fact overstated his case. His supposedly incontrovertible evidence of a foreign ministry conspiracy and double-dealing was none other than three letters from Émile Mauchamp. Written just weeks before his death, they held, he said, the secret to the doctor's murder.

In Jaurès's version of events, the foreign ministry sent Mauchamp as an official intermediary to open a channel to Moulay Hafid. This assertion brought vehement denials from the foreign minister Stephen Pichon, who claimed never to have met Mauchamp in person and never to have initiated any relations with Moulay Hafid beyond his capacity as viceroy of Marrakesh.[81]

Jaurès returned to the tribune four days later with the letters in hand. How he obtained the letters is still not clear. We can speculate that Mauchamp intended these letters, addressed only to "mon cher ami," for his closest friend in Marrakesh, the Italian merchant Berrino who, perchance, delivered them to Mauchamp's family. In the first letter, sent from Gibraltar on New Year's Day 1907 while en route to France for his vacation, Mauchamp merely alluded to his excellent reception in Tangier and his expectation of success in Paris.

Three weeks later, Mauchamp sent a second letter, dated January 22, from Paris. Here Jaurès identified the recipient of this letter only as an "Arabic-speaker" who had interpreted for Mauchamp in his conversations with Moulay Hafid. This too was likely to have been Berrino. Again Mauchamp alluded to his meeting "the minister," and again Pichon interjected that he had never met Mauchamp. (The unidentified minister would most certainly have been Regnault, with whom Mauchamp met in Tangier on his return to France.) Jaurès waved aside the objection. The letters, he said, spoke for themselves and admitted no "contradictory commentary."

"You can say to our friend," Jaurès quoted Mauchamp as writing, making an allusion to Moulay Hafid, "that starting now, he can be entirely assured as regards his persons and his belongings; no one will touch them. You understand that I cannot say specifically more in a letter."

The secretive and self-important Mauchamp tone is undeniable.

"His situation," the letter continued, "will be even more definitively and more clearly protected without anyone suspecting this situation. He ought already to have received from Tangier an official letter in which we say to him that we will not forget his services rendered."

Mauchamp concluded by saying that he was charged by the ministry in Paris to pick out a suitable gift, in this case a superb Beauvais rug. Jaurès's reading of the letter again brought denials of involvement from Pichon.

Dated February 6, 1907, and posted from Chalon-sur-Saône, the final letter spoke further of Mauchamp's gift, saying that the two rugs to be offered had been exhibited at the "Exposition de Saint-Louis." When presenting the rugs to Moulay Hafid, Mauchamp instructed his correspondent to inform the viceroy that these were the gifts of the French government and that "these types of rugs are not found anywhere in the market but are generally sent as a gift to sovereigns and great personages."

Over the objection of Pichon, who accused the orator of concocting a work of fiction, Jaurès drew his conclusion. Moulay Hafid had, in his rivalry with his brother Abdelaziz, sought and obtained French protection. These and other letters indicated, Jaurès insisted, "that there was a period where, as the Makhzan of Abdelaziz planned or committed violence against Europeans, apropos of the Lassallas affair and, a bit later, the death of Dr. Mauchamp himself, that France especially relied upon Moulay Hafid to protect the Europeans and the French."

The significant point missed by Jaurès was that the overtures to Moulay Hafid originated with Mauchamp and his friends in Marrakesh and not with the Quai d'Orsay in Paris. In this light, Pichon's rebuttal to Jaurès makes perfect sense. Moulay Hafid, the foreign minister asserted, was the sultan's functionary and the authority in Marrakesh where the acts of aggression against French nationals were committed. "Upon whom else would you want us to rely?" he asked Jaurès.

Jaurès resumed his attack:

> If you had supposed for Moulay Hafid the xenophobic passions which you speak about today, it's not sure that you would have counted on him to protect the foreigners. . . . It's possible that Moulay Hafid himself is only an adventurer born of the anarchy and incapable of repressing it. It's possible that he thought, having yielded to the popular movement that our intervention has unleashed, to limit this movement and to negotiate later with Europe. Of this I am unaware. I only have the present facts.

The *present facts* for Jaurès were that not a single Frenchmen or any other European had been harmed in Morocco since Moulay Hafid had undertaken his campaign some six months earlier.

As Jaurès intimated in his remarks, Moulay Hafid's conciliatory tone was motivated by a pragmatic realization. In order to succeed on the throne he could not further antagonize the Europeans. Indeed, throughout the four years of his reign, Moulay Hafid was dogged by an unsolvable dilemma. On the one hand, he was obliged to deal with Europeans, and particularly the French, not just because of their superior military strength, but because only Europe had the technical and financial resources needed to institute necessary fiscal and military reforms. On the other hand, Moulay Hafid had to placate those Moroccan supporters who had originally rallied to his cause because they saw in him someone who would reduce European influence. The new sultan's position thus resembled that of his brother who preceded him on the throne. Unable and unwilling to alienate the French, Moulay Hafid soon found himself surrounded on all sides by various claimants to the throne and leaders of jihad who sought his overthrow. Moulay Muhammad, an older brother popular among the rural population, represented the greatest threat. He was quickly arrested and imprisoned.

Moulay Hafid also moved preemptively against Muhammad al-Kattani, head of the Kattaniyya Sufi brotherhood. Architect of the Fez *baya*, or declaration of loyalty, the Fez Sufi shaykh and scholar had become disaffected and was rightly perceived by Moulay Hafid as an enemy. Apprehended in flight, al-Kattani was brought back to Fez, where he soon died of the beatings he had received. Meanwhile, the Ait Ndhir tribe, which had sheltered al-Kattani, was severely punished.

Moulay Hafid was also successful against Abu Himara, the so-called Rogui. Beginning in 1902, this pretender had dogged Moulay Hafid's predecessor, Abdelaziz, and now, with Spain's tacit approval, he ruled over the tribes of the eastern Rif mountains. In August 1909 forces loyal to Moulay Hafid defeated the pretender. Abu Himara was exhibited in a cage in the Fez palace and finally executed after an uncooperative lion deigned not to eat him.[82]

The treatment of Abu Himara and his fellow prisoners secured for the highly educated and scholarly Moulay Hafid a reputation for cruelty among Europeans. "We English had to put down the Indian mutiny with great severity," the British consul in Fez, MacLeod, observed at the time. "But to dismember prisoners was another matter. People in Europe had been hoping the Sultan would inaugurate a new and more civilized era in Morocco."

The consul argued that it was in Moulay Hafid's self-interest to show leniency. "These recent punishments would perpetuate hatred of himself and the Makhzan," he warned.

But the sultan found the consul's proposal ludicrous. "Who ever heard of anybody liking the Makhzan!" Moulay Hafid reportedly replied.[83]

A year later, in July 1910, Moulay Hafid's reputation was further darkened when it was widely reported that the governor of Meknes, Hajj bin Aissa, had been arrested and members of his family beaten. Ibn Aissa was a respected Makhzan official who had abetted Moulay Hafid in the capture of al-Kattani. Now he was accused of allegedly inciting the Zenmour region to revolt. According to reports widely published in the papers, one of his wives was tortured in the most heinous fashion in an effort to force her to divulge the location of her jewels. Yielding to pressure, Moulay Hafid agreed to allow the French doctor Weisgerber to examine Ibn Aissa's wife. The doctor reported that she suffered from a dislocated shoulder. Eventually, the governor's family members were freed on condition that they remain in Marrakesh while Ibn Aissa awaited trial.

While Moulay Hafid sought to placate European opinion, the damage to his reputation was irremediable. "It seems generally believed," the British minister in Tangier wrote, "that the excesses of drink, morphia, and debauchery to which he gives way are beginning to tell on his brain, and that his lust for cruelty and blood now amounts to a mania."[84]

Like the Mauchamp affair earlier, the Ibn Aissa affair became a cause célèbre among Europeans in Morocco. Coupled with a renewal of attacks upon Europeans, it provided the emotional context for the deepening French intervention in Morocco.[85]

10
Remains of the Day

Marrakesh sans Mauchamp

As for the handful of European businessmen and missionaries who
had fled to the coast in June 1907, they soon trickled back to Marrakesh. But there, only a few weeks after their return, the news of
the murdered European workers in Casablanca revived fears that
their lives too were in jeopardy. The Jews were especially frightened
by the two hundred or so Rahamna tribesmen who roamed the city.
Meekly, the Jews removed their shoes whenever they ventured outside the *mellah*. The guards who had been posted by Hajj Abdeslam
al-Warzazi in the aftermath of Mauchamp's death had by this point
disappeared. Despite his previous solicitude for the safety of the Europeans, Moulay Hafid warned that he might not be able to protect
them if he were obliged to wage a jihad against the French.

On August 9, news of the French bombardment of Casablanca
reached Marrakesh. Quickly a new evacuation was arranged, and
the following day at midnight the caravan departed. Its numbers
included six Germans, four English, four French, and one Swiss in
addition to three Jewish protégés from El-Jadida and eight Arabs
who were German protégés. Accompanying them were some forty
servants and muleteers and twelve soldiers provided by Moulay
Hafid. Two days later, weary from eighteen-hour days in the saddle,
the group arrived at Safi.[1]

Not until January 1908 did the British missionary Cuthbert Nairn
venture back to Marrakesh. Nairn, who made his visit in secret and
without official permission, disappointed the local Moroccan officials
with whom he met. They thought he might bear with him official

letters of recognition for Moulay Hafid from the British government. For his part, Nairn criticized the town's governor for the desecration of the European cemetery that had taken place. Having concluded that he "might be able to live quite safely in seclusion" but not do any real work, Nairn left Marrakesh after only five days. However, he wrote in a postscript, "I did not hear an uncivil word nor notice an antagonistic look neither by the way nor in the city."[2]

A full year later, in January 1909, Nairn finally returned to Marrakesh in the company of Misses Macarthur and Trainer, other longtime missionaries in the city. There they founded a booming business vaccinating children against smallpox. Writing in the May 1909 bulletin of the Southern Morocco Mission, Nairn reported having vaccinated 490 persons in a matter of months, the numbers limited only by their supplies of vaccine. The November issue of the Glasgow-based missionary bulletin put out an urgent request for a doctor to join Nairn's staff. Nairn reported seeing 2,000 patients a month pass through his dispensary and, owing to the lack of a fully-trained staff, he found himself turning away patients. By March 1910 Nairn reported record attendance for the previous year of 17,824 patients—18,000 if one included "stragglers unrecorded." He made no secret of the reasons for his success; the large numbers were attributable to "the absence of a French doctor."[3]

Nairn's success did not go unnoticed by the French, and in August 1909, more than two years after Mauchamp's death, Regnault in Tangier finally considered sending a replacement to Marrakesh. His chief candidates were Doctor Murat, the director of the hospital in Fez, and Guichard, the doctor in El-Jadida who had performed the postmortem on Mauchamp.[4] The post was evidently a coveted one, as earlier discussion of a replacement had included French doctors from as far away as Oran and Tunis. Significantly, Jonnart, the governor general of Algeria, advised against the candidature of a Parisian-trained Muslim doctor, one Mohamed Ben Larbey. "He is known as a mediocre physician," the governor general wrote. "Having neither professional value nor moral prestige . . . his presence in Morocco could cause prejudice against French prestige."

These arguments aside, the governor general revealed that the real reason for Ben Larbey's rejection was political. "He is a bad spirit and sets his co-religionists against French functionaries."

Not until 1910 did Guichard take up his post in Marrakesh. He was soon joined by a French-Algerian doctor, a woman named Françoise Legey. The pharmacist Mauchamp had first requested in

1906 did not arrive until 1912, when the French military occupied Marrakesh.[5] The Alliance school, meanwhile, was reopened in December 1908 with the support of Al-Madani al-Glawi, now vizier to Moulay Hafid.[6]

The Investigation

In the spring of 1909, two years after the death of his son, Pierre Mauchamp was still distraught. Apart from Émile's stolen ring that was recovered by Falcon, he had received none of his late son's personal effects. Nooman Kouri, the French consul in Essaouira, made inquiries on the father's behalf. Lassallas, Mauchamp's friend, confirmed that everything had been looted or destroyed.[7] Meanwhile, Mauchamp's father wrote to Kouri, saying that he had authorized Falcon to place in the Alliance school library whatever novels he had retrieved from his son's collection and to put aside any medical books for use in the hospital to be built in his son's name. He also gave Falcon permission to use any of his son's stores of preserved foods that had not yet gone bad.[8]

Writing to Regnault, the minister in Tangier, Pierre Mauchamp meanwhile complained that the Moroccan government had not made any effort to produce the promised reparations. The elder Mauchamp had his suspicions as to why the settlement of his son's affairs was taking so long. It was the Comte de Saint-Aulaire who was at fault. He "always showed himself an enemy to my unfortunate son and death has not calmed the hate of which we never understood the reason."[9]

The flurry of correspondence over the disposition of Émile's effects continued throughout the summer. Late in June, Kouri wrote apologetically to Mauchamp's father to say that he had been authorized back in February to settle his son's estate and had, at that time, asked Falcon to deliver to him whatever items remained from the late doctor. As for Saint-Aulaire, Kouri assured the elder Mauchamp, a former republican politician, that the aristocratic chargé d'affaires had nothing to do with the delays.[10]

In the spring of 1910, Kouri at last began his investigation into the death of the Émile Mauchamp. Three years had passed. Kouri started his investigation by gathering together copies of letters he had exchanged with Moulay Hafid, formerly the viceroy of the sultan in Marrakesh and now sultan. The letters, for the most part, dealt with the arrest of the ten locals who were accused by the Makhzan of murdering the French doctor. These supposed unfortunates continued to languish in prison in Tangier despite French requests that they now be forwarded to Essaouira for Kouri to examine.[11]

Then, at the end of May, Kouri ventured to Marrakesh. He had a dual mission. First, he was to scout locations for the hospital to be established in Mauchamp's name. Moulay Hafid agreed to honor his predecessor's commitment, but for uncertain motives, except perhaps as a means of annoying French officials, he tried to have the location changed to Safi.[12] Second, Kouri was to gather depositions from witnesses to the events of March 19, 1907, both Europeans and Moroccans. Complicating Kouri's task was the fact that Hajj Abdeslam al-Warzazi—the former governor of Marrakesh and the one whom the French government and press were originally inclined to blame for Mauchamp's death—was by now long since dead.

At the time of al-Warzazi's death in September 1907, the English paper *Al-Moghreb al-Aksa* wrote, "We lose an old acquaintance and quite a worthy, if somewhat fanatical man." Undoubtedly these were the sentiments verbatim of Alan Lennox, the British vice-consul, who served as the paper's Marrakesh correspondent. Lennox genuinely mourned his friend's demise and continued to defend the late pasha's memory at every opportunity when pressed by Kouri.

Indeed, a surprising number of people central to the story of Mauchamp's death and the ensuing events died soon in his wake. Bel Ghazi, who was sent by Abdelaziz to replace al-Warzazi as pasha of Marrakesh, died in June 1908 after a painful illness. The octogenarian Muhammad al-Turris, Abdelaziz's deputy in Tangier, died of old age in September of that same year. And fourteen months later, in December 1909, al-Turris's former boss, Abd al-Karim bin Sulayman, the foreign minister under sultan Abdelaziz, died in Fez, allegedly the victim of poison. Soon after his burial, vandals opened his grave and hung his head over one of the principal gates of the city. The desecration was intended as a warning to Moulay Hafid and his officials. An attached sign "warned of a similar fate to all those who compromised themselves with the Christians."[13]

In the three years following Mauchamp's death two rival theories as to who orchestrated the crime presented themselves. Their proponents tended to divide along national lines. First, the Englishmen in Marrakesh and Essaouira, among them Lennox, Nairn, and Spinney, defended the late governor al-Warzazi and tried to shift blame for Mauchamp's death to Moulay Hafid. French observers, on the other hand, chief among them Falcon and Gentil, recalled Moulay Hafid's efforts to safeguard their lives. Initially they tended to blame al-

Warzazi. Nevertheless, even among Frenchmen close to the event, there had been a change of heart as the murder receded in time. By 1910, French observers tended to view Mauchamp's death through the lens of subsequent events and especially Moulay Hafid's accession to the throne. Even Falcon now pointed to Moulay Hafid as the ultimate culprit, but the evidence was largely circumstantial.

In written statements to Kouri, Lassallas depicted Moulay Hafid as a kind of criminal mastermind.[14] He claimed that Moulay Hafid, knowing that al-Warzazi was hostile to the French, had cultivated good relations with Mauchamp and then deliberately did nothing to prevent the latter's death. According to Lassallas, Mauchamp had told Moulay Hafid the night before his murder of his fine practical joke (a *bonne blague,* as Gentil called it), namely, putting a fake telegraph pole on the roof of his house. Although (according to Lassallas) Moulay Hafid later said he had advised Mauchamp against it, what did he actually do to prevent Mauchamp's death the following morning? He sent unarmed men to rescue Mauchamp, knowing full well that they would arrive too late. He then blamed al-Warzazi and people connected with him. In other words, Moulay Hafid had set up the governor for the fall.

As further evidence, Lassallas said that he had suggested to Moulay Hafid that he interrogate the headman of the Arsa Moulay Musa quarter, Larbi bin Sahil. To this Moulay Hafid replied, "You can be certain that Ibn Sahil has had his throat slit ear to ear." The impression Moulay Hafid wanted to create, Lassallas wrote, was that al-Warzazi had divested himself of an inconvenient accomplice. However, the truth was that Ibn Sahil had merely fled Marrakesh, only to return immediately upon the proclamation of Moulay Hafid as sultan.

Finally, cementing Moulay Hafid's guilt in Lassallas's mind was the fact that the aspiring sultan, more than anyone else, stood to profit from Mauchamp's death. Lassallas even speculated that Moulay Hafid had made his decision to have Mauchamp murdered soon after his arrival in Marrakesh. Lassallas had no positive evidence of the plot, but he suspected that men close to the sharif, among them Driss bin Minu and al-Warzazi's son Abd al-Majid, knew of Moulay Hafid's intentions. These were the very men, of course, who were sent to rescue Mauchamp and who failed so miserably.

Lassallas's accusations did not end there. In another statement to Kouri, Lassallas saw Moulay Hafid as the mastermind behind the Casablanca port railroad murders as well. According to Lassallas, the viceroy had, through correspondence with his relatives, perfect intelligence of affairs in the Shawiya region. Lassallas wrote that when he first learned of the incident he went to talk to Moulay Hafid; the latter was already fully informed and "all smiles." According to Lassallas, Moulay Hafid compared his handling of the Mauchamp affair in Marrakesh with Moulay al-Amin's inept handling of events in Casablanca. If the European powers would confide to him the task of establishing order in the Haouz and the Shawiya, "he would turn the trick." More incriminating was the praise Moulay Hafid reportedly lavished on emissaries from the Shawiya and Moulay Hafid's willingness to pose as a leader of jihad. In the six months following Mauchamp's death, Moulay Hafid had, according to Lassallas, managed to put in place all the elements necessary for his proclamation as sultan. The irony that Mauchamp had supported Moulay Hafid's accession and then was alleged to be his victim seems to have been lost on the French doctor's erstwhile friend Lassallas.

Already inclined to blame Moulay Hafid, Kouri led his witnesses to adopt this conclusion when taking their depositions. This is apparent in his interview with Muhammad Sghir, the agent whom Abdeslam al-Warzazi sent to tell Mauchamp to remove his the pole from his roof.[15] But not everyone was willing to say that Moulay Hafid alone was the sole culprit. A money changer from the Arsa Moulay Musa quarter and an eyewitness to the attack accused both al-Warzazi and Moulay Hafid of complicity in the crime. He claimed that al-Warzazi's son Abd al-Majid had been stationed among the crowd, only to disappear once he assured himself that the deed was done. The retrieval of the corpse by al-Warzazi's other son, Muhammad, was merely a ploy to deter blame. Everyone in Marrakesh, this informant claimed, knew of the complicity of al-Warzazi and Moulay Hafid in planning Mauchamp's murder.[16]

Moroccan locals were not the only ones to indulge in conspiracy theories. European observers dismissed out of hand the possibility that the crowd may have erupted on its own in a spontaneous outburst of xenophobia. Nissim Falcon, in his deposition to Kouri, discounted the "fanatical mob" explanation.[17] He wrote, "One must before everything else set aside the so-called fanaticism of the population. It is impossible to conceive that a crowd, on a moment's notice and in perfect accord, would take itself with arms to the doctor's house on the pretext that there was a pole on the roof."

Falcon now blamed both al-Warzazi and Moulay Hafid. Al-Warzazi's motive was to wreak personal revenge; Moulay Hafid's, to seek political gain. But the plot thickened as Falcon dissected Mauchamp's relationship with Moulay Hafid. Falcon said he had long been apprehensive, concerned that the doctor had not taken adequate "precautions." For one thing, Mauchamp had relied on his Italian friend and confidant Berrino to translate for him during his audiences with Moulay Hafid. But Falcon had always known Berrino to be an intimate friend of Dr. Holzmann, Mauchamp's rival. Both Berrino and Holzmann had free access to the Dar al-Makhzan and had served as counselors to Moulay Hafid. "I found it strange," Falcon now recalled, "that the day after Berrino became a friend of the doctor, Holzmann was removed from the palace."

Falcon said he even warned Mauchamp that Holzmann was known to hide behind a tapestry in the palace and eavesdrop on his conversations with the viceroy. Mauchamp confirmed it, but attached little importance. Moulay Hafid was too "engaged," the doctor claimed, to shrink back now.

Falcon further saw evidence of Moulay Hafid's duplicity when the rumor circulated that the French were going to install a wireless telegraph in Marrakesh. Moulay Hafid knew about Mauchamp's little joke, Falcon insisted, and did nothing to dissuade him. Indeed, on the day of the murder Moulay Hafid's black slaves, Falcon insisted, were among the crowd in great numbers. When the viceroy did send his men to rescue Mauchamp, they went unarmed and even participated in the looting. As proof, Falcon said that one of his teachers, Miss Coriat, had bought Mauchamp's Ottoman decoration from the black man who had removed it.

Falcon further accused Mauchamp's friend Berrino of suspicious behavior after the death. Having helped Mauchamp and the visiting French engineer Quinson erect the pole, Berrino returned to the *mellah*, where he passed the rest of that fateful morning with Falcon, Quinson, Gentil, and Gentil's wife. When news of Mauchamp's death arrived, Berrino left, only to return an hour later. In the words of Falcon he looked ashen-faced and "defeated." He again disappeared till midnight the following day, when he joined the entourage accompanying Mauchamp's body to El-Jadida.[18] And lastly, Falcon added to the list of Moulay Hafid's alleged crimes the death of the governor, Abdeslam al-Warzazi. He too would have made a troublesome witness, and for that reason Falcon suspected that the viceroy had him done away.

As Nooman Kouri continued his investigation, he next turned his attention to Alan Lennox, the British vice-consul. Lennox had a reputation of being hostile to France, and Kouri wanted to make sure of where Lennox stood before contacting him directly. A French artillery captain named Jacquety, who directed the weapons depot in Marrakesh, reported in detail a conversation he had had with Lennox. According to the captain, Lennox—in a letter to Casablanca just after Mauchamp's murder—had said that he blamed Moulay Hafid for a plot against the doctor. The officer also quoted Lennox as deploring the attitude of the Germans in Marrakesh, whose actions he said further incited the population rather than calmed it after Mauchamp's murder. And finally, Jacquety said Lennox denied any knowledge of a diamond pendant that Moulay Hafid reportedly gave the wife of the German consul, Niehr, after the murder.[19]

Lennox endeavored to cooperate with the French investigation, but he had reservations as to the extent to which he should provide information. First, he knew that in French circles he was alleged to have had a "personal animosity" toward Mauchamp and to have manifested anti-French sentiments at the time of his death. He naturally denied these allegations, and having reassured Kouri, he contemplated having the consul write a dispatch to the French minister in Tangier in this regard to clear his name.

Second, in his capacity as British vice-consul, Lennox felt ill at ease offering testimony against Moulay Hafid, now the reigning Moroccan sultan. Kouri had at his disposal copies of letters Lennox had written to Spinney in El-Jadida at the time of the incident. In them, Kouri asserted, Lennox implied that Moulay Hafid was responsible for Mauchamp's death. As he informed his superiors, whether this was or was not the case, he certainly did not want to put his private views in writing now:

> I have my ideas on the matter drawn from private conversations with Hafid and from his subsequent actions, but are these sufficient to give evidence to a foreign power? . . . I don't feel favorable towards Hafid myself now, he has been most disappointing, and I can imagine you smiling as you remember my zeal for his cause, but I feel very reluctant to give any written declaration without sufficient evidence and without permission.[20]

Instructions came from Herbert White that Lennox should not include in his confidential testimony "any impressions, significance or conclusions that you might have arrived at. They would not be accepted in evidence in a law court and I could not see that they would be of any real use to the French government."[21]

Lennox was to stick to the facts, a point upon which he insisted in letters to Kouri.[22] He related a conversation held with Moulay Hafid shortly after the murder. At that time Moulay Hafid accused Hajj Abdeslam al-Warzazi of planning the attack but admitted that he had no proof of al-Warzazi's guilt. Regarding another conversation Lennox had held with Moulay Hafid on March 24, 1907, he added that "Drees wold Hadj Menou [Driss bin Minu, Hafid's military chief] gave such a minute and graphic account of the doctor's death that I became so indignant and began to state my feeling on the enormity of the crime and the guilt of the perpetrators in the strongest terms I could muster, but Mulai el-Haffid [*sic*] stopped me by saying 'Be calm, my friend, I did not murder the doctor.'"

Despite Lennox's statements in favor of Moulay Hafid's innocence, Kouri thought other information to be damning. Lennox confirmed that Moulay Hafid, on learning of the massacre of the workers in Casablanca at the end of July 1907, declared that he would continue his marriage celebration, then in progress, for another seven days. This demonstration of Moulay Hafid's anti-French sentiment further pointed to his alleged culpability.

In October 1910 Reginald Lister, the British minister in Tangier, made an extensive tour of southern Morocco that included a visit to Marrakesh. There he heard from Lennox his account of the Mauchamp murder and the subsequent Kouri investigation. According to Lennox (as Lister recorded in his journal), the pieces now all fit. Moulay Hafid had been plotting for more than six months before Mauchamp's death to discredit his brother Abdelaziz's government. After provoking a French intervention, he would then make his bid to become sultan. First, Moulay Hafid allegedly encouraged caravan robberies to create a climate of insecurity in the region. Then he instigated and exploited the murder of Mauchamp, originally attributed by the French to the governor, al-Warzazi, as a means of removing a staunch supporter of Abdelaziz. Moulay Hafid knew of Mauchamp's plan to hoist a false telegraph antenna as a joke upon the Germans and encouraged him, all the while informing Abdeslam al-Warzazi, who then told the neighborhood headmen to have the locals arm themselves and prepare for disturbances. Once Mauchamp was dead, according to Lennox, Moulay Hafid laid all responsibility upon al-Warzazi, who resigned and died shortly thereafter, replaced by his son, "a mere tool in Hafid's hands."

Having secured control of the city, Moulay Hafid's next step, according to Lister, was to antagonize the Rahamna tribe against his brother's government by his arrest of ten men, predominantly from the Rahamna. With the countryside riled up, Moulay Hafid convened a meeting of tribal leaders, hoping that they would proclaim him sultan. Nothing came of it. "Mr. Lennox tells me very confidentially that Moulai Hafid [*sic*], with whom he was on intimate terms, admitted that the whole thing was a failure."

But opportunity again knocked with the murder of the European railroad workers in Casablanca at the end of July 1907. "The news of Casa Blanca [*sic*] reached Marrakesh on the Thursday, the Europeans left at midnight on Saturday, and Moulai Hafid was proclaimed Sultan on the following Friday."

Lister's conclusion was clear. "M. Kouri, who had previously held the opinion that Dr. Mauchamp's murder was to be laid at the door of Hadj Abslam [*sic*] left Marrakesh convinced that Moulai Hafid had been the real instigator throughout."[23]

In assessing the outcome of Kouri's investigation, Lister was absolutely correct. In a coded letter Kouri wrote to his superiors on July 26 that he had officially terminated his investigation. "It establishes, I believe, the responsibility [Kouri or someone else crossed out the word "culpability"] of Hafid as the principal author in the doctor's murder."

However certain Kouri might have been of Moulay Hafid's guilt, he never succeeded in writing his final report. He became ill in Marrakesh, and not wanting to spend the remainder of the summer there, requested and received permission to take his three-month's leave in Vichy.[24] But before taking his leave, Kouri changed his mind. He wanted to finish his report first, if his health would allow. It didn't, and he soon died in Essaouira.

Thus Kouri's investigation petered to its conclusion without an official report. In September, a French diplomat stopped in Essaouira as Kouri lay dying and gathered together everything related to the investigation to send to Regnault in Tangier. In his cover letter he reconfirmed Kouri's conviction that Moulay Hafid was responsible for Mauchamp's murder.[25]

"Besides the written documents which he brought from Marrakesh, he said he had in his memory overwhelming proof regarding the Sultan." Kouri promised to tell him later, but his condition worsened. "As the doctor had ordered the most absolute rest, I refrained from questioning him about his mission. The day of my departure, however, Monsieur Kouri wished to speak to me about many subjects, this in particular, but he breathed and spoke so painfully that I was barely able to grasp some bits of phrase."

Reginald Lister, the British minister in Tangier, had the last word on Kouri's investigation. He wrote in his journal,

> There appears to be little doubt that M. Kouri was sent to Marrakesh to work up a crushing case against Hafid, whose attitude at that time was so unsatisfactory that the French Government seriously contemplated the possibility of a change of Sultan. Subsequently, however, his attitude changed entirely, his opposition collapsed on all points, and the matter was allowed to drop. The French have, however, kept the evidence collected up their sleeve, and may produce it at any moment should it prove necessary.[26]

Farewell Hafid, Hello Al-Hiba

For a variety of reasons, French diplomats never publicly produced their allegedly incriminating evidence. First, in 1910, as Kouri conducted his investigation, Moulay Hafid seemed to French eyes to have become suddenly more pliable. Without hesitation he accepted new loan agreements as well as French plans to reform the military. However, this honeymoon did not last long. The mistreatment of the wife of the Meknes governor, Ibn Aissa, and the brutality shown to the defeated rebel Abu Himara significantly damaged the sultan's reputation among Europeans. And in response to the growing French presence, rural insurrections continued throughout Morocco. Increasingly, Lyautey and other French policymakers lost patience with Moulay Hafid and his inability to establish order. In 1911, following a mutiny by Makhzan troops in Fez, French soldiers occupied the sultan's capital. Finally, at the end of March 1912, France succeeded in convincing Moulay Hafid to agree to the establishment of a French protectorate over Moroccan affairs. But having signed the protectorate agreement, Moulay Hafid withheld his signature from official decrees and refused to play along. Lyautey, in his new capacity as resident general, grew ever more impatient with Moulay Hafid's recalcitrance. He suspected that at any moment the sultan might slip away from Fez to join the tribes in revolt as the leader of a jihad against the French.

In order to keep a better eye on Moulay Hafid, Lyautey had the court transferred to Rabat. In the interim, French diplomats hunted for a replacement for the difficult sultan. They finally settled on a

younger brother, Moulay Youssef. In August 1912, after months of
negotiations concerning the terms of his abdication, Moulay Hafid
finally acceded to French demands that he leave the throne. As ex-
sultan Moulay Hafid would receive a pension amounting to fifteen
thousand pounds sterling. He also agreed to take a six-week tour
of France, an absence designed to ease the transition to Moulay
Youssef.[27] Eventually, Moulay Hafid would retire, like his brother
Abdelaziz before him, to Tangier. But he did allow himself one final
symbolic act of defiance before he departed Morocco. Before board-
ing the French cruiser *Du Chayla,* he destroyed the imperial seal and
parasol, emblems of his authority.[28]

In the end, when it came to deposing Moulay Hafid, there was
no longer any need to resort to Mauchamp's death as a reason. The
French government had held plenty of aces up its sleeve. Mauchamp's murder—which sparked the French military occupation of
Oujda and had led, in its fashion, to Moulay Hafid's accession—had
in fact been exhausted of all its political usefulness. It had been
superseded by other events almost too numerous to count—the
murder of the quarry workers in Casablanca and the French bombardment of the town, the war in the Shawiya, the conflict between
Abdelaziz and Moulay Hafid, the crushed rebellions of al-Kattani
and Abu Himara, the Fez mutiny and the French occupation. Tensions with Germany also continued to run high as Moulay Hafid
looked to Germany to buttress his position against the French. In
1911 Germany fomented another controversy with France when
Wilhelm II dispatched the *Panther* to the southern coastal town of
Agadir, ostensibly to protect German citizens there. In reality, Germany was simply trying to extort further concessions from France
(in this case, territorial gains in the Congo) in return for recognizing France's establishment of a protectorate over Morocco. Like the
murder of the French doctor in Marrakesh in 1907, these events
were largely unforeseen and difficult to control. They simultaneously delayed and assured what in hindsight appears to have been
inevitable—the French takeover of Morocco.

In Marrakesh, Hajj Driss bin Minu, Moulay Hafid's childhood
friend and one of the officers who quieted the city on the day
Mauchamp was murdered, became governor. However, responding
to pressure from Al-Madani al-Glawi, his vizier and principal supporter, Moulay Hafid soon appointed in his place Thami al-Glawi,
Al-Madani's younger brother. As Thami asserted control over the

city, life in the city remained generally calm for the small European colony. Al-Madani, however, fell out of favor, and on May 26, 1911, Muhammad al-Muqri took his place as grand vizier. Thami too fell into disgrace, but when the opportunity arose to return to favor, he seized it.[29]

In the summer of 1912 Saharan tribesmen, led by al-Hiba, a son of the late Mauritanian leader Ma al-Aynayn, briefly occupied the city and took a number of Frenchmen hostage. Proclaiming himself the legitimate sultan and declaring the French-appointed sultan Youssef to be a puppet, al-Hiba raised the specter of jihad against the French occupation. With many miracles attributed to him, at least some of al-Hiba's followers believed him to be the Mahdi, the Muslim messiah.[30]

The threat did not last long. On September 6, 1912, al-Hiba's ten-thousand-man force was intercepted at Sidi Abu Uthman by five thousand French troops led by Colonel Charles Mangin. Poorly armed and "confident in the promises of al-Hiba that French bullets would turn into water and French shells into watermelons," Moroccan tribesmen assailed the French troops, who were arrayed in the classic square formation with their artillery poised in the center. In little more than two hours it was all over, and the remaining Moroccan troops fled. "The battle was in effect a massacre," one historian has written. "More than two thousand Moroccans were killed outright and thousands more wounded, while Mangin suffered only four killed and twenty-three wounded."[31] That night Mangin dispatched a flying column under the command of Colonel Henri Simon to Marrakesh. The French arrived the next morning to discover that al-Hiba and the rest of his men had fled to the south.

The French continued to pursue al-Hiba and his men over the years. Many of his followers eventually submitted to French authority and some became wealthy *qaids*, but al-Hiba and a small group of followers continue to resist to the end. In 1919 al-Hiba died of illness in the Anti-Atlas at the age of 45.[32]

The month following Mangin's victory General Lyautey himself made a tour of Marrakesh. On October 11 he summoned the leading *qaids* of the south: Si Aissa bin Umar, Al-Madani al-Glawi, Al-Hajj Thami al-Glawi, Abdelmalik al-Mtouggi, Tayyib al-Goundafi, Al-Ayadi al-Rahmani, and a dozen leaders of less importance. He outlined the new order that he envisioned and solicited their collaboration. All of them understood the benefits they would derive from the new regime: an increase in their authority, security for their persons and their belongings, and an opportunity to serve alongside French forces in securing order. "The politics of the great *qaids*"—which gave a measure of autonomy to the Berber chiefs of the Atlas in return for their support of French domination over the sultan—"was inaugurated."[33]

Meanwhile, Thami al-Glawi, who had guaranteed the safety of the Europeans held hostage during al-Hiba's occupation of Marrakesh, earned the perpetual gratitude and trust of the French.[34] As the pasha of Marrakesh over the next four decades, Thami exploited his position to the hilt. In 1914 he already received 2 percent of the market revenues of Marrakesh as a guaranteed stipend to maintain his household, but he further demanded a sixty-thousand hassani peseta supplementary allowance (some twelve hundred dollars) annually.[35] This was just the beginning. After eliminating his rivals Goundafi and Mtouggi, the infamously rapacious Thami embarked on a career of loyal service to the French, who reciprocated by turning a blind eye to his excesses. He and his extended family amassed an unparalleled fortune. As the largest landowner in the country, Thami's holdings during the Protectorate exceeded those of the sultan, while his commercial and industrial investments were estimated at two billion francs in 1956. Either directly or indirectly through his sons, he held sway over slightly more than a million Moroccans for more than four decades.[36]

The European Presence in Marrakesh

After seven long years of twists and turns, the French takeover of Marrakesh and Morocco itself—first predicted by some Moroccans upon Mauchamp's arrival back in 1905—was now a fait accompli. Within the southern capital, the changes were felt immediately. In December 1912 Moulay Youssef, the pliable new sultan chosen as Moulay Hafid's replacement, was dispatched to Marrakesh and the surrounding region to shore up support for the Protectorate and to demonstrate his legitimacy by a visit to the ancestral Alawite *zawiya* in Tamesloht. In Marrakesh and throughout the south he received the *baya,* the oath of allegiance, from local dignitaries and tribal chiefs. His handler, Captain Berriau, head of the political bureau, sent favorable reports of the sultan's performance back to Lyautey in Rabat.[37] The sultan "never neglects to praise the benefits to the country extended by the protecting nation which, always scrupulously respectful of the customs and beliefs of Muslims, seeks to help them evolve toward a civilization and a superior social state which will give them more dignity and well-being."[38]

As early as March 1913—only six months after Mangin's victory over al-Hiba—some 350 Europeans, among them 250 Frenchmen, had taken up residence in Marrakesh. Each day a brisk traffic of automobiles from the coast deposited ever new arrivals outside the city gates.[39] In the month of November 1913 alone ninety Europeans arrived, among them seventy Frenchmen. Many of them took up residence in Mauchamp's former house, now dubbed l'Hotel de Champagne. The hotel's proprietor was Ernest Michel, who, by odd coincidence, had worked in Mauchamp's home town of Chalon-sur-Saône for Schneider et Cie., the parent firm of the Compagnie Marocaine, prior to his arrival in Morocco in 1908. Another of Michel's businesses was producing illustrated postcards. His collection, recently published by his grandson alongside contemporary views of the identical scenes in Marrakesh, provides a remarkable record of the city's transformation over a century.[40]

On October 5, 1913, *L'Atlas,* a French-language weekly, issued its first number to serve the growing European community.[41] In addition, in February 1913 the Marrakesh telegraph bureau also opened for international service.[42] Even before Mangin occupied Marrakesh, the Makhzan under Moulay Hafid planned to install a wireless telegraph there. This was a somewhat ironic development considering that Mauchamp's alleged installation of a telegraph antenna was often cited as the principal cause of his murder.[43]

Recognition of the growing European presence in Morocco was marked in other ways as well. In January 1913 the grand vizier, Muhammad al-Muqri, issued a royal edict from Marrakesh in the name of the sultan, Moulay Youssef. The edict regulated the establishment of public houses and the sale of alcohol. The prohibition on the drinking of alcohol would remain in effect for Muslims, while Europeans would enjoy the "tolerance which our non-Muslim subjects enjoy."[44]

Immediately, the French administration embarked on a program of public works that included paving roads, constructing sewers, and repairing city walls. In the eastern half of the Mamounia gardens, construction began on the Mauchamp hospital. "The garden of a sultan or a vizier?" the romantic writer André Chevrillon rhetorically asked when he recalled his visit to the famous Mamounia.

> I don't know; when I saw it, it was still all unviolated, all Muslim. But the French authority was getting ready to repair, [and] enlarge there an abandoned pavilion, in order to house a civil hospital, indispensable to Marrakesh—and which location could be happier? One ought to proceed with caution, to respect as best as possible the style,

the mauresque proportions that inspired the ancient forms: the chief who directs all of Morocco [i.e., Lyautey] has a fervent concern for beauty. But the soul of the place will not survive: it would not know how to accommodate utilitarian objects.[45]

Today, the celebrated five-star Mamounia Hotel occupies the western half of the gardens and is separated from the hospital grounds by a high wall.

Briefly interrupted at the outbreak of World War I (the entrepreneur overseeing construction was drafted), construction of the Mauchamp hospital continued till 1918, when the bulk of the various pavilions was completed and the hospital was officially opened.[46] In 1913, 224 Moroccans were hospitalized, the following year 416. Who would pay for it all was initially a mystery. In 1915 the occupation force military officer in charge of municipal services wrote to the Residence General requesting a greater contribution from the Protectorate treasury. Five thousand hassani pesetas was currently charged to the municipal budget for rent of the Mamounia property, but more than two-thirds of those treated, the officer complained, were strangers who did not reside in Marrakesh.[47]

Yet even as the buildings were going up, French officials foresaw an almost unlimited demand for medical services. An ophthalmology clinic established in Marrakesh reported 1,440 consultations in April 1917. "The increase of sick women who ask to be hospitalized for eye disorders will necessitate, in the very new future, the construction of a new pavilion for the hospitalization of women at the Mauchamp hospital alongside the one that exists there already."[48]

The doctors and nurses of the *Assistance médicale indigène* (Native Medical Aid) were busy, too. The number of monthly consultations with Moroccan patients climbed from 14,515 in December 1912 to 34,310 the following June. By June 1915 the *Groupe sanitaire mobile,* a roving team of military doctors that serviced the rural surroundings of Marrakesh, reported 57,923 consultations. Nearly a quarter of those seen received smallpox vaccinations. According to the report, "smallpox is not found in the high mountain areas, but the natives accept vaccination well. The population—very appealing, very trusting, poor but happy—only asks to have good relations with everyone."[49] The following year French health officials would inaugurate an intense anti-syphilis campaign. Marrakesh took the lead in 1920 with 24,121 consultations and 19,471 injections delivered.[50] Marrakesh's many prostitutes (from whose labor the governor Thami al-Glawi was said to receive substantial revenues) were also put under surveillance. By December 1935, 1,444 women were registered with the *Service des moeurs,* the "morals" police, and in the course of the year had been subjected to 37,310 visits.[51]

The completed Mauchamp hospital comprised many buildings: two medical and surgical buildings for Muslim men, a similar arrangement for Muslim women, a separate building for Jewish men and women, and a separate building for Muslim notables, both men and women. The ethnic segregation represented an effort to provide Moroccans with "scrupulous respect of their religion and customs." A separate building housed the operating room, a radiology service, and a laboratory. Finally, another building housed services such as the kitchen and laundry.

By the end of 1936 the hospital contained 320 beds. In 1938, 139,514 consultations were conducted. Some 4,747 individuals were hospitalized for a total of 65,292 days. Meanwhile 39,643 received anti-syphilis injections.[52] While it made inroads among the Moroccan population, the medicalization of society occurred at an uneven rate. The Jews of Marrakesh, accounting for only 10 percent of the population, nonetheless counted for 41 percent of the consultations at the Mauchamp hospital, according to the institution's report for 1944.[53] The willingness of the Jews to seek European medical care was noted elsewhere by doctors in various locales, especially in the cities along the coast. This success among Jews, however, encouraged the colonial administration to be even more forceful in its efforts to medicalize Moroccan society.

In the early decades of the Protectorate, the medical roles Mauchamp had always envisioned that he himself would play in Marrakesh—director of a hospital and educator of women in matters relating to childcare—were assumed by two individuals. The first role fell to Dr. Guichard. Like Mauchamp, he was one of the physicians appointed by Delcassé as part of the policy of peaceful penetration and, by coincidence, had examined Mauchamp's corpse in El-Jadida before it was sent on to France. The role of educator was assumed by the "Doctoresse" Françoise Legey. Born and educated in Constantine in Algeria, she received her medical degree from Paris in 1900 and returned to Algeria, where she gained prominence for her pioneering work treating Muslim women. In 1902 she set up a clinic for women in Algiers, and in the following year the government established twelve more clinics in other cities, all run by female physicians. In Marrakesh, Legey would oversee the establishment of a maternity hospital and a *gouttes de lait,* or infant nutrition program.

She also found time to write several respected volumes on Moroccan folklore. Thus, in a very real sense, her career—although played out with greater sensitivity to local norms and customs—was the successful culmination of Mauchamp's ambitions.

When Legey first visited Marrakesh in 1909, she was received, and indeed enthralled, by the young Thami al-Glawi, who had just been made the city's pasha. As al-Glawi's guest, "all the homes of Marrakesh were opened to me; I was dazzled, overcome with enthusiasm, I lived the most beautiful of dreams, and when we took our leave, I had to promise al-Glawi that I'd return."[54] In August 1910 the French ministry of foreign affairs, reportedly responding to a request from Thami himself, approved Dr. Legey's appointment to Marrakesh.[55] During World War I Dr. Legey temporarily left Marrakesh, first to direct a clinic for women in Salé and then later to organize the service for Moroccan women in a new hospital in Casablanca. Following the war she returned to Marrakesh, where she remained for the next three decades.

As early as 1900, while still in Algeria, Legey had proposed without success to the governor general, Paul Révoil, that the government create an independent medical service for native women. In Morocco, Lyautey viewed Legey's plans more favorably, and with al-Glawi's cooperation and the help of a young French midwife Legey succeeded in opening a medical office in Marrakesh. In her practice Legey eventually saw tens of thousands of Moroccan women and their children. Later, in 1926, Legey was joined by a young French doctor, Adrienne Decor, who eventually succeeded her. The following year Legey received funding to establish a separate maternity hospital.

Perhaps Legey's most dramatic accomplishment—again with al-Glawi's forceful connivance—was establishing oversight over local Moroccan midwives. Following a census, all the midwives in Marrakesh were summoned to the maternity hospital and examined. One hundred twenty-five *matrones,* or "matrons" as they were called, were issued licenses and put under Legey's control. All births and the circumstances of delivery were to be recorded, and the midwives were threatened with imprisonment if a mother were to die by their fault. French observers credited Legey on two accounts. First, women throughout the city would now know where to get help in the case of an abnormal labor, and second, native matrons were put under French supervision, a remarkable achievement considering how efforts to supervise native midwives in Algeria, dating back to 1902, had failed.[56]

Improved medical care for Moroccans of course was the ostensible reason why Mauchamp was sent to Marrakesh. While medicine provided the pretext for Delcassé's policy of peaceful penetration at the beginning of the century, Lyautey continued to see medicine as an instrument of pacification designed to win the hearts and minds of Moroccans. "If you can give me four doctors, I will send back companies," Lyautey said, paraphrasing his mentor Gallieni, who had pioneered in Madagascar the methods Lyautey would employ in Morocco. Throughout the Protectorate the French administration continued to make claims for the alleged public health benefits provided by the French occupation.[57]

Morocco was indeed racked by devastating epidemics of various kinds during the nineteenth century and well into the first half of the twentieth.[58] But French doctors such as Mauchamp were inclined to see the "great scourges menacing the native population as symptoms of the decadence of Islam and the degeneration of the Moroccan race."[59] While French successes against cholera, syphilis, typhoid, and smallpox were indeed considerable, one needs to bear in mind that Moroccans were not necessarily the intended beneficiaries. During the first decades of the Protectorate the primary objective of French medical efforts was to curb the epidemiological risk to the growing European population. The purpose of medicine was not so much the alleviation of individual suffering but rather the eradication of diseases that threatened to spill over from the native population. With its "mobile sanitation groups" and assorted campaigns against vermin, French efforts to eradicate disease borrowed the language and organizational methods of the military. The indigenous Moroccan was viewed as a "target bearing a menacing evil to the city" and was thus subjected to surveillance by the French medical authorities.[60] Health concerns—as much as other considerations such as the racism of the *colon* settlers or Lyautey's respectful desire to maintain Moroccan culture—underlay Lyautey's early policy of building separate European quarters, *les villes nouvelles,* alongside the existing *madina*s.[61]

By 1945, with the advent of the pesticide DDT and the success of various inoculation campaigns, the era of epidemics was largely over, and a new "medico-social" phase of French public health began. Moroccan rural migrants to the growing cities were no longer seen as germ bearers but as "the most exposed fraction of the neo-prole-tariat to be humanized, socialized and integrated."[62] Although the percentage of the total Protectorate budget devoted to public health remained relatively stable (vacillating from a low of 5.9 percent in 1928 to a high of 7.9 percent in 1945 and settling at 6.8 percent in 1951), greater attention was turned toward providing hospital beds. In 1926 there were 2,100 hospital beds in Morocco, 4,950 in 1939, and as many as 15,432 in 1955. The number of beds had tripled over the course of the preceding decade. "As for the number of consultations delivered by the hospital and medical units of the public health service, it swelled almost proportionally. Infinitesimally small in 1912, it reached a million in 1917, burst through to 10 million in 1941 and soared to almost 20 million in 1955." The numbers of medical personnel also grew. By 1956 there were upward of five hundred doctors attached to the public health service.[63]

Lest we succumb to the illusion that the expenditures for health-care were equitably distributed between European settlers and in-digenous Moroccans, the figures are sobering. In 1932, when only 4 percent of the total population of Morocco was French and another 1 percent "other" European, a loan was contracted from the French government for the purpose of financing schools and hospitals, to be repaid out of taxes and the profits of the phosphate industry. In each of the three predominantly Muslim cities of Marrakesh, Fez, and Meknes, European hospitals were allocated between four and five million francs, while Moroccan hospitals received five hundred thousand, eight hundred thousand, and five hundred thousand respectively. As one observer put it, "Natives outnumbered Euro-peans more than ten to one in the combined populations of these three cities, but got just over an eighth of the hospital facilities. A per capita ratio of eighty to one against the natives is excessive in a country where they pay most of the taxes. Less than a third of the loan provision for instruction went to institutions for natives. . . . Per child of school age, Europeans got over thirty times as much as Muslims."[64]

Despite French claims for its achievements in education and healthcare during the Protectorate, Moroccan nationalists were quick to point out the discriminatory practices that Moroccans were forced to endure in their own country. A 1953 publication of the Istiqlal (Independence) Party summarized the balance sheet in blunt terms.

After forty years of the French Protectorate, Moroccans are increasingly ill-housed, ill-fed, ill-clothed, deprived of civil rights and of equal and unrestricted access to education. While 94 percent of French children of school age attend schools in Morocco at the expense of the Moroccan people, only 6 percent of Moroccan children are permitted this luxury. Higher education is a virtual impossibility for Moroccans. Out of an indigenous population of over 8,500,000 there are less than a dozen Moroccan physicians and the number of people in Morocco per physician (of all nationalities) is 14,000. The average for Moroccans only is 1 physician for 43,300 Moroccans compared with the ratio of 1 to 1,300 persons in France and 1 to 1,100 non-Moroccans in Morocco.

Written three years before Morocco achieved its independence from France, the Istiqlal tract concludes, "The heritage of forty years of the French Protectorate offers nothing to justify French claims of assistance to the Moroccan people."[65]

Conclusion: The Old Morocco

Mourning and Memory

Mauchamp's memory was supposed to last forever. On that day in April 1907 when his mortal remains were laid to rest in the cemetery of Chalon-sur-Saône, one orator prophesied that Mauchamp's example would "sustain imitators among our generous and chivalrous French youth." Another promised that "this spilled blood that reddened the soil of Marrakesh will not remain infertile. It will give birth to converts." And for yet a third, Mauchamp's tragic death transcended partisan political differences. Mauchamp was "one of these modest and stubborn workers of pure science" who "fell victim to ignorance and fanaticism. . . . He died for the cause, three times holy and noble, of civilization."

Guillemin, the old schoolteacher and Mauchamp's future biographer, spoke the most ardently of all at the young doctor's funeral. He emphasized the selflessness of Mauchamp's mission:

> With the smiling fearlessness of the missionary who deliberately chose his path, [Mauchamp] looked on the art of healing as a force for moral penetration. He went among the peoples of the Orient not because of a thirst for novelty or a life of the picturesque but because he was convinced that there, more than any place else, there were victories to achieve over the ordinary, good deeds to do, human lives to save, and he figured that it was good that it was a Frenchman who would save them.[1]

To these eulogists, Mauchamp perished as a Frenchman bringing civilization to those who could not yet comprehend its benefit.

As Louis Gentil put it, capturing the exquisite irony of the doctor's martyrdom, "He died beneath the blows of those to whom he had dedicated his science and his devotion."

This is the image of Mauchamp, the selfless French martyr of science who would inspire French youth and Moroccans alike, that the memorializers attempted to keep alive. In the decade that followed his death, monuments of varying degrees of grandiosity, some built of words, others of bronze, were devoted to the late doctor's memory. Guillemin's biography of his former pupil came out in serial form within a year of his death. In 1910 Mauchamp's father saw to it that his son's notes on Moroccan magic were published posthumously as *Sorcery in Morocco*.[2]

Mauchamp's native Chalon repaid its loyal son well for his devotion. On April 14, 1908, nearly a year to the day after his funeral, the municipal council voted to name a street in his honor not far from his house in the place de Beaune.[3] Two years later and three years after Mauchamp was laid to rest, the foreign minister Pichon and other dignitaries again assembled in Chalon, on Sunday, August 21, 1910, this time to dedicate a monument to Mauchamp.[4] The "modest program"—as it was described in the minutes of the city council—was a virtual reenactment of the doctor's earlier funeral. The chief difference this time was the banquet that preceded the statue's unveiling. Costing the city three thousand francs, the banquet was described down to the smallest detail by the local republican daily *Le Progrès de Saône-et-Loire*. No effort was spared. In honor of the foreign minister, the city hall was decorated with potted plants. Carefully hidden in the corner, "a powerful electric fan brought a delicious freshness into the hall." The menu was lavish: chilled melon, cold salmon in a green sauce, filet of beef garnished *à la Richelieu*, green beans *à l'anglaise*, Bresse chicken baked in a brioche, crayfish *à la parisienne*, and a *bombe glacée*, or molded sherbet, for dessert.

The toasts were lavish, too—and decidedly partisan in tone. Pichon, the foreign minister, led the charge. "No other department," he proclaimed, "merits the sympathy of republican ministers more than yours." He recalled the sacrifices to the republican cause made by the department of Saône-et-Loire over the years and concluded that "the members of the government have no higher ambition than to serve the Republic and the Radical Party in which you have placed your confidence and which presides over the destiny of the country."[5]

Le Courrier—the rightist, pro-clerical paper—complained bitterly about Pichon's toast, but its republican rival, *Le Progrès*, was dismissive. "What do the snubs of malcontented clerics matter before this unanimity of spirit and hearts?"[6]

At two o'clock the procession formed outside the city hall. Occupying no less than eighteen cars, the entourage of dignitaries was preceded by a platoon of gendarmes on horseback, a brigade of firemen, and the municipal band. Members of various local societies marched in the rear. As the statue was unveiled, the assembled crowd heard a choir perform a "hymn to Doctor Mauchamp" and listened to more speeches praising Mauchamp's sacrifice.

The last to speak, Pichon used the opportunity to defend his government's policy in Morocco. Like that policy itself, Pichon's speech was both strained and contradictory. France's earlier diplomatic efforts were now seconded by the army, he said. Following the occupation of Casablanca, France was methodically taking military action in the south and the east. Resistance to French demands for reparation had been destroyed. French military victories in Morocco, like those earlier in Algeria, had won respect for France. Moreover, the native populations were profiting from "our beneficial protection and civilizing administration." France and Morocco were now working together, he claimed, while the international divisions that had posed a menace to peace in Europe had been resolved. "The only thing to do is to continue in peace—because we are the enemy of all militaristic adventures."

Pichon concluded by telling his listeners that only the day before Nooman Kouri, whom he had charged with investigating Mauchamp's murder, had himself died on his return from Marrakesh. The pursuit of France's policy in Africa would not be easy. Mauchamp's sacrifice—his "death on the field of honor"—was emblematic of the difficulty of the task.[7]

After the unveiling, the assembled crowd then proceeded to Chalon's Eastern Cemetery. There amid more speeches a wreath of roses was placed on Mauchamp's grave. Addressing his dead friend in the grave using the familiar *tu*, Jules Bois—the author of the introduction to Mauchamp's posthumous book—offered the most notable and moving eulogy. Mauchamp's siblings and brothers-in-law attended the ceremonies. His grief-stricken parents spent the day in their apartment.

As for the monument itself, the work was sculpted by Pierre Curillon, an award-winning sculptor from the nearby town of Tournus.

Figure 13. The Mauchamp Memorial in Chalon as it appeared prior to
World War II. Reproduction courtesy of *La Société d'histoire et d'archéologie de
Chalon-sur-Saône.*

A large bronze bust of the doctor rested on a tall stone stele. Before it stood a bronze, life-size statue of an incongruously bare-breasted Moroccan woman. With one arm outstretched toward Mauchamp's bust and the other holding an infant, she looked ardently at Mauchamp. "This Moroccan woman who clutches her infant below the bust of our friend," intoned Doctor Bauzon, "is the happy symbol of the gratitude of mothers and their children, returned to health." Mauchamp's eyes, turned to the horizon, seemed to look past the imploring woman.

Two bas-reliefs in bronze graced the side of the stele. One showed Mauchamp attending patients in his clinic. On the other, the furious mob was caught frozen in the act of murder. As one Arab plunged a dagger into the heart of the prostrate Mauchamp, another stood poised to smash in the Frenchman's head with a rock. Off to one side, a black man with a big knife waited his turn. The monument stands today in a mutilated condition. The mother and child were melted down by the Germans during their World War II occupation of Chalon.

Financed by voluntary subscription, the statue joined two other bronze monuments in the park and square adjacent to Chalon's present-day tourist office. The first bronze, dedicated in 1899, was a bust of François Chabas (1817–1882), a merchant and president of the local Chamber of Commerce who gained a reputation as a self-taught Egyptologist. The other, more extravagant monument was dedicated to the district's war dead and was unveiled in 1907, the same year as Mauchamp's death. It depicts in elaborate detail a mounted cavalryman of the Second Empire. He bears before him on his horse a dead or wounded comrade, while a woman leaning alongside wails her silent grief.[8] Thus, in a very real sense, Mauchamp united in his person two sentiments already abundantly felt in Chalon, a pride in scientific accomplishment and a sense of patriotic obligation.

Memorialization is something the French do particularly well. The phenomenon of erecting war monuments, undertaken on local initiative as in the case of Chalon after the defeat by Prussia in 1871, became a positive mania in France during and after World War I. As a result, less than 1 percent of France's thirty-eight thousand communes has no monument to its World War I dead.[9] But if Mauchamp's statue shares a common lineage with those of the anonymous soldier who bears arms in so many town squares of France, it also ironically echoes the Moroccan tradition of honoring saints.

The Moroccan countryside is dotted with whitewashed *qubba*s, the domed tombs of holy men whose intercessionary powers continue beyond the short span of their lives.

In Marrakesh, in the hospital that bore his name, Mauchamp's remaining effects became the centerpiece of a secular shrine. An early historian of French medicine in Morocco, René Cruchet, made the Mauchamp hospital his first stop during a 1929 visit to Marrakesh, and he devotes a good portion of his book *The Peaceful Conquest of Morocco and the Tafilalet* to the Mauchamp story. On a chimney mantle at the threshold of the examining room one could see a stucco bust of Mauchamp. Alongside it there lay "a sort of misshapened root that crudely resembled the end of a battered femur." Cruchet identified the object as a *zorouata,* a kind of Moroccan *matraque,* or bludgeon, displayed as a macabre reminder to Moroccan patients of the rationale for the hospital's existence.[10] Elsewhere, in the elegantly appointed hospital library, dominated by a large oriental rug and the photograph of the reigning sultan, Mohammed V, Cruchet discovered a veritable museum of Mauchamp artifacts. On one wall hung the doctor's portrait "with the thin, pointed mustache, his lively and determined small eyes, his hair, already thinning, parted on the right, divided toward the left in two unequal parts." Next to it was a photo taken in El-Jadida on March 26, 1907, of the crowd that accompanied his remains after they were examined by Dr. Guichard. Another photo showed the coffin being loaded upon the cruiser *Lalande.* In a far corner of the library Cruchet found on display remnants of Mauchamp's books and papers, discolored—he imagined—with the blood of Mauchamp's attackers.

"In this assortment of detached pages one forms an image of the abundant and varied cultural attainment of our unfortunate compatriot," Cruchet wrote. Alongside medical textbooks and a dictionary of Marrakesh Arabic, Cruchet uncovered a philosophical manual "on the union of body and the soul," a history of women during France's Second Empire, and various novels, including H. G. Wells's *First Men in the Moon.* In the margins of the scattered pages, Cruchet found notes in Mauchamp's handwriting. "Meager relics," he called these items, "of a past so close yet already so distant, poor vestiges of a peaceful conquest so tragically interrupted."[11]

"A past so close yet already so distant"

That Morocco had turned a corner, that the pre-Protectorate Morocco was qualitatively different from the country that existed under

French tutelage, was a conventional sentiment among French and European observers. Like many other writers from the Protectorate period, Cruchet conceived of his history of French medicine in Morocco as a series of *before* and *after* snapshots.[12] Emblematic of this perception is the title of Walter Harris's 1920 memoir, *Morocco That Was.* But the presentiment that change was inevitable could already be seen in such books as E. Ashmead-Bartlett's *The Passing of the Shereefian Empire,* published in 1910, two years before the Protectorate began. For many commentators, the "old Morocco," *le vieux Maroc,* had already passed in 1900 with the death of Abdelaziz's former regent, Ba Ahmed.

One might well anticipate that a posthumous reappraisal of Mauchamp's role would begin once Morocco regained its independence in 1956. In fact, Mauchamp's place in the narrative surrounding the French occupation of Morocco already had suffered a somewhat curious turn of fortune even during the Protectorate. Despite efforts like that of Cruchet to rally Frenchmen to the memory of the late doctor, more typically the story of Mauchamp's death was relegated to the footnotes of the historical narrative of France's occupation. In the emerging story of the French conquest of Morocco, it became clear that Mauchamp's violent death was part of the "old" Morocco, a coda to the old regime, rather than a preface or precursor to the new and future order.

Equally telling is the conspicuous absence of references to the doctor or his death in several works that refer to or specifically deal with Marrakesh. For example, in recounting his exploits as a doctor in the native medical service in the Atlas Mountains, Paul Chatinières starts with his arrival in Marrakesh in 1912. At that time Mauchamp's memory was still quite fresh. Nevertheless, given Chatinières's goal of glorifying the contributions toward pacification made by the military doctors of the mobile sanitary units, it is hardly surprising that the efforts of civilian "medical diplomats" who preceded them would receive short shrift. Mauchamp is entirely absent from his account.[13] Likewise, Mauchamp is conspicuously missing from both the Tharaud brothers' famous travelogue, *Marrakesh or the Lords of the Atlas,* and Edith Wharton's *In Morocco.*

What connects all three works by Chatinières, the Tharauds, and Wharton is the instrumental role of General Lyautey. In the case of Chatinières, the mobile sanitary units were Lyautey's innovation, and the general personally ordered Chatinières to Marrakesh. Writing an introduction to Chatinières's memoirs, Lyautey used the opportunity to justify the role of doctors in the pacification effort but did so without once mentioning Mauchamp. As for Jérôme and Jean Tharaud, Lyautey invited the brothers to Morocco in 1917 in the midst of World War I. After an extended stay they produced book-length portraits of Rabat, Fez, and Marrakesh, evocative and literate propaganda in support of the French Protectorate.[14] The American novelist Edith Wharton, also invited by Lyautey to Morocco in 1917, wrote an especially admiring account of France's civilizing mission in her travelogue, *In Morocco*. Like the Tharauds, Wharton left out of her account of Marrakesh all mention of Mauchamp.[15] Lyautey, whose fortunes materially benefited from the murder of Mauchamp and the occupation of Oujda, understood only all too well how the murder of a French doctor by Moroccans negated his arguments about pacification and the role of doctors in the "peaceful conquest" of Morocco. That Moroccans might hate Frenchmen, even the ones who ostensibly provided them with a benefit, was not a message that advocates of the French civilizing mission openly acknowledged.

In its March 21, 1937, issue, the French-language paper of Marrakesh, *Al-Atlas*, noted that the previous Friday marked the thirtieth anniversary of Mauchamp's death. The writer of "Echoes," a front-page feature regularly devoted to nostalgic tidbits, could not presume that his readers knew Mauchamp. He introduces the doctor as a "peaceful pioneer" on an official mission wherein he sought to "win hearts by a stubborn devotion to the Moroccan population." The account of his death in Marrakesh is boiled down to a handful of crucial details: unnamed German agents, underhanded intrigue, dagger blows, and the triumphant ululation of women watching the brutal attack from the neighboring rooftops. "A few days later, the French government, desirous of obtaining reparations, decided to occupy the city of Oujda." Nowhere is there mention of the inciting pole on the roof, the rumors about wireless telegraphy, or the alleged role of Moulay Hafid. With suitable bathos the article concludes with a reference to Mauchamp's posthumous book on Moroccan magic, lovingly compiled from his notes "by a friendly hand."

In short, for the French settlers of Marrakesh, Mauchamp's story had devolved into an item of antiquarian interest. The early years of conquest and even more recent examples of resistance such as the Rif War were already distant memories. And as if to confirm the distance traveled by Frenchmen and Moroccans alike, Mauchamp's anniversary shared the front page with a photograph showing French resident general Noguès and a compliant sultan Mohammed V arriving together to open Marrakesh's seventeenth agricultural fair.[16]

In later years, among the *colons,* or French settlers, of Morocco, there were some who could still remember the "old days." They formed clubs where they reveled in the nostalgia of their "pioneering" efforts. Paul Bouvier, one of the Frenchmen who had found himself under siege on the day Mauchamp was attacked, went on to become the leading industrialist of Casablanca. There he presided over the "Association of Frenchmen from before August 1907," that is, French *Casablancais* who dated their arrival to before the French occupation of the Shawiya. Another settler group called itself the "Association of Old Moroccans." It counted among its members more than seven hundred Frenchmen who dated their arrival to before 1914.[17]

In the 1940s and 50s, as the elderly Frenchmen who appropriated the name "old Moroccans" were beginning to pass away, a spate of books appeared that recalled the "good old days" of *le vieux Maroc.* Most notable among them were Madame Saint-René Taillandier's *The Vanished World,* Christian Houel's *My Moroccan Adventures,* Henri Croze's *Souvenirs of Old Morocco,*[18] Auguste de Saint-Aulaire's *In Morocco before and with Lyautey,* Felix Weisgerber's *On the Doorstep of Modern Morocco,* and Moïse Nahon's *About an Old Moroccan.*[19] Ironically, these books appeared just as a new generation of "genuine" Moroccans (as opposed to European settlers) experienced the resurgence of nationalism that would enable Morocco to gain its independence.

Marina López Gádor's relatively recent memoir, *The Casablanca Stagecoach,* gives a vivid account of emigrant life in Casablanca in the early decades of the Protectorate. In her introduction she recalls the remark, attributed, like so many other clever sayings, to Lyautey: "Morocco, spend eight days there, and you write a book. Live a month, and you produce an article. Live there your whole life, and you no longer know what to say about it."

"I found nothing to say about [Morocco] when I was living there with my family," López Gádor writes, explaining her belated urge to remember. "I believed that my entire life would unfurl itself there. . . . And since I left it—more than thirty years ago—not a day passes without my having it present in spirit, without my dreaming of it at night."[20]

Mauchamp may be forgotten, but for those who spent their childhood and productive years in Morocco, the passage of nearly half a century since the French departure has not dimmed the memory of the sun-drenched kingdom. The authors of a recent history entitled *Frenchmen in Morocco* compiled their work from the ardent testimony of nearly 150 former settlers.[21] In it, the nostalgia of French *colons* commingles with the nostalgia of Morocco's Jews, who, in the years following World War II, found their way into exile in Israel, France, Canada, and Spain.[22]

Alongside the latest production of nostalgia, a subgenre has emerged—memoirs by and about doctors recalling their humanitarian work during the Protectorate.[23] These books bear heroic titles such as *I Was Doctor to a 100,000 Berbers, Bush Doctor,* and *I Was a Doctor in Morocco.*[24] One might well imagine Mauchamp to have written such an autobiography himself had he survived to see the French prevail. Thus, while Mauchamp's image itself has blurred over the decades, the image of the heroic doctor in Morocco that his death helped create has been assiduously burnished.

Some doctors, such as Bouveret, who ran the hospital in Essaouira and created a flourishing institution out of nothing, became quite famous, even in their own lifetimes.[25] But serving as a physician in Morocco was not without risks. A long list of doctors, including both Bouveret and Chatinières, the mobile group doctor sent by Lyautey to the Atlas in 1912, died of contagious illnesses contracted while working in the public health service. Recognizing the dangers of service in Morocco, early in the Protectorate the French administration created a "Gold Medal for Epidemics." It was awarded to doctors and health workers—in some cases posthumously—for their having suffered typhus and other diseases while in the public health service.[26]

Many French doctors clearly served Morocco with devotion and formed deep personal attachments to the country. The depth of these emotional attachments as well as the success of French epidemiological campaigns waged against diseases such as typhus has made it difficult for some to accept the recently voiced criticisms of French medical practices under the Protectorate. One historian, Michel Lafon, was "astonished and shocked" to read his fellow historian Daniel Rivet's assertion that "repulsion, more often than compassion, inspired the medical discourse on Moroccans." Surely, Lafon objects, Rivet's source was the exception.[27]

Marie-Claire Micouleau-Sicault, the author of *French Doctors in Morocco, 1912–1956,* similarly objects to the increasingly negative portrayals of the Protectorate era. Her book has two aims: to com-

memorate her father, Georges Sicault, director of public health in
Morocco from 1946 to 1956, and to correct "the conventional and
largely false image" regarding France's colonial mission as propa-
gated by the French "intelligentsia." "Colonialism wasn't only a
matter of economic interests and strategic manipulations for power,"
she writes. "For the young people who were entering life, it was also
the fulfillment of destiny that they devote themselves to a people
consumed by anarchy and tribal struggles, decimated by epidemics
and infant malnutrition."

The balance sheet is difficult to assess. The Moroccan-born author
Tahar ben Jelloun can applaud the generous contributions of some
doctors (especially the Franciscan brothers and sisters) and speak
admiringly of those doctors who worked "outside of all political
calculus." These doctors provided what Moroccans so clearly lacked
and needed. But for Ben Jelloun there is always the overwhelming
fact that medicine served an ulterior motive, a fact that Lyautey
and his successors never denied. Medicine permitted the French
conquerors of Morocco to assume "a human face." Medicine was
the veil that hid from view France's military might, the true basis of
its power in Morocco.

"The Moroccans never challenged this humanitarian action,"
Ben Jelloun writes in regard to the Moroccan acceptance of the
Protectorate's medical practices. "It would be elsewhere, through
other actions, in other areas, that the wounds would imprint themselves."[28]

Against the backdrop of France's bloody war in Algeria, Morocco
regained its independence in 1956. The transfer of power was dramatic. In 1953 France, with the help of Thami al-Glawi, deposed the
Moroccan sultan, Mohammed V, and installed in his place a cousin,
Mohammed ben Arafa. Sent into exile, the popular Mohammed V
came to symbolize the country's aspirations for independence. In
August 1953, as if to confirm that the sultan in exile—and not the
imposter installed on the throne by the French—was the country's
genuine ruler, a group of women swore that they saw Mohammed
V's face in the moon. News of the miracle swept Morocco. In the
autumn of 1955 the true sultan triumphantly returned to reoccupy
the throne and to negotiate the end of the French Protectorate and
the return of the Spanish zone to Morocco.[29]

While the bloodbath that took place in neighboring Algeria was
avoided, violence nonetheless marred the transition to independence as terrorist groups on both sides engaged in a cycle of vicious

attacks and reprisals. The most notorious incident was the massacre at Oued Zem, a predominantly Berber town located northeast of Marrakesh, in which ninety-five French settlers were murdered on August 20, 1955. An estimated three hundred Moroccans were also killed. The tragic encounter took place just as talks devoted to ending the Protectorate were getting underway in the French town of Aix-les-Bains. As the attackers approached the door of the hospital in Oued Zem, the chief doctor, Fischbacher, pleaded in vain that they leave the hospital and its patients alone. Of the fourteen patients who were killed, eleven were Muslims.[30] Dr. Fischbacher himself was stabbed to death and dismembered. Thus, the French occupation of Morocco ended much as it began, with the murder of a French doctor in the street, arguing with Moroccans outside the door of his clinic.[31]

The irony of this coincidence should not mislead us into thinking that "nothing had changed." Moroccan independence did not and could not mean a return to the status quo that prevailed before the French occupation of Oujda. After forty-four years of the Protectorate, the "old" Morocco was indeed gone. Indeed, the Morocco of today would have been scarcely imaginable a century ago. This is most apparent not just in terms of political or economic stability but most obviously in the way Morocco and Moroccans interact with the world beyond its own borders. A hundred-year-ago Morocco was justifiably wary of foreigners and the world beyond its borders. In contrast, Morocco today is a country open to the outside world. It welcomes tourists; it sought (unsuccessfully) to host the World Cup in 2006; and, as an eager participant in the U.S.-sponsored Fulbright program, it actively promotes cultural exchanges. Together with Spain, Morocco is currently exploring the possibility of constructing a railway tunnel under the Straits of Gibraltar that would link Africa and Europe.[32] Not least, the ersatz Morocco exhibit at Disney's Epcot Center in Florida has allowed scores of Moroccans to experience life in America firsthand. Out of necessity, Morocco's population is proficient in many languages, and one finds in urban areas satellite dishes on virtually every balcony and an Internet boutique on every corner. Almost the first new word one learns in Arabic in Morocco is *al-awlama*, globalization, a word that carries in Morocco none of the negative connotations that it bears in some American circles.

Elsewhere, too, the image of Morocco has changed. In France, according to a poll reported in the Casablanca paper *Le Matin*, 88 percent of the French say they have a high opinion of Morocco's young new king, Mohammed VI, and 76 percent have a positive image of Morocco.[33] For this very reason the suicide bombings in Casablanca in May 2003 came to ordinary Moroccans as a devastating shock. Undertaken by their own fellow countrymen, the attacks conflicted with the pride most Moroccans take in theirs being a "moderate" Muslim country. As Moroccans frequently point out, their country is the very antithesis of their war-wracked neighbor, Algeria.[34]

Oblivion and the Erasure of Memory

But if time blurs memory, there has also been deliberate erasure.[35] With independence, the Moroccan state and its organs, both official and unofficial, sought to emphasize the nationalist myth of struggle and colonial resistance. The Mauchamp hospital, like so many other edifices and streets, was renamed. Now called the Ibn Zuhr Hospital after a medieval Arab ophthalmologist, it continues to serve as a kind of regional clinic. In the shade of its old pavilions poor women wait with their children to receive treatment. A high wall separates the dusty grounds of the old Mauchamp hospital from the immaculate gardens of the adjacent five-star Hotel Mamounia.

The fate of the little Mauchamp shrine so lovingly described by Cruchet is no mystery. The meager relics were thrown away along with the Protectorate. For my benefit, the public health ministry's representative in Marrakesh graciously called a retired administrator.[36] Yes, she told him over the phone, she had a distinct recollection of a suitcase in the corner of the hospital that contained papers belonging to the doctor. No, it was thrown in the trash when the hospital records were transferred to the larger, newer facility, the Ibn Tufayl hospital.

As for the Arsa Moulay Musa quarter of the *madina,* it looks today much as it did a hundred years ago when Mauchamp opened his clinic there—or possibly even worse. Many of the narrow, winding alleyways are still unpaved. Today in Marrakesh the very mention of the quarter's name causes old-timers to titter. In the 1930s Ars Moulay Musa enjoyed great renown as a red-light district. Mauchamp is indeed forgotten there, supplanted by other memories. A French doctor? Yes, there was one, a Dr. Roux, now long dead, who had a clinic there a half century ago. But Mauchamp, he has disappeared from Marrakesh.

Some of the characters who played a role in Mauchamp's story went on to become important personalities in the Protectorate of General Lyautey. But these too are by and large now forgotten. Gabriel Veyre—Abdelaziz's erstwhile instructor in photography—was the first entrepreneur to bring electricity to Casablanca. Veyre's tombstone in the Christian cemetery of Casablanca reads, "Here lies Docteur Gabriel Veyre (1871–1936). Officer of the Legion of Honor, first precursor of French civilization in Morocco."[37] Christian Houel founded—among other newspapers in his long career—*La Vigie Marocaine,* the settlers' principal mouthpiece. Louis Gentil established the Institut scientifique in Rabat and had an important phosphate mining town named after him. With independence, the city was renamed Youssoufia. The school for girls that once bore the name of the former chargé d'affaires Saint-Aulaire has been renamed for Ibn Battuta, the famed Moroccan traveler of the fourteenth century.[38] Only the French Lycée Regnault in Tangier continues to bear the name of the diplomat who signed the 1912 Fez treaty that established the Protectorate.

Moroccans have an ambivalent relationship with the past. It surrounds them but does not overwhelm them. "Have you been to the archeological museum?" I always ask my Moroccan friends in Rabat. "No," they reply. "Why should we? Our whole country is a museum." As one anthropologist has observed, "The nostalgia Arabs take as a given throughout most of the Middle East plays almost no role in Morocco, where the taxonomic emphasis on current relationships squeezes out the regretted past in favor of an existent or nonexistent impact in the world. Indeed, there is no real speculation as to how things might have been different."[39]

The museumification of Moroccan culture manifests itself in diverse ways. One sees it in the Berber dances staged to welcome dignitaries at the king's palace and in the internationally sponsored efforts to preserve the *madina*s of Fez and Marrakesh. Moroccans accept all this with a shrug. "What's it like?" I ask the taxi driver as he takes me to the Majorelle Garden in Marrakesh, a beautiful green spot laid out by a French artist famous for his travel posters and now owned and maintained by Yves Saint Laurent. "How should I know?" he replied. "That's for tourists."

Only in the context of family events or communal celebrations, when the passage of time is appropriately noted, do Moroccans typically engage in nostalgia.[40] Thus, at wedding celebrations even the most "Westernized" Moroccan women choose to wear stylish, updated caftans. Their husbands, on the other hand, conspicuously continue to wear suits—good suits—so as to display their success both materially and in terms of assimilation. At funerals, on the other hand, even male resistance breaks down, and, out of respect for the departed father or mother, the mourning son will cling to the old ways and don traditional Moroccan clothes. On Fridays and holidays, too, if he should attend the mosque, the Moroccan city dweller might put on a robe and slippers. After all, circumstances demand one dress for the part. This cultural cross-dressing was exemplified best by the late king Hassan II, who would change his clothes many times in the course of a day, appearing in one television clip in an elegant French suit and in the next in a flowing pastel robe.

The ability to live in the here-and-now and adapt to changes around him is symptomatic of another Moroccan trait, an ambivalent relationship to power. Confronted with a powerful figure, the Moroccan typically hedged his bets, playing both sides "just in case." Writing about the memory of French rule, Lawrence Rosen notes that "the French, as powerful figures, were regarded like other such rulers—as people you had to cleave to (in both senses of the word), staying close enough to them to predict and influence their actions without allowing that proximity to limit other attachments that may be of use."[41] After the initial period of resistance to the French, Moroccans made their accommodation with their colonizers.

Thus, a Berber chieftain who fought against the French invaders could later make his peace and receive a commission commanding native auxiliary troops during the Protectorate. Collaboration? At least during the Protectorate, things were not necessarily seen that way. The chieftain could continue to "enjoy the respect of his people because of his years fighting the French. By the same token, his past as a resistance hero guaranteed that he was never really trusted by French authorities." But in the nationalist period of the fifties and sixties, the same figure could be "despised and distrusted by the eager young nationalists."[42]

The American political scientist James C. Scott once put forth the argument that in the daily comportment of ordinary people one could uncover the "hidden transcripts" of resistance to colonialism.[43] And yet, in the case of Morocco, where the record of resistance was overt and well-documented, the interpretive challenge is just the opposite. In Morocco one must uncover the hidden transcripts of acceptance.

In its day, the murder of Émile Mauchamp signified many things to many people. For Moroccans, it was a demonstration against French imperialist designs and a symbolic display of violence directed at an inept ruler.[44] For the French, at least for those who

thought about these things, it was a glorious opportunity mas-
querading as a tragic event. And now, nearly a century later, a few
hundred yards from Arsa Moulay Musa, where he died, Moroccan
women wait patiently for treatment at the hospital that no longer
bears Mauchamp's name.

Nearby, conspicuously and centrally located across from the
Kutubiyya minaret and Marrakesh's Club Med, is the high-walled
French consulate building. The consul himself cordially answers my
questions. "No," he tells me, "there are no records of any historical
merit kept at the consulate. Everything is sent to Paris." The consul
listens intently to the story of Mauchamp. It was the first he had
ever heard of it. Later, when I tell Moroccans about how graciously
the French consul received me, they uniformly offer a hypothesis
for such unanticipated behavior. Obviously, they say, he must have
a Moroccan wife. Today Moroccans believe fervently in their own
version of a civilizing mission.

That the French consul in Marrakesh had never heard of Mauchamp was hardly a surprise. Only a few weeks earlier in Rabat, an
official attached to France's still considerable cultural mission lifted
his eyebrows in disbelief when, over dinner, he was told that French
warships had flattened Casablanca in 1907. This was news to him.
Postcolonial memory is obviously selective.

Only in his native town of Chalon-sur-Saône—where members
of the local historical society still refer to their once famous compatriot as "the poor" Mauchamp—has Mauchamp's memory managed
to survive. In the Musée Denon, a small neoclassical pile that sits in
the square across from the city hall where Mauchamp's body lay in
state, Mauchamp's bust graces a second-story landing. In a corner
of the museum devoted to North Africa, a display case offers an
exhibit of artifacts that had belonged once to the doctor. The items
entered the collection in 1938, following the death of Mauchamp's
father. It is almost impossible to imagine, but the old man Pierre
Mauchamp survived his son by thirty years and lived to the age of
ninety-nine.

If there are relatives of Mauchamp with private papers and family memoirs, no one in Chalon seems to know. Among the four or
five Mauchamps in the Paris phonebook, one is a sociologist and, by
an odd and somewhat befitting coincidence, the author of a series
of textbooks that explain French history to new immigrants. They
bear such grand, celebratory titles as *France Forever: Civilization* and
Without Borders: Civilization: France. From a family "too poor to have

produced any physicians," Nelly Mauchamp is no relation to Émile. But she knows his story well. As a small girl from Dijon, she would attend the annual carnival in Chalon, where her father would point out with pride the street placard that bore their family name.[45]

A street sign tacked on a wall, a half-broken statue, and a scattering of footnotes. A century after Mauchamp's death brought French troops into Morocco, these are the last traces of an event and a life that for an instant captured one country's imagination and literally changed the destiny of another. Moroccans are naturally indifferent to *Moshan*, as his name is rendered in Arabic. Contrary to the high-minded speeches made so long ago in Chalon about France's civilizing mission, there are no monuments to this or any other "martyred" French doctor today in Morocco. Why should there be? The high ideals that one nation professes cannot obliterate the indignity and sorrow that another nation feels when it no longer controls its fate.

Even so, Moroccans are not without a sense of humor in regard to their past. Today Morocco is a country of satellite dishes, cyber-cafés, and the ubiquitous *téléboutique*—the corner store where an array of phone booths serves the needs of people who have neither a cell phone or a home phone. One of these little shops, in a busy street in Rabat across from the *madina*, is appropriately called the *téléboutique* Bopp. Named for the Frenchman who brought the wireless telegraph to Morocco, it stands as an ironic milepost marking the distance traveled over a long century.

Notes

Abbreviations

AF	*Documents Diplomatiques, Affaires du Maroc*
AIU	Archives de l'Alliance Israélite Universelle (Paris)
BAIU	*Bulletin de l'Alliance Israélite Universelle*
BCAF	*Bulletin du Comité de l'Afrique Française*
BG	Bibliothèque Générale (Rabat)
BO	*Bulletin Officiel* (Protectorate du Maroc), Édition Français
BR	Bibliothèque Royale (Rabat)
DAR	Direction des Archives Royales (Rabat)
IJMES	*International Journal of Middle Eastern Studies*
JNAS	*Journal of North African Studies*
MAE	Ministère des Affaires Étrangères (Nantes)
PRO FO	Public Records Office, Foreign Office (Kew)

Introduction

1. William Hoisington, *Lyautey and the French Conquest of Morocco* (New York: St. Martin's, 1995), 30.

2. Jonathan G. Katz, *Dreams, Sufism and Sainthood: The Visionary Career of Muhammad al-Zawawi* (Leiden: E. J. Brill, 1996).

3. Émile Mauchamp, *La Sorcellerie au Maroc* (Paris: Dordon-Ainé, 1910).

4. Nina Epton, *Saints and Sorcerers, A Moroccan Journey* (London: Cassell, 1958), 128.

5. "Lettre de M. P. Mauchamp à M. Jules Bois," in Mauchamp, *Sorcellerie,* 3. Émile Mauchamp had met Bois in Jerusalem. The author of many books, including *La Satanisme et la magie,* Bois was well known in his lifetime for having participated in two sensational duels. Robert Baldick, *The Life of J.-K. Huysmans* (Oxford: Clarendon Press, 1955), 209–10.

6. With full justification Arabs and Muslims take umbrage with simplistic characterizations of an undifferentiated "Arab" or "Berber" mind. The critique of "Orientalism" in a 1978 book of the same name by the late Palestinian-American critic Edward Said had wide-reaching repercussions for the fields of Middle Eastern and Islamic studies. With views predicated on the epistemology of the French philosopher of history Michel Foucault,

Said describes Orientalism in all its forms—artistic, scholarly, and literary—as a single "discourse" of power in which the West substitutes for the reality of the East a representation of its own manufacture. Said's book aroused a rancorous debate at the time, and the many books and articles spawned by the appearance of *Orientalism* since then are too numerous to cite. A survey of the debate can be found in Zachary Lockman, *Contending Visions of the Middle East: The History and Politics of Orientalism* (Cambridge: Cambridge University Press, 2004).

7. Henri Guillemin, "Biographie du Docteur Émile Mauchamp," *Bulletin de la Société des Sciences Naturelles de Saône-et-Loire* 33 (1907): 252–68; 34 (1908): 33–40, 97–120, 154–68, 172–96; 35 (1909): 33–64, 91–120.

8. The point is emphasized in Joseph E. Stiglitz, *Globalization and Its Discontents* (New York: W. W. Norton, 2002).

9. On Moroccan attitudes toward science and the political basis of Mauchamp's murder, see Ellen Amster, "The Many Deaths of Dr. Emile Mauchamp: Medicine, Technology, and Popular Politics in Pre-Protectorate Morocco, 1877–1912," *IJMES* 36 (2004): 409–28. The article is drawn from her dissertation "Medicine and Sainthood: Islamic Science, French Colonialism and the Politics of Healing in Morocco, 1877–1935" (Ph.D. diss., University of Pennsylvania, 2003).

10. "Le protectorat, une parenthèse politique et un accident de l'Histore," *Le Matin du Sahara et du Maghreb, Spécial,* March 30, 2000.

11. Excellent summations of the Protectorate period are offered by Daniel Rivet in his *Le Maroc de Lyautey à Mohammed V: le double visage du Protectorat* (Paris: Denoël, 1999) and *Le Maghreb à l'épreuve de la colonization* (Paris: Hachette, 2002).

12. For the narrative of nineteenth-century events, I have relied extensively upon C. R. Pennell, *Moroco since 1830: A History* (New York: New York University Press, 2000), and Edmund Burke III, *Prelude to Protectorate in Morocco: Precolonial Protest and Resistance, 1860–1912* (Chicago: University of Chicago Press, 1976).

13. "By 1883 sugar made up just under 19% of all imports." Pennell, 76. On the history of tea consumption in Morocco see Abd al-Ahad al-Sabti and Abd al-Rahman Lakhsassi, *From Shai to Tea: Custom and History* [in Arabic] (Rabat: Université Mohammed V, 1999). Nineteenth-century trade relations are the subject of Jean-Louis Miège's monumental *Le Maroc et L'Europe (1822–1906),* 4 vols. (Paris: Presses Universitaires de France, 1961–1964; reprint with vol. 5, *Documents d'histoire économique et sociale* (Rabat: Éditions La Porte, 1989).

14. Thuraya Barrada, *The Moroccan Army and Its Transformation in the Nineteenth-Century* [in Arabic] (Rabat: Université Mohammed V, 1997); Bahija Simou, *Les Reformes Militaires au Maroc de 1844 à 1912* (Rabat: Université Mohammed V, 1995); Wilfrid John Rollman, "The 'New Order' in a Pre-colonial Muslim Society: Military Reform in Morocco, 1844–1904"

(Ph.D. diss., University of Michigan, 1983). See also Amira K. Bennison, "The 'New Order' and Islamic Order: The Introduction of the Nizami Army in the Western Maghrib and Its Legitimation, 1830–73," *IJMES* 36 (2004): 591–612.

15. See, for example, Felix Weisgerber, *Au Seuil du Maroc moderne* (Rabat: Éditions La Porte, 1947), 37, 107.

16. Mohammed Kenbib, *Les Protégés: Contributions à l'histoire contemporaine du Maroc* (Rabat: Université Mohammed V, 1996).

17. At the time 100 million Spanish pesetas was the equivalent of £4,000,000. *Encyclopedia Americana,* international ed., s.v. "Morocco." In calculating the amount of indemnity in today's dollars I relied on the conversion tools at http://www.eh.net/hmit/ (accessed Feb. 20, 2006).

18. Ellen Titus Hoover, "Among Competing Worlds: The Rehamna of Morocco on the Eve of French Conquest" (Ph.D. diss., Yale University, 1978).

19. Pennell, 114.

20. Nestor Larras to Auguste Thomas, Marrakesh, June 14, 1901, in Roger-Pierre Raoult, *Lettres d'un oncle, Contribution à l'Histoire du Maroc* (1887–1906), introduction and notes by Jean-Louis Miège (Rabat: Éditions La Porte, 1995), 269. Larras was a member of the French military mission to the Makhzan; Thomas was formerly a member.

21. Daniel Nordman, "L'Armée d'Algérie et le Maroc," in *Profils du Maghreb: Frontières, figures et territoires XVIIIᵉ–XXᵉ siècle* (Rabat: Université Mohammed V, 1996), 41–71.

22. French activities in southeastern Morocco and the indigenous response are the subjects of Ross E. Dunn, *Resistance in the Desert: Moroccan Responses to French Imperialism, 1881–1912* (London: Croom Helm, 1977).

23. Mannesmann's activities, which occasionally conflicted with the policies of the German foreign ministry, are outlined in Neil Sherwood Lewis, "German Policy in Southern Morocco during the Agadir Crisis of 1911" (Ph.D. diss., University of Michigan, 1977), and Jean-Claude Allain, *Agadir 1911: Une crise impérialiste en Europe pour la conquête du Maroc* (Paris: Sorbonne, 1976), 73–112. For details of the firm's mining operations see Al-Malki al-Malki, "Reinhard Mannesmann and the Sous: A Preliminary History of New Commerce in the Sous Region" [in Arabic], *Majallat tarikh al-Maghrib* 9 (1420/1999): 191–207.

24. Abdallah Laroui, "La conférence d'Algésiras," in *Esquisse historiques* (Casablanca: Centre Culturel Arabe, 1993), 73–79. See also Eugene N. Anderson, *The First Moroccan Crisis, 1904–1906* (Chicago: University of Chicago Press, 1930), for an account of the conference as told from the perspective of the European powers.

25. See Amira K. Bennison, *Jihad and Its Interpretations in Pre-colonial Morocco: State-Society Relations during the French Conquest of Algeria* (London: Routledge Curzon, 2002).

26. Alain Ruscio, *Le Credo de l'homme blanc: Regards coloniaux français, XIXᵉ et XXᵉ siècle* (Paris: Éditions Complexe, 1995), 71–74.

27. Auguste Félix Charles de Beaupoil, Comte de Saint-Aulaire, *Au Maroc avant et avec Lyautey, Extrait des Mémoires de l'ambassadeur publiés sous le titre:* Confession d'un vieux diplomate (Paris: Flammarion, 1954), 77.

1. Civilization's Martyr

1. *L'Illustration* (Paris), March 16, 1907.

2. A local Chalon historian, Henri Huet, believes that Mauchamp was buried in the coffin hastily assembled from packing crates in Marrakesh. He describes the coffin shown in the photo as being made from cedar, packed with charcoal and weighing 650 kg. Nevertheless, in Barthelmy's photo the coffin being loaded from the baggage car of the train onto the elaborately decorated, horse-drawn hearse appears to be a more refined structure than the crude coffin that appears in earlier pictures from Marrakesh and El-Jadida. Henri Huet, "Les Funérailles du Docteur Mauchamp: 11 avril 1907," *Mémoires de la Société d'histoire et d'archéologie de Chalon-sur-Saône* [1988–1989] 58 (1990): 67.

3. *Le Courrier* (Chalon), April 10, 1907, is the source of the details of the funeral that follow.

4. Mauchamp to unidentified friend, November 22, 1906, quoted in Guillemin (1908): 162. Mauchamp had another sister as well as a younger brother, Louis, an agriculturist who lived in Algeria and who returned to meet Émile's coffin on its arrival in Marseilles.

5. Quoted in Guillemin (1909): 52.

6. Ibid., 96–97.

7. Ibid., 111–14.

8. Ibid., 111.

9. Ibid., 116.

10. Similarly, "when engineers died in the course of performing their duty, they were referred to in obituaries as *morts au champs d'honneur,"* deaths on the field of honor. Robert A. Nye, "Honor Codes and Medical Ethics in Modern France," *Bulletin of the History of Medicine* 69 (1995): 99.

"The obsession with the notion of personal honor encouraged doctors to portray their profession as uniquely dangerous and to characterize themselves as endowed with personal qualities of great courage. Medicine was practiced on 'a field of honor' as exigent of bravery as military conflict, and virtually all the deontologies of the period make much of the courage, the ardor, and the virile steadfastness of the French doctor." Ibid., 108. Accounts of Mauchamp's death frequently comment on his keeping a cool head when faced by the mob.

See also Robert A. Nye, *Masculinity and Male Codes of Honor in Modern France* (New York: Oxford University Press, 1993); and idem, "Medicine and Science as Masculine 'Fields of Honor,'" *Osiris* 12 (1997): 60–79.

11. "Cette petite patrie à coté de la grande patrie française." Guillemin (1909): 101.

12. R. D. Anderson, *France, 1870–1914: Politics and Society* (London: Routledge and K. Paul, 1977), 35–39.

13. Guillemin (1909): 100–101.

14. See, for example, Rita Maran, "Torture during the French-Algerian War: The Role of the 'Mission Civilisatrice'" (Ph.D. diss., University of California, Santa Cruz, 1987).

15. From a debate in the chamber on July 9, 1925, quoted in Roger-Henri Guerrand, "Les clarions de la nostalgie," in *Au temps des colonies*, ed. Georges Balandier and Marc Ferro (Paris: L'Histoire, Éditions du Seuil, 1984), 8.

16. James Albert Paul, "Professionals and Politics in Morocco: A Historical Study of the Mediation of Power and the Creation of Ideology in the Context of European Imperialism" (Ph.D. diss., New York University, 1975), 110–14; Charles-André Julien, *Le Maroc face aux impérialismes, 1415–1956* (Paris: Editions J.A. 1977), 70–72; Allal el Khdimi, "L'Occupation d'Oujda," in *La Memorial du Maroc*, Tome 5: *1906–1934: Morcellement et résistance*, ed. Larbi Essakali (Rabat: Nord Publications, 1983–1985), 78–84.

17. Saliha Belmossous, "Assimilation and Racialism in Seventeenth and Eighteenth-Century French Colonial Policy," *American Historical Review* 110 (April 2005): 322–49; Tzvetan Todorov, *On Human Diversity: Nationalism, Racism, and Exoticism in French Thought*, trans. Catherine Porter (Cambridge: Harvard University Press, 1993), 1–89; Leon Poliakov, *The Aryan Myth*, trans. Edmund Howard (New York: Basic Books, 1974); William B. Cohen, *The French Encounter with Africans: White Response to Blacks, 1530–1880* (Bloomington: Indiana University Press, 1980).

18. Norbert Elias, *The Civilizing Process: The Development of Manners*, trans. Edmund Jephcott (New York: Urizen Books, 1978). *Kultur*—unlike *civilisation*—would seem to be an unlikely vehicle for a nation's expansionist policies. This benign understanding of *kultur*, with its relativistic and tolerant overtones, would of course all change a century later with the rise of Nazi doctrines of German racial superiority.

19. Michael Adas, *Machines as the Measure of Men: Science, Technology and Ideologies of Western Dominance* (Ithaca, N.Y.: Cornell University Press, 1989). The ambiguity of *métropole*-colony relations is a recurring theme in the anthology *Tensions of Empire: Colonial Cultures in a Bourgeois World*, ed. Frederick Cooper and Ann Laura Stoler (Berkeley: University of California Press, 1997). Also see Alice L. Conklin, *A Mission to Civilize: the Republican Idea of Empire in France and West Africa, 1895–1930* (Palo Alto, Calif.: Stanford University Press, 1997), and idem, "Colonialism and Human Rights, a Contradiction in Terms? The Case of France and West Africa, 1895–1914," *American Historical Review* 103 (1998): 419–42.

20. Patricia M. E. Lorcin, *Imperial Identities: Stereotyping, Prejudice and Race*

in Colonial North Africa (London: I. B. Taurus, 1995), 99–117. On Saint-Si-monianism and other intellectual currents, see also Kay Adamson, *Political and Economic Thought and Practice in Nineteenth-Century France and the Coloniza-tion of Algeria* (Lewiston, N.Y.: Edwin Mellen Press, 2002).

21. Bois, introduction to Mauchamp, *Sorcellerie,* 12–13. On efforts to shape public opinion regarding colonialism see Ruscio, *Le Credo de l'homme blanc,* and William H. Schneider, *An Empire for the Masses: The French Popular Image of Africa, 1870–1900* (Westport, Conn.: Greenwood, 1982).

22. Fanny Colonna, "Educating Conformity in French Colonial Algeria," in *Tensions of Empire,* 346–70.

23. Alfred Fouillée, *Psychologie du people français,* 6th ed. (Paris: Félix Alcan, 1914), 181, quoted in Raymond F. Betts, *Assimilation and Association in French Colonial Theory, 1890–1914* (New York: Columbia University Press, 1961), 25.

"There lives in French hearts a spontaneous piety (in the nature of a spiritual instinct) for the civilizing mission to which France has ever dedi-cated herself," wrote another theorist, Charles Castre, in *The Ideals of France* (New York: Abingdon Press, 1922), 34, quoted in Betts, 29.

24. John Ruedy, *Modern Algeria: The Origins and Development of a Nation,* 2nd ed. (Bloomington: Indiana University Press, 2005), 77.

25. Later, in the context of the French-Algerian War (1954–1962) and in an effort to effect a reconciliation between the French and the Algerians, the French offered a new paradigm called "integration." As elaborated by the last governor general of Algeria, Jacques Soustelle, integration called for the recognition of the cultural differences between the Arab, Berber, and French populations with the simultaneous extension of citizenship to all as Frenchmen. Instead of going its separate way, Algeria would continue to coexist alongside France. James D. LeSueur, *Uncivil War: Intellectuals and Identity Politics during the Decolonization of Algeria* (Philadelphia: University of Pennsylvania Press, 2001), 23–25.

26. Jules Bois, "Les anglais dans l'Inde," *Revue Bleue* 19 (April 11, 1903): 476–80. Bois is cited as Blois [*sic*] in Betts, 44.

27. Betts, 77.

28. Ibid., 107.

29. Tunisia, which officially became a French protectorate in 1884, was similarly never declared an official colony.

30. Robin Bidwell, *Morocco under Colonial Rule: French Administration of Tribal Areas, 1912–1956* (London: Frank Cass, 1973), xiv. On Lyautey's efforts to pursue a policy of indirect rule, see Hoisington, *Lyautey and the French Conquest of Morocco.* The practical advantages of an associationist policy were outlined at length in Jules Harmand, *Domination et Colonisation* (Paris: E. Flammarion, 1910).

31. Betts, 115.

32. Guillemin (1907): 254.

33. Quoted in ibid., 255.

34. A. Gautier, "Décès de M. P. Budin," *Bulletin de L'Academie Nationale de Médecine* (January 29, 1907): 163–67, reprinted as http://www.neonatology.org/classics/gautier.html (accessed Feb. 10, 2006); Elisa Guises, "Petit historique de la P.M.I," http://www.anpde.asso.fr/pmi1.html (accessed Feb. 10, 2006); "Histoire et patrimoine de l'Assistance Publique—Hôpitaux de Paris," http://www.aphp.fr/site/histoire/1901_hopitaux_pediatriques.htm (accessed Feb. 20, 2006).

35. Émile Mauchamp, *L'Allaitement artificiel des nourissons par le lait sterilisé: Conditions, Pratiques, Résultants, Indications* (Paris: Georges Carré et C. Naud, 1899).

36. Quoted in Guillemin (1907): 257.

37. Adolphe Pinard, "De la Puériculture," *Bulletin de la Société des Amis de l'Université de Lyon* (1907–1908): 262–85.

38. Mauchamp, *L'Allaitement,* 18.

39. Ibid., 572.

40. Ibid., 602.

41. Ibid., 603.

42. Ibid., 604. Recent scholarship puts the mortality rate for all infants in France sent out to wet nurses in 1897 and 1898 at 15.1 percent. This figure is lower than Mauchamp's estimates but still higher than the general infant mortality rate at the time. George D. Sussman, *Selling Mothers' Milk: The Wet-Nursing Business in France, 1715–1914* (Urbana: University of Illinois Press, 1982), 181. As Sussman's book indicates, Mauchamp was not alone in denouncing the use of wet nurses. The Parisian practice of sending infants to distant rural wet nurses fell off only during and after World War I, when communication with the countryside was disrupted and working mothers discovered that they could in fact rely on healthful infant foods as an alternative to breast milk. Ibid., 182–84.

43. Jack D. Ellis, *The Physician-Legislators of France: Medicine and Politics in the Early Third Republic, 1870–1914* (Cambridge: Cambridge University Press, 1990).

44. Ibid., 39.

45. William H. Schneider, *Quality and Quantity: The Quest for Biological Regeneration in Twentieth-Century France* (Cambridge: Cambridge University Press, 1990), 11–83; and Nye, *Masculinity and Male Codes,* 72–97.

46. Nancy Rose Hunt, "'Le bébé en brousse': European Women, African Birth Spacing, and Colonial Intervention in Breast Feeding in the Belgian Congo," in *Tensions of Empire,* 287–321; Anna Davin, "Imperialism and Motherhood," in *Tensions of Empire,* 87–151; and Nancy Rose Hunt, *A Colonial Lexicon: Of Birth Ritual, Medicalization, and Mobility in the Congo* (Durham, N.C.: Duke University Press, 1999).

47. In his biographical sketch of Mauchamp, Maxime Rousselle says that Mauchamp was named *médecin-aide-major de réserve* (August 15, 1899)

and assigned to a military hospital in Oran. There is no evidence that he actually held this post, and Rousselle himself assigns the date of his appointment as a naval medical officer as June 29, 1899. Rousselle, *Médecins, chirurgiens et apothicaires français au Maroc: 1577–1907* (France: M. Rousselle, 1996), 278 n. 443.

48. Mauchamp to consul [Auzépy], Chalon-sur-Saône, February 27, 1900, MAE 104, Jerusalem, Établisssements religieux (Hôpitaux).

49. Consul [Auzépy] to Mauchamp, Jerusalem, March 15, 1900, MAE 104, Jerusalem.

50. Mauchamp to consul [Auzépy], Chalon-sur-Saône, July 16, 1900, and reply (draft) July 30, 1900, MAE 104, Jerusalem.

51. Yehoshua Ben-Arieh, *Jerusalem in the Nineteenth Century, the Old City* (Jerusalem: Yad Itzhak Ben Zvi Institute and New York: St. Martin's Press, 1984), 353–58.

52. Martin Gilbert, *Jerusalem in the Twentieth Century* (New York: John Wiley and Sons, 1996), 10, and Ben-Arieh, 201.

53. Bernard Wasserstein, *Divided Jerusalem: The Struggle for the Holy City* (New Haven, Conn.: Yale University Press, 2001), 50, and Ben-Arieh, 184–89.

54. Ironically, just as Mauchamp's arrival in Jerusalem was preceded by the German monarch's visit there, so too would his arrival in Morocco be preceded by the kaiser's momentous 1905 stopover in Tangier.

55. Ada Goodrich-Freer, *Inner Jerusalem* (New York: E. P. Dutton, 1904).

56. Gilbert, 10.

57. "By 1914 there were an estimated 45,000 Jews in Jerusalem out of a total population of 70,000. Jerusalem at that point was the home of a majority of Jews in Palestine, who numbered at most 85,000 out of an estimated total population of 790,000." Wasserstein, 47.

As might be expected, the population figures for Palestine are subject to dispute. Using European estimates to adjust Ottoman census data, Justin McCarthy puts the 1914 Jewish population of Palestine at 56,754. This figure, he notes, is close to the 60,000 mark that the Palestine Zionist Office arrived at in its wartime estimate of Jewish population in 1914. McCarthy argues that the widely quoted 85,000 figure is inflated. The figure, which originated with Arthur Ruppin, an official with the Zionist Organization, was made—McCarthy believes—without reference to Ottoman statistics. Justin McCarthy, *The Population of Palestine: Population History and Statistics of the Late Ottoman Period and the Mandate* (New York: Columbia University Press, 1990), 18–24.

58. Gilbert, 11.

59. *Clinique Infantile*, January 1, 1905, quoted in Guillemin (1907): 263.

Despite occasional antagonism, Catholic missionaries and republican civilizers often shared the same language of proselytization. Working together they reinforced the idea of a national "French" civilizing mission. James Patrick Daughton, "The Civilizing Mission: Missionaries, Colonialists, and French Identity, 1885–1914" (Ph.D. diss., University of California, Berkeley, 2002).

60. Mauchamp to father, February 18, 1906, quoted in Guillemin (1908): 109.

61. Mauchamp, "Conseil aux mères pour élever leur infants," Hôpital Français de Saint-Louis à Jérusalem, MAE 104, Jerusalem.

62. Letter to French embassy in Constantinople, dated December 22, 1902. Text printed in "Le docteur Mauchamp," *Le Courrier* (Chalon), March 30, 1907; also excerpted in Guillemin (1907): 264–65.

63. Along with Mauchamp, another French doctor in Jerusalem, Mazinet, chief of the Hôpital Israélite, also received "la croix d'Ordre de l'Osmanié, 4ᵉ classe." Notice from unidentified Istanbul paper dated July 25, 1904 in MAE 104, Jerusalem.

64. Guillemin (1907): 266–68.

65. August 1902, cited without attribution in Rousselle, *Médecins,* 278.

66. Mauchamp to parents, June 1902, Jerusalem, quoted in Guillemin (1907): 266–67.

67. Guillemin (1907): 267.

68. Ibid., 267–68.

69. Born in Jerusalem in 1867, Holzmann studied medicine in Berlin from 1895 to 1898 and installed himself in Marrakesh the following year. Pierre Guillen, *L'Allemagne et le Maroc de 1870 à 1905* (Paris: Presses Universitaires de France, 1967), 488 n. 1.

70. Mauchamp to Boppe, December 1902, Jerusalem, MAE, 104, Jerusalem.

71. Mauchamp to mother, January 14, 1903, Jerusalem, quoted in Guillemin (1908): 33–34.

72. His account of the trip and his accompanying photographs appeared in two installments as Dr. Émile Mauchamp, "Un raid au Désert: Sinai, Arabie-Pétrée, Moab (note de voyages, 1902)," *Extrait du Bulletin de la Société des Science Naturelles de Saône-et-Loire* (1905), and idem, "Pétra (Impressions de Caravane)," *Extrait du Bulletin de la Société des Sciences Naturelles de Saône-et-Loire* (1905).

73. Guillemin (1907): 263–64 n. 1. The wealthy Abu Ghush [or Ghawsh] family were among the local lords of the area surrounding Jerusalem. Originally of Circassian origin, the Abu Ghush were said to have arrived in Palestine in 1516 with the Ottoman sultan Selim's conquest. Alexander Schölch, *Palestine in Transformation, 1856–1882, Studies in Social, Economic and Political Development,* trans. William C. Young and Michael C. Gerrity (Washington, D.C.: Institute for Palestine Studies, 1993), 187–88, 229–34.

74. Bois, introduction to *Sorcellerie,* by Mauchamp, 63.

75. Mauchamp, "Un raid," 20.

76. Mauchamp, quoted by Bois, introduction to *Sorcellerie,* by Mauchamp, 63.

77. Kathryn Tidrick, *Heart-Beguiling Araby* (Cambridge: Cambridge University Press, 1981), 124–25.

78. "Rapport du Dr. Émile Mauchamp, Médecin du gouvernement français, chargé du service d l'Hôpital St. Louis, sur l'exercise de sa mission du 15 November 1900 au 1 Janvier 1903 et sur la situation hospitaliêre de Jérusalem," May 1903, MAE 104, Jerusalem.

79. Mauchamp to father, June 15, 1905, Anvers, quoted in Guillemin (1908): 38.

80. Mauchamp to father, June 19, 1905, Amsterdam, quoted in Guillemin (1908): 40.

81. Guillemin (1908): 98. This was not a surprising hobby for Mauchamp given that the nineteenth-century inventor of photography, Nicéphore Niépce, also hailed from Chalon-sur-Saône.

2. The Road to Marrakesh

1. *Service Médical d'Assistance au Maroc.*

2. Jim Paul, "Medicine and Imperialism in Morocco," *MERIP Reports* 7 (September 1977): 5. Paul's article is drawn from his dissertation, "Professionals and Politics in Morocco." Both the article and the thesis remain good introductions to the subject despite the quaintness of Paul's unabashed Marxism ("But only the complete abolition of capitalism can clear the way for a society insuring good life and health for all." "Medicine and Imperialism," 12).

On European doctors in Morocco early in the nineteenth century, see Miège, *Le Maroc et L'Europe,* 2: 468–71.

3. Anne Marcovich, "French Colonial Medicine and Colonial Rule: Algeria and Indochina," in *Disease, Medicine, and Empire: Perspectives on Western Medicine and the Experience of European Expansion,* ed. Roy MacLeod and Milton Lewis (London: Routledge, 1988), 103.

4. During his 1889 visit to Fez in the company of Patenôtre, the French minister to Morocco, Pierre Loti stayed in one of two houses in Linarès's possession. Pierre Loti, *Au Maroc,* in *Maroc: Les Villes impériales,* ed. Guy Dugas (Paris: Omnibus, 1996), 72. For another account of the Patenôtre mission, see Raoult, 112–17.

5. Amster, "Many Deaths," 412–13.

Miège reproduces a letter to Linarès from the French legation indicating the kind of diplomatic tasks entrusted to the doctor. "Demande au Dr. Linarès" (Tangier, June 9, 1892) in Miège, *Le Maroc et L'Europe,* 5: 199–200, no. 44.

6. Ibid., 4: 192 n. 7.

7. Raoult, 271 n. 2.

8. Saint-Aulaire, *Au Maroc avant et avec Lyautey,* 79. In 1898 France and

England almost came to blows over the Sudan. A small French expedition led by Captain Jean-Baptiste Marchand had rebuilt the fort in Fashoda that had been abandoned by the British. After the British organized an expedition of some thirty thousand Egyptian troops to reoccupy the region now claimed by France, the French predictably withdrew.

9. Ibid., 80–81.

10. Paul, "Medicine and Imperialism," 4.

11. Ibid., 5.

12. Weisgerber, 46.

13. On the difficulties French doctors faced in earning a living at the turn of the century see Theodore Zeldin, *France, 1848–1945,* vol. 1: *Ambition, Love and Politics* (Oxford: Clarendon Press, 1973), 30–42.

14. Abdelaziz to Muhammad bin Yahya al-Jadidi called Ould al-Hamaduniyya, 8 Shawwal 1316/February 9, 1900, BG Rabat, Microfilm "Dal" 13/3.

15. Abd al-Karim Hafizi, "Manuscript Documents Preserved in the Manuscript Section of the Bibliothèque Générale" [in Arabic], in *Les archives du Protectorat, Première évaluation* (Rabat: Université Mohammed V, 1996), 14. This cash award encourages private individuals to contribute documents in their family's possession to the Moroccan nation. Latifa Benjelloun-Laroui, *Les bibliothèques au Maroc* (Paris: Maisonneuve and Larose, 1990), 246.

16. Marquis de Segonzac, *Au Coeur de l'Atlas, Mission au Maroc, 1904–1905* (Paris: Émile Larose, 1910), 213.

17. Muhammad al-Amin al-Bazzaz, "Constitution du Conseil Sanitaire International à Tanger" [in Arabic], *Revue Dar al-Niaba* 3 (Spring 1989): 39–46.

18. Miége, *Le Maroc et L'Europe,* 4: 393 n. 6.

19. Amster, "Many Deaths," 417. Amster sees vaccination and the use of needles as naturally related to the practice of tattooing and therefore a potentially suspect procedure in the hands of a European.

20. Dr. Honoré They, Archives Générales du Gouvernement Tunisien 817/61 (24 Safar al-Khayr 1284/June 27, 1867), quoted in Nancy Elizabeth Gallagher, *Medicine and Power in Tunisia, 1780–1900* (Cambridge: Cambridge University Press, 1983), 71.

21. Frantz Fanon, "Medicine and Colonialism," in *A Dying Colonialism,* trans. Haakon Chevalier (New York: Grove Press, 1967), 131.

22. "Whatever else it might have been, nineteenth-century Western medicine had a powerful ontology, finding confirmation, in bodies at home and abroad, for the universalist claims of European reason." John Comaroff and Jean Comaroff, *Ethnography and the Historical Imagination* (Boulder, Colo.: Westview Press, 1992), 232.

Beyond the usual arguments for medicine's place in the colonial enterprise, the French philosopher of history Michel Foucault has put forth the thesis that modernity itself is an expression of the state's recourse to "bio-power." Foucault identifies the latter as an intrusive and pervasive mechanism of surveillance and control. On the one hand modern medicine counts (or "unitizes") individuals. On the other, it regulates what had hitherto been private matters of life, procreation, and death. Michel Foucault, *The History of Sexuality*, vol. 1: *An Introduction*, trans. Robert Hurley (New York: Vintage Books, 1980). Also see Ann Laura Stoler, *Race and the Education of Desire: Foucault's History of Sexuality and the Colonial Order of Things* (Durham, N.C.: Duke University Press, 1995).

The extent to which the practice of medicine in the colonies through vaccination campaigns and other public health measures—these designed to protect the European colonists as much as if not more than the indigenous subjects—succeeded in replicating or extending the bio-power of the *métropole* is a subject open to debate. Megan Vaughan, *Curing their Ills: Colonial Power and African Illness* (Stanford, Calif.: Stanford University Press, 1991), 151.

23. Kim Pelis, "Pasteur's Imperial Missionary: Charles Nicolle (1866–1936) and the Pasteur Institute of Tunis" (Ph.D. diss., Johns Hopkins University, 1995).

24. Richard Fogarty and Michael A. Osborne, "Constructions and Functions of Race in French Military Medicine, 1830–1920," in *The Color of Liberty: Histories of Race in France*, ed. Sue Peabody and Tyler Stovall (Durham, N.C.: Duke University Press, 2003), 206–36.

25. Edmond Doutté, *Magie et religion dans l'Afrique du nord* (Paris: Maisonneuve, 1908; reprint, Paris: P. Guethner, 1984).

26. Mustapha Akhmisse, *Médecine, magie et sorcellerie au Maroc: ou L'art traditionnel de guérir* (Casablanca: Benchara, 1985). While Mauchamp parted ways with Moroccan healers, his attitude regarding "primitive mentalities" was not out of line with that of his French contemporaries. Espousing the rhetoric of the civilizing mission, French psychiatrists who followed Mauchamp to North Africa seized upon the region as a laboratory for the creation of an "empirically based ethnopsychiatric subfield." Burdened by large caseloads, these psychiatrists were "among the first to employ radical new somatic therapies for the treatment of mental illness, including cardiazol, insulin, and electro-convulsive therapies and psychosurgery." Richard Keller, *"Action Psychologique:* French Psychiatry in Colonial North Africa, 1900–1962" (Ph.D. diss., Rutgers [State University of New Jersey], 2001), 3–4.

Mauchamp's views on the differences between Arabs and Berbers, and particularly between men and women, may derive in part from the views of a Dr. Meilhon, director of the psychiatric hospital in Aix-en-Provence and author of "L'Aliénation chez les Arabes; études de nosologie comparée," *Annales Médico-Psychologique* 3 (1896): 17–32, 177–207, 365–77; 4 (1897?): 344–36. Meilhon's work is cited and discussed in Alice Bullard, "The Truth in Madness: Colonial Doctors and Insane Women in French North Africa," *South Atlantic Review* 66 (2001): 114–32.

27. Sander L. Gilman, *Difference and Pathology: Stereotypes of Sexuality, Race, and Madness* (Ithaca, N.Y.: Cornell University Press, 1985); idem, "Black Bodies, White Bodies: Toward an Iconography of Female Sexuality in Late Nineteenth-Century Art, Medicine, and Literature," *Critical Inquiry* 12 (1985): 204–42.

28. Malek Alloula, *The Colonial Harem*, trans. Myrna Godzich and Wald Godzich (Minneapolis: University of Minnesota Press, 1986).

29. The *mellah* of Marrakesh has been described in detail in Emily R. Gottreich, "Jewish Space in the Moroccan City: A History of the *Mellah* of Marrakesh, 1550–1930" (Ph.D. diss., Harvard University, 1999), and idem, "On the Origins of the Mellah of Marrakesh," *IJMES* 35 (2003): 287–305.

30. Mauchamp, *Sorcellerie*, 168. On masturbation's alleged deleterious health effects see Thomas W. Laqueur, *Solitary Sex: A Cultural History of Masturbation* (New York: Zone Books, 2003).

31. This point is emphasized in Amster, "Many Deaths."

32. Gallagher, *Medicine and Power in Tunisia*.

33. Dr. Mauran, "Considerations sur la medicine indigene actuelle au Maroc," *Bulletin de l'Institut des Hautes Etudes Marocains* 1 (December 1920): 83–91, quoted in translation in Amster, "Medicine and Sainthood," 53. Amster further argues that by emphasizing the ritualistic aspects of Moroccan traditional medicine, contemporary anthropologists are similarly prone to see indigenous practices as "magic" rather than "science" set within an Islamic paradigm.

Dr. Mauran also presented his views on Moroccan medicine in an earlier work written for the general public, *Le Maroc: d'aujourd'hui et de demain* (Paris: H. Paulin, 1909).

34. Vaughan, 151.

"The sociological theory," Frantz Fanon writes, "is that the 'native' entertains the hope of being cured once and for all. The native sees the ailment, not as progressing little by little but as assaulting the individual in a single swoop, so that the effectiveness of a remedy would not depend so much on its consistent, periodic and progressive repetition but on its total impact, its immediate affect; this accounts for the natives' preference for injections."

Believing that "two remedies are better than one," the native who has access to Western medicine might simultaneously seek recourse to traditional medicine. But as Fanon goes on to explain, the ambivalence of the colonized patient toward Western medicine is deeply rooted in the anxieties induced in the patient by recourse to the colonist's medicine. "The colonized obscurely realizes that penicillin is more effective, but for political, psychological, social reasons, he must at the same time give traditional medicine its due. . . . Every pill absorbed or every injection taken invites the application of a preparation or the visit to a saint." Fanon, 130–31.

35. Mauchamp, *Sorcellerie*, 72.

36. Tangier, May 4, 1889, quoted in Weisgerber, 7. In decrying the homogenization and cultural leveling of the modern world, Loti in fact shares the sentiments of Victor Segalen, a severe critic of Loti's travel writings and the chief exponent of the "new exoticism" that characterized French travel writing in the next generation. Todorov, *On Human Diversity*, 308–38. See also Daniel Rivet, "Exotisme et 'Pénétration scientifique': l'effort de découverte du Maroc par les Français au début du XXᵉ siècle," in *Connaissances du Maghreb: Sciences sociales et colonisation,* ed. Jean-Claude Vatin (Paris: Éditions du Centre nationale de la recherche scientifique, 1984), 95–109, and Abdeljlil Lahjomri, *Le Maroc des heures françaises* (1968; reprint Rabat: Marsam and Stouky, 1999).

37. See in particular Burke, *Prelude to Protectorate,* 19–40; Paul Pascon, *Le Haouz de Marrakech,* 2 vols. (Rabat: Centre Universitaire de la Recherche Scientifique, 1983); Miège, *Le Maroc et l'Europe;* and Abdallah Laroui, *Les Origines sociales et culturelles du nationalisme marocaine (1830–1912)* (Paris: F. Maspero, 1977; Casablanca: Centre Culturel Arabe, 1993).

38. Mauchamp, *Sorcellerie,* 76.

39. Durkheim argued that industrialization's emphasis on technological innovation and specialization was contributing to the disintegration of contemporary society and leading to individual alienation. Nonetheless, Durkheim saw a way out of the trap. "Modern" work—unlike that of earlier times—was not done in isolation; the need for individuals to collaborate would lead to a corresponding increase in collective effort and thus further link men (and women) together. In the social evolutionary scale, the supposed "organic" solidarity of higher societies represented a step up from the mere "mechanical" solidarity of primitive peoples. To support his argument, Durkheim specifically cited the Berbers of Kabylia. Because they were grouped in small clans, their communal organization represented a kind of arrested social development. Émile Durkheim, *The Division of Labor in Society,* trans. George Simpson (Glencoe, Ill.: Free Press, 1933), 177–78.

For French scholars who studied North Africa, the Durkheimian view of society soon began to supersede earlier ethnographic traditions, a clash that led to—as one intellectual historian has put it—"the first crisis of Orientalism." Nevertheless, Durkheim himself and his immediate circle paid little attention to Islam or North Africa, an omission some scholars characterize as a lost opportunity. Edmund Burke III, "The First Crisis of Orientalism, 1890–1914" in *Connaissances du Maghreb,* 213–26; Lucette Valensi, "Le Maghreb vu du centre sa place dans l'école sociologique française," in ibid., 227–44; and Manfred Halpern, "Emile Durkheim: Analyst of Solidarity but Not of Transformation," in ibid., 245–47.

Later—particularly British—anthropologists would elaborate upon Durkheim's rudimentary theory of segmentary kinship lineage. As the principal theoretical tool for explaining Berber society, segmentary theory maintained that small groups (the family, the clan) come together only rarely and principally for purposes of defensive alliance. Ernest Gellner, *Saints of the Atlas* (London: Wiedenfeld and Nichols, 1969), and Dunn, 39–41, 65–66.

40. Zeldin, 654.

41. Mauchamp, *Sorcellerie*, 81–85. See also Edmund Burke III, "The Image of the Moroccan State in French Ethnological Literature: A New Look at the Origin of Lyautey's Berber Policy," in *Arabs and Berbers: From Tribe to Nation in North Africa*, ed. Ernest Gellner and Charles Micaud (London: Duckworth, 1973), 175–200; Lorcin, *Imperial Identities.*

42. On Lyautey's efforts to pursue a policy of indirect rule, see Hoisington, *Lyautey and the French Conquest of Morocco*, and Rivet, *Le Maroc de Lyautey à Mohammed V.*

43. "Allocution à Casablanca, le 29 juillet 1924," cited in Betts, 118–19.

44. Mauchamp, *Sorcellerie*, 100.

45. It is possible that Mauchamp, through his friendship with Jules Bois, had a personal association with the "decadent" French writer J.-K. Huysmann, the author of *Là-Bas* and *À Rebours.* Huysmann wrote the preface to Bois's *Le Satanisme et la magie.*

46. Homi Bhabha, "Of Mimicry and Man: The Ambivalence of Colonial Discourse," in *Tensions of Empire*, 152–61.

47. Ann Laura Stoler, "Sexual Affronts and Racial Frontiers: European Identities and Cultural Politics of Exclusion in Colonial Southeast Asia," in *Tensions of Empire*, 198–238. On supposed biological implications of miscegenation, see Claude Blanckaert, "Of Monstrous Métis? Hybridity, Fear of Miscegenation, and Patriotism from Buffon to Paul Broca," in *The Color of Liberty*, 42–70.

48. De Segonzac, 214.

49. Delcassé to Tangier legation, January 6, 1905, Paris, MAE Tangier A 342.

50. The fact that few Europeans lived in Rabat also made it an attractive posting. Mauchamp's correspondent there offered him encouragement. Should Mauchamp "decide to reside here and to aid in the peaceful penetration of which medicine is one of the principal agents," he wrote, Mauchamp could expect a first-year income of 2,500 francs. He described Rabat and its companion city Salé in glowing terms. Together they were Morocco's second city after Fez, a picturesque place with a temperate climate and population of fifty thousand, among them three thousand Jews. He assured the doctor that many aristocratic families lived there. Leriche to Mauchamp, Rabat, April 30, 1905, MAE Tangier A 342.

51. June 1905, Telegram no. 54, MAE Tangier A 342.

52. Saint-René Taillandier, June 15, 1905, Telegram no. 116, MAE Tangier A 342. The minister also wrote that he expected to allocate 9,000 francs annually for the doctor's salary and budget.

53. Mauchamp, undated personal memo, MAE Tangier A 342.

54. Henri Brunschwig, *French Colonialism, 1871–1914, Myths and Realities,* trans. William Glanville Brown (New York: Frederick A. Praeger, 1966), 118–20. On the development of French colonialist ideology, see Raoul Girardet, *L'Idée coloniale en France de 1871 à 1962* (Paris: La Table Ronde, 1972); Stuart Michael Persell, *The French Colonial Lobby, 1889–1938* (Stanford, Calif.: Hoover Institution Press, 1983); Jacques Valette, "Note sur l'idée coloniale vers 1871," *Revue d'histoire moderne et contemporaine* 14 (1967): 158–72.

55. Eugène Etienne, *BCAF* (January 1904) 2, quoted in Brunschwig, 119.

56. Falcon to Mauchamp, Marrakesh, August 2, 1905, MAE Tangier A 342.

57. Christian Houel, *Mes Adventures Marocaines* (Casablanca: Éditions Maroc-Demain, 1954), 59.

58. Falcon to AIU President, October 10, 1907, AIU Maroc VII B microfilm.

59. Houel, 59.

60. Ibid., 59.

61. Ibid., 73.

62. Ibid., 73. German claims to racial and cultural superiority did not go unchallenged in the French press at the time. See the essay by the literary critic Ernest Seillière, "Une École d'impérialisme mystique: Les plus récents théoriciens du pangermanisme," *Revue des deux mondes* 50 (1909): 196–228.

63. Falcon to Mauchamp, Marrakesh, August 2, 1905, MAE Tangier A 342.

64. Ibid.

65. Mauchamp to Regnault, Chalon-sur-Saône, August 12, 1905, MAE Tangier A 342. The sharif married an English governess who later published her memoirs. Emily Keene, Shareefa of Wazan, *My Life Story,* ed. L. Bensusan (London: Edward Arnold, 1912).

66. Terrier to Mauchamp, September 20, 1905, MAE Tangier A 342. Moreover, he warned Mauchamp against his potential rival Holzmann, "who will make us palpitate like Rosen Révoil." The latter remark was a cryptic allusion to Paul Révoil, the French negotiator at the Algeciras conference, whom Terrier—by his wordplay—likened to the German minister in Tangier, Dr. Rosen.

67. Terrier to Mauchamp, Paris, October 28, 1905, MAE Tangier A 342.

68. Mauchamp, November 8, 1905, quoted in Guillemin (1908): 101–102. Guillemin mistakenly dates this letter and the preceding letter from October 30 as 1906.

69. Linarès to Mauchamp, November 1, 1905, MAE Tangier A 342.

70. Vice Consul to Saint-Aulaire, Fez, December 3, 1905, MAE Tangier A 342.

71. Fariau to Saint-Aulaire, December 4, 1905, MAE Tangier A 342,

no. 253; Tangier legation to Direction politique, draft telegram, no. 64, December 12, 1905, MAE Tangier A 342; Direction politique to Tangier legation, December 19, 1905, MAE Tangier A 342, no. 174; Vice-consul Jeannier to Tangier legation, draft telegram, Mogador, December 21, 1905, MAE Tangier A 342.

72. Tangier legation to Mauchamp, copy, December 21, 1905, MAE Tangier A 342.

73. Fariau to Mauchamp, Fez, October 19, 1905, MAE Tangier A 342.

74. Rouvier to Saint-René Taillandier, February 16, 1906 [no. 52, Au sujet du docteur Mauchamp], MAE Tangier A 342.

75. Saint-René Taillandier to Paris, telegram no. 82, Tangier, March 12, 1906, MAE Tangier A 342.

76. Mauchamp to Saint-René Taillandier, Marrakesh, March 25, 1906, MAE Tangier A 342.

3. Europeans and Jews

1. Despite Article 60 of the Act of Algeciras, which sanctioned land purchases in the interior by foreigners, the Makhzan put up many obstacles to Europeans' acquisition of land. The inability of French companies to find investment opportunities in Morocco, it has been argued, contributed to the abandonment of the policy of peaceful penetration. See Lawrence Abrams, Jr., "French Economic Penetration of Morocco, 1906–1914: The Economic Bases of Imperialist Expansion" (Ph.D. diss., Columbia University, 1977).

2. For samples of French writing specifically about Marrakesh, see Michel Berthaud, ed., *Marrakech: Années 20* (Marseilles: Éditions la croisée des chemins, 1996).

3. Jean-Claude Allain, "Les Européens au Maroc à la Veille du Protectorat: Quelques chiffres et quelques réflexions," *Revue Dar al-Niaba* 12 (1986): 1–8.

4. *La Dépêche Marocaine,* January 4, 1907.

5. Paul Pascon, *Capitalism and Agriculture in the Haouz of Marrakesh,* edited with introduction by John R. Hall, trans. C. Edwin Vaughan and Veronique Ingman (London: KPI, 1986), 46, and idem, *Le Haouz de Marrakech,* 2: 47–48. *Capitalism and Agriculture* is a slightly abridged translation of *Le Haouz de Marrakech,* vol. 2.

6. Pascon, *Capitalism and Agriculture,* 51–53. On the corrosive effects of the protection system see Kenbib, *Les Protégés,* and Miège, *Le Maroc et L'Europe,* 3: 263–92 and 4: 355–59.

7. On the Protestant missions, see Miège, *Le Maroc et L'Europe,* 4: 316–23.

8. Ibid., 4: 301–302.

9. Pascon, *Capitalism and Agriculture.* 64.

10. Guillemin (1908): 100–101.

11. MAE Direction Politique 1907 Série B. Carton 47, Dossier 2, tele-

gram no. 167, March 18, 1907, photocopy in DAR in bound volume, *Maroc, Politique Étranger, Relations avec L'Allemagne,* vol. 1: novembre 1896–décembre 1903 [*sic,* 1908].

12. Narcisse Leven, *Cinquante ans d'histoire: L'Alliance israélite universelle (1860–1910),* 2 vols. (Paris: Libraire Félix Alcan, 1920), 2: 99. More recent histories of the Alliance include Michael M. Laskier, *The* Alliance Israélite Universelle *and the Jewish Communities of Morocco: 1862–1962* (Albany: State University of New York Press, 1983); Aron Rodrigue, *Images of Sephardi and Eastern Jewries in Transition: The Teachers of the Alliance Israélite Universelle, 1860–1939* (Seattle: University of Washington Press, 1993); and Meir Ben Abraham, "The Impact of the 'Alliance Israélite Universelle' on Change and Modernisation of the Jewish Communities of Morocco, 1912–1956" (Ph.D. diss., Anglia Polytechnic University, 2000).

13. I thank Lawrence Rosen for this estimate of Sefrou's Jewish population.

14. Leven, 2: 99. Leven's negative impression of Marrakesh and its religious leadership undoubtedly owes much to Abraham Ribbi, who wrote that "the rabbis of Marrakesh are from the poor people, servile, fanatical, and stripped of all moral authority." *BAIU,* 2ème série (1900), quoted in José Bénech, *Essai d'explication d'un mellah (Ghetto marocain): Un des Aspects du Judaïsme* (Paris: Éditions Larose, 1940), 154.

15. Laskier, 56 and 66 n. 78, Jewish community leaders in Marrakesh to Alliance, Marrakesh, November 20, 1893, AIU XXXIV.E.582(a), in Hebrew. Reproduced in Laskier, 57. The leaders in Marrakesh also appealed to the British Board of Jewish Deputies in this case. Gottreich, "Jewish Space," 226–27.

16. Élizabeth Antébi, *Les Missionnaires Juifs de la France (1860–1939)* (Paris: Calmann-Lévy, 1999), 47, erroneously places the Azzagui incident as occurring in Marrakesh.

17. According to the *New York Times* (October 13, 1900), 6, the United States demanded an indemnity of £1,000.

18. Ribbi, Marrakesh, December 2, 1900, quoted in Antébi, 47. In his report on Marrakesh Ribbi estimated there to be about six hundred households in the *mellah. BAIU* 25 (1900): 9, cited in Gottreich, "Jewish Space," 134 n. 129. Gottreich believes this figure was "an exaggeration to justify the opening of an A.I.U. school."

19. Messody Coriat was born in Tetuan in 1881 and educated at the ENIO. A.-H. Navon, *Les 70 Ans de l'École Normale Israélite Orientale (1865–1935)* (Paris: Librairie Durlacher,1935), 164. On the training of women teachers for the Alliance, see Frances Malino, "The Women Teachers of the Alliance Israélite Universelle, 1842–1940," in *Jewish Women in Historical Perspective,* ed. Judith R. Baskin, 2nd ed. (Detroit: Wayne State University Press, 1998), 248–69.

20. *BAIU,* 3ème série, *Bulletin annuel* 30 (1905): 127–142. These numbers

would double to 255 boys and 135 girls five years later in 1906, although the proportion of paying students would decline owing to the increasingly difficult financial situation in Marrakesh. Leven, 99. Relying on information provided by Falcon, Bénech described the enrollment figures for 1904 as "very elastic," varying from 250 to 350 boys and 150 to 175 girls. Bénech, 293.

21. Moïse Lévy, Marrakesh, August 13, 1902, AIU France XIV.F. 25, quoted in translation in Rodrigue, *Images of Sephardi and Eastern Jewries*, 206–207.

22. Moïse Lévy, 1904 report, received February 15, 1904, AIU Maroc Microfilm VII.B. An extract of this letter appears in Élias Harrus, *L'Alliance en Action: Les écoles de l'Alliance israélite universelle dans l'Empire de Maroc (1862-1912)* (Paris: Nadir, 2001), 131–32.

Gottreich, "Jewish Space," 202 n. 111 cites additional correspondence related to this affair from Corcos to Gharnit, 4 Dhu al-Qa'ada 1321/January 22, 1904, DAR, Marrakesh 12.

Regarding the new copper coinage, Paul Pascon writes that "these new coins modified the copper/silver exchange rate in a manner very unfavorable to small coins. Before the establishment of the French monetary system in Morocco, two metal-based currencies (silver and copper) were in separate circulation. Copper coins were held in abundance by the popular classes while silver was held by the elites and the wealthy merchants." Pascon, *Capitalism and Agriculture*, 73–75, and idem, *Le Haouz de Marrakech*, 2: 435–37. Pascon calls this revolt "perhaps the first popular insurrection" in Morocco.

23. According to Pascon, Moulay Hafid met with the leader of the insurrection and agreed to recall the new copper coinage, dismiss the market inspector, and abolish the unpopular and non-Koranic *maks*, or gate tax. He states that the Jews were obliged to remove their shoes on leaving the *mellah* and that the governor al-Warzazi was deposed. As al-Warzazi stayed on in his post and Lévy says nothing about the shoe removal ordinance, Pascon's account does not seem entirely reliable. Even he finds it astonishing that the head of the insurrection would have been received by the viceroy, Moulay Hafid. Pascon, *Capitalism*, 74, and idem, *Le Haouz de Marrakech*, 436 and n. 121.

24. Aron Rodrigue, "Eastern Sephardi Jewry and New Nation-States in the Balkans in the Nineteenth and Twentieth Centuries," in *Sephardi and Middle Eastern Jewries: History and Culture in the Modern Era*, ed. Harvey E. Goldberg (Bloomington: Indiana University Press, 1996), 81–88.

25. Bigart to Carmona, Paris, May 1903, AIU Maroc I.C.1–2, quoted in Rodrigue, *Images of Sephardi and Eastern Jewries*, 211.

26. Falcon to President [Leven], Marrakesh, January 15, 1905, AIU Maroc XXVI.E.398–416.

27. Falcon to President [Leven], Marrakesh, January 16, 1905, AIU Maroc XXVI.E.398–416.

28. Houel, 54.

29. *BAIU,* 3ᵉᵐᵉ série, *Bulletin annuel* 30 (1905): 127–42.

30. Souessia to Mauchamp, Essaouira, April 29, 1906, and August 22, 1906, MAE Tangier A 342.

31. *BAIU,* 3ᵉᵐᵉ série, *Bulletin annuel* 31 (1906): 135.

32. Falcon, "Rapport bimestriel," Marrakesh. January to February 1905. March 5, 1905, AIU Maroc XXVI.E.398–416.

33. Falcon to President [Leven], Marrakesh, June 22, 1905, AIU Maroc XXVI.E.398–416.

34. Falcon to President [Leven], Marrakesh, August 9, 1905, AIU Maroc XXVI.E.398–416.

35. For a portrait of this Moroccan Rothschild who later financed Moulay Hafid's bid to become sultan, see Jérôme Tharaud and Jean Tharaud, *Marrakech ou les seigneurs de l'Atlas,* in *Maroc: Les Villes impériale,* 794–95, 814. The source of the Corcos fortune and the family's relationship to the Makhzan are discussed in Daniel J. Schroeter, *Merchants of Essaouira: Urban Society and Imperialism in Southwestern Morocco, 1844–1886* (Cambridge: Cambridge University Press, 1988), 34–42.

36. Bénech, 265. In contrast to Bénech's testimony, Emily Gottreich argues that the Alliance faced an uphill battle in Marrakesh owing to Corcos's resistance. "Although his contributions to the Alliance were consistently larger than those of his fellow Jews, his reluctance to abandon strong patronage ties to the local Muslim authorities made him untrustworthy in the eyes of the A.I.U., which accused him of 'selling out' his coreligionists." In subsequent disagreements with the Alliance directors, Corcos accused "them of trying to Christianize the *mellah's* children and inculcate them with 'irreligion.'" Gottreich, "Jewish Space," 212–13 and n. 139, 140, 141, citing Lévy, December 20, 1910, AIU C.10; Falcon, April 12, 1907, AIU Maroc XXVI.E.398–416 and Falcon, May 5, 1905, AIU Maroc XXVI.E.398–416.

37. Aubin, 298.

38. Corcos encouraged Falcon to leave on the supposition that the continued presence of Europeans in Marrakesh following Mauchamp's death would be harmful to the safety of the city's Jews. See Falcon, May 14, 1907, AIU Maroc XXVI.E.398–416. The partial text of Falcon's letter detailing Corcos's request is reprinted in Gottreich, "Jewish Space," 301 n. 136.

39. Alfred Goldenberg, *Souvenirs d'Alliance: Itinéraire d'un instituteur de l'Alliance Israélite Universelle au Maroc* (Paris: Éditions du Nadir, 1998), 108. The promise to keep the schools open was made after Falcon returned temporarily to Marrakesh later that summer. Falcon to Leven, Safi, July 10, 1907, AIU Maroc XXVI.E.398–419.

40. Falcon to President [Leven], August 20, 1905, AIU Maroc XXVI.E.398–416.

41. He was one of principal stockholders in la Société Immobilière du Maroc. Mohammed Kenbib, *Juifs et Musulmans au Maroc, 1859–1948:*

Contribution à l'histoire des relations inter-communitaires en terre d'Islam (Rabat: Université Mohammed V, 1994), 322–23.

42. "Outside of M. Holzmann, no one has ever come to me to complain about M. Souessia's conduct." Falcon to President [Leven], Marrakesh, December 9, 1905, copied January 23, 1906, AIU Maroc XXVI.E.398–416.

43. Falcon, "Rapport," Marrakesh [1st page missing], received January 23, 1906, AIU Maroc XXVI.E.398–416.

44. Falcon to President [Leven], Marrakesh, March 15, 1906, April 18, 1906, and copy of Falcon to Jeannier, Marrakesh, March 15, 1906, AIU Maroc XXVI.E.398–416. Falcon to Mauchamp, Marrakesh, March 19, 1906, MAE Tangier A 342. Falcon to President [Leven], Marrakesh, May 29, 1906, AIU Maroc XXVI.E.398–416.

45. Falcon to Mauchamp, Marrakesh, undated, MAE Tangier A 342, and Falcon to President [Leven], Marrakesh, June 21, 1906, AIU Maroc XXVI.E.398–419.

46. Falcon, "Rapport bimestriel," Marrakesh, October to December 1906, AIU Maroc XXVI.E.398–416.

47. For example, it was reported in 1893 that the *jizya*, the poll tax for which Jews as non-Muslims were liable under Islamic law, had not been collected in Essaouira for eighteen years. When the tax was reinstated, the community was responsible for paying the arrears. Benchimol, December 1893, AIU Maroc XXXIII.E.582, cited in Daniel J. Schroeter and Joseph Chetrit, "The Transformation of the Jewish Community of Essaouira (Mogador) in the Nineteenth and Twentieth Centuries," in *Sephardi and Middle Eastern Jewries,* 166 n. 37. Similarly, in 1905 when the Jewish banker Jacob Schiff sent American officials a memorandum on the alleged mistreatment of Jews, the secretary of the American delegation to Algeciras, Lewis Einstein, investigated the claims and submitted a report countering Schiff point by point. Kenbib, *Juifs et Musulmans,* 333–35.

48. Kenbib, *Juifs et Musulmans,* 309.

49. Ibid., 309–46.

50. Falcon to Leven, September 2, 1907, Tangier, AIU Maroc Microfilm VII.B.188/2. Part of this letter is reproduced in Gottreich, "Jewish Space," 207.

51. Bénech, 311.

52. AIU XXV.E.394.a, quoted in Ben Abraham, 154.

53. Laskier, 307, 312.

54. For a thoughtful discussion of the relative effect of modernization and Westernization on Moroccan Jews, see Schroeter and Chetrit, "The Transformation of the Jewish Community in Essaouira."

4. A Doctor in Marrakesh

1. Mauchamp to Comité du Maroc, Marrakesh, December 8, 1905, quoted in Guillemin (1908): 102–103.

2. Mauchamp to father, Marrakesh, December 29, 1905, quoted in Guillemin (1908): 103–104. The text erroneously reads "1906."

3. "Divers Mauchamp," January 4, 1906, MAE Tangier A 342.

4. Mauchamp to Jeannier, Marrakesh, January 6, 1906, copy, MAE Tangier A 342, quoted with some changes in Guillemin (1908): 104–107.

5. Jeannier to Saint-Aulaire, Essaouira, January 16, 1906, MAE Tangier A 342.

6. Mauchamp to father, Marrakesh, February 13, 1906, quoted in Guillemin (1908): 108–09; February 18, 1906, ibid., 109–110; March 4, 1906, ibid., 110–111. Members of the Jewish community in Essaouira and Marrakesh similarly addressed appeals to British consular officials for famine relief. See related correspondence in PRO FO 174/276.

7. Mauchamp to father, Marrakesh, April 1, 1906 and April 8, 1906, quoted in Guillemin (1908): 113.

8. Falcon to President [Leven], Marrakesh, May 17, 1906, AIU Maroc XXVI.E.398–416.

9. Mauchamp to father, Marrakesh, June 3, 1906, quoted in Guillemin (1908): 119.

10. Mauchamp, June 11, 1906, and table prepared by Mauchamp. MAE Tangier A 342.

11. Mauchamp report, Marrakesh, September 1, 1906, MAE Tangier A 342.

12. Mauchamp to Regnault, Marrakesh, September 12, 1906, MAE Tangier A 342.

13. Mauchamp to father, Marrakesh, December 14, 1906, quoted in Guillemin (1908): 167.

14. Mauchamp to Regnault, Marrakesh, May 16, 1906 and July 19, 1906, MAE Tangier A 342.

15. Guichard to Mauchamp, Chalon-sur-Saône, November 1, 1906, MAE Tangier A 342.

16. Guillemin (1908): 114. European diplomats also went in for "pig-sticking." See Susan Gilson Miller, "The Colonial Hunt in Nineteenth Century Tangier," in *Tanger, 1800–1956, Contribution à l'histoire récente du Maroc* (Rabat: Université Mohammed V, 1991), 191–203.

17. Saint-Aulaire, *Au Maroc avant et avec Lyautey*, 79–81.

18. In approving Regnault's request to expand Mauchamp's clinic into a hospital for Moroccans, foreign minister Pichon allocated 28,500 francs for 1907. Pichon to Regnault, Paris, February 16, 1907, MAE Tangier A 342.

19. Guillemin (1908): 114.

20. René-Leclerc to Mauchamp, Tangier, July 27, 1906, MAE Tangier A 342.

21. Jeannier to Saint-René Taillandier, Essaouira, June 5, 1906, and June 11, 1906, MAE Tangier A 262.

22. Guillemin (1908): 116. Guillemin does not identify the recipient by name, but in the letter Mauchamp encourages the recipient to appeal

to his brother-in-law Jonnart, the governor general in Algeria. In this case the letter's recipient was likely to be Raymond Aynard, the son of a former deputy from Lyon and Jonnart's former administrative aide. See Saint-Aulaire, *Au Maroc avant et avec Lyautey,* 123.

23. Ruedy, 101, and Charles-Robert Ageron, *Les Algériens Musulmans et la France (1871–1919),* 2 vols. (Paris: Presses Universitaires de France, 1968), 2: 891.

24. In reply, the Alliance Française noted Mauchamp's willingness to found a school in Marrakesh and said it would discuss the matter with M. Gautsch, the Alliance's director in Tangier. Alliance Français to Mauchamp, July 9, 1906, MAE Tangier A 342.

25. Guillemin (1908): 120, 154.

26. Signature illegible, October 18, 1906, Safi, and January 1, 1906 [*sic,* 1907], MAE Tangier A 342.

27. Maclean to Lowther, F.O. 174/251, No. 91, May 12, 1906, cited in Pascon, *Le Haouz de Marrakech,* 2: 288 n. 109. In the end, the sharif Moulay Hajj al-Misluhi, who led the *zawiya* for thirty-five years and died in 1908 (not in 1906 as it appears in Pascon) never acquired French protection. Instead he and his successors continued to rely on the support of the British legation as late as 1929, that is, long after the establishment of the French Protectorate at least in theory made the protégé system obsolete. Ibid., 2: 288–89.

28. Mauchamp to father, Marrakesh, March 25, 1906 and April 1, 1906, quoted in Guillemin (1908): 112–13; Weisberger, 110; Walter Harris, *Maroc That Was* (London: William Blackwood, 1921; reprint London: Eland Books, 1983), 230.

29. Mauchamp to Gouguet de Girac, Marrakesh, May 14, 1906, quoted in Guillemin (1908): 118–99.

30. Castro to Mauchamp, Marrakesh, March 1, 1906, MAE Tangier A 342.

31. Firbach to Mauchamp, Marrakesh, April 24, 1906, MAE Tangier A 342.

32. Mauchamp to parents, Marrakesh, March 4, 1905, quoted in Guillemin (1908): 111.

33. L. H. Sadok to Mauchamp, March 1907, Marrakesh, and Marie L. Nicolet, March 16, 1907, "Mission House," Marrakesh, MAE Tangier A 342.

34. Burke, *Prelude to Protectorate,* 74.

35. Al-Kattani's career and his relationship to the Hafidiyya revolt is discussed at length in Sahar Bazzaz, "Challenging Power and Authority in Pre-protectorate Morocco: Shaykh Muhammad al-Kattani and the Tariqa Kattaniyya" (Ph.D. diss., Harvard University, 2002). See also Henry Munson Jr., *Religion and Power in Morocco* (New Haven, Conn.: Yale University Press, 1993), 56–76; and Mohamed Tozy, *Monarchie et Islam politique au Maroc,* 2nd ed. (Paris: Presses de Science Po, 1999), 63–68.

36. Burke, *Prelude to Protectorate,* 85.

37. MacLeod to Lowther, Fez, June 3, 1906, Inclosure in Lowther to Grey, Tangier, June 9, 1906 [20530], and MacLeod to Lowther, June 5, 1906, Inclosure in Lowther to Grey, Tangier, June 10, 1906 [20533], PRO FO 413/42.

38. Burke, *Prelude to Protectorate*, 85, 88. See Laroui, "La conférence d'Algésiras," 73–79.

39. Mauchamp to parents, Marrakesh, March 4, 1906, quoted in Guillemin (1908): 110–11.

40. Mauchamp to father, Marrakesh, April 15, 1906, quoted in ibid., 114.

41. Jeannier to Saint-René Taillandier, Essaouira, March 10, 1906, MAE Tangier A 263.

42. Mauchamp to father, Marrakesh, February 25, 1906, quoted in Guillemin (1908): 110.

43. Mauchamp to father, Marrakesh, March 4, 1906, quoted in Guillemin (1908): 111–12. German consular sources refer to Holzmann as an Ottoman subject and not a German, and note that he was a convert to Islam. Rather than being in the employ of the Germans, Holzmann seems instead to have been a genuine supporter of Moulay Hafid's cause.

44. On the ongoing and clandestine "war of deceit" between the two brothers Moulay Hafid and the sultan Abdelaziz prior to Moulay Hafid's ascension to the throne, see A. G. P. Martin, *Quatre siècles d'histoire marocaine, au Sahara de 1504 à 1902, au Maroc de 1894 à 1912* (Paris: Félix Alcan, 1923, reprinted Rabat: Éditions la Porte, 1994), 415–28.

45. In December 1904 Holzmann had traveled to Berlin on Moulay Hafid's behalf and, to the great consternation of the French, allegedly offered to the Mannesmann group mining concessions in the Atlas Mountains in exchange for loans and political support. These ties bore fruit only later, when Moulay Hafid made his bid for the throne in 1907. Guillen, 448.

46. Falcon to President [Leven], Marrakesh, May 6, 1907, AIU Maroc XXVI.E.398–416.

5. False Starts and False Reports

1. Mohammed Essaghir al-Khalloufi, *Bouhmara, du Jihad à la compromission: Le Maroc oriental et le Rif de 1900 à 1909* (Rabat: El Maârif al-jadida, 1993).

2. Despite his initial support for Moulay Hafid, al-Kattani soon became disillusioned with the new sultan for failing to wage the promised jihad. Having criticized Moulay Hafid and fearful for his life, al-Kattani headed off into the Atlas mountains in the spring of 1909 with the hope that he might spark an armed resistance to the foreigners. He did not get far. Pursued by Moulay Hafid's men, he was arrested, brought back to Fez, and flogged to death.

3. Lennox to White, Marrakesh, August 6, 1906, PRO FO 174/281.

4. Hoover, 51–52. On the tumultuous relations between the Rahamna and the Makhzan, see Pascon, *Le Haouz de Marrakech*, 1: 186–215.

5. Hoover, 136–74.

6. Lennox to White, Marrakesh, August 6, 1906, PRO FO 174/281.

7. Jeannier to Regnault, "Rapport d'ensemble sur l'agitation séparatistes," Essaouira, August 19, 1906, MAE Tangier A262.

8. Souessia to Mauchamp, Essaouira, August 22, 1906, MAE Tanger A 342.

9. Communiqué, Safi, August 21, 1906, MAE Tangier A262.

10. Jeannier to Regnault, Essaouira, August 24, 1906, MAE Tangier A262.

11. Communiqué, Safi, August 29, 1906, MAE Tangier A262.

12. Mauchamp to parents, Marrakesh, October 7, 1906, quoted in Guillemin (1908): 160.

13. Mauchamp to Regnault, Marrakesh, November 6, 1906, and November 18, 1906, MAE Tangier A 342; Regnault to Mauchamp, Tangier, November 20, 1906, MAE Tangier A 342.

14. Mauchamp to unidentified friend, Marrakesh, November 22, 1906, quoted in Guillemin (1908): 161–62.

15. On the housing shortage in the Essaouira *mellah* and the subsequent rent inflation in the Muslim quarter, see Kenbib, *Juifs et Musulmans,* 338–39.

16. Bargash to al-Turris, Essaouira, French translation of telegram, August 31, 1906, enclosed with note from Saint-Aulaire to Bourgeois, Tangier, September 11, 1906, MAE Tangier A 262.

17. White to Grey, Tangier, October 4, 1906, PRO FO 413/42 [34513].

18. Burke, *Prelude to Protectorate*, 89.

19. Ibid., 61–62; Munson, 57–58. On the violation of sanctuary and its significance, see Mohamed El Mansour, "The Sanctuary (Hurm) in Precolonial Morocco," in *In the Shadow of the Sultan: Culture, Power, and Politics in Morocco,* ed. Rahma Bourqia and Susan Gilson Miller (Cambridge, Mass.: Harvard Center for Middle East Studies, 1999), 49–73.

20. Burke, *Prelude to Protectorate*, 66.

21. Ibid., 91, and Lowther to Grey, "Report by Mr. G. Lowther for the Year 1906," Inclosure in No. 19. PRO FO 413/44.

22. Mauchamp to Minister of Post, Marrakesh, June 22, 1906, MAE Tangier A 342; Mauchamp to Regnault, Marrakesh, June 25, 1906, MAE Tangier A 342; and Mauchamp to father, Marrakesh, April 8, 1906, quoted in Guillemin (1908): 113.

23. Mauchamp to father, Marrakesh, July 15, 1906, quoted in Guillemin (1908): 119–20.

24. Mauchamp to Regnault, Marrakesh, September 12, 1906, MAE Tangier A 342.

25. Mauchamp to Regnault, Marrakesh, November 22, 1906, MAE Tangier A 342.

26. Mauchamp to Regnault, Chalon-sur-Saône, January 27, 1907, MAE Tangier A 342.

27. Pascon, *Le Haouz du Marrakech*, 2: 425, and idem, *Capitalism and Agriculture*, 65. The diplomatic correspondence surrounding the affair is summarized in Abrams, 136–43.

28. White to Grey, Tangier, September 27, 1906, PRO FO 413/42 [33945]. According to the British diplomat, "It was imprudent of M. Lassallas to travel in those districts at the present time."

29. Madden to White, Essaouira, October 5, 1906, PRO FO 174/276.

30. Madden to White, Essaouira, October 27, 1906, PRO FO 174/276.

31. Allal Abdi, who came to Morocco from Algeria in 1890, died not long after these events, according to an obituary in *La Dépêche Marocaine*, March 15, 1908. He was reputedly an accomplished mathematician and astronomer. Albert Cousin and Daniel Saurin, *Le Maroc* (Paris: Librairie du Figaro, 1905), 159.

32. Mauchamp to father, Marrakesh, October 7, 1906, quoted in Guillemin (1908): 160.

33. Madden further reported that, according to the French diplomat Jeannier, "Lassallas did wrong in leaving the main road and going to the Zawia [*sic*]: and had acted inadvisedly in protecting a Moor against whom a criminal charge had been preferred without fully investigating it first." Madden to White, Essaouira, November 25, 1906, PRO FO 174/276. Pascon believes that it was Lassallas himself who suggested to the Tekna *qaid* during his detention that the ambush was really aimed at the German agent Niehr, his "only real competition in the Haouz." Pascon, *Capitalism and Agriculture*, 65.

34. Peffau-Garavini to Regnault, Tangier, October 14, 1906, MAE Tangier A 263; René-Leclerc to Mauchamp, Tangier, October 27, 1906, MAE Tangier A 342.

35. *La Dépêche Marocaine*, November 25, 1906, cited in translation in Abrams, 138–39. On the Compagnie Marocaine's response to the Lassallas affair, see ibid., 140–42.

36. Madden to White, Essaouira, October 30, 1905, PRO FO 174/276.

37. B. G. Martin, "Ma' al-'Aynayn al-Qalqami, Mauritanian Mystic and Politics," in *Muslim Brotherhoods in Nineteenth-Century Africa* (Cambridge: Cambridge University Press, 1976), 125–51.

38. Burke, *Prelude to Protectorate*, 46–47.

39. Madden to White, Essaouira, October 30, 1905, PRO FO 174/276.

40. Madden to Lowther, Essaouira, June 18, 1906, PRO FO 174/276.

41. Burke, *Prelude to Protectorate*, 90.

42. Ibid., 90.

43. The French merchant Firbach had also earlier lodged a complaint against Hajj Abdeslam.

44. Mauchamp to Regnault, Marrakesh, September 25, 1906, MAE Tangier A 342.

45. Mauchamp to father, Marrakesh, September 26, 1906, quoted in Guillemin (1908): 157.

46. Madden to White, Essaouira, November 17, 1906, PRO FO 174/276.

47. Saint-Aulaire to Mauchamp, Tangier, December 3, 1906, MAE Tangier A 342.

48. André Mevil in *L'Echo de Paris*, clipping enclosed with letter from Peffau-Garavini to Mauchamp, Paris, November 28, 1906, MAE Tangier A 342.

49. Peffau-Garavini to Mauchamp, Paris, December 4, 1904, and December 8, 1906, MAE Tangier A 342.

50. Pierre Mauchamp to Sarrien, Chalon-sur-Saône, December 5, 1906, MAE Tangier A 342; Pichon to Regnault, Paris, December 26, 1906, MAE Tangier A 342.

51. Guillemin (1908): 166.

52. Mauchamp to father, December 14, 1906, quoted in Guillemin (1908): 167.

53. Jean d'Arbaumont, "Emile Mauchamp (1870–1907)," extract from *Société des Amis des Arts, Sciences, Archéologie et Histoire locale de la Bresse louhan-naise* 13 (1985): 56. The details surrounding the gifts do not appear in the published *Documents Diplomatiques*. I have not seen the MAE documents to which d'Arbaumont alludes.

54. Berrino to Mauchamp, Marrakesh, January 20, 1907, MAE Tangier A 342.

55. Mauchamp to Regnault, Chalon-sur-Saône, February 3, 1907, MAE Tangier A 342.

56. Paul Pascon, "Le rapport 'secret' d'Edmond Doutté: Situation politique du Haoûz, 1er janvier 1907," *Hérodote* (1978): 132–59.

57. Bouvier to Mauchamp, Marrakesh, January 12, 1907, MAE Tangier A 342.

58. MacLeod to Lowther, Fez, March 28, 1907, Inclosure in Lowther to Grey, Tangier, April 2, 1907, PRO FO 371/285.

6. March 19, 1907

1. *La Dépêche Marocaine*, February 7, 1907.

2. Lewis Pyenson, *Civilizing Mission: Exact Sciences and French Overseas Expansion, 1830–1940* (Baltimore, Md.: Johns Hopkins University Press, 1993), 141.

3. Louis Gentil, *Titres et travaux scientifiques* (Paris, 1922), 25–27, quoted in ibid., 141.

4. Pyenson, 142–43.

5. E. Doutté, "Les causes de la chute d'un sultan," *Renseignements coloniaux*, supplément au *BCAF* 7 (1909) 132, 134, cited in Daniel Rivet, *Lyautey et l'institution du protectorat français au Maroc, 1912–1925*, 3 vols. (Paris: L'Harmattan, 1988), 1:19.

6. Alfred le Chatelier's intellectual legacy is discussed in detail in Mohamed Mahfoud Chkouri, "L'Anthropologie Coloniale Française et le Maroc" (thèse de Doctorat nouveau régime, Université Paris VIII Vincennes-Saint-Denis, 1997–1998).

7. Edmund Burke III, "La Mission Scientique au Maroc: Science sociale et politique dans l'âge de l'impérialisme," in *Recherches récentes sur le Maroc moderne (Actes de Durham, 13–15 Juillet 1977)* (Rabat: Bulletin Economique et social du Maroc, 1978), 37–56.

8. The exception to the rule was Edmond Doutté, who worked hard to align himself with Émile Durkheim's circle of sociologists. See Valensi, "Le Maghreb vu du centre," 241–43.

9. Nye, *Masculinity and Male Codes of Honor,* 211 and 281 n. 183.

10. Mauchamp to Guillemin, El-Jadida, March 2, 1907, quoted in Guillemin (1908): 173.

11. In Limoun the *qaid* was the protégé of Mateo, the Italian vice-consul in El-Jadida; from there, Mauchamp's friend, the French officer Jacquety, had arranged for the chiefs of the Oulad Ferj to conduct them safely through that tribe's region; in the area of Djebel Lakdar, Aouna tribe protégés of Spinney, the English vice-consul in El-Jadida, would take over; elsewhere protégés of Lassallas among the Menabha would provide safe conduct.

12. Mauchamp to father, El-Jadida, March 6, 1907, quoted in Guillemin (1908): 174–75.

13. *La Dépêche Marocaine,* March 26, 1907.

14. Gentil to Pichon, Paris, April 23, 1907, MAE Tangier A 269, p. 4. A copy of Gentil's typed report can also be found in the Papiers Lyautey, Archives Nationales (France), 475 AP 60.

15. Ibid., 39.

16. Edited version published in *Documents Diplomatiques, 1907, Affaires du Maroc* III (1906–1907), no. 261, 235.

17. "I saw the supposed pole," the British vice-consul in Marrakesh, Lennox, wrote to his counterpart in El-Jadida. "It is only two or three reeds bound together, about 5½ yards long, and there were two small cross-pieces near the top." Lennox to Spinney, Marrakesh, March 20, 1907, Inclosure 1 in Lowther to Grey, Tangier, March 26, 1907, PRO FO 371/285.

18. See especially Allal el-Khdimi, "L'Occupation d'Oujda," in *La Memorial du Maroc,* tome 5: *1906–1934: Morcellement et résistance,* ed. Larbi Essakali (Rabat: Nord Publications, 1983–1985), 74–78.

19. Julien, 71.

20. Jacques Cagne, *Nation et nationalisme au Maroc: Aux racines de la nation marocaine* (Rabat: Institute Universitaire de la Recherche Scientifique, 1988), 283 and 284 n. 326. In making this interpretation, Cagne relied on the published and therefore edited version of Gentil's report.

21. White to Grey, Tangier, November 28, 1906, PRO 413/42 [41317].

22. In an effort to establish independent communications with France, the French had also established at the turn of the century an undersea telegraph cable to Oran. J.-C. Allain, "Le double enjeu de Tangier dans la stratégie française des telecommunications sous-marines au debut du XXème siècle," in *Tanger, 1800–1956*, 217–36; and idem, *Agadir 1911*, 131–35.

23. Lowther to Grey, Tangier, February 22, 1907, PRO FO 413/44 [6845].

24. *Al-Moghreb al-Aksa*, March 2, 1907.

25. Lowther to Grey, Tangier, March 7, 1907, PRO FO 413/44 [8455].

26. Abdelaziz to Muhammad al-Turris, Fez, 19 Muharram 1325/March 4, 1907. Text in French translation in M. Allouche, "Lettres chérifiennes inédites relatives à l'assasinat du Dr. Mauchamp et à l'occupation d'Oujda en 1907," *Actes du XXI^eCongrès international des orientalistes* (Paris, 23–31 Juillet 1948) (Paris: Imprimerie Nationale, 1949), 302–304. I was unable to locate the Arabic text of this letter. These letters are also cited in d'Arbaumont. Al-Turris wrote to the sultan just the day before Mauchamp's murder, acknowledging receipt of the sultan's letter warning about the possible installation of a telegraph in Marrakesh. Al-Turris to Abdelaziz, Tangier, 3 Safar 1325/March 18, 1907, copy in BG Kunnash 2720, p. 274.

27. Abdelaziz to Tetuan Custom Agents, Fez, 19 Muharram 1325/March 4, 1907, DAR Sijil 21592.

28. Abd al-Rahman Lahlu and Hajj Abd al-Rahman al-Ufir to Abdelaziz, Tangier, 3 Safar 1325/March 18, 1907, DAR.

29. Gentil to Pichon, Paris, April 23, 1907, MAE Tangier A 269, p. 30.

30. Bargash to al-Turris, Essaouira, 1 Safar 1325/March 16, 1907, DAR.

31. Abdelaziz to al-Warzazi, Fez, 1 Muharram 1325/February 14, 1907, published in French translation in Allouche, 304. Allouche's translation erroneously implies that Gentil was already in Marrakesh. In reality, Gentil arrived in the city only the following month.

32. *La Dépêche Marocaine*, March 2, 1907.

33. Lowther to Grey, Tangier, March 8, 1907, PRO FO 413/44 [8459].

34. *Al-Moghreb al-Aksa*, March 23, 1907.

35. In addition to published accounts of Mauchamp's murder, details of the narrative that follows are derived largely from documents collected in MAE Tangier A 269. In particular, two sets of so-called depositions, all recorded in French, were taken in Marrakesh. The first set of depositions was taken by Louis Gentil in the days immediately following the murder. The second set was taken three years after the incident, in May 1910 by Nooman Khouri, the French consul in Essaouira.

36. Reference to a dispute with Ibn Sahil comes from Muhammad Hassani Zailachi's deposition, taken on March 28, 1907 by French vice-consul Hoff in Safi. MAE Tangier A 269. Muhammad Hassani gave another undated deposition in Marrakesh soon after the murder. MAE Tangier A 269.

37. Deposition of M. Benchimol, March 24, 1907, MAE Tangier A 269. This is possibly the Algerian Jew whom Mauchamp had accused of running a brothel the previous year.

38. Deposition of Muhammad al-Sghir ould [bin] al-Bidawi to Nooman Kouri, witnessed by Nairn, May 24, 1910. MAE Tangier A 269.

39. Muhammad Hassani, undated deposition and deposition taken by Hoff in Safi on March 28, 1907, and another on March 28, 1907, MAE Tangier A 269.

40. Si Ali bin Ibrahim, deposition taken by Paul Bouvier, March 30, 1907, MAE Tangier A 269. Ali bin Ibrahim gave a second deposition given to Kouri on June 8, 1910, at which point he said he did not hear the conversation between Muhammad Sghir and Mauchamp. MAE Tangier A 269. According to Alan Lennox, Muhammad Sghir pleaded with Mauchamp "to return to the dispensary and send one of the men to take down the pole." Lennox to Spinney, Marrakesh, March 19, 1907, Inclosure in Lowther to Grey, Tangier, March 23, 1907, PRO FO 371/285.

41. Brahim bin Touggani, deposition before Kouri and Nairn, May 26, 1910, MAE Tangier A 269.

42. Lennox's initial accounts of Mauchamp's murder are found in a series of correspondence beginning with Lennox to Spinney, Marrakesh, March 19, 1907, Inclosure in Lowther to Grey, Tangier, March 23, 1907, PRO FO 371/285.

43. Aisha [Aicha], undated deposition, MAE Tangier A 269.

44. Al-Mukhtar al-Susi's account of his 1355/1935–1936 conversation with Driss bin Minu appears in his book, *Around the Dinner Table* [in Arabic] (Rabat: Al-Sahil, n.d.), 50.

45. Lennox to Madden, Marrakesh, March 19, 1907, Inclosure in Lowther to Grey, Tangier, March 24, 1907, PRO FO 371/285.

46. In his telling of the story, Driss bin Minu took credit for recovering the corpse. Al-Susi, 50.

47. Paul Bouvier, deposition, March 20, 1907, MAE Tangier A 269.

48. Gentil to Pichon, Paris, April 23, 1907, MAE Tangier A 269, 3.

49. Lennox to Spinney, Marrakesh, March 20, 1907, Inclosure 1 in Lowther to Grey, Tangier, March 26, 1907, PRO FO 371/285.

50. Lennox to Madden, Marrakesh, March 20, 1907, Inclosure 1 in No. 1 Lowther to Grey, Tangier, March 24, 1907, PRO FO 371/285. Amster errs when she says that the home of a "Dr. Assiegeait" was also attacked. "Many Deaths," 422.

51. Autopsy Report, signed Dr. Guichard, Dr. V. Herzen, and Vice-Consul Huytèza, March 24, 1907, MAE Tangier A 269.

52. Falcon to President [Leven], March 20, 1907, AIU Maroc XXVI. E.398–416.

53. Al-Warzazi to al-Turris, Marrakesh, 4 Safar 1325/March 19, 1907, DAR.

54. Brives to Regnault, Misfiwa, March 23, 1907, MAE Tangier A 269.

According to Gentil, Brives also wrote to Bouvier the very same day that "everyone" unanimously says, "Doctor Mauchamp was murdered because he flew a French flag on his terrace." Gentil to Pichon, Paris, April 23, 1907, MAE Tangier A 269, p. 32.

55. Al-Warzazi to al-Turris, Marrakesh, 4 Safar 1325/March 19, 1907, DAR.

56. Al-Warzazi to al-Turris, Marrakesh, 19 Safar 1325/April 3, 1907, DAR Sijil 30271.

57. Falcon to President [Leven], Marrakesh, March 20, 1907, AIU Maroc XXVI.E.398–416.

58. *La Dépêche Marocaine,* March 26, 1907.

59. The wealthy Casablanca merchant Carl Ficke was associated with the efforts of the Mannesmann brothers to extend their commercial interests in the south of Morocco. Later he was accused of espionage and executed along with five other Germans early in World War I. In her memoirs, Marina López Gádor recalls how her Spanish-born father, a naturalized French citizen who had been conscripted into the French army, was a member of the firing squad that shot Ficke. According to López Gádor, Ficke and her father had had close relations before the war. Her father reported averting his aim after Ficke had nodded to him in recognition. Ficke's large villa was confiscated and turned into a home for sick children. Maria López Gádor, *La diligence de Casablanca, souvenirs du début du siècle* (Talence, France: Maxime Rousselle, 1998), 74–75.

Saint-Aulaire claims that Ficke had been a correspondent of Jaurès. The socialist politician, who opposed the French military intervention in Morocco, was assassinated in July 1914. His assailant, a French nationalist, thought Jaurès's pacifism played into the hands of the Germans. Saint-Aulaire similarly considered him a traitor. Saint-Aulaire, *Au Maroc avant et avec Lyautey,* 227.

60. Gentil to Regnault, Marrakesh, March 20, 1907, midnight, typed copy, MAE Tangier A 269.

61. The explanation that Mauchamp placed the bamboo pole on his roof to aid Gentil in his measurements also appears in Segonzac, 213.

62. Gentil to Pichon, Paris, April 23, 1907, MAE Tangier A 269, 18.

63. Lennox to Madden, Marrakesh, March 21, 1907, PRO FO 174/253. Also see Lennox to Madden, Marrakesh, March 19, 1907, and Lennox to Spinney, Marrakesh, March 20, 1907, French translation, MAE Tangier A 269.

64. In his brief account of the Mauchamp affair, the Moroccan historian Ibn Zaydan errs in placing an aggrieved Abdeslam al-Warzazi at the scene when Mauchamp was being laid in his coffin. Abd al-Rahman bin Zaydan, *A Presentation of Luminous Men with the Most Beautiful Reports of the City of Meknes* [in Arabic], 5 vols. (Fes: n.p., 1930; reprint Casablanca: Ideal, 1990), 1: 416.

65. Lennox to Lowther, Marrakesh, April 17, 1907, PRO FO 174/281.

66. Text of article appears in ibid. The English journalist Ashmead-Bartlett similarly made a point of retaining his boots when visiting Moulay Hafid in 1910. E. Ashmead-Bartlett, *The Passing of the Shereefian Empire* (Edinburgh: William Blackwood, 1910; reprint Westport, Conn.: Negro Universities Press, 1970), 248.

67. Gentil to Pichon, Paris, April 23, 1907, MAE Tangier A 269, pp. 24–27.

68. Lennox to Lowther, Marrakesh, April 17, 1907, PRO FO 174/281.

69. Ibid.

70. Al-Warzazi to al-Turris, Marrakesh, 9 Safar 1325/March 24, 1907, DAR.

71. Lennox to Spinney, Marrakesh, March 20, 1907, Inclosure 1 in Lowther to Grey, Tangier, March 26, 1907, PRO FO 371/285 [10507].

72. Lennox to Madden, Marrakesh, March 21, 1907, Inclosure 2 in Lowther to Grey, March 26, 1907, PRO FO 371/285 [10507] and PRO FO 174/253.

73. Gentil to Pichon, Paris, April 23, 1907, MAE Tangier A 269, p. 28.

7. In Morocco, No One Dies without a Reason

1. Ibn Zaydan reports, for instance, that Mauchamp raised the French tricolor above his door. Ibn Zaydan, 1: 415. Abdelaziz's letter is discussed in chapter 8.

2. *The British Medical Journal,* March 30, 1907, 785.

3. Segonzac, 214.

4. *Al-Saada,* April 4, 1907/20 Safar 1325. This may be a reference to an incident that occurred in 1892 during a visit of the British minister Sir Charles Euan Smith. See Raoult, 180.

5. For example, Julien, *Le Maroc face aux impérialisme.*

6. Allouche, 302–304, and André Adam, *Histoire de Casablanca (des origins à 1914)* (Aix-en Provence: Éditions Ophrys, 1968), 107.

7. Houel, 60.

8. Lennox to Madden, Marrakesh, March 21, 1907. PRO FO 371/285 and PRO FO 174/253.

9. *Al-Moghreb al-Aksa,* April 20, 1907.

10. Houel, 110. Abu Amama, a marabout, or holy man, of Oulad Sidi Cheikh origin, led a tribal revolt in the Sud Oranais in 1881. Taking refuge in Morocco, neither he nor the Oulad Sidi Cheikh submitted to the jurisdiction of the Makhzan. Burke, *Prelude to Protectorate,* 29. His several insurrections are recounted in Dunn, 140–43 and 158–59.

11. Houel, 63–64.

12. Burke, *Prelude to Protectorate,* 132 and 253–54 n. 17.

13. Graf Sternberg, *The Barbarians of Morocco,* trans. Ethel Peck, illustrations by Douglas Pitt-Fox (London: Chatto and Windus, 1908), 74–75.

14. Sternberg at this point continues with his own diatribe against the French, whom he calls "the barbarians of the twentieth century."

15. R. B. Cunningham Grahame recounted his 1897 adventures in *Mogreb-El-Acksa: A Journey in Morocco* (London: 1898; reprint New York: National Travel Club, 1930).

16. *Al-Moghreb al-Aksa,* April 13, 1907. According to Pascon, a syndicate of French financiers had sent an engineer as early as 1897 to explore the possibility of establishing a telegraph in Marrakesh. Schlumberger, Marrakesh to Ministry of War, June 1, 1896, Archives Générales Vincennes. C.9. cited in Pascon, *Le Haouz,* 2: 439–40 and 439 n. 132. Pascon says that in 1902 and again in 1905 the same group of financiers made an attempt to install a wireless telegraph relay between Marrakesh and Essaouira. See also idem, *Capitalism,* 76.

17. *Al-Saada,* June 20, 1907/8 Jumada I 1325, reprinted as Appendix 89, "Concerning the Wireless Telegraph Venture in Morocco," in Muhammad al-Manuni, *Aspects of the Awakening of Modern Morocco* [in Arabic], 2 vols. (Casablanca: al-Madaris, 1985), 2: 577–79.

18. Louis Gentil, "L'Insecurité actuelle dans le sud marocain," *BCAF* 17 (April 1907): 128.

19. *Al-Moghreb al-Aksa,* March 30, 1907.

20. *La Dépêche Marocaine,* March 25/26, 1907.

21. *L'Express de Lyon,* April 2, 1907. These allegations also appear in Segonzac, 214.

22. Lascelles to Grey, Berlin, May 6, 1907, PRO FO 174/253 [15494]. Photocopy in DAR.

23. Langwerth to Auswärtiges Amt, Tangier, Telegram No. 266, August 20, 1907, received August 24, 1907, No. 13243, Photocopy in "Sultan von Marokko," 3 vols. in DAR.

24. Gavin Maxwell, *Lords of the Atlas: The Rise and Fall of the House of Glaoua, 1893–1956* (London: Pan Books, 1966), 104. For further allegations of Holzmann's instigation see Ibn Zaydan, 1: 418.

25. Houel, 56–57.

26. Ibid., 57.

27. Al-Susi, 50.

28. Houel, 88–90, provides a portrait of Saurin, an Algerian lawyer turned journalist.

29. *L'Éclair,* March 25, 1907.

30. "Chambre des Députés, Séance du 26 Mars 1907," *Journal officiel du Débats parlementaires* (March 23, 1907): 831.

31. Ibid.

32. Georges Oved, *La Gauche française et le nationalisme marocaine, 1905–1955,* 2 vols. (Paris: L'Harmattan, 1984), 1: 33.

33. Regnault to Pichon, March 26, 1907, *AF* 3: 197–98, No. 226. The workers demanded "notable reparations be accorded to France, whose prestige has suffered from the purely platonic demonstrations made till now in reparation of the committed crimes. They expressed their confidence in the public powers and told the metropolitan authorities that they can count in

Morocco on the energy of the French workers ready to defend all claims which we are in our right to demand."

34. Oved, 1: 43.

35. Lowther to Grey, Tangier, April 4, 1907, FO PRO 371/285 [11705].

36. The speeches of Regnault, Braunschvig, and Spivacoff are excerpted in Guillemin (1909): 50–57.

8. Negotiations

1. Georges Saint-René Taillandier, *Les Origines du Maroc Français, Récit d'une mission (1901–1906)* (Paris: Plon, 1930).

At the time of his posting, the diplomat was in his early fifties. His colleague Saint-Aulaire later described him as an "ascetic of diplomacy" and a "secular saint" who, at the outbreak of World War I and at the age of sixty-two, enlisted as a junior lieutenant in the reserves. He died in 1942 at the age of ninety. Comte de Saint-Aulaire, "Guillaume II à Tanger," *Les oeuvres libres* 70 (March 1952), 74–77.

Saint-René Taillandier's wife, the sister of the writer André Chevrillon, published her memoirs more than forty years after leaving Tangier. Madeleine Saint-René Taillandier, *Ce monde disparu, Souvenirs: Syrie-Palestine-Liban-Maroc* (Paris: Librarie Plon, 1947).

2. G. Saint-René Taillandier, *Les Origines*, 5, 44–45. The pre-Protectorate structure of the Moroccan government is discussed in a number of books: Cousin, *Le Maroc;* Abdallah Laroui, *Les Origines sociales et culturelles du nationalisme Marocaine;* Mustafa al-Shabi, *The Makhzan Elite in Nineteenth-Century Morocco* [in Arabic] (Rabat: Université Mohammed V, 1995); Muhammad al-Saghir al-Khallufi, *Morocco's Suicide at the Hands of Its Rebels: Samples of al-Hajawi's Political Writings Regarding the Start of the Twentieth-Century* [in Arabic] (Rabat: El Maarif Al-Jadida, 1995).

3. Cousin, 159.

4. Ramón Lourido Diaz, "Le Sultan Sidi Muhammad b. Abd Allah et l'institution de la représentation consulaire à Tanger," in *Tanger, 1800–1956,* 9–27.

5. Miège, *Le Maroc et L'Europe,* 2: 570 n. 3; ibid., 4: 54–55 n. 9.

6. G. Saint-René Taillandier, *Les Origines,* 16.

7. Especially after the death of Moulay Hassan, there was a marked increase in European naval demonstrations and other displays of European pressure. Kenbib, *Les Protégés,* 84–92.

8. Ibid., 92.

9. Al-Turris to Ibn Sulayman, Tangier, 9 Safar 1325/March 24, 1907, BG Kunnash 2720, p. 277.

10. Ibn Sulayman to al-Turris, Fez, 12 Safar 1325/March 27, 1907, DAR Sijil 16195.

11. Al-Turris to Ibn Sulayman, Tangier, 12 Safar 1325/March 27, 1907, BG Kunnash 2720, p. 278.

12. Ibn Sulayman to al-Turris, Fez, 14 Safar 1325/March 29, 1907, DAR Sijil 18647.

13. Bargash to Abdelaziz, Essaouira, 15 Safar 1325/March 30, 1907, reprinted as CXIII in M. Nehlil, *Lettres chérifiennes* (Paris: E. Guilmoto, 1915).

14. Bargash to al-Turris, Essaouira, 3 Rabi I 1907/April 16, 1907, DAR; Abdelaziz to Bargash, Fez [draft], 9 Rabi I 1325/April 22, 1907, DAR.

15. Lister to Grey, Paris, March 26, 1907, PRO FO 413/44 [9894].

16. Al-Turris to Ibn Sulayman, Tangier, 14 Safar 1325/March 29, 1907, BG Kunnash 2720, p. 283.

17. In 1904 the Oulad Sidi Cheikh tribe threw its support behind the pretender, Abu Himara, but the sultan, Abdelaziz, was able to buy off Tayyib, Abu Amama's son and successor. Mohammed Essaghir al-Khalloufi, *Bouhmara, du Jihad à la compromission: Le Maroc oriental et le Rif de 1900 à 1909* (Rabat: El Maârif al-jadida, 1993), 97.

18. Ibn Karrum al-Jaburi to al-Turris, Oujda, 13 Safar 1325/March 28, 1907, DAR.

19. "The force will be composed as follows: three battalions of infantry; two squadrons of Spahis; one or two mounted batteries; one section of Engineers; one goum [*sic*] of 200 Arab horse. It is hoped that Oujda will be occupied on the 29th, or at latest the 30th of this month." Lister to Grey, Paris, reporting on conversation with Pichon, March 27, 1907, PRO FO 413/44 [10015].

Lyautey telegraphed Paris to report that there were two battalions of 2ᵉ Zouaves, a batallion of 2ᵉ *tirailleurs*, two squadrons of 2ᵉ spahis, an artillery battery, and 200 *goumiers* commanded by Colonel Félineau of the 2ᵉ Zouaves and seconded by Lieutenant-Colonel Reibell. *BCAF* 17 (April 1907): 137. Also see Jonnart to Pichon, Algiers, March 29, 1907, *AF* 3: 204–205, no. 234.

20. *BCAF* 17 (March 1907): 137.

21. Ukasha Burhab, "The Moroccan Government and the Frontier Problem in the Early Twentieth Century: Oujda Province, 1900–1912," [in Arabic], 2 vols. (Ph.D. diss., Université Mohammed V, 1996), 1: 102.

22. *Al-Moghreb al-Aksa*, March 30, 1907.

23. Al-Manuni, *Aspects*, 2: 479, no. 71. The occupation forces would soon grow. One historian puts the number of French soldiers in Oujda under Félineau's command at 2,500. J. Frémeaux, "Les trois occupations d'Oujda par l'armée française," *Revue Maroc Europe* 5 (1995): 44. Later, when Reibell became commander, 7,000 troops were stationed there. Burhab, 1: 103.

24. Al-Turris to Muhammad al-Tazi, Tangier, 12 Safar 1325/March 27, 1907, BG Kunnash 2720, p. 278; al-Turris to al-Tayyib al-Muqri, Tangier, 12 Safar 1325/March 27, 1907, ibid., p. 281; al-Turris to Muhammad al-Mufaddil Gharnit, Tangier, 12 Safar 1325/March 27, 1907, ibid., p. 281; al-Turris to Abd al-Rahman bin Abd al-Sadiq and al-Amin bin Buzid, Tangier, 12 Safar 1325/March 27, 1907, ibid., p. 283.

25. Al-Turris to Ibn Sulayman, 16 Safar 1325/March 31, 1907, BG Kunnash 2720, p. 284.

26. Ibn Sulayman to al-Turris, 18 Safar 1325/April 2, 1907, DAR Sijil 11704.

27. Al-Turris to Ibn Sulayman, 24 Safar 1325/April 8, 1907, BG Kunnash 2720, p. 289.

28. "Copy of Letter Sent by Army Officers in Oujda to the Minister of War," 13 Rabi I 1325/April 26, 1907, DAR.

29. Abd Rabihi Muhammad Barrada to al-Turris, Oujda, 18 Safar 1325/April 2, 1907, DAR.

30. Abdelaziz to Muhammad al-Turis, Fez, 1 Rabi II 1325/May 14, 1907, DAR.

31. Pichon to Regnault, Paris, March 29, 1907, *AF* 3: 203, no. 233.

32. Burhab, 1: 103.

33. Ibid., 1: 105–106.

34. Various versions of this letter survive. See Nehlil, CXIV; Abdelaziz, 20 Safar 1325/April 4, 1907, DAR Sijil 19190; 19 Safar 1325/April 3, 1907, DAR Sijil 18654; Abdelaziz to Buzgawi, Fez, 18 Safar 1325/April 2, 1907, DAR; Abdelaziz to Buzgawi, Fez, 19 Safar 1325/April 3, 1907, DAR; Abdelaziz to al-Jilani bin Hassan al-Harbili, Fez, 20 Safar 1325/April 4, 1907, BG Microfilm 1, Ref. 22/105, No. 144.

35. J. M. MacLeod to Edward Grey, Fez, April 9, 1907, PRO 371/285 [12674].

36. "Shereefian Letter respecting Occupation of Oujdah, read in Karuin Mosque, Fez, April 2, 1907," Inclosure in No. 137. Unnumbered photocopy from PRO FO in DAR.

37. *La Dépêche Marocaine*, April 10, 1907.

38. Also see Regnault to Pichon, Tangier, April 8, 1907, *AF* 3: 211, no. 242.

39. Anonymous to Moulay Hafid, Fez, 18 Safar 1325/April 2, 1907. DAR Sijil 11707.

40. Regnault to Pichon, Tangier, April 27, 1907, and Annexe, Gaillard to Regnault, Tangier, April 20, 1907, *AF* 3: 240–41, no. 267.

41. Lowther to Grey, Tangier, April 5, 1907, PRO FO 371/285 [11706].

42. Muhammad al-Buzgawi to al-Turris, 20 Safar 1325/April 4, 1907, DAR.

43. Muhammad al-Buzgawi to Abdelaziz, 8 Rabi I 1325/April 21, 1907/ DAR Sijil 11716.

44. Muhammad Rida al-Zakrawi to Abdelaziz, April 21, 1907/8 Rabi I 1325 DAR Sijil 11725.

45. Hashim bin Abu Bakr al-Sadani al-Fasi, quoted in al-Manuni, *Aspects*, 1: 489–90.

46. Al-Manuni, *Aspects*, 2: 500, no. 76.

47. MacLeod to Grey, Fez, April 2, 1907, PRO FO 371/285 [11764].

48. Al-Turris to Abdelaziz, Tangier, 16 Rabi 1325/May 29, 1907, BG Kunnash 2720, p. 319.

49. Lowther to Grey, Tangier, May 26, 1907, PRO FO 371/286 [17779].

50. Lowther to Grey, Tangier, April 5, 1907, PRO FO 371/285 [11706].

51. Lowther to Grey, Tangier, April 5, 1907, PRO FO 371/285 [11707].

52. Regnault to Pichon, Tangier, March 28, 1907, *AF* 3: 201, no. 229.

53. Compare, for example, Madeleine Saint-Rene Tallandier's admiring account (*Ce Monde Disparu*, 195–96) with Gustave Babin, *Au Maroc: Par les Camps et par les Villes* (Paris: Bernard Grasset, 1912), 354. In a later book, Babin accused Ben Ghabrit of procuring Parisian women—"birds of more or less great luxury . . . experienced and guaranteed"—for Thami al-Glawi. Gustave Babin, *"Son Excellence": Le Maroc sans masques* (Paris: Éditions G. Ficker, n.d.), 153.

54. The obituary notice in the *Bulletin mensuel des questions musulmanes*, June 5, 1954, in the Archives d'Outre Mer, 16 H 81, cited in Allen Christelow, "Algerian Dimensions of France's Middle East Policy 1916," in *Franco-Arab Encounters: Studies in Memory of David C. Gordon*, ed. L. Carl Brown and Matthew S. Gordon (Beirut: American University of Beirut, 1996), 288 and n. 41. Jalila Sbai gives November 1, 1868, as the date of Ben Ghabrit's birth. Jalila Sbai, "Trajectoire d'un homme et d'une idée: Si Kaddour Ben Ghabrit et l'Islam de France 1892–1926," *Hespéris-Tamuda* 39 (2001): 51. Christelow says Ben Ghabrit first entered government service in 1891. According to Sbai, Ben Ghabrit started his career in September 1892.

55. Algerian emigration as a form of religious and political protest is one of the themes Ageron takes up in his mammoth study, *Les Algériens musulmans et la France*, 2: 1079–83. The phenomenon was well-documented at the time. For many years the French legation in Tangier had extended "patents of nationality" and protection to Algerians residing in Morocco. E. Michaux-Bellaire, "Les musulmans d'Algérie au Maroc," *Archives Marocaines* 11 (1907): 38.

56. On his diplomatic service at this time, see Sbai, 52–53.

57. Saint-Aulaire, *Au Maroc avant et avec Lyautey*, 47.

58. The texts of these plays no longer seem extant.

59. Laskier, 72–73. The school and its curriculum are described in Cousin, 157.

60. Saint-Aulaire, *Au Maroc avant et avec Lyautey*, 90.

61. Madeleine Saint-René Taillandier, 195–96.

62. Christelow, 270–305.

63. http://www.mosquee-de-paris.net/cat_index_41.html (accessed Feb. 20, 2006) and Derri Berkani, Director, "Une résistance oubliée, La mosquée de Paris, 1940–1944."

64. Regnault to Ibn Sulayman, Tangier, March 28, 1907, Annexe to Regnault to Pichon, Tangier, March 28, 1907, *AF* 3: 199–200, no. 228.

65. Bertie to Gray, Paris, April 1, 1907, PRO FO 371/285 [10691]. The 1901–1902 Franco-Moroccan border accords called for a mixed commission to examine frontier interests between Algeria and Morcco. Without waiting for a Moroccan reply, the French government appointed Destailleur, who had previously negotiated the accords for France, as the commissioner for settlement of frontier questions.

66. Ibn Zaydan writes that al-Warzazi's son Muhammad was tried in Tangier and that he and his family were exonerated of any wrongdoing. Ibn Zaydan, 1: 418. I have not come across any record of a hearing.

67. Ibn Sulayman to Regnault, Fez, 18 Safar 1325/April 2, 1907, AF 3: 212–13, no. 243, and Annexe. Also printed in *Documents Diplomatiques Français*, 10:737–39, no. 456, Annexe.

68. Regnault to Pichon, Tangier, April 9, 1907, AF 3: 213–17, no. 244.

69. Pichon concurred with Regnault's approach. "Following your suggestion which I approve entirely, I authorize you not to accept any conversation with the Makhzan before it accepts in principle and without any restrictions all our demands." Pichon to Regnault, Paris, April 9, 1907, AF 3: 217, no. 245.

"The Sharifian delegates tried several attempts, under the pretext of offering explanations, to discuss the affair. It was easy for me not to fall for this manoeuvre and I gave them leave to depart well disconcerted." Regnault to Pichon, Tangier, April 10, 1907, AF 3: 218, no. 247.

70. Ibn Sulayman to Regnault, Fez, 24 Rabi I 1325/May 9, 1907, Annex to MacLeod to Grey, Fez, May 16, 1907, PRO FO 371/286 [17792]. Also see Gaillard to Regnault, Fez, April 20, 1907, Annex to Regnault to Pichon, Tangier, April 27, 1907, AF 3: 240–41, no. 267; and Ibn Sulayman to al-Turris, 21 Rabi II 1325/June 3, 1907, DAR Sijil 28974.

71. MacLeod to Grey, Fez, May 25, 1907, PRO FO 371/286 [19108].

72. Gaillaird to Regnault, Fez, April 20, 1907, Annexe to Regnault to Pichon, Tangier, April 27, 1907, AF 3: 240–42, no. 267.

73. Regnault to Pichon, Tangier, April 20, 1907, AF 3: 223–25, no. 255.

74. Regnault to Pichon, Tangier, April 22, 1907, AF 3: 227–28, no. 259; Pichon to Daeschner [chargé d'affaires in Madrid], Paris, April 23, 1907, AF 3: 237, no. 262; Pichon to Regnault, Paris, April 26, 1907, AF 3: 239–40, no. 266; Pichon to Daeschner, Paris, May 2, 1907, AF 3: 244, no. 272; Pichon to Ambassadors in London, Berlin, St. Petersburg, Vienna, Rome, and Washington, May 3, 1907, AF 3: 244–45, no. 273.

75. Regnault to Pichon, Tangier, April 26, 1907, AF 3: 238–39, no. 264.

76. Pichon to Regnault, Paris, April 30, 1907, AF 3: 242–43, no. 269.

77. Writing to his superior, Edmund Grey, in London, Lowther boasted that he had had a copy of Ibn Sulayman's reply to Regnault even before Regnault received it. Lowther to Grey, Tangier, April 20, 1907, PRO FO 371/285 [13493].

78. "Prospects of Settlement," *Times* (London), May 4, 1907.

79. *Times* (London), May 22, 1907.

80. *Al-Moghreb al-Aksa,* June 29, 1907.

81. Ibn Sulayman to al-Turris, Fez, 18 Safar 1325/April 2, 1907, DAR Sijil 11705.

82. Abdelaziz to al-Turris, Fez, 19 Safar 1325/April 3, 1907, DAR Sijil 18653.

83. According to Ibn Sulayman, transferring al-Warzazi to Tangier, as Regnault demanded, would condemn the former governor to death. Instead, he asked for the French government to send a doctor to Marrakesh to ascertain the true state of al-Warzazi's health. Regarding the establishment of the port police, Ibn Sulayman announced that al-Ghibbas had just received additional powers relative to the agreement made at Algeciras. As for resolving the border issue and sending a Makhzan agent to Oujda, the Makhzan had every intention of seeking French aid in its establishing posts to police the border. To Regnault's earlier assertion that the Makhzan was "fomenting trouble" in the Adrar region, Ibn Sulayman insisted that the Morocco wanted only to be a "good neighbor" with the French and that, in this regard, Moulay Idriss bin Abd al-Rahman had been recalled. As for the alleged arms shipments to Ma al-Aynayn, Ibn Sulayman again asserted that these shipments were only for the defense of the Moroccan garrison at Tarfaya. And lastly, Ibn Sulayman reported progress regarding bringing to justice those accused of the attacks on French nationals. The prisoners arrested in connection with the Mauchamp affair had been ordered to Tangier, people connected with the Lassallas affair were now imprisoned in Marrakesh, Gironcourt's assailants were similarly imprisoned in Fez, and one of two suspects involved in the Charbonnier murder was already under arrest in Tangier. Ibn Sulayman to Regnault, Fez, 24 Rabi I 1325/May 7, 1907, Annexe to Regnault to Pichon, Tangier, May 15, 1907, *AF* 3: 252–54, no. 287.

84. White to Grey, Tangier, August 4, 1907, PRO FO 413/43 [27524].

85. Apart from the claim for Mauchamp's murder, the family valued the pillaged contents of his house at 4,500 francs. Telegramme Déchiffrés, no. 242, Paris, June 11, 1907, MAE Tangier A 342.

86. Qaada 1325/December 9, 1907, and mid-Safar 1325/April 1907, BR Kunnash 568, pp. 53, 66.

87. F. Arin, "Le Talion et le prix du sang chez les Berbères Marocains" in *Les Archives Berbères* 1 (1915–16; reprint, Rabat: 1987), 62–83.

88. Regnault to Pichon, Tangier, May 30, 1907, *AF* 3: 257–58, no. 292; and "Four PM, Tuesday 15 Rabi II 1325," 15 Rabi II 1325/May 28, 1907, DAR.

89. Lascelles to Grey, Berlin, March 29, 1907, PRO FO 371/285 [10420].

90. Just seven years before the outbreak of World War I, to which the Franco-German rivalry over Morocco contributed so materially, the *Times*

gave a positive assessment of the future. Was the *Times'* correspondent startlingly naïve or—more likely—displaying a sly sense of irony?

"The brilliant international position which France now occupies has, no doubt, had its effect on the Moorish Sovereign and his counsellors. Never since the war of 1870 has France enjoyed the prestige and authority in the council of nations which she does to-day. Evidence of this is daily forthcoming. Large states and small vie with each other in seeking friendly relations with the Republic, with the result that the prospect that peace will be maintained for some time to come has materially improved. . . . No wonder then that the Sultan of Morocco should court the good will of the great Continental Republican Power that attracts so many friendships and that shows no signs of intending to abuse its strength."

"The Position of France," *Times* (London), May 30, 1907, 5.

91. Saint-Aulaire to Pichon, Tangier, June 14, 1907; *AF* 3: 269–71, no. 313; and Ibn Sulayman to Regnault, Fez, 21 Rabi II 1325/June 3, 1907. Annexe.

92. James C. Scott, *Domination and the Arts of Resistance: Hidden Transcripts* (New Haven, Conn.: Yale University Press, 1990).

93. Houel, 57.

94. What the sociologist Pierre Bourdieu writes in the case of individual honor among Kabyle Berbers applies equally in the case of nations as well. "To make someone a challenge is to credit him with the dignity of a man of honor, since the challenge, as such, requires a riposte and therefore is addressed to a man deemed capable of playing the game of honor and playing it well." Pierre Bourdieu, *Outline of a Theory of Practice,* trans. Richard Nice (Cambridge: Cambridge University Press, 1972), 10–15. See also idem, "The Sentiment of Honour in Kabyle Society," trans. Philip Sherrard, in *Honour and Shame: The Values of Mediterranean Society,* ed. J. G. Peristiany (Chicago: University of Chicago Press, 1966), 191–241.

Writing of the Bedouin in the Sinai desert, Stewart similarly emphasizes that honor between equals or "horizontal honor" depends upon mutual recognition. Frank Henderson Stewart, *Honor* (Chicago: University of Chicago Press, 1994). The theme of honor is further explored in Jonathan G. Katz, "The 1907 Mauchamp Affair and the French Civilizing Mission in Morocco," *JNAS* 6 (2001): 143–66 (reprinted in *North Africa, Islam and the Mediterranean World: From the Almoravids to the Algerian War,* ed. Julia Clancy-Smith [London: Frank Cass, 2001]). For a discussion of how the French military's sense of honor in part contributed to the bombardment of Casablanca, see André Adam, "Sur l'action du Galilée à Casablanca en Août 1907," *Revue de l'Occident Musulman et de la Méditerranée* 69 (1969): 9–21.

95. Laroui, "Conférence d'Algeciras."

96. Guillemin (1908): 119.

97. Edward Westermarck, *Ritual and Belief in Morocco,* 2 vols. (London: Macmillan, 1926; reprint New Hyde Park, N.Y.: University Books, 1968), 2:

518. For critiques of Westermarck's interpretation of the *'ar,* see Kenneth L. Brown, "The "Curse" of Westermarck," *Acta Philosophica Fennica* 34 (1982): 219–59; and David M. Hart, "Muslim Ritual Models in Two Pre-colonial Moroccan Berber Societies: Covenant, Conditional Curse, Shame Compulsion and Sacrifice," *JNAS* 6 (2001): 81–94.

98. *BCAF* 17 (April 1907): 370; Saint-Aulaire, *Au Maroc avant et avec Lyautey,* 78; and Burke, *Prelude to Protectorate,* 109.

99. Hans Speier, "Honour and Social Structure," *Social Order and the Risks of War* (New York: George W. Stewart 1952), 36–52.

9. The Crisis of the Month

1. Al-Warzazi to al-Turris, Marrakesh, 9 Safar 1325/April 3, 1907, DAR Sijil 30270. I was unable to locate the affidavits mentioned by al-Warzazi.

2. The names of the prisoners appear in Bargash to al-Turris, Essaouira, 6 Jumada I 1325/June 17, 1907, DAR, and Bargash to al-Turris, Essaouira, 12 Jumada I 1325/June 23, 1907, DAR Sijil 29273. The names also appear with some variations in the entry for 15 Jumada I 1325/June 26, 1907, BG Kunnash 2720, p. 332, and al-Turris to Ibn Sulayman, Tangier, 17 Jumada I 1325/June 28, 1907, BG Kunnash 2720, p. 335.

1. Ahmad bin Muhammad bin al-Hajj Abd Allah al-Wazgiti al-Marrakshi

2. Abd al-Rahman Abd al-Kabir al-Darawi al-Marrakshi (from Riyad al-Zaytun)

3. Al-Mahjub bin al-Mahjub al-Misfiwa al-Gadji al-Marrakshi (from Arsa Moulay Musa)

4. Al-Najim bin al-Hasan al-Misfiwi al-Gadji al-Marrakshi (from Riyad al-Zaytun)

5. Al-Thami bin Qadur al-Zamrani al-Bakruni al-Marrakshi (from Arsa Moulay Musa)

6. Al-Sayyid Muhammad bin al-Hasan al-Zemrani al-Marrakshi (from Bab Doukkala)

7. Al-Sayyid Ahmad bin Abd al-Rahman al-Rahami al-Marrakshi (from Arsa Moulay Musa)

8. Al-Hassan bin al-Hajj Muhammad bin Allal al-Misfiwi al-Kadji al-Marrakshi)

9. Al-Hassan bin Muhammad al-Susi al-Akuri al-Marrakshi

10. Deaf-mute, "no one knows his name"

3. "Note au sujet des individus arrêtés à Marrakesh connus coupables de Meurtre du Dr. Mauchamp," MAE Tangier A 342.

4. Lowther to Grey, Tangier, June 28, 1907, PRO FO 371/286 [22489].

5. In *Le Consul et l'Indigène, Bras de fer à Tanger,* a 1999 novel based loosely on the Charbonnier affair, the Moroccan writer Ahmed Beroho imagines the staging of an execution in Tangier. In the novel a corrupt

European consul frames an innocent young Moroccan for murder so as to acquire his farm.

6. Hoover, 144–74.

7. Al-Warzazi to Abdelaziz, Marrakesh, 21 Rabi I 1325/May 4, 1907, DAR.

8. Falcon to President [Leven], Marrakesh, May 5, 1907, AIU Maroc XXVI.E.398–416.

9. *Al-Moghreb al-Aksa*, May 11, 1907.

10. Tayyib al-Tazi and Muhammad Abd al-Qadir Banis to Abdelaziz, Marrakesh, 21 Rabi I 1325/May 4, 1907, DAR; Al-Jilani bin Muhammad al-Harbili to Abdelaziz, Marrakesh, 21 Rabi 1325/May 5, 1907, DAR Sijil 28897.

11. Moulay Hafid to Abdclaziz, Marrakesh, 23 Rabi I 1325/May 7, 1907, DAR.

12. Lennox to Madden, Marrakesh, May 6, 1907, PRO FO 371/286. Inclosure 1 in No. 118.

13. Lennox to Madden, Marrakesh, May 7, 1907, PRO FO 371/286, Inclosure 2 in No. 118.

14. Lowther to Grey, Tangier, May 7, 1907, PRO FO 371/286 [15650].

15. *L'Illustration*, May 11, 1907.

16. Accompanying Lennox and his family were the British missionaries Cuthbert Nairn and his sister Jessie, Misses Trainer and Hancock, Mr. Muir, and Miss Hood. A Spanish family, a Swiss lady missionary, a Syrian woman, and one German were also in the party. Lennox to unknown recipient, Safi, May 14, 1907, PRO FO 174/253.

Subsequently, British merchants sought indemnification for losses to their businesses caused by the inability of the Makhzan to provide security after Mauchamp's murder. Lowther to Grey, Tangier, May 29, 1907, PRO 371/286 [18962].

Similarly, in January 1908, a French businessman (identified by Paul Pascon only as Jean B.) entered into a correspondence with Saint-Aulaire in Tangier and the consul in Essaouira, seeking support in his efforts to recover money he had lent his Moroccan partners as well as losses he suffered in the wake of the Mauchamp affair. These losses totaled 57,554 hassani pesetas. At a 1905 exchange rate of one hassani peseta to 1.5 francs, this was not a small claim. The diplomats offered the businessman little encouragement, citing the anarchy that prevailed in the south of the country and the consulate's lack of communication with the pasha of Marrakesh. Pascon, *Le Haouz du Marrakech*, 2: 419–23, and idem, *Capitalism and Agriculture*, 62–63.

17. Lennox to Madden, Marrakesh, May 6, 1907, Inclosure 1 in Lowther to Grey, Tangier, May 12, 1907, PRO 371/286 [16180].

18. Falcon to President [Leven], Safi, May 14, 1907, AIU Maroc XXVI.E.398–416.

19. Falcon to President [Leven], Safi, July 10, 1907, AIU Maroc XXVI.E.398–416.

20. Lennox to Madden, Marrakesh, May 7, 1907, Inclosure 2 in No. 1, Lowther to Grey, Tangier, May 12, 1907, PRO 371/286 [16180].

21. Lowther to Grey, Tangier, May 12, 1907, PRO FO 371/286 [16180].

22. According to Mohammed Kenbib, Holzmann was replaced as Moulay Hafid's physician by a French Jew named Dr. Magny. In return, Moulay Hafid promised Holzmann that he would be the director of the munitions factory, or "Makina," in Fez, but this promise went unfulfilled. Kenbib, *Juifs et Musulmans au Maroc,* 360. It is unclear whether this development resulted from a falling out between Holzmann and Moulay Hafid or whether Moulay Hafid was pursuing a more politically expedient course vis-à-vis the French.

23. Houel, 64.

24. Lyautey to Couget [consul general in Tangier], January 3, 1915; Lyautey to Couget, July 12, 1915; Couget to Lyautey, July 15, 1915, MAE Tangier A 342.

In the Protectorate Archives housed in the Bibliothèque générale in Rabat, "Docteur Holtzmann ou Outhman" appears on a list of dossiers, but the file could not be located and may no longer exist. "Surveillance des suspects: autorisation de séjours pour les autriciens et les allemands: 1910–1918, 1924–1926," BG, Archives Protectorate B50.

25. Hunot to Madden, Safi, May 20, 1907, Inclosure in Lowther to Grey, Tangier, May 24, 1907 PRO FO 371/286 [17775]. See also Louis Arnaud, *"Au Temps de Mehallas," ou le Maroc de 1860 à 1912* (Casablanca: Éditions Atlantides, 1952), 235.

26. Qadur bin al-Ghazi [Kaddour bel Ghazi] to Abdelaziz, Safi, 29 Rabi I 1325/May 12, 1907, DAR. He sent nearly identical versions of the letter to Muhammad al-Muffadal Gharnit, the minister of war, and Muhammad al-Turris. On rumors, see also Bargash to al-Turris, 18 Rabi I 1325, May 1, 1907, DAR.

27. *Al-Moghreb al-Aksa,* May 18, 1907.

28. *Al-Moghreb al-Aksa,* June 15, 1907, and June 22, 1907.

29. *Al-Moghreb al-Aksa,* September 21, 1907. A month later, in October, Bel Ghazi was sent to Essaouira to command a reinforced garrison of 1,500 troops. *Al-Moghreb al-Aksa,* November 2, 1907.

30. Lowther continues, "In reply to inquiries as to the effect produced on the population by the occupation of Ujda [*sic*], Mr. Lennox said that he had anticipated that it would produce none, but that he had been impressed by the fact that, so far from the action of the French having inspired respect, it had only produced an irritating effect." Lowther to Grey, Tangier, May 29, 1907, PRO FO 371/286 [18691].

31. Miège, *Le Maroc et L'Europe,* 4: 67 n. 5.

32. Bou Bakr Ghanjowy [*sic*] to Lowther, Marrakesh, 23 Rabi II 1325/ June 5, 1907, Inclosure in Lowther to Grey, Tangier, June 15, 1907, PRO FO 371/286 [20791].

33. Abdelaziz was kept abreast of Rahamna developments by his own intelligence sources. One Ibn al-Mahjub reported that the "riffraff" of the Saraghna tribe camped outside the Bab al-Ahmar and then scattered on Tuesday, June, 11, after being mollified by the distribution of five hundred riyals. Qabur bin al-Mahjub al-Rahamni al-Bubakr to Abdelaziz, Marrakesh, 7 Jumada I 1325/June 18, 1907, DAR.

34. Lowther to Grey, Tangier, June 23, 1907, PRO FO 371/286 [21631].

35. Writing to his brother on June 25, Moulay Hafid reported that the news from the Rahamna gathered at Dar al-Zafiri was contradictory. First they were intent on plunder and taking revenge on Thami al-Glawi for transferring the prisoners. When the tribesmen learned that troops were posted in the city, calm was restored. Moulay Hafid to Abdelaziz, Marrakesh, 14 Jumada I 1325/June 25, 1907, DAR.

36. Abdelaziz to Moulay Hafid, Fez, 12 Jumada I 1325/June 23, 1907, DAR Sijil 29272. In a letter dated the same day Moulay Hafid wrote to Abdelaziz about the restoration of order. Moulay Hafid to Abdelaziz, Marrakesh, 12 Jumada I 1325/June 23, 1907, DAR.

37. Abdelaziz to al-Warzazi, Fez 12 Jumada I 1325/June 23, 1907, DAR.

38. See Moulay Hafid to Abdelaziz, Marrakesh, 12 Jumada I 1325/June 23, 1907, DAR; Abdelaziz to al-Warzazi, Fez, 20 Jumada I 1325/July 1, 1907, DAR; Abdelaziz to Moulay Hafid, Fez, 20 Jumada I 1325/July 1, 1907, DAR. British commercial interests were especially vociferous in their complaints about security in Marrakesh

39. Abdelaziz to Moulay Hafid, Fez, 20 Jumada I 1325/July 1, 1907, DAR.

40. Ibn Sulayman to al-Turris, 9 Jumada I 1325/June 20, 1907, DAR Sijil 29280.

41. Kouri to Regnault, Essaouira, July 17, 1907, MAE Tangier A 262.

42. Falcon to President [Leven], October 10, 1907, AIU Maroc Microfilm VII B.

43. Hamza Ben Driss Othmani, *Essaouira, Une cité sous les alizeés, des origines à 1939* (Rabat: Éditions La Porte, 1997), 227.

44. Bargash to al-Turris, Essaouira, 6 Jumada I 1325/June 17, 1907, DAR; and Bargash to al-Turris, Essaouira, 12 Jumada I 1325/June 23, 1907, DAR Sijil 29273.

45. *Al-Moghreb al-Aksa*, June 29, 1907.

46. Moulay Hafid to Kouri, Marrakesh 15 Jumada I 1325, June 26, 1907, MAE Tangier A 269.

47. Abd al-Rahman Bargash to al-Turris, Essaouira, 6 Jumada I 1325/ June 17, 1907, DAR; Moulay Hafid to Abdelaziz, Marrakesh, 11 Jumada I 1325/June 22, 1907, DAR Sijil 29269.

48. Moulay Hafid to Rahamna *qaids*, 11 Jumada I 1325/June 22, 1907,

DAR Sijil 29265; Moulay Hafid to Abdelaziz, Essaouira, 11 Jumada I 1325/ June 22, 1907, DAR Sijil 29269.

49. Ibn Sulayman to Regnault, Fez, 27 Jumada I 1325/July 8, 1907, MAE Tangier A 342.

50. Abdelaziz to al-Turris, Fez, 8 Rajab 1325/August 17, 1907, DAR Sijil 29458; Abdelaziz to Bargash, Fez, 8 Rajab 1907/August 17, 1907, facsimile in Nehlil, CXXI; and text quoted in Ibn Zaydan, 1: 419.

51. Gaillard to Regnault, Fez, April 21, 1910, Annexe to Regnault to Pichon, Tangier, April 27, 1910, AF 5: 374–75, no. 454.

52. Al-Turris to Ibn Sulayman, Tangier, 17 Rajab 1325/July 26, 1907, BG Kunnash 2720, p. 360.

53. *Al-Moghreb al-Aksa,* July 20, 1907.

54. Later it emerged that Perdicaris—born in Greece to an American mother and a Greek father (he was reared in Trenton, New Jersey)—had actually renounced his American citizenship in 1862 in an effort to protect his mother's South Carolina property from confiscation by the Confederacy. Jon Blackwell, "1904: 'Perdicaris alive or Raisuli dead!'" *Trentonian,* reprinted in http://www.capitalcentury.com/1904.html (accessed Feb. 20, 2006). The kidnapping of Perdicaris became the subject of the 1975 adventure epic *The Wind and the Lion.* Al-Raisuli as depicted by Sean Connery has a Scottish accent, while Perdicaris—turned into a woman by Hollywood—is played by Candace Bergman.

55. Maclean to Lowther, September 11, 1907, Inclosure in Lowther to Grey, September 14, 1907, Unidentified photocopy in DAR, probably PRO FO 174/253 [31452].

56. Some accounts offer eight victims, with the apportionment of nationality varying.

57. Madden to Lowther, Casablanca, July 30, 1907, FO 174/253.

58. Houel provides an eyewitness account of events at the French consulate in *Mes Aventures Marocaines,* 9–44. For other versions of the bombardment of Casablanca see Georges Bourdon, *Les journées de Casablanca* (Paris: P. Lafitte, 1908); and Saint-Aulaire, *Au Maroc avant et avec Lyautey.* André Adam is best at sorting out the inconsistencies among the various eyewitness accounts. Adam, *Histoire de Casablanca,* 103–35, and idem, "Sur l'action de Galilée." Other recent works that treat the event include Douglas Porch, *The Conquest of Morocco* (New York: Random House, 1983), 149–58, and Allal al-Khdimi, *Foreign Intervention and Resistance in Morocco (1894–1910)* [in Arabic] (Casablanca: Ifriqiya al-Sharq: 1994).

59. Ollivier to Naval Minister, *Le Galilée* (Casablanca), August 2, 1907, copy in DAR deposited by Allal al-Khdimi.

60. Murdoch, Butler, and Co. to Lloyd's, Casablanca, August 10, 1907, PRO FO, unidentified photocopy in DAR.

61. Moulay al-Amin to al-Turris and al-Ghibbas, 27 Jumada II 1325/August 7, 1907, DAR Sijil 28626.

62. *Encyclopaedia Britannica*, 11th ed., s.v. "Morocco."

63. *Al Moghreb al-Aksa*, August 10, 1907.

64. "Israélites du Maroc," *BAIU* 35 (July–August 1907): 67–76.

65. *L'Illustration*, August 24, 1907.

66. Adam, "Sur l'action du *Galilée*."

67. Hoover, 153.

68. "Account of the Ceremony on the Occasion of the Proclamation of Mulai Hafid as Sultan," Inclosure in Lowther to Grey, Tangier, August 28, 1907, PRO FO, unidentified photocopy in DAR.

69. Munson, 67–68.

70. Ibid., 69–71.

71. Its other terms called for Moulay Hafid to do his utmost to restore Morocco's territorial integrity; bring about the evacuation of French troops from Casablanca and Oujda; abolish the *maks* (an unpopular tax); restore and revivify the practice of Islam; abolish foreign privileges and capitulations; and seek a closer cooperation with other Muslim powers, especially the Ottoman state. Burke, *Prelude to Protectorate*, 115–16.

72. Ibid., 121.

73. Moulay Hafid to British minister in Tangier, Marrakesh, 27 Rajab 1325/September 5, 1907, DAR, and Lowther to Grey, September 25, 1907, PRO FO [33295], photocopy in DAR.

74. Holzmann was instrumental in securing financing for Moulay Hafid from the German industrial group Mannesmann in exchange for mining and territorial concessions in the south. Guillen, 488. Equally desperate for cash, the sultan Abdelaziz pawned the royal jewels in Paris in October 1907.

75. Harris, *Morocco That Was*, 120.

76. Burke, *Prelude to Protectorate*, 119–21.

77. Ibid., 125.

78. Moulay Hafid to White, January 29, 1908, PRO FO 413/48, Inclosure 2 in no. 91, quoted in Burke, *Prelude to Protectorate*, 125.

79. Moulay Hafid to King Edward VIII, Inclosure in Moulay Hafid to Grey, communicated by Ashmead-Bartlett, August 24, 1908, PRO FO 413/50 [29451].

80. Burke, *Prelude to Protectorate*, 129.

81. Jaurès, Chamber des Députés, January 24, 1908, in *Oeuvres de Jean Jaurès*, vol. 3: *Le Guêpier marocain (1906–1908)* (Paris: Les Éditions Rieder, 1933), 232–33.

82. Burke, *Prelude to the Protectorate*, 128–38.

83. MacLeod to Grey, Fez, August 16, 1909, PRO FO 413/52 [32664]. Also see Frank Rattigan to Grey, Tangier, August 18, 1909, PRO FO 413/52 [32653].

84. Lister to Grey, Tangier, June 8, 1910, PRO FO 413/53 [21756].

85. *Al-Moghreb al-Aksa*, July 4, 1910; Burke, *Prelude to Protectorate*, 146–47.

10. Remains of the Day

1. Falcon to President [Leven], Safi?, October 10, 1907, AIU Maroc Microfilm VII B.

2. Nairn to Madden, Essaouira, January 20, 1908, PRO FO 174/255.

3. *Southern Morocco Mission* (March 1909): 1, 4; (May 1909): 3; (November 1909): 2; (January 1910); (March 1910): 6. Nairn remained in Marrakesh for the rest of his life. He was murdered there in 1944. Miège, *Le Maroc et L'Europe,* 4: 318 n. 5.

4. Regnault, draft, August 25, 1909, MAE Tangier A 342.

Other candidates under consideration included Drs. Fauvel, Laborde, Tibaudeau, and Louet. Rouselle, *Médecins,* 283.

5. Ibid., 283 n. 458.

6. Leven, 2: 100.

7. Lassallas to Kouri, Marrakesh, April 12, 1909; Kouri to Lassallas, Essaouira, May 18, 1909; Lassallas to Kouri, Marrakesh, May 31, 1909, MAE Tangier A 342.

8. Pierre Mauchamp to Kouri, Chalon-sur-Saône, June 8, 1909, MAE Tangier A 342.

9. Pierre Mauchamp to Regnault, Chalon-sur-Saône, June 8, 1909, MAE Tangier 342.

10. Kouri to Pierre Mauchamp, Essaouira, June 21, 1909, MAE Tangier A 342.

11. Kouri to Regnault, Essaouira, April 21, 1910, MAE Tangier A 269.

12. Gaillard to Renault, Fez, April 21, 1910. Annexe to Regnault to Pichon, Tangier, April 27, 1910, *AF,* 5: 374, no. 454.

The request for a hospital in Safi is found in DAR Kunnash 1327–29, p. 5. The capture of Marrakesh in 1912 by the pretender al-Hiba postponed the start of construction till the following year.

13. Burke, *Prelude to Protectorate,* 133.

14. Lassallas to Kouri, Marrakesh, two letters dated May 22, 1910, MAE Tangier A 269.

15. Muhammad Sghir. Deposition signed before Kouri and Nairn, May 24, 1910, MAE Tangier A 269.

Muhammad Sghir himself was not entirely free of suspicion. Another local, Brahim Baga, who had formerly conducted business on Moulay Hafid's behalf, testified that Hajj Abdeslam al-Warzazi and Muhammad Sghir were the ones responsible for Mauchamp's death. While having little to add about Mauchamp's murder, Baga claimed that Moulay Hafid was involved in the murder of the European quarry workers in Casablanca. Brahim Baga. Deposition before Kouri and Lassallas, May 31, 1910, MAE Tangier A 269.

One of Mauchamp's servants, an eyewitness to the attack, also implicated Muhammad Sghir. He noted that Muhammad Sghir momentarily stepped outside into the street after he had first come to the dispensary to get the French doctor. "You think then," Kouri asked, "that Muhammad Sghir, in returning to take the doctor, had for a goal to deliver him to the crowd to kill?" The servant replied that there could not be any doubt. Ali bin Brahim de Mzouda. Deposition before Kouri and Muhammad bin al-Majjad, correspondent of the consulate of France, June 8, 1910, MAE Tangier A 269.

16. Brahim bin Muhammad Touggani. Deposition to Kouri witnessed by Nairn, May 26, 1910, MAE Tangier A 269.

17. Falcon to Kouri, Marrakesh, MAE Tangier A 269, June 18, 1910, MAE Tangier A 269. In a letter Falcon sent to Paris seven months after Mauchamp's murder, the schoolmaster called Holzmann and Moulay Hafid the real perpetrators of Mauchamp's murder, labeling Hajj Abdeslam al-Warzazi as an unwitting accomplice. Falcon to President [Leven], Safi?, October 10, 1907, AIU Maroc Mircofilm VII B.

18. Later, in El-Jadida, Falcon said he asked Berrino why he did not return to Marrakesh. Berrino allegedly replied that he didn't dare because al-Warzazi had accused him of entering a mosque. This excuse seemed insufficient to Falcon, who ventured the guess that Berrino was afraid Moulay Hafid might make him "disappear" to prevent him from talking.

19. Jacquety to Kouri, Marrakesh, June 16, 1910, MAE Tangier A 269.

André Puel, a teacher at the Alliance school, offered additional confirmation regarding Lennox's alleged views. On a social visit that Puel made to Lennox and his wife, he heard Lennox declare "spontaneously" that it was his opinion that Moulay Hafid was one of the instigators of Mauchamp's murder. Puel to Kouri, Marrakesh, June 20, 1910, MAE Tangier A 269.

20. Lennox to White, Marrakesh, June 19, 1910, PRO FO 174/281.

21. White to Lennox, June 27, 1910, PRO FO 174/281.

22. Lennox to Kouri, Marrakesh, July 13, 1910, and July 15, 1910, MAE Tanger A 269.

23. "Diary of Mr. Lister's Journey in Southern Morocco," October 29, 1910, entry, Inclosure in Lister to White, December 4, 1910, PRO FO 413/53 [44688].

24. Kouri to Regnault, Marrakesh, July 7, 1910; and telegram, Essaouira, July 10, 1910, MAE Tangier A 269.

25. Unknown [illegible signature] to Regnault, Essaouira, October 1, 1910, MAE Tangier A 269.

26. "Diary of Mr. Lister's Journey in Southern Morocco," October 29, 1910, entry.

27. Walter Harris gives an account of Moulay Hafid's trip to Europe in *Morocco That Was*.

28. Burke, *Prelude to Protectorate*, 197–98.

29. Pascon, *Le Haouz du Marrakech*, 1: 318–20.

30. Munson, 99–101.

31. Burke, *Prelude to Protectorate*, 206–207, and Weisgerber, 348–58.

32. Munson, 100.

33. Weisgerber, 356–57.

Pascon goes to great lengths to distinguish "qaidalism" from feudalism, with which it has often been compared. Pascon, *Le Haouz du Marrakech*, 1: 293–99.

34. Lyautey, Ordre général no. 12 bis. *BO* (November 8, 1912): 5.

35. Simon to Directeur, Service du Renseignement, February 8, 1914, SGP no. 239 inclosed in Simon to Secrétaire Générale du Protectorat, no. 139, February 10, 1914, Archives du Protectorate, BG A 491 Marrakesh 1914 (Comptabilité municipale. Budgets. Marrakech).

Gustave Babin's *"Son Excellence"* is an impassioned diatribe against Thami al-Glawi. He maintains that Driss bin Minu was really responsible for saving the Europeans and that Thami al-Glawi had cleverly appropriated the credit.

36. For a popular account of the Glawi family, see Maxwell, *Lords of the Atlas*. On the family's origins and rise to power, also see Pascon, *Le Haouz de Marrakech*, 1: 299–342.

37. Berriau to Lyautey, Marrakesh, December 24, 1912, DAR Sijil 29196; December 29, 1912, DAR Sijil 29797; January 2, 1913, DAR Sijil 29198.

38. Berriau to Lyautey, Marrakesh, December 29, 1912, DAR Sijil 29797.

39. *Rapport mensuel d'Ensemble de Protectorat et Situation Politique de Maroc Occidental* (Archives du Protectorat, BG Rabat) (March 1913): 10.

40. Claude Michel, *Marrakech d'un siècle à l'autre* (Paris: Maisonneuve and Larose, Malika Éditions, 2003).

41. *Rapport mensuel* (October 1913): 6.

42. Ibid. (February 13, 1913): 12; and *BO* (January 31, 1913): 71.

43. S. Biarnay [Directeur des Télégraphes Chérifiens] to al-Muqri, [in French] December 21, 1911, DAR Sijil 30081, and [in Arabic] 23 Muharram 1330/January 13, 1912, DAR Sijil 20449.

44. Dahir chérifien, 1 Safar 1331/January 10, 1913, in *BO* (February 7, 1913).

45. A. Chevrillon, *Marrakech dans les palmes*, 13th ed. (Paris: Calman-Lévy, 1921), 44.

46. *BO* (November 1914): 24, and Mohamed Ghoti, *Histoire de la Médecine au Maroc, le XXᵉ Siècle (1896–1994)* (Morocco: 1995). An early description of the hospital and an admiring account of doctors Legey, Guichard, and a more recent arrival, Dr. Madelaine, can be found in Noel Fiessinger, *La Médecine Française au Maroc* (Paris: A. Maloine and Fils, 1923).

47. Le Chef de Bataillon Nancy to Résidence Général, July 1, 1915; Saint-Aulaire to Gaillard, August 10, 1915. Archives du Protectorat, BG A 492 C6 Marrakech.

48. *BO* (April 1917): A23–24.

49. *BO* (June 1915): 27.

50. *BO* (November 1916): A18–19, and Fiessinger, 36.

51. *La Médicine au Maroc* (Casablanca: 1939), 176.

52. Ibid., 178–79.

53. Rivet, *Le Maroc de Lyautey,* 300 and 448 n. 52.

54. Legey quoted in R. Arlette Butavaud, "Les femmes médecins missionaires" (*thèse médicale,* Lyon, 1930), quoted in Jean Péraud, *La femme médecin en Afrique du Nord, Son rôle d'éducatrice* (Bordeaux: Imprimerie de l'université, 1932), 42–43.

55. The doctor Robert Debré reports that when he visited Marrakesh in the winter of 1911 in the company of the French deputy Abel Ferry, Françoise Legey was the sole French woman in Marrakesh. Robert Debré, *L'Honneur de vivre* (Paris: Herman et Stock, 1974), 149. She was named "Adjunct to the chief of medicine at the Mauchamp Hospital in Marrakesh in charge of women's services" in 1913. *BO* (May 23, 1913): 146.

56. Péraud, 44–45.

Doctor Legey had many admirers, but Gustave Babin, the author of an anti-Glawi polemic, was not one of them. Her close relationship with her patron Thami al-Glawi led Babin to make the most scurrilous accusations. "I've sometimes dreamt of a passionate conversation where, relieved of professional secrecy, Madame Doctor Legey, the household physician to al-Glawi—and the only stranger without a doubt in the world who knows all the frightening mysteries—would unveil all that she has seen, the hideous pleas which she heard, and the sad cadavers whose eyes she charitably shut." Babin, *"Son Excellence,"* 31–32.

57. See Marie-Claire Micouleau-Sicault, *Les médecins français au Maroc (1912–1956)* (Paris: L'Harmattan, 2000). The author is the daughter of Georges Sicault, who headed the public health service in Morocco from 1946–1956.

58. Muhammad al-Amin al-Bazzaz, *The History of Epidemics and Famines in Morocco in the 18th and 19th Centuries* [in Arabic] (Rabat: Université Mohammed V, 1992).

59. Rivet, *Le Maroc de Lyautey à Mohammed V,* 292.

60. Ibid., 291.

61. On French policies of urban development in Morocco see Janet Abu-Lughod, *Rabat: Urban Apartheid in Morocco* (Princeton, N.J.: Princeton University Press, 1980); Paul Rabinow, *French Modern: Norms and Forms of the Social Environment* (Cambridge, Mass.: MIT Press, 1989); and Gwendolyn Wright, "Tradition in the Service of Modernity: Architecture and Urbanism in French Colonial Policy, 1900–1930," in *Tensions of Empire,* 322–45. Rabinow stresses the idea of Morocco's role as a "laboratory" for modern design and social policy.

62. Rivet, *Le Maroc de Lyautey,* 297.

63. Ibid., 298.

64. Abu-Lughod, *Rabat,* 194–95 and 195 n. 19. Data are drawn from the *BO,* supplement to No. 1027, July 1, 1932, 14, as cited in Melvin Knight, *Morocco as a French Economic Venture* (New York: D. Appleton-Century, 1937), 105. The editorial comment is Knight's, quoted in Abu-Lughod, 195.

65. *Morocco under the Protectorate: Forty Years of French Administration: An Analysis of Facts and Figures* (New York: Istiqlal [Independence] Party of Morocco, 1953), 8. Further statistics on education and healthcare are found in ibid., 52–58.

Conclusion

1. Guillemin (1909): 100–101.

2. A brief notice of the book appeared in the *Times Literary Supplement* (London), April 14, 1910. "This book is certainly of great interest to anthropologists, but it is by no means one for general reading. It gives a terrible picture of Moorish cruelty and superstition."

Mauchamp's book later makes an appearance as a prop in Julien Duvivier's 1932 *Cinq Gentlemen Maudit* (Five Damned Tourists), one of the first full-length features shot in Morocco and a film that pokes fun at the supposed superstitious nature of Moroccans. David Henry Slavin, *Colonial Cinema and Imperial France, 1919–1939* (Baltimore, Md.: Johns Hopkins University Press, 2001), 113.

3. The proposal, however, was not without controversy. Some members of the council opposed the dominant *Bloc républicain* and, by implication, Mauchamp's anticlericalism. Robert Tatheraux, "Émile Mauchamp: la vie généreuse et la fin tragique d'un médecin chalonnais," *Images de Saône et Loire* 56 (1983): 17–19.

4. *Association des Anciens élèves du collège de Chalon-sur-Saône, Bulletin annuel,* 2ᵉsérie, illustrée (1910, numéro 4): 71–84; "Rapport de M. Duverne, Inauguration du monument de M. le docteur Mauchamp." *Bulletin municipal, Chalon-sur-Saône* (July 8, 1910): 235–37.

5. *Le Progrès de Saône-et-Loire,* August 23, 1910.

6. *Le Progrès de Saône-et-Loire,* August 24, 1910.

7. *Le Progrès de Saône-et-Loire,* August 23, 1910.

8. Eugène LeClerc, "Note historique sur trois monument situés près de l'Office du Tourisme, Chalon-sur-Saône," June 20, 1980, typed ms. Deposited in Bibliothèque municipal, Chalon-sur-Saône.

9. Antoine Prost, "Monuments to the Dead," in *Realms of Memory,* vol. 2: *Traditions,* under the direction of Pierre Nora, English language ed., ed. Lawrence D. Kritzman, trans. Arthur Goldhammer (New York: Columbia University Press, 1997), 307–30, 532 n. 4.

10. René Cruchet, *La Conquête pacifique du Maroc et du Tafilalet,* 2nd ed. (Paris: Éditions Berger-Levrault, 1934), 120.

11. Ibid., 121–23.

12. See for example the long front-page article by J. du Pac, "Vingt-cinq ans de Protectorat Français," in the *L'Atlas* (Marrakesh), February 21, 1937.

13. Paul Chatinières, *Dans le Grand Atlas Marocain: Extraits du carnet du route d'un Médecin d'assistance médicale indigène, 1912–1916*, introduction du Général Lyautey (Paris: Librairie Plon, 1919).

14. Mohammad Bakkali-Yedri, "L'Esthétique baroque dans *Marrakech ou Les Seigneurs de l'Atlas*. Portraits et Caricatures," in *Maroc: Littérature et peinture coloniales (1912–1956)* (Rabat: Université Mohammed V, 1996), 83–98.

15. Edith Wharton, *In Morocco* (New York: Scribners, 1920), and Fouzia Rhissassi, "Le Voyage d'Edith Wharton au Maroc," in *Maroc: Littérature et peinture coloniales*, 173–82.

16. *Al-Atlas* (Marrakesh), March 21, 1937.

17. Houel, 237–38.

18. "With Lyautey, a new page in Moroccan history began." Henri Croze, *Souvenirs du vieux Maroc* (Paris: Éditions du Deux Monde, 1952), 47.

19. Moïse Nahon, *Propos d'un vieux Marocain* (Paris: Larose, 1930).

20. López Gádor, 9. López Gádor's memoirs are part of a series entitled "Documents" published in the past decade by Maxime Rousselle, a former doctor in Morocco, who has devoted much energy to documenting the French experience in Morocco.

21. Yvonne Knibiehler, Geneviève Emmery, and Françoise Leguay, eds., *Des Français au Maroc: La présence et la mémoire* (Paris: Denoël, 1992).

22. Lucette Valensi, "From Sacred History to Historical Memory and Back: The Jewish Past," in *Between History and Memory*, ed. Marie-Noëlle Bourguet, Lucette Valensi, and Nathan Wachtel (Chur, Switz.,: Harwood, 1990), 77–100.

23. R. P. Michel Lafon, "Le Témoignage des médecins français au Maroc," in *Maroc: Littérature et peinture coloniales*, 143–53.

24. Nicolas Dobo, *J'étais le médecin de cent mille Berbères: Un Médecin francais dans le bled marocain de 1955–1958* (Paris: Éditions du Scorpion, 1964); Maxime Rousselle, *Médecin du bled* (Talence: M. Rousselle, 1990); Henri Dupuch, *J'étais médecin au Maroc, 1942–1958* (Paris: France-Empire, 1985).

25. See the admiring account of Dr. Bouveret and his hospital in Essaouira in Eleanor Elsner, *The Magic of Morocco* (New York: Dodd, Mead, 1928), 75–77.

26. Micouleau-Sicault, *Les médecins français au Maroc*, 28.

27. *Lyautey et l'institution du Protectorate français*, 2: 230. Quoted in Michel Lafon, "Le Témoignage des médecins français au Maroc," in *Maroc: Littérature et peinture coloniales*, 152.

28. Micouleau-Sicault, 23; Tahar ben Jelloun, "Preface," in *Des Français au Maroc*, 12–13.

29. Pennell, 268–96; Julien, 245–454; Stéphane Bernard, *The Franco-*

Moroccan Conflict, 1943–1956 (New Haven, Conn.: Yale University Press, 1968); Pierre July, *Une République pour un roi* (Paris: Fayard, 1974).

30. Julien, 434.

31. July, 169–70.

32. "World Briefing: Europe-Africa Tunnel," *New York Times*, December 16, 2003.

33. *Le Matin*, February 16, 2000.

34. As Khalid Belyazid wrote in the Casablanca periodical *L'Economiste* (May 20, 2000), "They launched bombs because we opened the doors. . . . These suicide bombers, who were true Moroccans, had been infantilized— by years of Arabization of the education system, by the vain presentation of our history, and by the negation of the role of Jews, Europe, and the positive values of liberty and tolerance." Cited in http://www.worldpress. org/Mideast/1113.cfm (accessed Feb. 20, 2006).

35. Recently, anthropologists have written about a "post-colonial memory crisis" in Africa. As new generations become further removed from the era of direct colonial occupation, they tend to forget the actual and symbolic violence of the experience. The past, or at least specific aspects of it, disappears down a "memory hole." See such works as Jennifer Cole, *Forget Colonialism? Sacrifice and the Art of Memory in Madagascar* (Berkeley: University of California Press, 2001); Richard Werbner, ed., *Memory and the Postcolony: African Anthropology and the Critique of Power* (London: Zed Books, 1998).

36. I thank Dr. Mohammed Benchaou of the Ministry of Public Health for his efforts on my behalf.

37. The Institut Français occasionally makes an effort to remind Moroccans of France's historic contribution. Before settling in Morocco in 1901, Veyre, who trained as a pharmacist, traveled the world making and displaying movies for the Lumière brothers. In the winter of 2000 Veyre's greatgrandson, the French filmmaker Philippe Jacquier, lectured in Marrakesh at an exhibit of his ancestor's Moroccan photography legacy. Kijû Yoshida, "L'Homme qui a vu la naissance et la mort du cinéma," French translation by Rose-Marie Makino-Fayolle, in *Gabriel Veyre, Opérateur Lumière: Autour du monde avec le Cinématographe, Correspondance (1896–1900)*, ed. Philippe Jacquier and Marion Pranal (Lyon: Institute Lumière/Actes Sud, 1996).

38. Jean-Claude Karmazyn, *Le Maroc en cartes postales 1900–1920* (Cahors: Publi-fusion, 1994), 24.

39. Lawrence Rosen, "Memory in Morocco," in *The Culture of Islam: Changing Aspects of Contemporary Muslim Life* (Chicago: University of Chicago Press, 2002), 92.

40. Annarose Pandey, "Nostalgic Lives: Memories of Maria in Sidi Ifni, Morocco," *JNAS* 8 (2003): 92–113, offers a case study of Moroccans in one town who tie their recollections of the colonial past to the memory of the town's last Spanish resident.

41. Rosen, 92.

42. Edmund Burke III, "Mohand N'Hamoucha: Middle Atlas Berber," in *Struggle and Survival in the Modern Middle East,* ed. Edmund Burke III (Berkeley: University of California Press, 1993), 112–13.

43. Scott, *Domination and the Arts of Resistance.*

44. One thinks of the printshop apprentices killing their employer's pet cat in Robert Darnton, *The Great Cat Massacre and Other Episodes in French Cultural History* (New York: Basic Books, 1984).

45. Personal communication, October 25, 2001.

Bibliography

Archives

Archives de l'Alliance Israélite Universelle, Paris, France
Archives du Ministère des Affaires Étrangères, Nantes, France
Bibliothèque Générale, Rabat, Morocco
Bibliothèque Royale (Hassaniya), Rabat, Morocco
Direction des Archives Royales, Rabat, Morocco
Public Records Office, Foreign Office Correspondence, Kew, United Kingdom

Newspapers and Periodicals

Al-Atlas (Marrakesh)
The British Medical Journal
Bulletin Annuel, Association des Anciens élèves du collège de Chalon-sur-Saône
Bullétin Municipal (Chalon-sur-Saône)
Le Courrier (Chalon-sur-Saône)
La Dépêche Marocaine (Tangier)
L'Éclair (Paris)
L'Express de Lyon
L'Illustration (Paris)
Al-Moghreb al-Aksa (Tangier)
New York Times
Le Progrès de Saône-et-Loire
Al-Saada (Tangier)
Southern Morocco Mission (Glasgow)
Times (London)
Times Literary Supplement (London)

Unpublished Works

Hajawi, Muhammad al-. *Kunashsha al-Hajawi.* Bibliothéque Générale, Rabat, H 128.

Kunnash 2720. Bibliothéque Générale, Rabat.

Kunnash 2721. Bibliothéque Générale, Rabat.

Kunnash Makhzani 1327–1329 A.H. Direction des Archives Royales, Rabat.

LeClerc, Eugène. "Note historique sur trois monument situés près de l'Office du Tourisme, Chalon-sur-Saône." 20 June 1980, typed ms. Deposited in Bibliothèque Municipal, Chalon-sur-Saône.

Mauchamp, Èmile. "Conseil aux mères pour élever leur infants," Dispensaire français de Marrakech (texts in French and Arabic). Archives du Ministère des Affaires Étrangères, Nantes. Carton A 342, Tangier.

————. "Conseil aux mères pour élever leur infants," Hôpital Français de Saint-Louis à Jérusalem. Archives du Ministère des Affaires Étrangères, Nantes. Carton 104, Jerusalem.

————. "Rapport du Dr. Émile Mauchamp, Médecin du gouvernement français, chargé du service d l'Hôpital St. Louis, sur l'exercise de sa mission du 15 November 1900 au 1 Janvier 1903 et sur la situation hospitalière de Jérusalem," May 1903, Archives du Ministère des Affaires Étrangères, Nantes. Carton 104, Jerusalem.

Published Works

Abrams, Lawrence, Jr. "French Economic Penetration of Morocco, 1906–1914: The Economic Bases of Imperialist Expansion." Ph.D. diss., Columbia University, 1977.

Abu-Lughod, Janet. *Rabat: Urban Apartheid in Morocco.* Princeton, N.J.: Princeton University Press, 1980.

Adam, André. *Histoire de Casablanca (des origins à 1914).* Aix-en Provence: Éditions Ophrys, 1968.

————. "Sur l'action du Galilée à Casablanca en Aôut 1907." *Revue de l'Occident Musulman et de la Méditerranée* 69 (1969): 9–21.

Adamson, Kay. *Political and Economic Thought and Practice in Nineteenth-Century France and the Colonization of Algeria.* Lewiston, N.Y.: Edwin Mellen Press, 2002.

Adas, Michael. *Machines as the Measure of Men: Science, Technology and Ideologies of Western Dominance.* Ithaca, N.Y.: Cornell University Press, 1989.

Ageron, Charles-Robert. *Les Algériens Musulmans et la France (1871–1919).* 2 vols. Paris: Presses Universitaires de France, 1968.

Akhmisse, Mustapha. *Médecine, magie et sorcellerie au Maroc: ou L'art traditionnel de guérir.* Casablanca: Benchara, 1985.

Allain, Jean-Claude. *Agadir 1911: Une crise impérialiste en Europe pour la conquête du Maroc.* Paris: Sorbonne, 1976.

————. "Le double enjeu de Tangier dans la stratégie française des telecommunications sous-marines au debut du XXème siècle." In *Tanger, 1800–1956, Contribution à l'histoire récente du Maroc.* Rabat: Université Mohammed V, 1991.

————. "Les Européens au Maroc à la Veille du Protectorat: Quelques chiffres et quelques réflexions." *Revue Dar al-Niaba* 12 (1986): 1–8

Allouche, M. "Lettres chérifiennes inédites relatives à l'assasinat du Dr. Mauchamp et à l'occupation d'Oujda en 1907." *Actes du XXIe Congrès international des orientalistes* (Paris, 23–31 Juillet 1948), 302–304. Paris: Imprimerie Nationale, 1949.

Alloula, Malek. *The Colonial Harem.* Trans. Myrna Godzich and Wald Godzich. Minneapolis: University of Minnesota Press, 1986.

Amster, Ellen. "The Many Deaths of Dr. Emile Mauchamp: Medicine, Technology, and Popular Politics in Pre-Protectorate Morocco, 1877–1912." *International Journal of Middle Eastern Studies* 36 (2004): 409–28.

———. "Medicine and Sainthood: Islamic Science, French Colonialism and the Politics of Healing in Morocco, 1877–1935." Ph.D. diss., University of Pennsylvania, 2003.

Anderson, Eugene N. *The First Moroccan Crisis, 1904–1906.* Chicago: University of Chicago Press, 1930.

Anderson, R. D. *France, 1870–1914: Politics and Society.* London: Routledge and K. Paul, 1977.

Antébi, Élizabeth. *Les Missionnaires Juifs de la France (1860–1939).* Paris: Calmann-Lévy, 1999.

Arin, F. "Le Talion et le prix du sang chez les Berbères Marocains." *Les Archives Berbères* 1 (1915–1916): 62–83. Reprinted, Rabat: 1987.

Arnaud, Louis. *"Au Temps du Mehallas," ou le Maroc de 1860 à 1912.* Casablanca: Éditions Atlantides, 1952.

Ashmead-Bartlett, E. *The Passing of the Shereefian Empire.* Edinburgh: William Blackwood, 1910. Reprinted, Westport, Conn.: Negro Universities Press, 1970.

Babin, Gustave. *Au Maroc: Par les Camps et par les Villes.* Paris: Bernard Grasset, 1912.

———. *"Son Excellence": Le Maroc sans masques.* Paris: Éditions G. Ficker, n.d.

Bakkali-Yedri, Mohammad. "L'Esthétique baroque dans *Marrakech ou Les Seigneurs de l'Atlas.* Portraits et caricatures." In *Maroc: Littérature et peinture coloniales (1912–1956).* Rabat: Université Mohammed V, 1996.

Baldick, Robert. *The Life of J.-K. Huysmans.* Oxford: Clarendon Press, 1955.

Barrada, Thuraya. *The Moroccan Army and Its Transformation in the Nineteenth-Century* [in Arabic]. Rabat: Université Mohammed V, 1997.

Bazzaz, Muhammad al-Amin al-. "Constitution du Conseil Sanitaire International à Tanger" [in Arabic]. *Revue Dar al-Niaba* 3 (Spring 1989): 39–46.

———. *The History of Epidemics and Famines in Morocco in the 18th and 19th Centuries* [in Arabic]. Rabat: Université Mohammed V, 1992.

Bazzaz, Sahar. "Challenging Power and Authority in Pre-protectorate Morocco: Shaykh Muhammad al-Kattani and the Tariqa Kattaniyya." Ph.D. diss., Harvard University, 2002.

Belmossous, Saliha. "Assimilation and Racialism in Seventeenth and Eighteenth-Century French Colonial Policy." *American Historical Review* 110 (April 2005): 322–49.

Ben Abraham, Meir. "The Impact of the 'Alliance Israélite Universelle' on Change and Modernisation of the Jewish Communities of Morocco, 1912–1956." Ph.D. diss., Anglia Polytechnic University, 2000.

Ben-Arieh, Yehoshua. *Jerusalem in the Nineteenth Century, the Old City.* Jerusalem: Yad Itzhak Ben Zvi Institute and New York: St. Martin's Press, 1984.

Ben Jelloun, Tahar. "Preface." In *Des Français au Maroc: La présence et la mémoire,* ed. Yvonne Knibiehler, Geneviève Emmery, and Françoise Leguay. Paris: Denoël, 1992.

Bénech, José. *Essai d'explication d'un mellah (Ghetto marocain): Un des Aspects du Judaïsme.* Paris: Éditions Larose, 1940.

Benjelloun-Laroui, Latifa. *Les bibliothèques au Maroc.* Paris: Maisonneuve and Larose, 1990.

Bennison, Amira K. *Jihad and Its Interpretations in Pre-colonial Morocco: State-Society Relations during the French Conquest of Algeria.* London: Routledge Curzon, 2002.

———. "The 'New Order' and Islamic Order: The Introduction of the Nizami Army in the Western Maghrib and Its Legitimation, 1830–73." *International Journal of Middle Eastern Studies* 36 (2004): 591–612.

Bernard, Stéphane. *The Franco-Moroccan Conflict, 1943–56.* New Haven, Conn.: Yale University Press, 1968.

Beroho, Ahmed. *Le Consul et l'Indigene, Bras de fer à Tanger.* Tangier: Editions Sophia, 2000.

Berthaud, Michel, ed. *Marrakesh: Années 20.* Marseilles: Éditions la croisée des chemins, 1996.

Betts, Raymond F. *Assimilation and Association in French Colonial Theory, 1890–1914.* New York: Columbia University Press, 1961.

Bhabha, Homi. "Of Mimicry and Man: The Ambivalence of Colonial Discourse." In *Tensions of Empire: Colonial Cultures in a Bourgeois World,* ed. Frederick Cooper and Ann Laura Stoler. Berkeley: University of California Press, 1997.

Bidwell, Robin. *Morocco under Colonial Rule: French Administration of Tribal Areas, 1912–1956.* London: Frank Cass, 1973.

"Biographie de Si Kaddour Ben Ghabrit." La Grande Mosquée de Paris. http://www.mosquee-de-paris.net/cat_index_41.html. Accessed February 20, 2006.

Blackwell, John. "1904: 'Perdicaris alive or Raisuli dead!'" *Trentonian,* n.d. Reprinted in http://www.capitalcentury.com/1904.html. Accessed February 20, 2006.

Blanckaert, Claude. "Of Monstrous Métis? Hybridity, Fear of Miscegenation, and Patriotism from Buffon to Paul Broca." In *The Color of Liberty: Histories of Race in France,* ed. Sue Peabody and Tyler Stovall. Durham, N.C.: Duke University Press, 2003.

Bois, Jules. "Les anglais dans l'Inde." *Revue Bleue* 19 (April 11, 1903): 476–80.

Bourdieu, Pierre. *Outline of a Theory of Practice.* Trans. Richard Nice. Cambridge: Cambridge University Press, 1972.

———. "The Sentiment of Honour in Kabyle Society." Trans. Philip Sherrard. In *Honour and Shame: The Values of Mediterranean Society,* ed. J. G. Peristiany. Chicago: University of Chicago Press, 1966.

Bourdon, Georges. *Les journées de Casablanca.* Paris: P. Lafitte, 1908.

Bourqia, Rahma, and Susan Gilson Miller, eds. *In the Shadow of the Sultan: Culture, Power, and Politics in Morocco.* Cambridge, Mass.: Harvard Center for Middle East Studies, 1999.

Brown, Kenneth L. "The 'Curse' of Westermarck." *Acta Philosophica Fennica* 34 (1982): 219–59.

Brunschwig, Henri. *French Colonialism, 1871–1914, Myths and Realities.* Trans. William Glanville Brown. New York: Frederick A. Praeger, 1966.

Bullard, Alice. "The Truth in Madness: Colonial Doctors and Insane Women in French North Africa." *South Atlantic Review* 66 (2001): 114–32.

Burhab, Ukasha. "The Moroccan Government and the Frontier Problem in the Early Twentieth Century: Oujda Province, 1900–1912" [in Arabic]. 2 vols. Ph.D. diss., Université Mohammed V, 1996.

Burke, Edmund, III. "The First Crisis of Orientalism, 1890–1914." In *Connaissances du Maghreb: Sciences Sociales et Colonisation,* ed. Jean-Claude Vatin. Paris: Éditions du Centre nationale de la recherche scientifique, 1984.

———. "The Image of the Moroccan State in French Ethnological Literature: A New Look at the Origin of Lyautey's Berber Policy." In *Arabs and Berbers: From Tribe to Nation in North Africa,* ed. Ernest Gellner and Charles Micaud. London: Duckworth, 1973.

———. "La Mission Scientique au Maroc: Science sociale et politique dans l'âge de l'impérialisme." In *Recherches récentes sur le Maroc moderne (Actes de Durham, 13–15 Juillet 1977).* Rabat: Bulletin Economique et social du Maroc, 1978.

———. "Mohand N'Hamoucha: Middle Atlas Berber." In *Struggle and Survival in the Modern Middle East,* ed. Edmund Burke III. Berkeley: University of California Press, 1993.

———. *Prelude to Protectorate in Morocco: Precolonial Protest and Resistance, 1860–1912.* Chicago: University of Chicago Press, 1976.

Cagne, Jacques. *Nation et nationalisme au Maroc: Aux racines de la nation marocaine.* Rabat: Institute Universitaire de la Recherche Scientifique, 1988.

Chatinières, Paul. *Dans le Grand Atlas Marocain: Extraits du carnet du route d'un Médecin d'assistance médicale indigène, 1912–1916.* Introduction du Général Lyautey. Paris: Librairie Plon, 1919.

Chevrillon, A. *Marrakech dans les palmes.* 13th ed. Paris: Calmann-Lévy, 1921.

Chkouri, Mohamed Mahfoud. "L'Anthropologie Coloniale Française et le Maroc." Thèse de Doctorat nouveau régime, Université Paris VIII Vincennes-Saint-Denis, 1997–1998.

Christelow, Allen. "Algerian Dimensions of France's Middle East Policy 1916." In *Franco-Arab Encounters: Studies in Memory of David C. Gordon,* ed. L. Carl Brown and Matthew S. Gordon. Beirut: American University of Beirut, 1996.

Cohen, William B. *The French Encounter with Africans: White Response to Blacks, 1530–1880.* Bloomington: Indiana University Press, 1980.

Cole, Jennifer. *Forget Colonialism? Sacrifice and the Art of Memory in Madagascar.* Berkeley: University of California Press, 2001.

Colonna, Fanny. "Educating Conformity in French Colonial Algeria." In *Tensions of Empire: Colonial Cultures in a Bourgeois World,* ed. Frederick Cooper and Ann Laura Stoler. Berkeley: University of California Press, 1997.

Comaroff, John, and Jean Comaroff. *Ethnography and the Historical Imagination.* Boulder, Colo.: Westview Press, 1992.

Conklin, Alice L. "Colonialism and Human Rights, a Contradiction in Terms? The Case of France and West Africa, 1895–1914." *American Historical Review* 103 (1998): 419–42.

————. *A Mission to Civilize: The Republican Idea of Empire in France and West Africa, 1895–1930.* Palo Alto, Calif.: Stanford University Press, 1997.

Cooper, Frederick, and Ann Laura Stoler, eds. *Tensions of Empire: Colonial Cultures in a Bourgeois World.* Berkeley: University of California Press, 1997.

Cousin, Albert, and Daniel Saurin. *Le Maroc.* Paris: Librairie du Figaro, 1905.

Croze, Henri. *Souvenirs du vieux Maroc.* Paris: Éditions du Deux Monde, 1952.

Cruchet, René. *La Conquête pacifique du Maroc et du Tafilalet,* 2nd ed. Paris: Éditions Berger-Levrault, 1934.

Cunningham Grahame, R. B. *Mogreb-El-Acksa: A Journey in Morocco.* London: 1898. Reprinted, New York: National Travel Club, 1930.

D'Arbaumont, Jean. "Emile Mauchamp (1870–1907)." *Extrait du Société des Amis des Arts, Sciences, Archéologie et Histoire locale de la Bresse louhannaise* 13 (1985).

Darnton, Robert. *The Great Cat Massacre and Other Episodes in French Cultural History.* New York: Basic Books, 1984.

Daughton, James Patrick. "The Civilizing Mission: Missionaries, Colonialists, and French Identity, 1885–1914." Ph.D. diss., University of California, Berkeley, 2002.

Davin, Anna. "Imperialism and Motherhood." In *Tensions of Empire: Colonial Cultures in a Bourgeois World,* ed. Frederick Cooper and Ann Laura Stoler. Berkeley: University of California Press, 1997.

Debré, Robert. *L'Honneur de vivre.* Paris: Herman et Stock, 1974.

Dobo, Nicolas. *J'étais le médecin de cent mille Berbères: Un Médecin francais dans le bled marocain de 1955–1958.* Paris: Éditions du Scorpion, 1964.

Documents Diplomatiques, 1907, Affaires du Maroc. Vol. 3, 1906–1907. Paris: Imprimerie nationale, 1947.

Doutté, Edmond. *Magie et religion dans l'Afrique du nord.* Paris: Maisonneuve, 1908. Reprinted, Paris: P. Guethner, 1984.

Dugas, Guy, ed. *Maroc: Les Villes impériales.* Paris: Omnibus: 1996.

Dunn, Ross E. *Resistance in the Desert: Moroccan Responses to French Imperialism, 1881–1912.* London: Croom Helm, 1977.

Dupuch, Henri. *J'étais médecin au Maroc, 1942–1958.* Paris: France-Empire, 1985.

Durkheim, Émile. *The Division of Labor in Society.* Trans. George Simpson. Glencoe, Ill.: Free Press, 1933.

Duverne, M. "Rapport de M. Duverne, Inauguration du monument de M. le docteur Mauchamp." *Bulletin Municipal, Chalon-sur-Saône* (8 July 1910): 235–37.

Elias, Norbert. *The Civilizing Process: The Development of Manners.* Trans. Edmund Jephcott. New York: Urizen Books, 1978.

Ellis, Jack D. *The Physician-Legislators of France: Medicine and Politics in the Early Third Republic, 1870–1914.* Cambridge: Cambridge University Press, 1990.

Elsner, Eleanor. *The Magic of Morocco.* New York: Dodd, Mead, 1928.

Epton, Nina. *Saints and Sorcerers: A Moroccan Journey.* London: Cassell, 1958.

Fanon, Frantz. "Medicine and Colonialism." In *A Dying Colonialism.* Trans. Haakon Chevalier. New York: Grove Press, 1967.

Fiessinger, Noel. *La Médecine Française au Maroc.* Paris: A. Maloine and Fils, 1923.

Fogarty, Richard, and Michael A. Osborne. "Constructions and Functions of Race in French Military Medicine, 1830–1920." In *The Color of Liberty: Histories of Race in France,* ed. Sue Peabody and Tyler Stovall. Durham, N.C.: Duke University Press, 2003.

Foucault, Michel. *The History of Sexuality.* Vol. 1: *An Introduction.* Trans. Robert Hurley. New York: Vintage Books, 1980.

Frémeaux, J. "Les trois occupations d'Oujda par l'armée française." *Revue Maroc Europe* 5 (1995): 41–46.

Gallagher, Nancy Elizabeth. *Medicine and Power in Tunisia, 1780–1900.* Cambridge: Cambridge University Press, 1983.

Gautier, A. "Décès de M. P. Budin." *Bulletin de L'Academie Nationale de Médecine* (January 29, 1907): 163–67. Reprinted in http://www.neonatology.org/classics/gautier.html. Accessed Feb. 20, 2006.

Gellner, Ernest. *Saints of the Atlas.* London: Wiedenfeld and Nichols, 1969.

Gentil, Louis. "L'Insecurité actuelle dans le sud marocain." *Bulletin du Comité du Maroc Française* 17 (April 1907): 128–29.

Ghoti, Mohamed. *Histoire de la Médecine au Maroc, le XXᵉ Siècle (1896–1994).* Morocco: 1995.

Gilbert, Martin. *Jerusalem in the Twentieth Century.* New York: John Wiley and Sons, 1996.

Gilman, Sander L. "Black Bodies, White Bodies: Toward an Iconography of Female Sexuality in Late Nineteenth-Century Art, Medicine, and Literature." *Critical Inquiry* 12 (1985): 204–42.

———. *Difference and Pathology: Stereotypes of Sexuality, Race, and Madness.* Ithaca, N.Y.: Cornell University Press, 1985.

Girardet, Raoul. *L'Idée coloniale en France de 1871 à 1962.* Paris: La Table Ronde, 1972.

Goldberg, Harvey E., ed. *Sephardi and Middle Eastern Jewries: History and Culture in the Modern Era.* Bloomington: Indiana University Press, 1996.

Goldenberg, Alfred. *Souvenirs d'Alliance: Itinéraire d'un instituteur de l'Alliance Israélite Universelle au Maroc.* Paris: Éditions du Nadir, 1998

Goodrich-Freer, Ada. *Inner Jerusalem.* New York: E. P. Dutton, 1904.

Gottreich, Emily R. "Jewish Space in the Moroccan City: A History of the *Mellah* of Marrakesh, 1550–1930." Ph.D. diss., Harvard University, 1999.

———. "On the Origins of the Mellah of Marrakesh." *International Journal of Middle East Studies* 35 (2003): 287–305.

Guerrand, Roger-Henri. "Les clarions de la nostalgie." In *Au temps des colonies,* ed. Georges Balandier and Marc Ferro. Paris: L'Histoire, Éditions du Seuil, 1984.

Guillemin, Henri. "Biographie du Docteur Émile Mauchamp." *Bulletin de la Société des Sciences Naturelles de Saône-et-Loire* 33 (1907): 252–68; 34 (1908): 33–40, 97–120, 154–68, 172–96; 35 (1909): 33–64, 91–120.

Guillen, Pierre. *L'Allemagne et le Maroc de 1870 à 1905.* Paris: Presses Universitaires de France, 1967.

Guises, Elisa. "Petit historique de la P.M.I." http://www.anpde.asso.fr/pmi1. html. Accessed Feb. 20, 2006.

Hafizi, Abd al-Karim. "Manuscript Documents Preserved in the Manuscript Section of the Bibliothèque Générale" [in Arabic]. In *Les archives du Protectorat, Première évaluation.* Rabat: Université Mohammed V, 1996.

Halpern, Manfred. "Emile Durkheim: Analyst of Solidarity but Not of Transformation." In *Connaissances du Maghreb: Sciences Sociales et Colonisation,* ed. Jean-Claude Vatin. Paris: Éditions du Centre nationale de la recherche scientifique, 1984.

Harmand, Jules. *Domination et Colonisation.* Paris: E. Flammarion, 1910.

Harris, Walter. *Morocco That Was.* London: William Blackwood, 1921. Reprinted, London: Eland Books, 1983.

Harrus, Élias. *L'Alliance en Action: Les écoles de l'Alliance israélite universelle dans l'Empire de Maroc (1862–1912).* Paris: Nadir, 2001.

Hart, David M. "Muslim Ritual Models in Two Pre-colonial Moroccan Berber Societies: Covenant, Conditional Curse, Shame Compulsion and Sacrifice." *Journal of North African Studies* 6 (2001): 81–94.

"Histoire et patrimoine de l'Assistance Publique—Hôpitaux de Paris." http://www.aphp.fr/site/histoire/1901_hopitaux_pediatriques.htm. Accessed Feb. 20, 2006.

Hoisington, William. *Lyautey and the French Conquest of Morocco.* New York: St. Martin's, 1995.

Hoover, Ellen Titus. "Among Competing Worlds: The Rehamna of Morocco on the Eve of French Conquest." Ph.D. diss., Yale University, 1978.

Houel, Christian. *Mes Adventures Marocaines.* Casablanca: Éditions Maroc-Demain, 1954.

Huet, Henri. "Les Funérailles du Docteur Mauchamp: 11 avril 1907." *Mémoires de la Société d'histoire et d'archéologie de Chalon-sur-Saône* [1988–1989] 58 (1990): 64–75.

Hunt, Nancy Rose. *A Colonial Lexicon: Of Birth Ritual, Medicalization, and Mobility in the Congo.* Durham, N.C.: Duke University Press, 1999.

———. "'Le bébé en brousse': European Women, African Birth Spacing, and Colonial Intervention in Breast Feeding in the Belgian Congo." In *Tensions of Empire: Colonial Cultures in a Bourgeois World,* ed. Frederick Cooper and Ann Laura Stoler. Berkeley: University of California Press, 1997.

Ibn Zaydan, Abd al-Rahman. *A Presentation of Luminous Men with the Most Beautiful Reports of the City of Meknes* [in Arabic]. 5 vols. Fes, 1930. Reprinted, Casablanca: Ideal, 1990.

Jean, Jaurès. *Oeuvres de Jean Jaurès.* Vol. 3: *Le Guêpier marocain (1906–1908).* Paris: Les Éditions Rieder, 1933.

Journal officiel du Débats parlementaires. Paris: Imp. des Journaux officiels, 1882–1920s.

Julien, Charles-André. *Le Maroc face aux impérialismes, 1415–1956.* Paris: Éditions J.A. 1977.

July, Pierre. *Une République pour un roi.* Paris: Fayard, 1974.

Karmazyn, Jean-Claude. *Le Maroc en cartes postales 1900–1920.* Cahors: Publi-fusion, 1994.

Katz, Jonathan G. *Dreams, Sufism and Sainthood: The Visionary Career of Muhammad al-Zawawi.* Leiden: E. J. Brill, 1996.

———. "The 1907 Mauchamp Affair and the French Civilizing Mission in Morocco." *Journal of North African Studies* 6 (2001): 143–66. Reprinted in *North Africa, Islam and the Mediterranean World: From the Almoravids to the Algerian War,* ed. Julia Clancy-Smith. London: Frank Cass, 2001.

[Keene], Emily, Shareefa of Wazan. *My Life Story.* Ed. L. Bensusan. London: Edward Arnold, 1912.

Keller, Richard. "*Action Psychologique:* French Psychiatry in Colonial North Africa, 1900–1962." Ph.D. diss., Rutgers (State University of New Jersey), 2001.

Kenbib, Mohammed. *Juifs et Musulmans au Maroc, 1859–1948: Contribution à l'histoire des relations inter-communitaires en terre d'Islam.* Rabat: Université Mohammed V, 1994.

———. *Les Protégés: Contributions à l'histoire contemporaine du Maroc.* Rabat: Université Mohammed V, 1996.

Khadimi, Allal al-. *Foreign Intervention and Resistance in Morocco (1894–1910)* [in Arabic]. Casablanca: Ifriqiya al-Sharq, 1994.

———. [Khdimi, Allal el-]. "L'Occupation d'Oujda." In *La Memorial du Maroc: Tome 5: 1906–1934: Morcellement et résistance,* ed. Larbi Essakali. Rabat: Nord Publications, 1983–1985.

Khalloufi, Mohammed Essaghir al-. *Bouhmara, du Jihad à la compromission: Le Maroc oriental et le Rif de 1900 à 1909.* Rabat: El Maarif Al-Jadida, 1993.

———. [Khallufi, Muhammad al-Saghir al-.] *Morocco's Suicide at the Hands of its Rebels: Samples of al-Hajawi's Political Writings Regarding the Start of the Twentieth Century* [in Arabic]. Rabat: El Maarif Al-Jadida, 1995.

Knibiehler, Yvonne, Geneviève Emmery, and Françoise Leguay, eds. *Des Français au Maroc: La présence et la mémoire.* Paris: Denoël, 1992.

Lafon, R. P. Michel. "Le Témoignage des médecins français au Maroc." In *Maroc: Littérature et peinture coloniales (1912–1956).* Rabat: Université Mohammed V, 1996.

Lahjomri, Abdeljlil. *Le Maroc des heures françaises.* Rabat: Marsam and Stouky, 1999. Originally published as *L'image du Maroc dans la littérature française (de Loti à Montherlant).* Algiers: SNED, 1968.

Laqueur, Thomas W. *Solitary Sex: A Cultural History of Masturbation.* New York: Zone Books, 2003.

Laroui, Abdallah "La conférence d'Algésiras." In *Esquisse historiques.* Casablanca: Centre Culturel Arabe, 1993.

———. *Les Origines sociales et culturelles du nationalisme marocaine (1830–1912).* Paris: F. Maspero, 1977. Reprinted, Casablanca: Centre Culturel Arabe, 1993.

Laskier, Michael M. *The* Alliance Israélite Universelle *and the Jewish Communities of Morocco: 1862–1962.* Albany: State University of New York Press, 1983.

LeSueur, James D. *Uncivil War: Intellectuals and Identity Politics during the Decolonization of Algeria.* Philadelphia: University of Pennsylvania Press, 2001.

Leven, Narcisse. *Cinquante ans d'histoire: L'Alliance israélite universelle (1860–1910).* 2 vols. Paris: Libraire Félix Alcan, 1911, 1920.

Lewis, Neil Sherwood. "German Policy in Southern Morocco during the Agadir Crisis of 1911." Ph.D. diss., University of Michigan, 1977.

Lockman, Zachary. *Contending Visions of the Middle East: The History and Politics of Orientalism.* Cambridge: Cambridge University Press, 2004.

López Gádor, Maria. *La diligence de Casablanca, souvenirs du début du siècle.* Talence, France: Maxime Rousselle, 1998.

Lorcin, Patricia M. E. *Imperial Identities: Stereotyping, Prejudice and Race in Colonial North Africa.* London: I. B. Taurus, 1995.

Loti, Pierre. *Au Maroc.* In *Maroc: Les Villes impériales,* ed. Guy Dugas. Paris: Omnibus, 1996.

Lourido Diaz, Ramón. "Le Sultan Sidi Muhammad b. Abd Allah et l'institution de la représentation consulaire à Tanger." In *Tanger, 1800–1956: Contribution à l'histoire récente du Maroc.* Rabat: Université Mohammed V, 1991.

Malino, Frances. "The Women Teachers of the Alliance Israélite Universelle, 1842–1940." In *Jewish Women in Historical Perspective,* ed. Judith R. Baskin. 2nd ed. Detroit, Mich.: Wayne State University Press, 1998.

Malki, Al-Malki al-. "Reinhard Mannesmann and the Sous: A Preliminary History of New Commerce in the Sous Region" [in Arabic]. *Majallat tarikh al-Maghrib* 9 (1420/1999): 191–207.

Mansour, Mohamed El. "The Sanctuary (Hurm) in Precolonial Morocco." In *In the Shadow of the Sultan: Culture, Power, and Politics in Morocco,* ed. Rahma Bourqia and Susan Gilson Miller. Cambridge, Mass.: Harvard Center for Middle East Studies, 1999.

Manuni, Muhammad al-. *Aspects of the Awakening of Modern Morocco* [in Arabic]. 2 vols. Casablanca: al-Madaris, 1985.

Maran, Rita. "Torture during the French-Algerian War: The Role of the 'Mission Civilisatrice.'" Ph.D. diss., University of California, Santa Cruz, 1987.

Marcovich, Anne. "French Colonial Medicine and Colonial Rule: Algeria and Indochina." In *Disease, Medicine, and Empire: Perspectives on Western Medicine and the Experience of European Expansion,* ed. Roy MacLeod and Milton Lewis. London: Routledge, 1988.

Maroc: Littérature et peinture coloniales (1912–1956). Rabat: Université Mohammed V, 1996.

Martin, A. G. P. *Quatre siècles d'histoire marocaine, au Sahara de 1504 à 1902, au Maroc de 1894 à 1912.* Paris: Félix Alcan, 1923. Reprinted, Rabat: Éditions La Porte, 1994.

Martin, B. G. "Ma' al-'Aynayn al-Qalqami, Mauritanian Mystic and Politics." In *Muslim Brotherhoods in Nineteenth-Century Africa.* 125–51. Cambridge: Cambridge University Press, 1976.

Mauchamp, Émile. *L'Allaitement artificiel des nourissons par le lait sterilisé: Conditions, Pratiques, Résultants, Indications.* Paris: Georges Carré et C. Naud, 1899.

———. *La Sorcellerie au Maroc.* Paris: Dordon-Ainé, 1910.

———. "Pétra (Impressions de Caravane)." *Extrait du Bulletin de la Société des Sciences Naturelles de Saône-et-Loire* (1905).

———. "Un raid au Désert: Sinai, Arabie-Pétrée, Moab (note de voyages, 1902)." *Extrait du Bulletin de la Société des Science Naturelles de Saône-et-Loire* (1905).

Mauran, Dr. *Le Maroc: d'aujourd'hui et de demain.* Paris: H. Paulin, 1909.

Maxwell, Gavin. *Lords of the Atlas: The Rise and Fall of the House of Glaoua, 1893–1956.* London: Pan Books, 1966.

McCarthy, Justin. *The Population of Palestine: Population History and Statistics of the Late Ottoman Period and the Mandate.* New York: Columbia University Press, 1990.

Michaux-Bellaire, E. "Les musulmans d'Algérie au Maroc." *Archives Marocaines* 11 (1907).

Michel, Claude. *Marrakech d'un siècle à l'autre.* Paris: Maisonneuve and Larose, Malika Éditions, 2003.

Micouleau-Sicault, Marie-Claire. *Les médecins français au Maroc (1912–1956).* Paris: L'Harmattan, 2000.

Miège, Jean-Louis. *Le Maroc et L'Europe (1822–1906).* 4 vols. Paris: Presses Universitaires de France, 1961–1964. Reprinted with vol. 5: *Documents d'histoire économique et sociale,* Rabat: Éditions La Porte, 1989.

Miller, Susan Gilson. "The Colonial Hunt in Nineteenth Century Tangier." In *Tanger, 1800–1956, Contribution à l'histoire récente du Maroc.* Rabat: Université Mohammed V, 1991.

Morocco under the Protectorate: Forty Years of French Administration: An Analysis of Facts and Figures. New York: Istiqlal (Independence) Party of Morocco, 1953.

Munson, Henry, Jr. *Religion and Power in Morocco.* New Haven, Conn.: Yale University Press, 1993.

Nahon, Moïse. *Propos d'un vieux Marocain.* Paris: Larose, 1930.

Navon, A.-H. *Les 70 Ans de l'École Normale Israélite Orientale (1865–1935).* Paris: Librairie Durlacher, 1935.

Nehlil, M. *Lettres chérifiennes.* Paris: E. Guilmoto, 1915.

Nordman, Daniel. "L'Armée d'Algérie et le Maroc." In *Profils du Maghreb: Frontières, figures et territoires XVIIIᵉ–XXᵉ siècle.* Rabat: Université Mohammed V, 1996.

Nye, Robert A. "Honor Codes and Medical Ethics in Modern France." *Bulletin of the History of Medicine* 69 (1995): 91–111.

———. *Masculinity and Male Codes of Honor in Modern France.* New York: Oxford University Press, 1993.

———. "Medicine and Science as Masculine 'Fields of Honor.'" *Osiris* 12 (1997): 60–79.

Othmani, Hamza Ben Driss. *Essaouira, Une cité sous les alizeés, des origines à 1939.* Rabat: Èditions La Porte, 1997.

Oved, Georges. *La Gauche française et le nationalisme marocaine, 1905–1955.* 2 vols. Paris: L'Harmattan, 1984.

Pandey, Annarose. "Nostalgic Lives: Memories of Maria in Sidi Ifni, Morocco." *Journal of North African Studies* 8 (2003): 92–113.

Pascon, Paul. *Capitalism and Agriculture in the Haouz of Marrakesh.* Edited with introduction by John R. Hall. Trans. C. Edwin Vaughan and Veronique Ingman. London: KPI, 1986.

———. *Le Haouz de Marrakech,* 2 vols. Rabat: Centre Universitaire de la Recherche Scientifique, 1983.

———. "Le rapport 'secret' d'Edmond Doutté: Situation politique du Haoûz, 1er janvier 1907." *Hérodote* (1978): 132–59.

Paul, James Albert. "Professionals and Politics in Morocco: A Historical Study of the Mediation of Power and the Creation of Ideology in the Context of European Imperialism." Ph.D. diss., New York University, 1975.

Paul, Jim [James Albert]. "Medicine and Imperialism in Morocco." *MERIP Reports* 7 (September 1977).

Peabody, Sue, and Tyler Stovall, eds. *The Color of Liberty: Histories of Race in France.* Durham, N.C.: Duke University Press, 2003.

Pelis, Kim. "Pasteur's Imperial Missionary: Charles Nicolle (1866–1936) and the Pasteur Institute of Tunis." Ph.D. diss., Johns Hopkins University, 1995.

Pennell, C. R. *Moroco since 1830: A History.* New York: New York University Press, 2000.

Péraud, Jean. *La femme médecin en Afrique du Nord: Son rôle d'éducatrice.* Bordeaux: Imprimerie de l'université, 1932.

Persell, Stuart Michael. *The French Colonial Lobby, 1889–1938.* Stanford, Calif.: Hoover Institution Press, 1983.

Pinard, Adolphe. "De la Puériculture." *Bulletin de la Société des Amis de l'Université de Lyon* (1907–1908): 262–85.

Poliakov, Leon. *The Aryan Myth.* Trans. Edmund Howard. New York: Basic Books, 1974.

Porch, Douglas. *The Conquest of Morocco.* New York: Random House, 1983.

Prost, Antoine. "Monuments to the Dead." In *Realms of Memory,* vol. 2: *Traditions,* under the direction of Pierre Nora; English language edition by Lawrence D. Kritzman; trans. Arthur Goldhammer. New York: Columbia University Press, 1997.

Pyenson, Lewis. *Civilizing Mission: Exact Sciences and French Overseas Expansion, 1830–1940.* Baltimore, Md.: Johns Hopkins University Press, 1993.

Rabinow, Paul. *French Modern: Norms and Forms of the Social Environment.* Cambridge, Mass.: MIT Press, 1989.

Raoult, Roger-Pierre. *Lettres d'un oncle, Contribution à l'Histoire du Maroc (1887–1906).* Introduction and notes by Jean-Louis Miège. Rabat: Éditions La Porte, 1995.

Rhissassi, Fouzia. "Le Voyage d'Edith Wharton au Maroc." In *Maroc: Littérature et peinture coloniales (1912–1956)*. Rabat: Université Mohammed V, 1996.

Rivet, Daniel. "Exotisme et 'Pénétration scientifique': l'effort de découverte du Maroc par les Français au début du XXᵉ siècle." In *Connaissances du Maghreb: Sciences sociales et colonisation*, ed. Jean-Claude Vatin. Paris: Éditions du Centre nationale de la recherche scientifique, 1984.

———. *Lyautey et l'institution du protectorat français au Maroc, 1912–1925*. 3 vols. Paris: L'Harmattan, 1988.

———. *Le Maghreb à l'épreuve de la colonization*. Paris: Hachette, 2002.

———. *Le Maroc de Lyautey à Mohammed V: le double visage du Protectorat*. Paris: Denoël, 1999.

Rodrigue, Aron. "Eastern Sephardi Jewry and New Nation-States in the Balkans in the Nineteenth and Twentieth Centuries." In *Sephardi and Middle Eastern Jewries: History and Culture in the Modern Era*, ed. Harvey E. Goldberg. Bloomington: Indiana University Press, 1996.

———. *Images of Sephardi and Eastern Jewries in Transition: The Teachers of the Alliance Israélite Universelle, 1860–1939*. Seattle: University of Washington Press, 1993.

Rollman, Wilfrid John. "The 'New Order' in a Pre-colonial Muslim Society: Military Reform in Morocco, 1844–1904." Ph.D. diss., University of Michigan, 1983.

Rosen, Lawrence. "Memory in Morocco." In *The Culture of Islam: Changing Aspects of Contemporary Muslim Life*. Chicago: University of Chicago Press, 2002.

Rousselle, Maxime. *Médecin du bled*. Talence: M. Rousselle, 1990.

———. *Médecins, chirurgiens et apothicaires français au Maroc: 1577–1907*. [France]: M. Rousselle, 1996.

Ruedy, John. *Modern Algeria: The Origins and Development of a Nation*. 2nd ed. Bloomington: Indiana University Press, 2005.

Ruscio, Alain. *Le Credo de l'homme blanc: Regards coloniaux français, XIXᵉ et XXᵉ siècle*. Paris: Éditions Complexe, 1995.

Sabti, Abd al-Ahad al-, and Abd al-Rahman Lakhsassi. *From Shai to Tea: Custom and History* [in Arabic]. Rabat: Université Mohammed V, 1999.

Saint-Aulaire, Auguste Félix Charles de Beaupoil, Comte de. *Au Maroc avant et avec Lyautey, Extrait des Mémoires de l'ambassadeur publiés sous le titre:* Confession d'un vieux diplomate. Paris: Flammarion, 1954.

———. "Guillaume II à Tanger." *Les oeuvres libres* 70 (March 1952).

Saint-René Taillandier, Georges. *Les Origines du Maroc Français, Récit d'une mission (1901–1906)*. Paris: Librarie Plon, 1930.

Saint-René Taillandier, Madeleine. *Ce monde disparu, Souvenirs: Syrie-Palestine-Liban-Maroc*. Paris: Librarie Plon, 1947.

Sbai, Jalila. "Trajectoire d'un homme et d'une idée: Si Kaddour Ben Ghabrit et l'Islam de France 1892–1926." *Hespéris-Tamuda* 39 (2001): 45–58.

Schneider, William H. *An Empire for the Masses: The French Popular Image of Africa, 1870–1900*. Westport, Conn.: Greenwood, 1982.

————. *Quality and Quantity: The Quest for Biological Regeneration in Twentieth-Century France.* Cambridge: Cambridge University Press, 1990.

Schölch, Alexander. *Palestine in Transformation, 1856–1882: Studies in Social, Economic and Political Development.* Trans. William C. Young and Michael C. Gerrity. Washington, D.C.: Institute for Palestine Studies, 1993.

Schroeter, Daniel J. *Merchants of Essaouira: Urban Society and Imperialism in Southwestern Morocco, 1844–1886.* Cambridge: Cambridge University Press, 1988.

Schroeter, Daniel J., and Joseph Chetrit. "The Transformation of the Jewish Community of Essaouira (Mogador) in the Nineteenth and Twentieth Centuries." In *Sephardi and Middle Eastern Jewries: History and Culture in the Modern Era,* ed. Harvey E. Goldberg. Bloomington: Indiana University Press, 1996.

Scott, James C. *Domination and the Arts of Resistance: Hidden Transcripts.* New Haven, Conn.: Yale University Press, 1990.

Segonzac, Marquis de. *Au Coeur de l'Atlas, Mission au Maroc, 1904–1905.* Paris: Émile Larose, 1910.

Seillière, Ernest. "Une École d'impérialisme mystique: Les plus récents théoriciens du pangermanisme." *Revue des deux mondes* 50 (1909): 196–228.

Shabi, Mustafa al-. *The Makhzan Elite in Nineteenth-Century Morocco* [in Arabic]. Rabat: Université Mohammed V, 1995.

Simou, Bahija. *Les Reformes Militaires au Maroc de 1844 à 1912.* Rabat: Université Mohammed V, 1995.

Slavin, David Henry. *Colonial Cinema and Imperial France, 1919–1939.* Baltimore, Md.: Johns Hopkins University Press, 2001.

Speier, Hans. "Honour and Social Structure." In *Social Order and the Risks of War.* New York: George W. Stewart, 1952.

Sternberg, Graf. *The Barbarians of Morocco.* Trans. Ethel Peck. Illustrations by Douglas Pitt-Fox. London: Chatto and Windus, 1908.

Stewart, Frank Henderson. *Honor.* Chicago: University of Chicago Press, 1994.

Stiglitz, Joseph E. *Globalization and Its Discontents.* New York: W. W. Norton, 2002.

Stoler, Ann Laura. *Race and the Education of Desire: Foucault's History of Sexuality and the Colonial Order of Things.* Durham, N.C.: Duke University Press, 1995.

————. "Sexual Affronts and Racial Frontiers: European Identities and Cultural Politics of Exclusion in Colonial Southeast Asia." In *Tensions of Empire: Colonial Cultures in a Bourgeois World,* ed. Frederick Cooper and Laura Ann Stoler. Berkeley: University of California Press, 1997.

Susi, Al-Mukhtar al-. *Around the Dinner Table* [in Arabic]. Rabat: Al-Sahil, n.d.

Sussman, George D. *Selling Mothers' Milk: The Wet-Nursing Business in France, 1715–1914.* Urbana: University of Illinois Press, 1982.

Tanger, 1800–1956, Contribution à l'histoire récente du Maroc. Rabat: Université Mohammed V, 1991.

Tatheraux. Robert. "Émile Mauchamp: la vie généreuse et la fin tragique d'un médecin chalonnais." *Images de Saône et Loire* 56 (1983): 17–19.

Tharaud, Jerôme, and Jean Tharaud. *Marrakesh ou les seigneurs de l'Atlas.* In *Maroc: Les Villes impérials,* ed. Guy Dugas. Paris: Omnibus, 1996.

Tidrick, Kathryn. *Heart-Beguiling Araby.* Cambridge: Cambridge University Press, 1981.

Todorov, Tzvetan. *On Human Diversity: Nationalism, Racism, and Exoticism in French Thought.* Trans. Catherine Porter. Cambridge: Harvard University Press, 1993.

Tozy, Mohamed. *Monarchie et Islam politique au Maroc.* 2nd ed. Paris: Presses de Science Po, 1999.

Valensi, Lucette. "From Sacred History to Historical Memory and Back: The Jewish Past." In *Between History and Memory,* ed. Marie-Noëlle Bourguet, Lucette Valensi, and Nathan Wachtel. Chur, Switz.: Harwood, 1990.

———. "Le Maghreb vu du centre sa place dans l'école sociologique française." In *Connaissances du Maghreb: Sciences Sociales et Colonisation,* ed. Jean-Claude Vatin. Paris: Éditions du Centre nationale de la recherche scientifique, 1984.

Valette, Jacques. "Note sur l'idée coloniale vers 1871." *Revue d'histoire moderne et contemporaine* 14 (1967): 158–72.

Vatin, Jean-Claude, ed. *Connaissances du Maghreb: Sciences Sociales et Colonisation.* Paris: Éditions du Centre nationale de la recherche scientifique, 1984.

Vaughan, Megan. *Curing Their Ills: Colonial Power and African Illness.* Stanford, Calif.: Stanford University Press, 1991.

Wasserstein, Bernard. *Divided Jerusalem: The Struggle for the Holy City.* New Haven, Conn.: Yale University Press, 2001.

Weisgerber, Felix. *Au Seuil du Maroc moderne.* Rabat: Éditions la Porte, 1947.

Werbner, Richard, ed. *Memory and the Postcolony: African Anthropology and the Critique of Power.* London: Zed Books, 1998.

Westermarck, Edward. *Ritual and Belief in Morocco.* 2 vols. London: Macmillan, 1926. Reprinted, New Hyde Park, N.Y.: University Books, 1968.

Wharton, Edith. *In Morocco.* New York: Scribners, 1920.

Wright, Gwendolyn. "Tradition in the Service of Modernity: Architecture and Urbanism in French Colonial Policy, 1900–1930." In *Tensions of Empire: Colonial Cultures in a Bourgeois World,* ed. Frederick Cooper and Ann Laura Stoler. Berkeley: University of California Press, 1997.

Yoshida, Kijû. "L'Homme qui a vu la naissance et la mort du cinéma." French translation by Rose-Marie Makino-Fayolle. In *Gabriel Veyre, Opérateur Lumière: Autour du monde avec le Cinématographe, Correspondance (1896–1900),* ed. Philippe Jacquier and Marion Pranal. Lyon: Institute Lumière/Actes Sud, 1996.

Zeldin, Theodore. *France, 1848–1945.* Vol. 1: *Ambition, Love and Politics.* Oxford: Clarendon Press, 1973.

Index

Segalen, Victor, 292n36
Segonzac, Marquis de, 49, 61, 63, 74, 83, 100, 128, 130
Service des moeurs (Marrakesh), 257
Service Médicale d'Assistance au Maroc, 46
Sghir, Muhammad, 139–40, 142, 144, 246, 325n15
Shawiya, 13, 48, 114, 228, 246; campaign, 232–33, 252, 264, 270
Sibai, Muhammad (sons), 93, 126
Smith, Charles Euan, 310n4
La Sorcellerie au Maroc (Mauchamp), 3–5, 52–61, 263
Souessia (Alliance teacher), 83, 87, 93, 111
Soustelle, Jacques, 284n25
Southern Morocco Mission. *See* missionaries
Souvenirs du vieux Maroc (Croze), 270
Spinney, Robert, 148, 151, 244, 248
Spivacoff (physician), 184
Sternberg, Graf: *The Barbarians of Morocco,* 169–70, 310n14
Stewart, Frank Henderson, 318n94
Strauss, Paul, 34
Susi, Al-Mukhtar al-, 175

Tamesloht, 101, 112, 155, 254, 301n27
Tangier: Alliance Israélite school, 79, 82; Bel Ghazi, governor of, 208; Bel Ghazi mission, 220–21; Braunschvig, 87, 184; Casablanca bombardment, 228–31; *Dar al-niaba,* 186–88; dockside ceremony, 20, 22, 182–84; European population, 74–75; foreign warships, 8, 176, 187, 227; French legation, 47, 61–63, 67–70, 72–73, 92, 95, 97–99, 116, 122, 124, 130–31, 178–80; Grand Café, 119; Jewish population, 78; news of murder, 148, 153, 171–73, 175–76, 188; prisoners, 215–16, 225; Wilhelm II's visit, 13, 104, 185; wireless telegraph, 135–38. *See also* Charbonnier affair; Eugène Regnault; Muhammad al-Turris
Tazi, Muhammad and Umar al-, 197, 199, 204
Tekna. *See* Lassallas affair
telegraph: undersea cable, 307n22. *See also* wireless telegraph
Terrier, Auguste, 62, 66–67
Tetuan: 1903 siege, 82; Alliance Univer-

selle Israélite, 187; Bel Ghazi, governor of, 208; European population,75; Jewish population 78–79; al-Turris family, 187; war, 8
Tharaud, Jean and Jerôme, 74, 268
Times (London), 198, 206, 209, 218
Times Literary Supplement, 329n2
Touggani, Brahim bin Muhammad, 142
Trainer (missionary), 242, 320n16
Trouin, César, 178
Tschirschky, Heinrich von, 209
Turjuman, Samuel, 86–87, 95
Turris, Ahmad al-, 182–83, 188
Turris, Muhammad al-: and Alliance Israélite Universelle, 81, 186; and Bel Ghazi, 220; complaints about press, 198–99; death, 244; and Moulay al-Amin, 230; negotiations, 201, 204, 206, 209; Oujda occupation, 188–94, 197; Saint-René Taillandier's description, 186; as sultan's delegate, 136, 182, 186–89, 216, 226; and al-Warzazi, 152–53, 158–59

Utting (German merchant), 153–54, 219

vaccinations, 50, 95, 242, 256, 289n19, 290n91
Vaffier-Poulet, Ernest, 25, 109, 119, 126, 168–69
Variot, Gaston, 33–35, 39
Verdon, Egbert, 47, 196
Verdon, Navil, 47
Veyre, Gabriel, 25, 275, 331n37
La Vigie Marocaine (Casablanca), 275
Von Maur (German merchant), 76
Von Tschudi (German military mission), 135

Warzazi, Abd al-Majid al-, 144–47, 150, 245–46
Warzazi, Abdeslam al-: and Abdelaziz, 244; and Bel Ghazi, 219, 244; counterfeiting, 122; day of murder, 138–39, 148–50, 246; death, 244, 246, 249; demand for dismissal, 201, 219, 232; and Europeans, 103,152–59, 166, 178, 240; and Ibn Sulayman, 203, 205; Lennox's opinion, 159–61; and Ma al-Aynayn, 119; Mauchamp's impression, 125; and prisoners, 215–18, 225; shoemakers'

Jonathan G. Katz is Professor of History at Oregon State University. He is author of *Dreams, Sufism, and Sainthood: The Visionary Career of Muhammad al-Zawawi.*